STUDIES IN IMPERIALISM

General Editor: Andrew S. Thompson

Founding Editor: John M. MacKenzie

When the 'Studies in Imperialism' series was founded by Professor John M. MacKenzie more than twenty-five years ago, emphasis was laid upon the conviction that 'imperialism as a cultural phenomenon had as significant an effect on the dominant as on the subordinate societies'. With well over a hundred titles now published, this remains the prime concern of the series. Cross-disciplinary work has indeed appeared covering the full spectrum of cultural phenomena, as well as examining aspects of gender and sex, frontiers and law, science and the environment, language and literature, migration and patriotic societies, and much else. Moreover, the series has always wished to present comparative work on European and American imperialism, and particularly welcomes the submission of books in these areas. The fascination with imperialism, in all its aspects, shows no sign of abating, and this series will continue to lead the way in encouraging the widest possible range of studies in the field. 'Studies in Imperialism' is fully organic in its development, always seeking to be at the cutting edge, responding to the latest interests of scholars and the needs of this ever-expanding area of scholarship.

Exhibiting the Empire

Manchester University Press

WRITING IMPERIAL HISTORIES
ed. Andrew S. Thompson

MUSEUMS AND EMPIRE
Natural history, human cultures and colonial identities
John M. MacKenzie

MISSIONARY FAMILIES
Race, gender and generation on the spiritual frontier
Emily J. Manktelow

THE COLONISATION OF TIME
Ritual, routine and resistance in the British Empire
Giordano Nanni

BRITISH CULTURE AND THE END OF EMPIRE
ed. Stuart Ward

SCIENCE, RACE RELATIONS AND RESISTANCE
Britain, 1870–1914
Douglas A. Lorimer

GENTEEL WOMEN
Empire and domestic material culture, 1840–1910
Dianne Lawrence

EUROPEAN EMPIRES AND THE PEOPLE
Popular responses to imperialism in France, Britain, the Netherlands,
Belgium, Germany and Italy
ed. John M. MacKenzie

SCIENCE AND SOCIETY IN SOUTHERN AFRICA
ed. Saul Dubow

Exhibiting the Empire

CULTURES OF DISPLAY
AND THE BRITISH EMPIRE

Edited by
John McAleer and John M. MacKenzie

MANCHESTER UNIVERSITY PRESS

Published by MANCHESTER UNIVERSITY PRESS
ALTRINCHAM STREET, MANCHESTER M1 7JA, UK
www.manchesteruniversitypress.co.uk

British Library Cataloguing-in-Publication Data
A catalogue record for this book is available from the British Library

ISBN 978 1 5261 1835 6 *paperback*

First published by Manchester University Press in hardback 2015

This edition first published 2017

Typeset in Trump Medieval by
Koinonia, Manchester

CONTENTS

FIGURES, MUSIC EXAMPLES
AND TABLES

Figures

[vii]

Music examples

Tables

ACKNOWLEDGEMENTS

We would like to acknowledge the Carl H. and Martha S. Lindner Center for Art History at the University of Virginia for its generous support in acquiring the images and copyright permissions for Chapter 3. More broadly, and on behalf of all the contributors, we are grateful to the staff at a range of libraries, archives and galleries around the world for permission to quote from sources and reproduce images from their collections.

The editors would like to thank all of the contributors to this volume. In addition to friends and colleagues in a number of institutions, we are particularly grateful to Dr Nigel Dalziel for his assistance and support.

We are much indebted to the entire team at Manchester University Press for their help, encouragement and support at every stage of the publication process. John Banks, Andrew Kirk and Lianne Slavin provided invaluable assistance and advice on numerous occasions. And we are especially grateful to Emma Brennan for her interest in the project.

NOTES ON CONTRIBUTORS

Jeffrey Auerbach is Professor of History at California State University, Northridge. He is the author of *The Great Exhibition of 1851: A Nation on Display* (1999) and co-editor of *Britain, the Empire, and the World at the Great Exhibition of 1851* (2008). He has published articles on such varied topics as British imperial art, boredom and the British Empire, nineteenth-century women's magazines and the legacy of imperialism in modern advertising.

Stephanie Barczewski is Professor of History at Clemson University. Her publications include *Myth and National Identity in Nineteenth-century Britain: The Legends of King Arthur and Robin Hood* (2000), *Titanic: A Night Remembered* (2004) and *Antarctic Destinies: Scott, Shackleton and the Changing Face of Heroism* (2007). Her book on country houses in Britain and Ireland and their relationship to the British Empire between 1700 and 1945 was published by Manchester University Press in 2014.

Douglas Fordham is Associate Professor of Art History at the University of Virginia, where he teaches and advises students on British art, the visual culture of empire and eighteenth-century European topics. He is currently working on a series of essays dealing with printmaking and reception in Britain and the empire, which will culminate in a book on Asia and Africa in British print culture of the long eighteenth century. He is the author of *British Art and the Seven Years' War: Allegiance and Autonomy* (2010).

Nalini Ghuman is an ethno/musicologist whose research focuses on orientalism, nationalism and identity. Her book *Resonances of the Raj: India in the English Musical Imagination, 1897–1947* was published by Oxford University Press in July 2014. She has presented her work on BBC Radio and has published essays in *Western Music and Race* (2007), in *Elgar and His World* (2007) and in the *Elgar Society Journal*. Ghuman is Associate Professor of Music at Mills College, California, and was educated at The Queen's College, Oxford, King's College, London, and the University of California at Berkeley. She is also an active performer (pianist, singer, violinist) in the San Francisco Bay Area.

Eleanor Hughes is Deputy Director for Art & Program at the Walters Art Museum, Baltimore. Before that she was Associate Director of Exhibitions and Publications, and Associate Curator, at the Yale Center for British Art, New Haven, where she curated a number of major exhibitions. She has taught at the University of California at Berkeley, the Open University and Yale University. Her publications include essays in *Art and the British Empire* (2009), *The English Prize: The Capture of the Westmorland, An Episode of the Grand Tour* (2012), *The Pleasure Garden, from Vauxhall to Coney Island* (2013) and *The British School of Sculpture, c. 1760–1832* (forthcoming).

Ashley Jackson is Professor of Imperial and Military History at King's College, London, and a Visiting Fellow of Kellogg College, Oxford. He is the author of numerous books, including *Mad Dogs and Englishmen: A Grand Tour of the British Empire at Its Height, 1850–1945* (2009), *Illustrating Empire: A Visual History of British Imperialism* with David Tomkins (2011), *The British Empire: A Very Short Introduction* (2013) and *Buildings of Empire* (2013).

Sarah Longair received her PhD from Birkbeck, University of London, and currently works in the Department of Africa, Oceania and the Americas at the British Museum. Her research explores British colonial history in East Africa and the Indian Ocean world through material and visual culture. Her first monograph is *Cracks in the Dome: Fractured Histories of Empire in the Zanzibar Museum, 1897–1964* (2015). She has also published several book chapters, articles and edited volumes, including *Curating Empire: Museums and the British Imperial Experience* (2012), co-edited with John McAleer.

John McAleer is a Lecturer in History at the University of Southampton. His work focuses on the British encounter and engagement with the wider world in the eighteenth and nineteenth centuries, situating the history of empire in its global and maritime contexts. He was previously Curator of Imperial and Maritime History at the National Maritime Museum, Greenwich. He is the author of *Representing Africa: Landscape, Exploration and Empire in Southern Africa, 1780–1870* (2010) and *Monsoon Traders: The Maritime World of the East India Company* (2011). A collection of essays, co-edited with Sarah Longair, on *Curating Empire: Museums and the British Imperial Experience* was published by Manchester University Press in 2012.

John M. MacKenzie is emeritus professor of imperial history at Lancaster University and holds honorary professorships of Aberdeen, St Andrews and Edinburgh Universities. Among his many publications are 'Art and the Empire' in the *Cambridge Illustrated History of the British Empire* (1996) and *Museums and Empire* (2009). He is the Editor-in-Chief of the Wiley–Blackwell *Encyclopedia of Empire* (forthcoming) and has been editing the Manchester University Press 'Studies in Imperialism' series for the past thirty years.

Berny Sèbe is Senior Lecturer in Colonial and Postcolonial Studies at the University of Birmingham. His research examines the relations between metropolitan and colonial history in Britain and France since the nineteenth century, as well as the modern history of the Sahara. He has written extensively about the role and place of imperial heroes, and is the author of *Heroic Imperialists in Africa: The Promotion of British and French Colonial Heroes, 1870–1939* (2013) and the co-editor of *Echoes of Empires: Identity, Memory and Colonial Legacies* (2014). Since 2012, he has led the AHRC-funded project 'Outposts of conquest: the history and legacy of the fortresses of the Steppe and the Sahara in comparative perspective (1840s to the present day)' (www.birmingham.ac.uk/forts).

David Tomkins has led a number of high-profile digitisation, content creation and crowd-sourcing projects for the Bodleian Library at the University of Oxford, including *Queen Victoria's Journals, What's the Score?, Mapping Crime* and *Electronic Ephemera*. Before joining the Bodleian, he worked at the Victoria & Albert Museum, the Institute of Historical Research and the Courtauld Institute of Art. He is co-author (with Ashley Jackson) of *Illustrating Empire: A Visual History of British Imperialism* (2011), and has written a number of book chapters and articles.

INTRODUCTION

Cultures of display and the British Empire

John M. MacKenzie and John McAleer

Britain's overseas empire had a profound impact on people in the United Kingdom, their domestic spaces and rituals, and their perceptions of, and attitudes towards, the wider world. The country's imperial status seemed to pervade almost every aspect of British culture from exhibitions, panoramas and theatrical performances to art, literature and music.[1] Such influences and impacts were multiple and complex, and frequently became deeply embedded in British domestic culture. New academic approaches, adopting multi- and interdisciplinary forms of analysis, have heightened our awareness of, and sensitivity towards, the influences of colonialism, imperialism and empire on British life, in terms of not only 'high' culture but also the popular culture experienced by the vast majority of the population. Indeed, in some respects, this was a Europe-wide phenomenon, though this book concentrates on the British experience.[2] Thus many recent studies have provided a more nuanced view of how empire impinged upon the everyday lives and imaginations of British (and other) people and the complex ways in which they interacted with, and against, the imperial state. Furthermore, these approaches have illuminated the multifaceted ways in which imperialism was interwoven with a whole host of different phenomena, from the development of academic disciplines to the growth of institutions like museums and botanic gardens.[3] And the Empire had far-reaching and long-lasting effects, not least through its relations with the churches and their attendant missionary societies, and its role in forming aspects of national character, identity and public self-image.[4] The churches and missionary societies were important in transmitting visual propaganda for their work, through their magazines, through lectures and magic lantern slides, through exhibitions and publications such as postcards.

However, despite these advances in our understanding of the ways in which an awareness of empire permeated British culture, less attention has been paid to the literal display and exhibition of empire (and the idea of empire) in the imperial metropolis. Until recently, as Christopher Pinney has pointed out, the historiography of empire has largely ignored questions of materiality. The phenomena and process of empire were often discussed without paying any attention to the visual art, architecture, sculpture, costume and interior decor that have sustained all empires. In doing so, Pinney has highlighted the ways in which 'representation' and the 'material history' of the British Empire are more than mere supplements to 'politics', 'society' or 'culture'. In fact, they offer 'an alternative mode of historiography'.[5] Nevertheless, the plethora of material culture, publications, visual images, theatrical performances and even people exhibited and displayed in Britain as a result of imperial expansion, consolidation and exploration remains to be comprehensively investigated, explained and contextualised. Discussion tends to be constrained within disciplinary boundaries or confined to particular media. Historians are apt to overlook the mechanics, practicalities and significance of putting empire-related subjects and material culture on display, on to exhibition walls, or into print, both in books and in the press. *Exhibiting the Empire* seeks to begin the process of correcting that imbalance. The chapters collected here explore and contextualise the ways in which the practices, results and complexities of Britain's extra-European activities were 'exhibited' (in the broadest sense of the word) to British people. And, as a whole, the collection addresses issues of central concern to historians of empire: the relationship between those in Britain (i.e. the metropole) and the wider world; the impacts and influences of the Empire on British society and its significance for British people.

Exhibiting the Empire suggests that the history of empire also needs to be, to a large degree, a history of display and of reception. As the contributions from a range of scholars and a variety of disciplinary traditions attest, a whole host of cultural products – paintings, prints, photographs, panoramas, 'popular' texts, ephemera, newspapers and the press, theatre and music, exhibitions, institutions and architecture – were used to record, celebrate and question the development of the British Empire.

In addition to these, atlases and maps became increasingly influential sources for exhibiting the world to the British public. Atlases sold in large numbers and were available in all libraries, while maps appeared on the walls of many schoolrooms.[6] Geographical societies were founded in many regional port cities (including Liverpool, Manchester, Hull, Newcastle, Southampton, Glasgow, Edinburgh, Dundee and Aberdeen) in the 1880s. These became influential in arranging lectures, with maps and slides, as well as organising many events for schools.[7] In these and many other ways, the Empire was visualised, exhibited and displayed for a variety of reasons: to promote trade and commerce; to encourage emigration and settlement; to assert and cement imperial authority; to exhibit the curious and the marvellous; to digest and display the data and specimens derived from various voyages of exploration and missionary endeavours undertaken in the name of empire; to celebrate and commemorate important landmarks, people or events in the imperial pantheon; to prove the positive impact of British rule; and, often, to provide evidence of having been somewhere foreign and faraway. Captain James Cook offered practical reasons for bringing artists on his voyages. The images they produced would 'serve to make the result of our voyages entertaining to the generality of readers, as well as instructive to the sailor and scholar'. John Webber, an Anglo-Swiss painter, was employed on Cook's third voyage 'for the express purpose of supplying the unavoidable imperfections of written accounts, by enabling us to preserve, and to bring home, such drawings of the most memorable scenes of our transactions, as could be executed by a professed and skilful artist'.[8]

By considering a broad sweep of different media and 'imperial moments', this collection highlights the essentially contingent and changing nature of imperial display through time and in a variety of contexts. It foregrounds the continuing impact and cultural valency of empire in Britain throughout (and beyond) the country's imperial meridian. As such, *Exhibiting the Empire* confirms the importance of considering the cultural implications of 'empire' for wider British history. While this collection focuses primarily on how the Empire was exhibited in the British Isles, even here, in the 'metropolis', there were competing 'visions' and experiences of empire. Similarly, many of the media employed to 'exhibit' empire were inherently mobile and, almost by definition, international in their character; their reach and impact often transcended national boundaries. The phenomenon of exhibiting empire might also, therefore, be considered in a transnational context. The exhibition and display of empire and imperial themes was prevalent throughout the geographical sweep of the British Empire. Indeed, perhaps the architecture of buildings, addressed only tangentially in this book in the contributions of Barczewski and MacKenzie, represents one of the supreme means of exhibiting empires, both in the colonies and in the metropole. Such buildings conveyed ideological messages, as well as representing different facets of the imperial experience, political, military, technological, social, and recreational.[9] They remain as one of the most visible manifestations of empire, as they do not only for all the empires of Europe and the United States but also for many historic empires. And among historic empires we should identify those of the Ancient World and also those of the global peoples among whom Europeans established their power. Indeed, in the Middle East, India and South-East Asia, Europeans sought to incorporate and assimilate such earlier displays of empire into their own exhibiting and self-awareness of power.[10] The whole question of architecture and monumental remains, however, is so vast that it would require a further volume or volumes to treat it adequately. Similarly, parallel visual phenomena, related to the areas that are treated here, can also be identified across Europe and the United States. In all these ways, ideas and concepts of empire were conveyed to a wide variety of people, migrants and travellers, officials and military, as well as indigenous at every level.

We should, however, also note the silences of empire. Empires always seek to exhibit themselves as a means to underpinning their power. But they also attempt to obscure, in both documentary and visual ways, anything that might undermine that power or bring their reputations into disrepute. There are various examples of this. One would be the involvement in the slave trade and the practice of slavery, highlighted particularly by abolitionist movements, but often apparently written out of documentary and visual records until modern times. Another would be the massacres and instances of near-genocide that tragically occur in all empires. Where there are, for example, visual representations of individuals, such as the indigenous Tasmanians, they tend to be presented within a Darwinian framework of inevitable, evolutionary extinction and consequently as quaint final examples of a disappearing race. Resistance to empire can also sometimes be expunged, particularly in the modern period. Earlier revolts, such as that in India in 1857, could be presented as hopeless, obscurantist, anti-modern and non-progressive acts of resistance, thus chiming with the ideological thrust of imperial propaganda. But modern nationalist revolts were treated differently and in some cases documentation was conveniently 'lost' or destroyed while visual representations were played down. When dealing with the multiple forms of exhibiting empires, we should also be alert to these attempted obscuring acts of omission.

Early exhibitions of empire

The exhibition of objects and images garnered from British overseas activities has a long history. In 1599, Thomas Platter, a visitor to London from Basle, described Sir Walter Cope's renowned collection of curiosities. One particular apartment in Cope's 'fine house' was 'stuffed with queer foreign objects in every corner'.[11] Platter acknowledged that there were many people in London interested in curios but 'this gentleman is superior to them all for strange objects, because of the Indian voyage he carried out'.[12] One of those who displayed objects resulting from overseas commercial ventures was Thomas Smythe, known as 'Customer Smythe' because of his close connections with Queen Elizabeth's customs service. An 'Esquimau canoe' brought back from one of the north-west voyages of which Smythe was an untiring promoter hung in the hall of his son Thomas, who became the first governor of the East India Company.[13] Perhaps the most renowned early collectors were the Tradescants, whose collection today forms the basis of the Ashmolean Museum in Oxford. Indeed, many British museum collections owe their origins to the networks of global trade and maritime endeavour that developed at this time.[14]

This interest in displaying material derived from increasingly global interactions was not just restricted to private connoisseurs. Writing at the end of James I's reign, for example, Samuel Purchas remarked that a great map representing Francis Drake's circumnavigation was 'presented to Queen Elizabeth, [and is] still hanging in His Majestie's Gallerie at White Hall'.[15] The exhibiting of this object in the great spaces of state highlights the close connection between display and power, exhibition and empire. Later in the century, the triumphal arches erected for the coronation of James's grandson, Charles II, carried 'living figures' of the four continents and prominently displayed the arms of the chartered companies trading there. On the pediment above, a crouching figure of Atlas bore the globe surmounted by a model ship in full sail.[16] Of course, such display was not just an English or British phenomenon. Philip II of Spain showed keen interest in the visual representation of the natural history of his American dominions. He sent his court physician, Francisco Hernández, on five expeditions in the 1570s to collect and visually record the flora and fauna of New Spain. Philip then decorated his chambers at San Lorenzo del Escorial with paintings derived from these drawings. In 1632, his son, Philip III, who was then also ruler of Portugal, directed the Viceroy of India to send him views of all 'the coasts, ports, harbours and anchorages of this State'. The Count of Linhares assigned the responsibility to Captain Pedro Barreto de Resende, who produced *Livro do Estado da India Oriental*, a survey of Iberian interests ranging from the Indian to the Pacific Ocean. It showed towns, ports and fortresses, as well as individual buildings, fortifications and schematic plots of vegetation from a high bird's-eye view.[17] The Dutch East India Company also maintained a 'Secret Atlas' in manuscript form – 'a systematic pictorial inventory of all of the islands, cities, and towns associated with Dutch commercial interests, rendered in explicit detail and brilliant, beautiful colours' – apparently to impress visiting dignitaries.[18]

And the European engagement with the wider world was not just confined to images or objects. William Dampier returned to England in September 1691 with a tattooed man, 'a Painted Prince, whose Name was Jeoly', in tow. Considering 'what might be gain'd by shewing him in England', Dampier soon sold him to new owners who 'exposed [him] to publick view every day' and privately by appointment to 'persons of quality'.[19] James Cook's voyages in the second half of the eighteenth century continued this penchant for bringing people back from the Pacific to be exhibited in Europe. The most famous example of this was Mai, who arrived in London 1774 and was famously depicted by Sir Joshua Reynolds in a grand portrait, itself exhibited in 1776.[20] And this appetite for displaying and observing people as a result of imperial activity continued into the nineteenth century.[21]

By the eighteenth century, empire was increasingly exhibited in Britain in visually arresting two-dimensional form. William Hodges, the artist on Captain Cook's second voyage to the Pacific, exhibited regularly at the Free Society of Artists and the Royal Academy.[22] Hodges subsequently travelled in India, exhibiting eight Indian landscapes at the Academy exhibition of 1786.[23] As the importance of India to Britain's Empire rose, so the subcontinent became the focus of an immense project of visualisation.[24] Indian pictures appear in as many as 20 per cent of all the house sales managed by Christie's, for example.[25] Lady Mary Wortley Montagu described her London apartments as 'like an Indian warehouse' and her dressing room as 'like the temple of some Indian god'.[26] Popular panoramas, history paintings treating of the death of Tipu Sultan, a profusion of lithographs, aquatints and engravings, exhibitions and photography constructed a new India.[27] Francis Swain Ward, who had gone to India in 1757 as a lieutenant, exhibited Indian landscapes at the Society of Artists between 1765 and 1773. When he was re-commissioned as a captain in the Madras Army in 1773, he gratefully gave the East India Company ten landscapes which it hung in the Committee of Correspondence's meeting room at East India House in Leadenhall Street in London.[28] The fall of Tipu Sultan in 1799 inspired much visual as well as political interest in Britain. Robert Ker Porter capitalised on this curiosity by painting a 200-feet-long panorama in just six weeks. Depicted on a semicircular (some say three-quarter-circle) plane, the *Taking of Seringapatam* was a pictorial reconstruction of the fourth Anglo-Mysore War. When it went on display at Somerset House, on the Strand, it transported viewers to the scene. One contemporary, Thomas Frognall Dibdin, commented that 'you seemed to be listening to the groans of the wounded and the dying', whose 'red hot blood' was spilled all over the canvas. The realism of the scene produced 'a sight that was altogether as marvellous as it was novel. You carried it home, and did nothing but think of it, talk of it, and dream of it.'[29]

India continued to be an important site of imperial representation into the nineteenth century. In 1808, objects from Seringapatam were brought to London to be housed with other material in an 'Oriental repository' kept by the East India Company.[30] At the Great Exhibition of 1851, the British political presence in the subcontinent was powerfully represented by the exhibition of regalia such as palanquins, thrones, crowns and sceptres, as well as the crown of the Raja of Oudh and the regal dress of the Raja of Bundi. The ivory throne of the Raja of Travancore, a present to the Queen, was even used by Prince Albert for the closing ceremonies.[31] In 1855, the Company's 'repository' was remodelled to reflect changing political imperatives about the value, utility and purpose of empire in the mid-nineteenth century. As a result, although it still contained 'monumental and artistic records of the progress of the British Empire in the East', it also aimed 'to illustrate the productive resources of India and to give information about the life, manners, the arts and industry of its inhabitants'.[32]

Domestic display

The exhibition of empire was not solely undertaken by public institutions: the role of individuals in displaying objects was one of the most powerful ways in which empire was brought home, in many cases quite literally. Valentine's Mansion in Ilford was occupied by a succession of merchants connected with the East India Company. In 1771, it was said that '[it] may, with great propriety, be called a Cabinet of Curiosities', with goods from the Orient 'especially conspicuous'.[33] Outside, secretary birds roamed the gardens. Lawrence Dundas's home in Kerse, near Falkirk, also had a wealth of Indian articles. An inventory of 1763 lists twenty-eight 'Indian pictures' in the gallery, 'two Indian Cabinets' and 'one settee with blew Indian Sattin Work'd', among other things.[34]

Lord Caledon, a returning governor of the Cape Colony, provides another example. Through networks nurtured by patronage and local connections, Caledon could exhibit imperial connections in his country estate in County Tyrone. His dinner table boasted 'new wine and Cape Madeira ... purchased from Messrs De Vos and Schaadu' by Robert Crozier, an Ulsterman whom Caledon had patronised at the Cape. Crozier provided Caledon with animal skins by the same consignment, including one which he packed up with 'camphire [camphor] and pepper which I thought a necessary precaution in order to prevent the hair falling off'. He also had a box of stuffed birds in his possession, which he also duly dispatched.[35] Perhaps the most spectacular impact on the earl's estate was made by the Norfolk Island pine trees that another local contact, John Campbell, sent to Caledon from his posting in New South Wales. Campbell reported that he had a box containing 'about a half a dozen of the young Norfolk pines' and was sure that 'if they should reach your Lordship's demesne at Caledon', they would 'be considered beautiful exotics'.[36] In describing their peculiar charm, Campbell set out very clearly their prospective impact and effect on his patron's estate in Ulster: 'On some of the eminences of Your Lordship's domain at Caledon these trees would cast a most commanding and beautiful appearance, and it would give me the greatest pleasure to find that they flourished there.'[37]

But the ostentatious display of empire-related objects, or the wealth derived from overseas commercial activities, was not always welcome. The example of the Nabob was often held up as the epitome of vulgar wealth and conspicuous consumption. Nabobs were criticised by contemporaries for their 'opulence' and 'Asiatic luxury', and their activities as 'importers of foreign gold'.[38] Perhaps the most glaring example of this was in their penchant for showing off the diamonds that helped them remit their earnings from India. When Thomas Rumbold's estate was sold off after his death in 1793, the listing from Christie's auction house included 'a cameo ring set with brilliants', 'an emerald cameo ring set with brilliants', 'a brilliant sipher [*sic*] cameo', 'a large single stone rose diamond' and 'a ditto brilliant with 11 rubies'. Nabobs flaunted their jewels: Robert Clive spent a fortune giving 'his Lady a new set of jewels' in 1768, while Warren Hastings's wife appeared at a party in Tunbridge Wells in 1784 wearing diamonds worth an estimated £20,000.[39] T.B. Macaulay provided a damning assessment of their baleful influence by connecting it very directly with their conspicuous consumption and exhibition of opulence:

> The Nabobs soon became a most unpopular class of men ... That they had sprung from obscurity, that they had acquired great wealth, that they exhibited it insolently, that they spent it extravagantly, that they raised the price of everything in their neighbourhoods, from fresh eggs to rotten boroughs, that their liveries outshone those of dukes, that their coaches were finer than that of the Lord Mayor, that the examples of their large and ill-governed households corrupted half the servants of the country, that some of them, with all their magnificence, could not catch the tone of good society, but, in spite of the stud and the crowd of menials, of the plate and the Dresden china, of the venison and Burgundy, were still low men; these were the things which excited, both in the class from which they had sprung and in the class in which they attempted to force themselves, the bitter aversion which is the effect of mingled envy and contempt.[40]

The Nabob, as an example of the 'integration of the imperial world into the fabric of British national culture' through the exhibition of empire, was presented in almost wholly negative terms.[41]

Images and objects not only exhibited wealth or commercial success, however. Their display could be used to convey other imperial themes, such as civilisation and improvement, that gained momentum and attracted support as the nineteenth century progressed. For example, the London Missionary Society (LMS) established a museum in 1814 to display objects donated by King Pomare of Tahiti. Pomare claimed that he wished 'to send these idols to Britain, for the Missionary Society, that they may know the likeness of the gods that Tahiti worshipped'. But the missionaries themselves were also keen to return to Britain with evidence of the conversion of the unbelievers. They referred to these objects as 'trophies of Christianity': 'They call our ship, a ship of God, and truly it is. It has carried the Gospel to distant lands, and brought back the trophies of its victory.'[42] The extraordinary juxtaposition of objects in this museum from an aesthetic or scientific perspective – an engraving which appeared in the *Lady's Newspaper* for 1853 showed a twelve-foot god brought from the island of Rarotonga by the Reverend John Williams standing beside a giraffe shot in Griqualand, South Africa, in 1814 – was perfectly comprehensible from the point of view of the LMS. That so many objects were on display, and that the artefacts covered terrain ranging from the domestic to the natural, apparently demonstrated the extent to which Christian civilisation could replace existing belief systems. The display of traditional Pacific costumes or indigenous religious artefacts was a clear indication that the people from whom these objects originated now adhered to European standards of taste, decorum and domestic habits. And, more importantly, the fact that they worshipped a Christian god.[43]

Later flowerings

The exhibitionary impulse is often assumed to have reached its apogee in the Great Exhibition of 1851. But many more exhibitions on explicitly imperial themes followed in its wake, continuing well into the twentieth century.[44] Many see the climax of this movement as occurring at Wembley in 1924–25, but the imperial exhibitions continued right up until the Second World War. These exhibitions occurred throughout the British Empire and other parts of the world.[45] In Britain itself, the Glasgow Empire Exhibition of 1938 was the last of these great shows. It adopted contemporary Art Deco architecture and by that time its message could be propagated through a whole variety of media, including newsreel. Many of these exhibitions, including those before the First World War and the great show at Wembley, included massive Pageants of Empire which conveyed imperial events to a large public, in the latter instance taking place in the new Wembley Stadium. But exhibitions ranged from these large-scale, international shows to smaller-scale affairs that promoted the activities of specific societies or indeed one company by using explicitly imperial iconography.

The recently formed Imperial Airways, for example, used exhibitionary techniques to promote its activities and advertise the imperial connections that it offered to customers. In 1929 at London's Olympia, at the seventh international aeronautical exhibition, the company occupied two stalls, both of which incorporated suitably imperial motifs. At one, a slow-moving painted panorama of scenes on the England–Egypt–India route passed behind the windows of an airliner cabin section. At the second stall, aircraft models were moved along a map of the route.[46] Five years later, in 1934, the airline mounted its own exhibition, entitled 'Flying over the Empire'. The exhibition, which comprised a large folding screen on which was mounted a map, models of Imperial aircraft, photographs depicting imperial scenes and several dioramas, toured the provinces and was remounted for a two-month Christmas show at the Science Museum in December 1935 (renamed 'Empire's Airway' with free admission). It was subsequently sent to Canada, South Africa and Australia and, by 1937, an estimated one million people had seen the exhibition.[47]

The Empire Marketing Board (EMB) provides another illuminating example of the exhibition of empire in the early twentieth century. Although its existence was brief – from May 1926 to September 1933 – it managed to publish around 800 different poster designs to promote the consumption of goods and products produced in the Empire. These images and their exhibition were conceived in an effort to 'move the hearts and minds' and 'touch the imagination of the people' by 'bringing the Empire alive'.[48] By December 1927, a thousand frame-poster hoardings had been erected, many of them at sites which had never carried advertising before. By the time of the EMB's demise, there were 1,800 such hoardings in 450 towns across the country. Images produced by the EMB had widespread appeal and far-reaching impact. Commercial companies used them for stationery, and made them into pictures for jigsaw puzzles or designs for card games. Eight designs were reprinted in 5,000 sets by the EMB and issued as Christmas cards. MacDonald Gill's 'Highways of Empire' map was reprinted in miniature and 26,000 copies were distributed at the Schoolboy's Own Exhibition in 1929. The visually persuasive qualities of the images published by the EMB certainly seemed to have the desired effect. One teacher thought the posters were a 'god-send' because 'they vivify and intensify the very impression we wish our pupils to receive with respect to the resources and potentialities of our empire'.[49]

As Catherine Hall and Sonya Rose remind us, 'Britain's imperial role and its presence within the metropole shaped peoples' identities as Britons and informed their practical, daily activities'.[50] Through a series of examples, drawn from a wide chronological sweep and expressed in a variety of different media, *Exhibiting the Empire* shows the diverse ways in which Britain's Empire was displayed and exhibited to people in the United Kingdom. Taken together, the collection suggests the complex interpretative contexts in which British people experienced and responded to the Empire as it waxed and waned from the late seventeenth century to the early decades of the twentieth.

Contributions range across a gamut of international, national, regional and domestic contexts. Traditional exhibitionary practices associated with artistic media like oil paintings and prints, such as those considered in the chapters by Eleanor Hughes and Douglas Fordham, offered a ready-made channel for disseminating information, ideas and ideologies about empire. The chapters by Jeffrey Auerbach, Sarah Longair, Nalini Ghuman and John MacKenzie explore the opportunities for exhibiting and celebrating empire provided by grand, organised, set-piece occasions. The Festival of Empire which took place in 1911, for example, offered a panoply of tangible representations of empire to its visitors: scale models of the Dominions' parliament buildings connected by the 'all-red tour' of the miniature railway; replicas of a Jamaican sugar plantation and a Malay village; an Indian section complete with jungle, palace and bazaar. The centrepiece event – the 'Pageant of London and the Empire' – traced the development of empire from the 'Dawn of British History' to a 'Grand Imperial Finale', in which hundreds of visitors from the Dominions joined with thousands of British performers to provide a 'living picture' that illustrated the vastness of the Empire on which the sun famously never set.

But empire was manifest in Britain in other ways and in other circumstances. Stephanie Barczewski, in her chapter on the iconography of British country houses, argues that the display of this imagery in domestic architectural contexts is connected to the growth, both in territorial scale and in metropolitan cultural significance, of the British Empire in the eighteenth century. John MacKenzie offers a detailed look at the ways in which the Delhi Durbar of 1911 – taking place half the world away in India – was represented in Britain, becoming the subject of major news reports across the United Kingdom. Newspapers around the country carried extensive reports of the ceremonial, often with 'library photographs' of the key sites in which they took place, as well as stories of the journeys of the King-Emperor and Queen-Empress from Europe to India and around India itself. This serves to demonstrate the significance of the press, after the removal of controls and taxes in the mid-nineteenth century, in circulating more widely material and ideas about the British Empire, initially through reading rooms in libraries and other institutions, later in personal copies, creating a profound visual effect both through print information and through the increasing use of illustrations.[51] Turning to aural representations, Nalini Ghuman, in her chapter, explores the musical contribution of Sir Edward Elgar, the newly appointed Master of the King's Musick, to the British Empire Exhibition held at Wembley in the mid-1920s – a reminder that empire was often 'exhibited' and experienced in Britain in intangible, as well as physical, forms. Through the performance of bands in public places, various forms of concerts and music in churches, as well as through the considerable sales of sheet music, such musical expressions of empire were everywhere, the imperial content invariably highlighted through highly charged texts.[52]

And empire could be exhibited on much more modest scales than these powerful public examples. Several of the chapters that follow show how the Empire was 'exhibited', both visually and textually, in a variety of printed material. John McAleer and Berny Sèbe consider the importance of printed books in disseminating ideas about Britain's engagement with the wider world, as well as the ideas about empire this inspired and provoked. David Tomkins and Ashley Jackson explore yet another type of documentary evidence – ephemera. Drawing principally on the riches of the John Johnson Collection at the Bodleian Library, they argue that the printed ephemera that proliferated as a result of technical and social changes – programmes, postcards, tickets, posters, playbills, paper bags, cigarette cards, food labels and advertisements to name but a few – were one of the most important ways in which ideas about empire and the wider world were introduced to the public in Britain.

Exhibiting the Empire sheds light on the complex interplay between 'metropole' and 'periphery', both within the United Kingdom and in the wider Empire beyond. Clearly London, as the beating heart of the global British Empire, played a huge role in exhibiting that phenomenon to the general public. Jeffrey Auerbach considers the Great Exhibition of 1851 and the Festival of Empire (held at the rebuilt Crystal Palace in Sydenham) which celebrated the coronation of George V in 1911. The British Empire Exhibition, held at Wembley in 1924 and 1925 where it attracted some twenty-seven million visitors, provides the backdrop for the themes explored by Sarah Longair and Nalini Ghuman in their respective chapters. But the Empire was exhibited beyond London. Monuments to James Cook's endeavours appeared in rural Buckinghamshire, while objects collected by those who sailed with him were displayed in Cambridge and Dublin, among other places. Museums throughout the country sought to exhibit artefacts derived from voyages of exploration,[53] while later in the nineteenth century some shipping companies actually commissioned captains to supply ethnographic materials.[54] And exhibiting the Empire in Britain could have important ramifications beyond the shores of the United Kingdom. Sarah Longair's chapter shows how the authorities in Zanzibar tried to use the opportunity presented by the British Empire Exhibition in Wembley to present carefully calibrated images about the protectorate to the British public.

Contributions range widely over time and across space. Jeffrey Auerbach demonstrates in his chapter on the exhibitions held in the Crystal Palace that even a relatively short period of sixty years could make a great deal of difference to the ways in which empire was displayed and interpreted. No single collection of essays on such a wide-ranging subject, therefore, can claim to be comprehensive or all-encompassing. And the British Empire was not exhibited just in the United Kingdom; it was also displayed and experienced throughout the territories of that Empire and in the wider world beyond. Besides, while some representations of empire were clearly conscious acts, others were not. Representations of imperial events in ephemera might have been, as Ashley Jackson and David Tomkins point out, incidental, almost 'accidentally' expressing some association with empire. As such, *Exhibiting the Empire* does not claim to offer a comprehensive evaluation of the myriad ways in which the British Empire was imbricated in British domestic life and culture over the centuries. By offering a series of detailed case studies, however, the collection hopes to promote further research into the ways in which the Empire was made manifest and tangible to those living with it as a real political, social and cultural entity. All of this reflects the extent to which the phenomenon some art historians have described as 'the visual turn' has come to be significant in imperial studies.[55] Several recently published books demonstrate the commitment of the 'Studies in Imperialism Series' to this important historiographical trend, emphasising materiality, ritual, monuments, memory, and various ways of visualising and imagining empire.[56] It is quite clear that many more such studies will follow. It is hoped that the essays in *Exhibiting the Empire* will make a significant contribution to such developments, while also suggesting the potential riches remaining to be unlocked.

Notes

1 For exhibitions, art and music, see below. For panoramas, see Denise Blake Oleksijczuk, *The First Panoramas: Visions of British Imperialism* (Minneapolis: University of Minnesota Press, 2011), and for the theatre, Marty Gould, *Nineteenth-Century Theatre and the Imperial Encounter* (New York: Routledge, 2011), which convincingly overturns any idea that the British stage was somehow bereft of empire. For the cinema, James Chapman and Nicholas J. Cull's *Projecting Empire: Imperialism and Popular Cinema* (London: I.B. Tauris, 2009) is a notable addition to the literature.

2 See, for example, John M. MacKenzie (ed.), *European Empires and the People: Popular Responses to Imperialism in France, Britain, The Netherlands, Belgium, Germany and Italy* (Manchester: Manchester University Press, 2011).

3 On museums, see John M. MacKenzie, *Museums and Empire: Natural History, Human Cultures and Colonial Identities* (Manchester: Manchester University Press, 2009), and Sarah Longair and John McAleer (eds), *Curating Empire: Museums and the British Imperial Experience* (Manchester: Manchester University Press, 2012). Botanic gardens, as well as displaying plants and tropical products from colonised regions, often additionally displayed exotic botanical illustrations which conveyed visions of the botanical riches of the empire to a wider public. Some of these became popular in interior decor. See, for example, H.J. Noltie, *Indian Botanical Drawings, 1793–1868 from the Royal Botanic Gardens, Edinburgh* (Edinburgh: Royal Botanic Garden, 1999), and H.J. Noltie, *The Dapuri Drawings: Alexander Gibson and the Bombay Botanic Gardens* (Edinburgh: Royal Botanic Gardens, 2002).

4 Among a growing literature on the public exposure of missions and missionaries, see Susan Thorne, *Congregational Missions and the Making of an Imperial Culture in Nineteenth-Century England* (Stanford, CA: Stanford University Press, 1999).

5 Christopher Pinney, 'The Material and Visual Culture of British India', in Douglas M. Peers and Nandini Gooptu (eds), *India and the British Empire* (Oxford: Oxford University Press, 2012), pp. 231–61 (pp. 232–3).

6 The archive of the great map and atlas publisher John Bartholomew and Son is now deposited in the National Library of Scotland, and reveals just how extensive the sales of these products were. See also James McCarthy, *Journey into Africa: The Life and Death of Keith Johnston, Scottish Cartographer and Explorer (1844–79)* (Caithness: Whittle Publishing, 2004).

7 John M. MacKenzie, 'The Provincial Geographical Societies in Britain, 1884–1914', in Morag Bell, Robin Butlin and Michael Heffernan (eds), *Geography and Imperialism, 1820–1940* (Manchester: Manchester University Press, 1995), pp. 93–124. See also Felix Driver, *Geography Militant: Cultures of Exploration and Empire* (Oxford: Blackwell, 2001), and Anne Godlewska and Neil Smith (eds), *Geography and Empire* (Oxford: Blackwell, 1994).

8 James Cook and James King, *A Voyage to the Pacific Ocean … for Making Discoveries in the Northern Hemisphere, in the Years 1776, 1777, 1778, 1779, and 1780*, 3 vols (London: G. Nicol and T. Cadell, 1784), vol. 1, p. 5.

9 See Ashley Jackson, *Buildings of Empire* (Oxford: Oxford University Press, 2013). See also the imperial chapters of Jeffrey Richards and John M. MacKenzie, *The Railway Station: A Social History* (Oxford: Oxford University Press, 1986).

10 See, for example, Astrid Swenson and Peter Mandler (eds), *From Plunder to Preservation: Britain and the Heritage of Empire, c. 1800–1940* (Oxford: Oxford University Press, 2013).

11 Quoted in Daniela Bleichmar, 'Seeing the World in a Room: Looking at Exotica in Early Modern Collections', in Daniela Bleichmar and Peter C. Mancall (eds), *Collecting across Cultures: Material Exchanges in the Early Modern Atlantic World* (Philadelphia: University of Pennsylvania Press, 2011), pp. 15–30 (p. 22).

12 Quoted in Arthur MacGregor, 'A Cabinet of Wonder', in *The World of 1607* (Williamsburg, VA: Jamestown-Yorktown Federation, 2007), pp. 144–9 (pp. 144–5).

13 William Foster, *The East India House: Its History and Associations* (London: John Lane, 1924), p. 3.

14 See Sarah Longair and John McAleer, 'Curating Empire: Museums and the British Imperial Experience', in Sarah Longair and John McAleer (eds), *Curating Empire: Museums and the British Imperial Experience* (Manchester: Manchester University Press, 2012), pp. 1–16 (pp. 2–3).

15 Samuel Purchas, *Hakluytus Posthumus*, 20 vols (Glasgow, 1905–7), vol. 13, pp. 3–4. The map probably perished in the Whitehall fires of 1694 and 1697. See R.A. Skelton, 'The Royal Map Collections of England', *Imago Mundi* 13 (1956), pp. 181–3.

16 Olivia Horsfall Turner, 'Introduction', in Olivia Horsfall Turner (ed.), *'The Mirror of Great Britain': National Identity in Seventeenth-Century Britain* (Reading: Spire, 2012), pp. 9–14 (p. 13).

17 See John E. Crowley, *Imperial Landscapes: Britain's Global Visual Culture, 1745–1820* (New Haven, CT: Yale University Press, 2011), pp. 20–1. The *Livro* remained in manuscript form and is currently housed at the British Library, London.

18 Crowley, *Imperial Landscapes*, p. 31.

19 Neil Rennie, *Far-Fetched Facts: The Literature of Travel and the Idea of the South Seas* (Oxford: Clarendon Press, 1998), p. 64.

20 See McAleer, 'Exhibiting Exploration', p. 50 below. See also Harriet Guest, 'Ornament and Use: Mai and Cook in London', in Kathleen Wilson (ed.), *A New Imperial History: Culture, Identity, and Modernity in Britain and the Empire, 1660–1840* (Cambridge: Cambridge University Press, 2004), pp. 317–44.

21 See Sadiah Qureshi, *Peoples on Parade: Exhibitions, Empire, and Anthropology in Nineteenth-Century Britain* (Chicago: University of Chicago Press, 2011).

22 See John Bonehill, '"This Hapless Adventurer": Hodges and the London Art World', in Geoff Quilley and John Bonehill (eds), *William Hodges, 1744–1797: The Art of Exploration* (London: National Maritime Museum, 2004), pp. 9–14. See also Giles Tillotson, *The Artificial Empire: The Indian Landscapes of William Hodges* (Richmond: Curzon, 2000), pp. 53–4.

23 Crowley, *Imperial Landscapes*, p. 179.

24 See Hermione de Almeida and George H. Gilpin, *Indian Renaissance: British Romantic Art and the Prospect of India* (Aldershot: Ashgate, 2005).

25 Natasha Eaton, *Mimesis across Empires: Artworks and Networks in India, 1765–1860* (Durham, NC: Duke University Press, 2013), p. 30.

26 Ibid., p. 24.

27 Pinney, 'The Material and Visual Culture of British India', p. 241.

28 Crowley, *Imperial Landscapes*, p. 171.

29 Richard Altick, *The Shows of London* (Cambridge, MA: Harvard University Press, 1978), p. 135.

30 Carol A. Breckenridge, 'The Aesthetics and Politics of Colonial Collecting: India at World Fairs', *Comparative Studies in History and Society* 31 (1989), pp. 195–216 (p. 198).

31 Ibid., pp. 203–4.

32 Eaton, *Mimesis across Empires*, p. 292, n. 12.

33 Georgina Green, 'Valentines, the Raymonds and Company Material Culture', *The East India Company at Home*, http://blogs.ucl.ac.uk/eicah/files/2013/02/Valetines-case-study-Final-Website-Draft-2.pdf (accessed 5 July 2013), pp. 5, 6.

34 Helen Clifford, 'Accommodating the East: Sir Lawrence Dundas as Northern Nabob? The Dundas Property Empire and Nabob Taste', *The East India Company at Home*, http://blogs.ucl.ac.uk/eicah/files/2013/02/Aske-Hall-Final-PDF-Version2.pdf (accessed 5 July 2013), p. 19.

35 Public Record Office of Northern Ireland (PRONI), Caledon papers, D2431/17/3/3, Robert Crozier to Lord Caledon, 20 December 1812.

36 PRONI, Caledon papers, D2433/C/11/26, John Campbell to Lord Caledon, 2 November 1812.

37 PRONI, Caledon papers, D2433/C/11/26, Campbell to Caledon, 15 August 1813.

38 See Philip Lawson and Jim Phillips, '"Our Execrable Banditti": Perceptions of Nabobs in Mid-Eighteenth Century Britain', *Albion* 16 (1984), pp. 225–41 (p. 238).

39 Tillman W. Nechtman, 'A Jewel in the Crown? Indian Wealth in Domestic Britain

in the Late Eighteenth Century', *Eighteenth Century Studies* 41 (2007), pp. 71–86 (p. 78).

40 Thomas Babington Macaulay, *Macaulay's Essay on Lord Clive*, ed. William Henry Hudson (London: George G. Harrap, 1910), pp. 94–5.

41 Nechtman, 'A Jewel in the Crown?', p. 72.

42 Sujit Sivasundaram, *Nature and the Godly Empire: Science and Evangelical Mission in the Pacific, 1795–1850* (Cambridge: Cambridge University Press, 2005), pp. 178, 185. For more on the London Missionary Society and its museum, see Chris Wingfield, 'The Moving Objects of the London Missionary Society: An Experiment in Symmetrical Anthropology', unpublished PhD thesis, University of Birmingham, 2012.

43 Sivasundaram, *Nature and the Godly Empire*, p. 177.

44 See Jeffrey A. Auerbach, *The Great Exhibition of 1851: A Nation on Display* (New Haven, CT: Yale University Press, 1999); Jeffrey A. Auerbach and Peter H. Hoffenberg (eds), *Britain, the Empire, and the World at the Great Exhibition of 1851* (Aldershot: Ashgate, 2008); Paul Greenhalgh, *Ephemeral Vistas: The Expositions Universelles, Great Exhibitions and World's Fairs, 1851–1939* (Manchester: Manchester University Press, 1990).

45 Such exhibitions included those at Paris Vincennes, 1931, Johannesburg, South Africa, 1936–37 and Wellington, New Zealand, 1939–40.

46 Gordon Pirie, *Cultures and Caricatures of British Imperial Aviation: Passengers, Pilots, Publicity* (Manchester: Manchester University Press, 2012), p. 177.

47 Ibid., pp. 184–5.

48 Stephen Constantine, *Buy and Build: The Advertising Posters of the Empire Marketing Board* (London: HMSO, 1986), pp. 1, 6–7. See also Melanie Horton, *Empire Marketing Board Posters* (London: Scala, 2010).

49 Constantine, *Buy and Build*, pp. 11, 17.

50 Catherine Hall and Sonya O. Rose, 'Introduction: Being at Home with the Empire', in Catherine Hall and Sonya Rose (eds), *At Home with the Empire: Metropolitan Culture and the Imperial World* (Cambridge: Cambridge University Press, 2006), pp. 1–31 (p. 22).

51 See Simon J. Potter, *Newspapers and Empire in Ireland and Britain: Reporting the British Empire, c. 1857–1921* (Dublin: Four Courts Press, 2001), and Chandrika Kaul (ed.), *Media and the British Empire* (London: Palgrave 2006).

52 See Jeffrey Richards, *Imperialism and Music* (Manchester: Manchester University Press, 2001).

53 William Hunter acquired material from Captain Cook, now in the Hunterian Museum of the University of Glasgow. See Lawrence Keppie, *William Hunter and the Hunterian Museum in Glasgow, 1807–2007* (Edinburgh: Edinburgh University Press, 2007). See also Eileen Hooper-Greenhill, *Museums and the Shaping of Knowledge* (London: Routledge, 1992), and Amiria Henare, *Museums, Anthropology and Imperial Exchange* (Cambridge: Cambridge University Press, 2005) for many other examples.

54 For this phenomenon, see Zachary Kingdon and Dmitri von den Bersselaar, 'Collecting Empire? African Objects, West African Trade and a Liverpool Museum', in Sheryllynne Haggerty, Anthony Webster and Nicholas J. White (eds), *The Empire in One City? Liverpool's Inconvenient Imperial Past* (Manchester: Manchester University Press, 2008), pp. 100–22.

55 Earlier work on visual aspects of the British Empire includes John M. MacKenzie, 'Art and the Empire', in P.J. Marshall (ed.), *Cambridge Illustrated History: The British Empire* (Cambridge: Cambridge University Press, 1996), pp. 296–315; Tim Barringer, Geoff Quilley and Douglas Fordham (eds), *Art and the British Empire* (Manchester: Manchester University Press, 2007); and Tim Barringer and Tom Flynn (eds), *Colonialism and the Object: Empire, Material Culture and the Museum* (London: Routledge, 1998). For collecting, see Maya Jasanoff, *Edge of Empire: Conquest and Collecting in the East, 1750–1850* (London: Fourth Estate, 2005), and Holger Hoock, *Empires of the Imagination: Politics, War and the Arts in the*

British World, 1750–1850 (London: Profile, 2010). For photography, see James R. Ryan, *Picturing Empire: Photography and the Visualisation of the British Empire* (London: Reaktion, 1997); Anne Maxwell, *Colonial Photography and Exhibitions: Representations of the 'Native' People and the Making of European Identities* (Leicester: Leicester University Press, 1999); and Paul S. Landau and Deborah D. Kaspin (eds), *Images and Empires: Visuality in Colonial and Postcolonial Africa* (Berkeley, CA: University of California Press, 2002).

56 Stephanie Barczewski, *Country Houses and the British Empire, 1700–1930* (Manchester: Manchester University Press, 2014); Pamila Gupta, *The Relic State: St Francis Xavier and the Politics of Ritual in Portuguese India* (Manchester: Manchester University Press, 2014); Dominik Geppert and Frank Lorenz Müller (eds), *Sites of Imperial Memory: Commemorating Colonial Rule in the Nineteenth and Twentieth Centuries* (Manchester: Manchester University Press, 2015).

CHAPTER ONE

An elite imperial vision: Eighteenth-century British country houses and four continents imagery

Stephanie Barczewski

Just north of York, Castle Howard casts its imposing gaze over the North Yorkshire Moors. Built by the third Earl of Carlisle in the early eighteenth century, the house was intended as a lasting monument to the power and prominence of the Howard family, even though – or perhaps because – Carlisle came from a minor branch with little connection to his more renowned ancestors. If any added motivation was needed, it came from Carlisle's summary dismissal from the upper reaches of the political world in 1702, when the pro-Whig King William III was succeeded by the pro-Tory Queen Anne. The staunchly Whig Carlisle, who had risen to First Lord of the Treasury under William, suddenly found himself out of favour and out of office. He had already embarked upon plans for a grand house in the hopes of enticing the king to visit; now he had little else to do but concentrate on his new seat, which if all went well would dazzle his contemporaries with its splendour and display of the highest standards of taste and erudition. His creaky old castle at Naworth in Cumbria would simply no longer do as a seat for a man of his stature and – at this point thwarted – ambition.

For the job, he hired a man with no previous architectural experience, the erstwhile soldier John Vanbrugh, whom Carlisle had met at the Kit-Kat Club in London and who was at the time enjoying considerable success as a playwright. From this unlikely pairing sprang a country house that many architectural historians have since proclaimed to be England's greatest. Castle Howard's most famous feature is the dome over its central block, the first on a private house in Britain. Soaring seventy feet into the air, the dome is surmounted by an eight-windowed lantern that serves as the main source of light, while inside massive Corinthian columns bracket huge arches that open on to flanking stairways. In 1709, Carlisle commissioned the Italian artist Gianantonio Pellegrini to decorate the interior of the dome with a painting of the fall of Phaethon surrounded by representations of the four elements – fire, earth, air and water.

Although it is unknown precisely why Phaethon was selected as the centrepiece of the decorative scheme, one explanation is that the theme referenced Antonio Verrio's paintings for the Queen's Staircase at Windsor Castle, which depicted Apollo giving his wayward son permission to drive the Chariot of the Sun across the sky.[1] In the late seventeenth and early eighteenth centuries, Apollo was closely linked to the French King Louis XIV, who had identified himself with the Greek god from the earliest days of his reign and who had dedicated his magnificent throne room at Versailles to him. In English eyes, this reference to Louis XIV would have had negative associations with absolute monarchy and the divine right of kings. In his study of the building of Castle Howard, Charles Saumarez Smith asserts that early eighteenth-century Britons would have seen Pellegrini's painting 'as an image of the collapse of such ambitions, of the detestation of the English for French forms of government and a celebration of the individual liberty established by the Glorious Revolution'.[2] It is presumably this meaning that William III, victor of the Glorious Revolution, intended it to have at Windsor.

Contemporary English visitors to Castle Howard, however, would have seen Phaethon not only as Louis XIV but also as the recently deposed James II, whose popish and autocratic agenda had led to his downfall. The presence of Phaethon at the centre of the Great Hall's decorative scheme would have thus been read by contemporary visitors to Castle Howard as a political message referencing recent events close to home as well as on the European continent. From the perspective of a member of the Whig political elite like Carlisle, that message was clear: overreaching monarchs will bring about their own destruction. This was in keeping with the reason for building Castle Howard itself: to serve as a symbol of the power, wealth and discernment of its owner, and by extension of the right of his fellow members of the elite to govern the nation, with the limited assistance of a monarchy kept within strict constitutional limits. Carlisle intended the Phaethon painting to remind his monarch – now Queen Anne, another Stuart – of the real balance of political power in the British nation.

The other components of the great hall were part of the same decorative and iconographic scheme. The staircase walls featured large scenes, also by Pellegrini, depicting Apollo and the Muses on one side and Apollo and Midas on the other. Lower down on the staircases, meanwhile, were smaller allegorical representations of the four known continents at the time. (Though a 'great southern continent' had existed in imagined form since classical times, Australia and Antarctica had not yet been discovered by Europeans.) Pellegrini represented the continents in female form. A robed Europe holds a model of a church in her right hand, while a cornucopia leans against her left side, symbolising the Christian religious faith and plenty of the continent. In the background, a collection of helmets, spears and flags proclaims Europe's military prowess. Standing before a camel, Asia dangles an incense burner from her right hand while a sheaf of wheat lies to her left. A dark-skinned Africa is seated, her right elbow leaning on a lion, while in her left hand she clutches a scorpion. And finally, America is a barely clothed, muscular Indian, with a bow dangling loosely from her left hand and a number of arrows grasped in her right. An alligator peers from beneath her feet. The combination of Apollo and the four continents was a frequent one in baroque decorative schemes; Svetlana Alpers and Michael Baxandall write that 'the four continents below a heaven ruled by the sun-god' was 'the ultimate cliché of baroque iconography'.[3] In this context, however, it had specific political and imperial meanings that the remainder of this chapter will explore.

By the early eighteenth century, the use of the four continents motif had a long history in European iconography.[4] In 1593, the Italian artist Cesare Ripa published an allegorical emblem book titled the *Iconologia overo Descrittione Dell'imagini Universali cavate dall'Antichità et da altri luoghi* that came to serve as the prototype for representing the continents throughout Europe.[5] Ripa's depiction was not politically neutral. His Europe is crowned and seated in monarch-like fashion, with the surrounding frame crammed with symbols of the continent's bounty, power and cultural sophistication, including the church and cornucopia seen at Castle Howard. His other three continents, meanwhile, are all standing, with far less cluttered backgrounds in demonstration of their relative poverty of civilisation; only Asia is fully dressed, while Africa and America are almost naked. The representation of Europe is dominated by human inventions such as books and musical instruments, while the others feature native flora and fauna or commodities derived from them, suggesting that only in Europe has human ingenuity triumphed fully over nature.[6]

Beyond its establishment of a global hierarchy of peoples and nations, four continents iconography had explicitly imperial connotations from an early stage. In the Netherlands, it was used as an expression of the nation's commercial and imperial ambitions when it appeared on the west tympanum of Amsterdam's City Hall, which featured a relief carving dating from the 1650s entitled *The Four Continents Bring Their Tribute to the City of Amsterdam* by Artus Quellinus the Elder.[7] By the eighteenth century, four continents iconography had been incorporated into 'the European Enlightenment's moral geography in which Europe ... represented the summit of civilization, and other continents represented various levels of savagery and barbarism'.[8] This view was evident in the ceiling paintings over the central staircase of the Residenz of the Prince-Bishop of Würzburg, executed by Gianbattista Tiepolo in the early 1750s. A sumptuously dressed Europe is surrounded by emblems of moral, technological, cultural and military superiority: a cross, a telescope, architectural elements and a cannon, while a globe represents the continent's growing imperial reach. In contrast, America rides a crocodile through an untamed wilderness, while Africa, mounted on a camel, proffers textiles, spices and ivory, signifying that Europeans now envisioned their relationship to these continents as colonial. Bestriding an elephant and surrounded by armed men, Asia is depicted as a threat. A naked, bound male figure in the foreground suggested that Asians were barbarous and cruel. The allegorical representations of the continents are arranged in a manner that, no matter where the viewer stands, he or she sees the others in relation to Europe.[9]

In Britain, use of the four continents motif did not become common until the late seventeenth century, when allegorical figures inspired by it began to appear in theatrical productions.[10] By that point, the representation of America in particular was more than a symbolic exercise, for the eastern seaboard of the continent had become a British colonial possession. As Castle Howard's staircase illustrates, Ripa's iconography continued to be used as the basis for visual representations. Now, however, it had a more specific context: demonstrating the growing role that imperial expansion was playing in Britain's colonial and commercial endeavours. Carlisle's decision to include Phaethon as a prominent part of the great hall could be seen as an attempt to wrest control of a prominent, politically charged myth from royal hands and to use it to express the burgeoning power of the Whig elite. His decision to include the four continents was the product of a similar impulse, demonstrating the placement of the house's owner at the centre not only of his estate but of the entire world.

Royal use of the four continents

Between 1690 and 1720, there were a number of royal-sponsored efforts to use the four continents in artistic projects. These projects were intended not only to inspire loyalty to the British state but also to convey the authority of the monarchy by emphasising the expanse of the territory over which it now ruled. Occurring as they did at a moment in British history when the scope of royal power was still very much a subject of debate, these examples show how contemporary monarchs attempted to turn the nation's imperial expansion to their advantage, by overtly displaying how their power extended beyond the boundaries of the British Isles to a global realm. British monarchs did not entirely abandon their efforts to increase their political power after the calamities of the seventeenth century; instead they developed new strategies to win the argument. What they had been forced to concede at home could perhaps be recovered abroad, through the reconfiguration of the British monarchy in a more overtly imperial mode.[11]

Four continents iconography played an important role in this process. Completed between 1688 and 1692, Antonio Verrio's mural at the west end of the Great Hall of the Royal Hospital, Chelsea, in London depicts Charles II on horseback, surrounded by representations of the four continents. The re-establishment of royal authority after 1660 was a complex process that required considerable dexterity and ruthlessness on Charles's part. Belying the image of the decadent and lackadaisical 'Merry Monarch', Charles devoted significant attention to cultural methods of promoting his authority.[12] Decorative painters like Verrio and his pupils Louis Laguerre and James Thornhill had key roles to play in the campaigns of Charles and other late Stuart monarchs to project the power of the dynasty in the complex political circumstances of the post-Restoration era. Verrio's painting for the Royal Hospital depicts a mounted Charles II trampling on a dragon, while Victory and Hercules place a laurel wreath on his head. To the king's left, her head entwined by a serpent, a black female Africa holds a sheaf of wheat; behind her a white female Asia carries a censer, clearly referencing Ripa's iconography. Also echoing Ripa, a white female Europe proffers an overflowing cornucopia, while in the background additional female figures encircle a large globe. In the bottom right corner, a bare-breasted female Indian represents America. She wears a feathered headdress and holds a bow loosely in her left hand, while a quiver of arrows lies harmlessly beside her on the ground as she kneels in supplication to the king.

This was not the first time that Verrio had employed the motif of the four continents to represent the royal majesty and authority of Charles II. In the King's Presence Chamber at Windsor, his ceiling painting, since destroyed, featured a portrait of the king being 'shown by Mercury to the four quarters of the world, who are introduced by Neptune'.[13] Verrio's use of similar iconography at the Royal Hospital suggests that it was seen as relevant to contemporary representations of royal power. Kevin Sharpe and Steven Zwicker observe that Charles II could not simply return to older forms of royal representation following the 'violent assault on the iconicity of Renaissance monarchy' that had occurred in 1649:

Thereafter, whatever the force of royalist polemics and however limited the success of republican representation, the mystery of kingship was irreparably fractured ... Charles II himself appears to have recognized that his authority could not simply be reconstituted out of the old pieties.[14]

Instead, he turned to new modes of representation. The four continents motif had the advantage of combining the display of royal power in relation to a traditional arena, represented visually by Europe, with images that could show its expansion into new realms such as Asia, Africa and, most immediately, America. Thus could it be reconstructed as an iconographical form that on the one hand hearkened back to pre-Civil-War modes of displaying royal authority as encompassing the globe in an absolutist but abstract manner, but on the other could be adapted to the contemporary context by showing the expansion of royal sovereignty over a real-life imperial realm.

The four continents motif continued to be used by the English monarchs who followed Charles II. Shortly after ascending to the throne, William III concluded that a new royal residence was needed, as the poor quality of London's air and the damp riverside site of White-hall Palace aggravated his chronic asthma. The king wanted, however, to remain sufficiently close to the capital as not to isolate himself from the business of government. The village of Kensington on the city's western edge was ideal in both location and air quality, and so the purchase of Nottingham House, previously owned by William's Secretary of State, the Earl of Nottingham, was arranged. Christopher Wren was commissioned to transform the house into Kensington Palace. The most prominent feature of the new palace was the 96-foot-long King's Gallery. In 1694, a wind-vane was installed on the palace roof and connected to a dial over the gallery's fireplace. Set in a central position in Kensington's most splendid room, the dial was intended as more than a mere decorative device. By showing the king the direction of the wind, it allowed him to track the comings and goings of his naval and merchant fleets. The commercial and imperial purpose of the device is confirmed by its artwork. The dial features a map of north-western Europe, made by Robert Morden, with England at its centre. In the corners are scenes of the four continents, probably painted by the London artist Robert Robinson, that are less allegorical and more naturalistic than Ripa's iconography. Represented by a pastoral scene, Europe is at top left, while Asia at top right features several colourfully dressed figures in turbans and flowing robes, accompanied by monkeys and a camel. In the bottom left corner, Africa is represented by a group of half-naked, dark-skinned men and women; a pile of ivory tusks lies on the ground beside them. And finally, America is at bottom right,

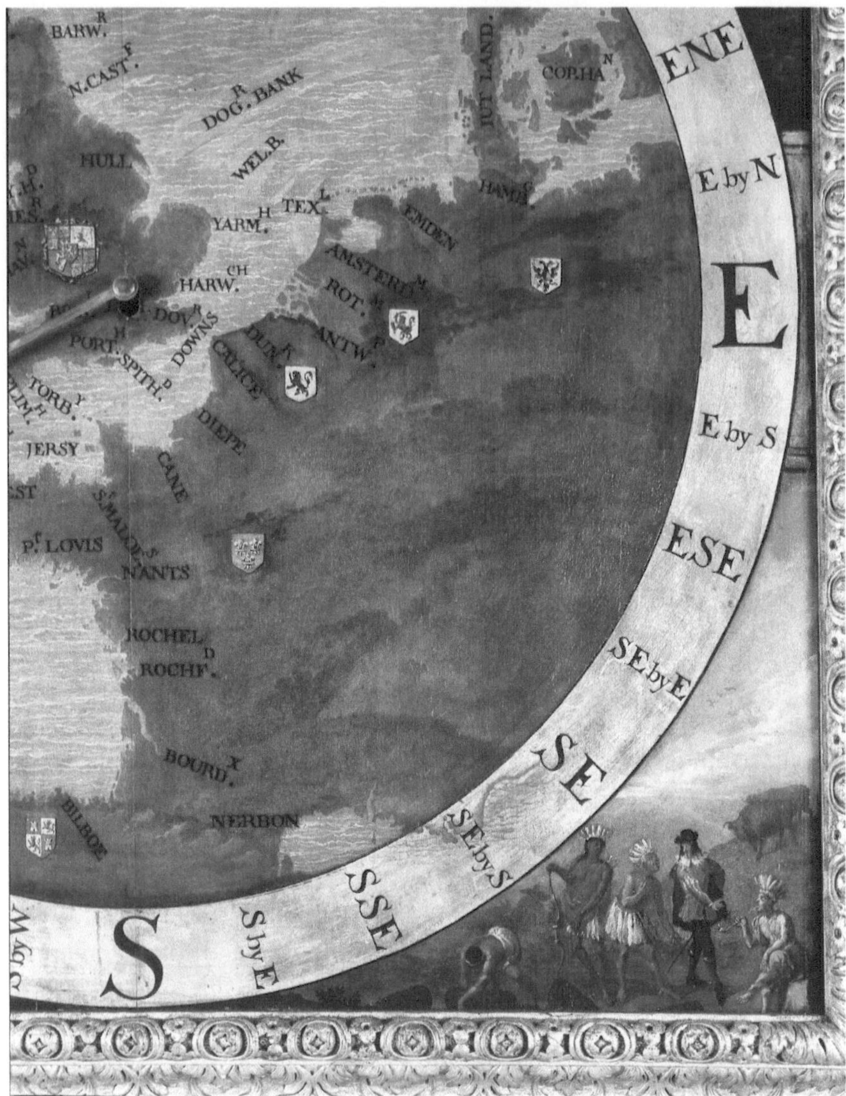

Figure 1.1 A detail from the 'America' section of the wind-vane in the King's Gallery at Kensington Palace (1694), depicting an encounter between American Indians and English colonial settlers

represented by a scene depicting a colonial encounter between a party of east-coast Indians and an English settler. One of the Indians bows and extends his hand in friendship to the Englishman, while another sits with his legs crossed as he smokes a pipe (see Figure 1.1). The overall impression is one of peace and harmony between the two peoples; there is no sign of tension or violence.

By depicting the scene in such an idealised form, the artist reflected the aspirations of the English for their American colonies, with the Indians represented as willing partners rather than hostile adversaries. The inclusion of the tobacco pipe, symbolising the colonies' most profitable commodity, was no coincidence. Nor was the presence of the windvane in the King's Gallery, for the accompanying artwork presented visual evidence of the destinations of and the economic reasons for – as represented by ivory and tobacco – the voyages of the sailing ships that were carried on their global trade routes by the winds measured by the exterior vane. As an example of the four continents motif, the vane is significant for its major adjustment of the conventional iconography, based upon Ripa's century-old engravings, that had dominated previous English uses of the motif. The representations of Africa and America in particular had been altered to reflect the more overtly imperial context of the late seventeenth century, when these continents were seen primarily as providing opportunities for profit. The English had thus adopted an iconographic motif that was popular all over Europe to their specific circumstances, and it was in this form that the four continents would continue to be used in subsequent decades.

In the immediate future, the use of the motif would continue to be the province of the monarchy. Like her predecessors, Queen Anne 'made extensive use of the arsenal of ceremonial paraphernalia' to bolster her power.[15] In 1703, shortly after ascending to the throne, she decided to redecorate one of the most important rooms at Hampton Court, the Queen's Drawing Room, in which on a weekly basis she mixed with her courtiers and other distinguished guests. For the redecoration, she hired Antonio Verrio. Over the next two years, he painted the ceiling and walls with scenes celebrating Britain's growing naval and imperial power. The ceiling depicts Anne in the guise of Justice, being crowned by Britannia and Neptune and surrounded by the Virtues. At her feet rests a cornucopia to show the bounty she brings to Britain. The two side walls of the room feature Anne's husband, George of Denmark, in his role as Lord High Admiral of the British fleet. The left-hand wall (as one faces the windows) is a conventional depiction of George wearing armour as he stands beneath a crimson tent and points to a group of warships in the background. The right-hand wall is more bizarre: floating above a group of mythological figures in the foreground, a nude George sits daintily side-saddle on a dolphin that leaps from the sea before the distant British fleet.

It is the wall opposite the windows that is of greatest relevance here, however. There, Anne appears as Britannia, with Religious

Truth, Hercules (representing strength), Mars (victory) and Minerva (wisdom) on her right and a prophetess of promise for Britain on her left. At her feet in a clockwise direction are female figures representing the four continents: a dark-skinned Africa, Asia carrying a basket and a crowned Europe. Behind Europe and closest to Anne is a tawny America, bare-breasted and wearing a headdress with feathers of red, white and blue, the colours of the Union Jack. She extends her left hand towards the Queen, offering her a gift of a pearl necklace, while her right hand clutches a tobacco plant. As in the wind-vane artwork at Kensington, this rendition of the four continents thus emphasises the commodities and corresponding riches that America was producing. It also duplicates the explicit connection between colonisation and monarchy made in Verrio's earlier painting at the Royal Hospital. It represents, therefore, the first use of the four continents motif to bring together the themes of royal power, empire and profitable trade in a single work.

This fusion can be seen also in the largest-scale artistic project of Anne's reign. In the mid-1690s, Christopher Wren embarked upon a new royal commission: the construction of a hospital for infirm sailors, a naval equivalent of the Royal Hospital, Chelsea, to be located at Greenwich. The ceremonial centrepiece of the complex was the Painted Hall, named for its decorations by James Thornhill and completed between 1708 and 1727. In Thornhill's own description of the work, he described the central scene as follows:

> In the Middle of the great Oval, under a Canopy of State, and attended by the four Cardinal Virtues, are King William and Queen Mary, Concord sitting between, Cupid holding the Sceptre, while King William presents Peace and Liberty to Europe, and tramples on Tyranny and Arbitrary Power. Underneath is a Figure of Architecture holding a Drawing of Part of the Hospital, and pointing up to the Royal Founders. Near them is Time bringing Truth to Light: below them is Wisdom and Virtue represented by Pallas and Hercules destroying Calumny, Detraction and Envy, with other Vices. In the Circumference of the Oval are the twelve Signs of the Zodiac with their proper Attitudes, over which preside the four Seasons of the Year ... Apollo on high, drawn by four white Horses, the Hours, &c. flying round him, Dews falling before him, going his Celestial Course thro' the Zodiac, and giving Light to the whole Ceiling. The Oval Frame is supported by Stone Figures, and grouped with all Sort of marine Trophies in Stone Colour.[16]

While useful in explaining the iconography of the painting, this account does not convey the intensity of its Francophobic patriotism: as at Windsor and Castle Howard, Apollo has been wrested from the French monarchy and transferred to an English context, with the intention of demonstrating where true national superiority now rests. If this was somehow missed by the viewer, there was no mistaking the figure cowering with his broken sword beneath William's foot: Louis XIV, clad in yellow to show his cowardice. Beyond the central oval at the ends of the hall, Thornhill painted two ships, one a captured 'Spanish galley filled with Trophies' and the second a 'British Man of War, with a Figure of Victory filling her with Spoils and Trophies taken from the Enemy'. Beneath these ships flow 'the four great Rivers of England': the Thames, being brought 'Treasures' by the Tyne ('pouring forth his plenty of Coals'); the Severn ('with her Lampreys'); and the Humber ('with his Piggs of Lead'). In the corners of the room are 'the Four Elements, Fire, Air, Earth and Water, with their several symbols, offering their various Productions to King William and Queen Mary, while Fame at one End of the Oval descends sounding the Praise of the Royal Pair'.[17] In the Lower Hall, Thornhill thus rendered in literal form the nationalist themes that had emerged after the Glorious Revolution: virtue, commerce, liberty and naval might, with a healthy dose of Francophobia added to the mix.

In the Upper Hall, Thornhill displayed even more explicitly the benefits of Britain's maritime power, carried forward into the reign of Queen Anne. In the central panel of the ceiling, Anne and Prince George are 'supported by Virtue Heroick, Concord Conjugal, Liberality, Piety, Victory, &c.'. Neptune surrenders 'his Trident to the Prince as Lord High-Admiral of the British Seas'; the god is attended by 'Tritons and other Deities of the Sea, bringing their respective Offerings, while Juno or the Air, with Aeolus, God of the Winds, are commanding a Calm'. Surrounding this scene are images of 'the four Quarters of the World', depicted 'with their several Attitudes, &c. admiring our Maritime Power'.[18] Reminiscent of Ripa, three of the continents have an animal companion: Europe has a white horse, Asia a camel and Africa a lion. Only America is alone, represented as a female Indian in a feathered headdress equipped with a bow and arrows.

In some ways, Thornhill's choice of iconography is less interesting than Verrio's, representing a regression to Ripa's more allegorical style rather than providing America with new attributes more suited to the realities of the contemporary imperial context. What gives it greater significance, however, is its placement in Thornhill's composition. In the Painted Hall, the four continents motif was incorporated into an explicit statement of contemporary British nationalism, emphasising the naval power and imperial expansion upon which national greatness was increasingly based. The Queen's Drawing Room at Hampton Court and the Painted Hall at Greenwich are two striking examples of the fusion of the exuberance of the baroque style with more immediate and pragmatic political needs of the British monarchy. There is nothing else like them in the British Isles; both products of a time when the monarchy eagerly sought ways to assert its declining power, they today come off as stunningly over-the-top in their blatant, xenophobic nationalism and their association of monarchy with divinity. But their aggressiveness is not without purpose: they both represent attempts to wrest the genre of history painting from its long-standing associations with continental and Catholic absolutism and enable it to express the Protestant vision of constitutional – but far from impotent – monarchy that prevailed in post-1688 Britain.[19]

There is one more adaptation of the four continents motif from the reign of Queen Anne that merits mention. In honour of the completion of Wren's new St Paul's Cathedral in 1710, a statue of Queen Anne was placed outside the west front two years later. The statue features the Queen standing on an elliptical plinth surrounded by female figures representing Britain, France, Ireland and North America, with the latter depicted as a seated, bare-breasted Indian holding a bow in her left hand.[20] Returning once again to Ripa's iconography, she is accompanied by a reptilian creature, and a severed head lies at her feet. Here, the four continents motif has been adapted to a specifically British context, and for a specifically royal purpose: to show the four realms over which the monarchy claimed sovereignty. The motif's journey from abstract allegory to specific political statement was thus complete.

Elite appropriation of the four continents

When scholars note the increasing use of four continents imagery in eighteenth-century Britain, they tend to focus on its links to mercantilist visions of global relations, and to growing popular enthusiasm for empire.[21] Designed by John Wood the Elder and opened in 1743, the Exchange in Bristol featured iconography that reflected the city's reliance on colonial trade as its economic lifeblood. The tympanum in the central courtyard featured relief carvings by Thomas Paty of the four continents, with representations of the non-European parts of the globe that emphasised their commercial products and natural resources. Eric Frederick Gollannek writes that 'as merchants stood in this open space to negotiate the value of goods from faraway lands, they took the place of Britons symbolically at the center of the world, with portals to the Crown's global colonies surrounding them'.[22] Such interpretations miss, however, the main context in which four continents iconography was deployed after 1800: the country houses of the British elite.

It might be argued that the social exclusiveness of country houses, which were built and owned by a narrow group of elite males, limits their ability to serve as a means by which to examine broader cultural developments such as the impact of empire upon metropolitan culture. Country houses, however, transcended this narrow perspective as both absorbers and conveyers of cultural influences. In terms of gender, they clearly felt the influence of wives and other female family members on their design and decoration, and in numerous cases saw the financial impact of female fortunes acquired through inheritance. And if country houses were not exclusively male realms, nor were they solely the province of the elite. Their design and decor received input from a bevy of sources, including middle-class architects and landscape architects. The estates that surrounded them, meanwhile, served as the homes of tenant farmers, agricultural labourers and domestic servants. And finally, country houses were visited by a wide range of people, including, in increasing numbers by the late eighteenth century, tourists. Peter Mandler observes:

> the urge to show off the booty of erudition and travel posed an interesting problem for the culturally ambitious country-house owner. … His collections had to be seen and admired for his skill and taste as a connoisseur to be fully appreciated; he had therefore to ensure that his impregnable fortifications were just sufficiently permeable to admit any visitors able to assess, appreciate and, preferably, report on his achievements.[23]

All of these constituencies would have thus seen, and in some cases played a role in the decision to feature, four continents iconography in a country-house context. The increasing employment of a motif formerly favoured by the royal Stuarts was deliberate in an era in which elite politicians alternated between boycotting royal ceremonial events and attempting to appropriate them for their own ends. In the wake of the Hanoverian Succession, which propelled them to a position of dominance in the British political universe that lasted almost half a century, the Whigs in particular made a determined attempt to 'adapt Baroque court art to the exigencies of the post-revolutionary state'.[24] One of the most prominent examples can be found in the famous landscape garden at Stowe in Buckinghamshire. Stowe was the creation of Richard Temple, first Viscount Cobham, a leading member of the 'Patriot Whigs' who increasingly opposed the leadership of Robert Walpole. His garden was intended not only to revolutionise English garden design but to inscribe his political views on to the English landscape.[25] Stowe was an example of what Stephen Bending has termed the 'coercive structuring' of the first stage of development of the English landscape style, which was intended to produce a 'shared and stable interpretation'.[26] In other words, the message was intended to be unmistakable and prescriptive, a clear declaration of Cobham's Whig political views. But if Stowe has long been recognised as a Whig landscape, it has come in recent years to be interpreted as an imperial one as well. The opposition of the Patriot Whigs to Walpole was due not only to his purported corruption and venality but also to his perceived failure vigorously to defend Britain's imperial interests in America and the Caribbean, particularly against the Catholic powers France and Spain. These pro-imperial views are reflected in the iconographic landscape at Stowe. The now vanished structure by Vanbrugh known as Nelson's Seat in honour of Stowe's head gardener featured inscriptions copied from the Arch of Constantine in Rome that linked Britain's growing imperial might to that of the ancient Romans:

> Ultra Euphratem et Tigrim
> Usq ad Oceanum propagata ditione,
> Orbis Terrarum Imperium Romae adsignat optimus Princeps
> Cui super advolat Victoria
> Laurigerum fertum hinc inde
> Utraq manu extendens
> Comitantibus Pietate et Abundantia.[27]

These imperial sentiments were more overtly applied to the more recent British context in the Temple of British Worthies, designed by William Kent in the mid-1730s. Among the sixteen busts that occupy the temple were Sir Walter Raleigh and Sir Francis Drake, both included for their staunch Protestantism and fierce opposition to Spain in the era of the Armada. This was implicitly compared to what the Patriot Whigs saw as Walpole's betrayal of the national interest – and the Protestant faith – by refusing to go to war with Spain in the present. The Temple recognised that the roots of the British Empire lay in the Elizabethan age. Drake's inscription described him as a man who 'through many Perils, was the first of Britons that adventur'd to sail round the Globe and carried into unknown Seas and Nations the Knowledge and Glory of the English name'.[28] The inscription beneath Raleigh's bust, meanwhile, made it clear that his execution at the hands of James I was due to a corrupt court's failure to apprehend the true nature of the Spanish threat:

> A valiant Soldier, and an able Statesman; who endeavouring to rouze the Spirit of his Masters for the Honour of his Country, against the Ambition of Spain, fell a Sacrifice to the Influence of that Court, whose Arms he had vanquish'd and whose Designs he opposed.

According to Christine Gerrard, Stowe's 'valorization of the Elizabethan age' was linked to 'the tradition of trade and empire which Elizabeth was credited with initiating', a tradition that the Patriot Whigs wanted to see preserved in the present.[29] The current conflict with Spain was after all an imperial one, for it was over trade in North America and the West Indies, and in particular the right of the Spanish to board British ships in order to ensure that they were not trading illegally with Spain's colonies.

Warfare to defend empire would be further commemorated at Stowe in 1749, when Cobham added to the Elysian Fields a column honouring his nephew Captain Thomas Grenville, who had been killed two years earlier while commanding HMS *Defiance* in the First Battle of Finisterre during the War of the Austrian Succession. This, too, was an essentially imperial conflict, for the French were attempting to keep the shipping lanes open to their colonies on the Indian subcontinent and in the West Indies. After Cobham's death, Stowe would see the addition of two more imperial monuments: an obelisk to General James Wolfe, victor of the Battle of Quebec during the Seven Years War, in 1759, and a globe celebrating Captain James Cook's voyages to the South Pacific in 1778. Finally, it is worth mentioning the wooden Chinese House of the late 1730s, the earliest Chinese-style garden building in England, which reflects the fascination with Asia that was beginning to develop as the nation's commercial and imperial interest in the continent expanded.[30]

It is in this context that the use of four continents iconography at Stowe needs to be interpreted. In the late 1730s, the architect James Gibbs added a Palladian bridge to Stowe's landscape, in imitation of an earlier example at Wilton House in Wiltshire. The bridge featured a carved relief by Peter Scheemakers entitled *The Four Quarters of the World Bringing Their Various Products to Britannia*. At the far left, America is embodied by a half-naked Indian female carrying a bow in one hand and a severed human head in the other. She is accompanied by an alligator, a sea-turtle, a large, mountain-lion-like cat and an iguana. Next to her, Asia is represented by a robed and turbaned figure holding the reigns of a camel, while in the background is a bare-chested male wearing a grass skirt with a basket of fruit on his head. Flanking Britannia on the right side is a crowned female Europe holding a cornucopia, with a horse behind her. And finally, on the far right is a bare-breasted female Africa and a lion, with a bale of cargo floating in the foreground.

The iconography of the relief is clearly taken from Ripa. What differs, however, is that the centre of the composition is occupied by Britannia, with the classical gods Neptune and Minerva at her feet, along with pelicans symbolising charity and plenty. The four continents have thus been recast in a subordinate and colonial relationship to the

British metropolis, in the immediate political service of bolstering the
Patriot Whigs' cause by displaying their commitment to empire. The
sculpture won the approval of contemporary observers, both for its
content and for its display of artistic skill. In 1750, George Bickham
wrote:

> it is a vaulted Fabric, where you see the different Parts of the World
> bringing their several Products to Britannia, to whom they seem to pay
> Homage. A great many of these Figures are extremely striking. There is
> so much Art required, and so much Difficulty attends doing any thing in
> this Way, as it ought to be, that when we do meet with a good Piece of
> Workmanship of this Kind, it affords us an extreme Pleasure.[31]

In its original position on the Palladian Bridge, the relief was bracketed
by lifesize portraits by Francesco Sleter of Sir Walter Raleigh 'with a
map of Virginia in his Hand' – another indication of his popularity with
the Patriot Whigs – and William Penn 'holding the laws of Pennsylvania', which were thought by the Patriot Whigs to offer a model of
government and religious toleration.[32]

Figure 1.2 The pediment sculpture from the Temple of Concord and
Victory in the garden of Stowe House. Originally dating from the late
1730s, Peter Scheemakers's work depicts the four continents delivering
their riches to the seated Britannia in the centre

[32]

These figures reinforced the importance of empire, as did the relief's second location on the pediment of the Temple of Concord and Victory, to which it was moved in the early 1760s when it was decided to open up the sides of the Palladian Bridge (see Figure 1.2). Originally built in the 1740s, the Temple was converted in 1761 to a celebration of Britain's recent victories in the Seven Years War. The mason William Emberly altered Scheemakers's relief to a triangular shape, requiring the addition of several sculptures by William Stevenson in order to fill the small corner spaces. A large statue of Victory with a laurel wreath was placed atop the pediment, and the interior walls were adorned with fourteen terracotta medallions, based on designs by James 'Athenian' Stuart and depicting the war's key military and naval battles. We have seen Britannia at the centre of the four continents before, in Verrio's murals at Hampton Court, but there she was a stand-in for Queen Anne, and the political message was to reinforce the authority of monarchy by making the current ruler synonymous with the nation. At Stowe, the message was very different: to oppose the power of the monarchy and the current administration with which it was associated, and to posit the moral superiority of a group of elite politicians who offered an alternative vision of national leadership. It was also to proclaim the importance of empire to Britain's welfare, and to castigate those leaders who were not felt to be defending it with sufficient ardour.

Eighteenth-century country houses and the four continents

In addition to its manifestation at Stowe, the four continents motif made a number of other country-house appearances in the eighteenth century. A variant of it appears at Blenheim Palace in Oxfordshire, which like Castle Howard was designed by Vanbrugh. Funded by a grateful Queen Anne as a reward for Marlborough's victory over the French at the Battle of Blenheim during the War of the Spanish Succession in 1704, Blenheim is not only one of England's grandest houses but also one of its most bombastic in its celebration of military triumph. In the enormous and ornate saloon, the French artist Louis Laguerre painted a series of murals on the walls between 1718 and 1720. The murals depict emissaries from Europe, Asia and Africa, who peer through *trompe l'oeil* colonnades as they offer admiration and homage to the Duke, portrayed on the ceiling in a chariot holding a thunderbolt of war, with Peace restraining his other arm in reference to the Treaty of Utrecht. Like the use of the Phaethon myth, the scheme was derived from Versailles, in this case from Charles LeBrun's work in the Escalier des Ambassadeurs. So, as at Castle Howard, here we see a Whig aristocrat appropriating a decorative motif from Versailles, with the same tripartite purpose: to express English superiority over France, to express the power of the English elite and its successful resistance to absolutist monarchical ambitions and finally to express the global aspirations, via military conquest and imperial expansion, of that selfsame elite.

Another, more conventional appearance of the four continents was at Osterley Park in Middlesex, which was acquired by the London goldsmith-turned-banker and major East India Company investor Sir Francis Child in 1713. The Child family gradually transformed the house into a grand neoclassical residence, culminating in the decision of Sir Francis's grandson, also named Francis Child, to hire the eminent Scottish architect Robert Adam to undertake a major renovation of the exterior and interior in 1761. In the dining room at the top of the stairs on the first floor, Adam's frequent artistic collaborator Antonio Zucchi depicted representations of the four continents in rectangular panels over the doors. All four are represented by female figures. Europe is shown seated in a chariot drawn by four white horses. Another female figure in the right foreground proffers a cornucopia, out of which pour crowns and books, while on the left three women hold paintbrushes and artists' palettes, an indication of the continent's cultural achievements. In the background is a temple resembling the Pantheon in Rome. Also in a chariot, a turbaned Asia accepts tribute in the form of gold and textiles from a group of male figures, while camels placidly survey the scene. On the left, a man stands with his hands tied behind his back, possibly a reference to European perceptions of Asian despotism. Next, a light-skinned Africa rides on an elephant while a muscular male figure in the foreground restrains two chained lions. On the right, dark-skinned figures offer her a variety of goods. And finally, America is also a white female figure, in this case almost nude. A group of men carry examples of the continent's natural bounty, including birds, a large turtle and a selection of plants. On the far left, another male figure stands with a bow.

Zucchi's paintings of the four continents at Osterley Park represent the world beyond Britain as a source of bounty in the form of various commodities, an indication of the rising importance of commerce in the contemporary British global vision. Among the continents, America is the most 'natural': its emblematic figure wears scarcely any clothing, and its products are directly obtained from the native flora and fauna. Zucchi's depiction thus implies not only that its people await the benefits of European civilisation but also that its wealth requires European intervention to transform it to commercially useful ends. When it is taken into account that the room was created by a family whose wealth derived in significant part from imperial invest-

Figure 1.3 Gerald Lanscroon's *Peace Banishing War from the Four Continents* (1705), from the saloon (now the blue drawing room) of Powis Castle

ment, the selection of the four continents motif seems something more than random or purely aesthetic, and instead becomes suffused with greater, and more specific, meaning. Other uses of the four continents also came to be instilled with more specifically imperial meanings. In 1705, Gerard Lanscroon painted the ceiling of the saloon (now the blue drawing room) of Powis Castle in Wales with an allegory of *Peace Banishing War from the Four Continents* (see Figure 1.3).[33] After Lady Henrietta Herbert, daughter of the first Earl of Powis, married Edward Clive, second Lord Clive, in 1784, the painting could be linked to the British conquest of India via the familial connection to Clive's father Robert, the prime architect of that conquest after his victory at the Battle of Plassey in 1757 secured the East India Company's control of Bengal. Edward Clive, too, became involved with the administration of India via his term as Governor of Madras from 1798 to 1803. Though I have been unable to discover any contemporary comment on the relationship between the painting and the prominent imperial history of the Clive family, contemporary visitors to the house almost certainly would have noted it. The bare-breasted figure of a seated Asia proffers an olive branch in supplication to the central figure of Peace, who could all too easily be seen as a stand-in for Britannia.

By the second half of the eighteenth century, the four continents had become a common feature of the iconography of British country houses. In the 1770s, John Mortimer included representations of the four continents in his ceiling paintings for the saloon at Brocket Hall in Hertfordshire, seat of Sir Matthew Lamb.[34] Echoing his work at Osterley, Zucchi painted oval panels of Africa, Asia, America and Europe for the ceiling of Kedleston House in Derbyshire in 1777. They replaced the roundels of Sculpture, Painting, Music and Architecture that had been installed as part of Robert Adam's original decorative scheme in the late 1760s, suggesting that Lord Scarsdale specifically wanted the four continents to be used.[35] The motif was used for tapestries, as at Nostell Priory in Yorkshire and Packwood House in Warwickshire; for bronzes, as at Wimpole in Cambridgeshire; for sculptures, as at Claydon House in Buckinghamshire; and for porcelain figurines, as at Saltram House in Devon, Wallington House in Northumberland, Upton House in Warwickshire and again at Packwood and Wimpole.[36]

Some of these uses of the four continents in country-house context were deliberately and specifically linked to imperial expansion. Adam began his work on the interior decor at Kedleston in 1759, the 'Year of Victories' in which Britain won a series of victories around the globe. He inserted seahorses and mermaids into the ceiling plasterwork, while blue damask upholstery and wall hangings completed the nautical effect.[37] Lord Scarsdale's subsequent incorporation of Zucchi's paintings into the house's decorative scheme can be seen as a complement to these expressions of Britain's growing imperial might. Designed by James Wyatt, the great hall of Ragley Hall in Warwickshire, seat of the Viscounts Conway, was begun in 1756, the first year of the Seven Years War. Its iconography features plasterwork figures of War and Peace over the fireplaces, martial trophies in the arched coves of the vaulted ceiling and a central roundel of a spear-carrying Britannia in the ceiling's centre, all executed by Giuseppe Artari. Emphasising the imperial dimension of the war, busts of a black slave, representing the West Indies, and an Indian, representing North America, top the side doors.[38] The use of the four continents motif at Ragley Hall represented the culmination of the motif's appropriation by the British elite. The fact that aristocrats like Lord Carlisle, Lord Cobham and Lord Conway thought it worthwhile to wrest control of the four continents from the monarchy and use it for their own purposes confirms the motif's potency. In the process, the motif was transformed from a general representation of early modern European views of the world to a means of depicting Britain's increasingly imperial sense of the globe. The emergence of the four continents motif as a decorative embellishment in country houses in the eighteenth century shows that, in their modes of architectural and artistic expression as well in their political and economic lives, their owners were looking beyond the confines of their estates to a more global realm of opportunity and power.

This vision was in keeping with a growing enthusiasm for imperial expansion among the British elite in the eighteenth century. This was due to a recognition not only of the potential commercial value that could accrue from colonial possessions but also of a desire to shift the nation's external commitments away from continental European entanglements and towards a 'blue-water' policy that would secure British power and independence through an Atlantic and Asiatic empire. By the early 1750s, patriotic calls for swift and decisive action against French incursions upon Britain's overseas interests had become a powerful voice driving the foreign policy emanating from Westminster. There were, to be sure, limits to this imperial vision of elite political action and ruling authority. Of the country houses that utilised the four continents motif in a prominent manner, only Powis Castle was not located in England; none was located in Scotland or Ireland. This suggests two things. First, as Linda Colley has so clearly established, a sense of British national identity was not completely 'forged' until the end of the eighteenth century.[39] And second, the Empire was not yet fully 'British' in elite conceptions of identity, and it was primarily the English aristocracy and gentry who thought of it as a venue for the extension of their domestic power. Though the term 'British Empire' was occasionally used prior to the Seven Years War, it was not until the 1750s that it came to be widespread, or that Scottish, Welsh and Irish people began participating in imperial ventures, both commercial and military, in India, the West Indies and elsewhere in substantial numbers.[40]

In England, however, the four continents were seen as a means of expressing an increasingly global vision of elite power. This was confirmed when its usage began to spread to the colonies. Among all colonial settlers, West Indian planters were perhaps the most eager to emulate elite landowners in Britain. Turning absentee as quickly as they acquired sufficient wealth, they returned home, purchased landed estates and settled into the lives of country gentlemen, albeit ones who kept a close eye on the price of sugar and slaves. Amassing a fortune adequate to support elevation to the gentry, however, could take decades, and so they began the process of emulation sooner both by imitating the British elite as best they could on their plantations and by adopting transatlantic lifestyles for themselves and their heirs while still in the West Indies. An example was Sir Charles Price, a wealthy Jamaican planter, who lived in an impressive mansion called The Decoy in the parish of St Mary in the north-eastern part of the island. There, he created an English-style landscape garden, complete with fallow deer, which he decorated, as an English aristocrat would have done, with architectural embellishments. These included a triumphal arch, dating from the 1760s, from which a fragment of a column that was discovered hidden in the tropical undergrowth in 1932 probably derives. The base of the column featured relief carvings of the four continents; if a local sculptor executed them in a cruder style than would have been the case had they adorned a similar structure in a landscape garden in England, their message was similar. Price was a fierce defender of planters' rights on both sides of the Atlantic. When in England, he vigorously lobbied Parliament to protect West Indian interests, while back home in Jamaica he fiercely resisted efforts by the colonial government to curb the planters' power. In the 1750s, when Jamaica's governor, Admiral Charles Knowles, attempted to move the capital from Spanish Town, where the planters held sway, to Kingston, Price led the resistance. Joan Coutu describes him and his fellow planters as playing 'the role of disgruntled Whig magnates'; they succeeded in blocking the move and in getting Knowles recalled to London. His activities on the planters' behalf earned Price the nickname 'the Patriot', a further link to Cobham's rebellious Whigs of a few decades earlier.[41] Price's employment of the four continents thus can be connected to the Scheemakers relief carving at Stowe as an expression of the power and independence of the landed elite. That he chose to use it in Jamaica serves as further confirmation that that elite now saw their power in a truly global context.

Notes

1 The Phaethon myth was popular in contemporary residential iconography, appearing at Montagu House in London and twice at Chatsworth in Derbyshire.
2 Charles Saumarez Smith, *The Building of Castle Howard* (London: Pimlico, 1997), p. 105. This interpretation was first proposed by Kerry Downes in his biography *Vanbrugh* (London: A. Zwemmer, 1977), p. 33.
3 Svetlana Alpers and Michael Baxandall, *Tiepolo and the Pictorial Intelligence* (New Haven, CT: Yale University Press, 1994), p. 110.
4 For the history of the earliest uses of four continents iconography, see Peter Mason, *Infelicities: Representations of the Exotic* (Baltimore, MD: Johns Hopkins University Press, 1998), pp. 106–8.
5 The illustrated version of the *Iconologia* was not published until 1603.
6 Michael Wintle writes, 'Compared with the cultured and civilized sophistication of Europe, the exotic, primitive and even bestial projections of the other continents is an archetypal example of an "Othering" process.' Michael Wintle, 'Visual Representations of Europe in the Nineteenth Century: The Age of Nationalism and Imperialism', in Stefan Berger (ed.), *A Companion to Nineteenth-Century Europe* (London: John Wiley, 2008), p. 12. See also Michael Wintle, 'Europe's Image: Visual Representations of Europe from the Earliest Times to the Twentieth Century', in Michael Wintle (ed.), *Culture and Identity in Europe: Perceptions of Divergence and Unity in Past and Present* (Aldershot: Avebury Press, 1996), pp. 52–95.

7 Jan Nederveen Pieterse, *White on Black: Images of Africa and Blacks in Western Popular Culture* (New Haven, CT: Yale University Press, 1995), p. 19. See also Michael Wintle, 'Visualizing Commerce and Empire: Decorating the Built Environment of Amsterdam', in Marco de Waard (ed.), *Imagining Global Amsterdam: History, Culture and Geography in a World City* (Amsterdam: Amsterdam University Press, 2012), pp. 68–70.

8 Bruce Buchan, 'Asia and the Moral Geography of European Enlightenment Thought c.1600–1800', in Cary J. Nederman and Takashi Shogimen (eds), *Western Political Thought in Dialogue with Asia* (Lanham, MD: Lexington Books, 2009), p. 70. See also Mark Ashton, 'Allegory, Fact and Meaning in Giambattista Tiepolo's Four Continents in Würzburg', *Art Bulletin* 60 (1978), pp. 109–25.

9 Anthony Pagden, 'Europe: Conceptualizing a Continent', in Anthony Pagden (ed.), *The Idea of Europe: From Antiquity to the European Union* (Cambridge: Cambridge University Press, 2002), p. 51.

10 See Stephanie Pratt, *American Indians in British Art, 1700–1840* (Norman, OK: University of Oklahoma Press, 2013), p. 15.

11 Historians have increasingly come to emphasise the transatlantic aspects of the Stuart monarchy. See, for example, the essays in Allan I. Macinnes and Arthur H. Williamson (eds), *Shaping the Stuart World, 1603–1714: The Atlantic Connection* (Leiden and Boston: Brill, 2006).

12 See Joyce Lee Malcolm, 'Charles II and the Reconstruction of Royal Power', *Historical Journal* 35 (1992), pp. 307–32, and Anna Keay, *The Magnificent Monarch: Charles II and the Rituals of Royal Power* (London and New York: Continuum, 2008).

13 Charles Knight, *Guide to Windsor* (London, c.1811). See also Keay, *The Magnificent Monarch*, p. 189. Most of Verrio's work at Windsor was destroyed by George IV's redecoration schemes of the early nineteenth century. Only three of his ceilings survive, in the Queen's Presence Chamber, the Queen's Audience Chamber and the King's Eating Room.

14 Kevin Sharpe and Steven N. Zwicker, 'Introduction: Refiguring Revolutions', in Kevin Sharpe and Steven N. Zwicker (eds), *Refiguring Revolutions: Aesthetics and Politics from the English Revolution to the Romantic Revolution* (Berkeley and Los Angeles: University of California Press, 1998), p. 5.

15 R.O. Bucholz, '"Nothing but Ceremony": Queen Anne and the Limitations of Royal Ritual', *Journal of British Studies* 30 (1991), p. 289.

16 James Thornhill, *An Explanation of the Painting in the Royal Hospital at Greenwich* (London, [1726]), pp. 5–8.

17 Ibid., pp. 10–12.

18 Ibid., pp. 12–14.

19 Paul Monod writes that 'the taint of Stuart royalism, Jacobitism and Roman Catholicism discouraged the flow of continental styles in England. Politics damaged "history" painting in particular; portraiture and landscape were much safer channels for artistic endeavour.' Paul Monod, 'Painters and Party Politics in England, 1714–60', *Eighteenth-Century Studies* 26 (1993), p. 377.

20 In 1340, Edward III became the first English monarch to claim the French throne, in the wake of the death of his uncle King Charles IV of France. At the end of the Hundred Years War, England's only remaining French possessions were Calais and the Channel Islands, but English kings and queens continued to assert their claim even after the former was lost in 1558. It was not until 1801, by which point France had become a republic, that the claim was formally relinquished.

21 Eliga H. Gould writes that 'the pursuit of empire held a tremendous appeal for the metropolitan public throughout the eighteenth century', while Kathleen Wilson argues that the British mercantile community in the mid-eighteenth century demanded a 'bellicose foreign policy geared to colonial expansion'. See Eliga H. Gould, *The Persistence of Empire: British Political Culture in the Age of the American Revolution* (Chapel Hill, NC: University of North Carolina Press, 2000), p. xvii; Kathleen Wilson, 'Empire, Trade and Popular Politics in Mid-Hanoverian Britain: The Case of Admiral Vernon', *Past and Present* 121 (1988), p. 97. Much recent schol-

arly attention has focused on the popular impact of empire in eighteenth-century Britain. See, for example, Gerald Jordan and Nicholas Rogers, 'Admirals as Heroes: Patriotism and Liberty in Hanoverian England', *Journal of British Studies* 28 (1989), pp. 201–24; Philip Lawson, '"The Irishman's Prize": Views of Canada from the British Press, 1760–1774', *Historical Journal* 28 (1985), pp. 575–96; Philip Lawson, '"Arts and Empire Equally Extend": Tradition, Prejudice and Assumption in the Eighteenth-Century Press Coverage of Empire', in Karl Schweizer and Jeremy Black (eds), *Politics and the Press in Hanoverian Britain* (Lewiston, NY: Edwin Mellen Press, 1989), pp. 119–46; P.J. Marshall, '"Cornwallis Triumphant": War in India and the British Public in the Late Eighteenth Century', in Lawrence Freedman, Paul M. Hayes and Robert O'Neill (eds), *War, Strategy and International Politics: Essays in Honour of Sir Michael Howard* (Oxford: Oxford University Press, 1992), pp. 57–74; Nicholas Rogers, *Whigs and Cities: Popular Politics in the Age of Walpole and Pitt* (Oxford: Oxford University Press, 1989); and Kathleen Wilson, '"Empire of Virtue": The Imperial Project and Hanoverian Culture, c.1720–1785', in Lawrence Stone (ed.), *An Imperial State at War: Britain from 1689 to 1815* (London: Routledge, 1994), pp. 128–64.

22 Eric Frederick Gollannek, '"Empire Follows Art": Exchange and the Sensory Worlds of Empire in Britain and Its Colonies, 1740–1775', PhD dissertation, University of Delaware, 2008, p. 75.

23 Peter Mandler, *The Fall and Rise of the Stately Home* (New Haven, CT: Yale University Press, 1997), pp. 8–9. See also Dana Arnold, 'The Country House and its Publics', in Dana Arnold (ed.), *The Georgian Country House: Architecture: Landscape and Society* (Stroud: Sutton, 1998), pp. 20–42.

24 Monod, 'Painters and Party Politics in England', p. 378.

25 See G.B. Clarke, 'Grecian Taste and Gothic Virtue: Lord Cobham's Gardening Programme and Iconography', *Apollo* 97 (1973), pp. 566–71; Christine Gerrard, *The Patriot Opposition to Walpole: Politics, Poetry and National Myth, 1725–42* (New York: Clarendon, 1994), pp. 125–31; Christopher Hussey, *English Gardens and Landscapes, 1700–1750* (New York: Funk & Wagnalls, 1967), pp. 89–106; and John Martin Robinson, *Temples of Delight: Stowe Landscape Gardens* (London: George Philip, 1990).

26 Stephen Bending, 'Re-Reading the Eighteenth-Century Landscape Garden', *Huntington Library Quarterly* 55 (1992), p. 380.

27 The most excellent Prince / Having extended his power beyond the Euphrates and Tigris, / As far as the ocean, / Assigns the empire of the world to Rome: / Over whom flies victory, / Stretching forth a laurel crown / On each side with both hands, / Accompanied with piety and plenty.

28 *A Description of the Gardens of Lord Viscount Cobham at Stow in Buckinghamshire* (Northampton, 1747), p. 21.

29 Gerrard, *Patriot Opposition to Walpole*, p. 9. For more on the 'Raleigh cult' in the first half of the eighteenth century, see Gerrard, pp. 157–61.

30 The Chinese House was moved to the garden of Lord Cobham's nephew Richard Grenville in 1748 and subsequently to Harristown House in County Kildare, Ireland, and was only recently returned to Stowe.

31 George Bickham, *The Beauties of Stow* (London, 1750), p. 30.

32 *A Description of the Gardens of Lord Viscount Cobham*, pp. 23–4. In a mock dialogue between two visitors to Stowe that was published in 1748, one tells the other that 'our Sailors mention [Penn's] Colony as a very happy set of People; they live entirely at Peace amongst themselves; and (bred up in a strict Observance of Probity) without any knowledge of an Art Military amongst them, are able to preserve the most sociable Terms with their Neighbours'. *A Dialogue upon the Gardens of the Right Honourable the Lord Viscount Cobham, at Stow in Buckinghamshire* (London, 1748), pp. 38–9.

33 Christopher Rowell, *Powis Castle* (Swindon: National Trust, 2000), p. 28.

34 Christopher Hussey, *English Country Houses: Mid Georgian, 1760–1800* (Woodbridge: Antique Collectors' Club, 1984), p. 106.

35 See /www.nationaltrustcollections.org.uk/object/108934 (accessed 13 November 2013).
36 See the National Trust's collections database: www.nationaltrustcollections.org.uk.
37 Eileen Harris, *The Country Houses of Robert Adam* (London: Aurum, 2008), pp. 39–40.
38 Geoffrey Tyack, *Warwickshire Country Houses* (Chichester: Phillimore, 1994), p. 168.
39 Linda Colley, *Britons: Forging the Nation, 1707–1837* (New Haven, CT: Yale University Press, 1992).
40 See James Truslow Adams, 'On the Term "British Empire"', *American Historical Review* 27 (1922), pp. 485–9.
41 Joan Coutu, *Persuasion and Propaganda: Monuments and the Eighteenth-Century British Empire* (Montreal: McGill-Queen's University Press, 2006), pp. 51–3.

CHAPTER TWO

Exhibiting exploration:
Captain Cook, voyages of exploration
and cultures of display

John McAleer

Writing in 1777, it appeared to Edmund Burke as if all the regions and people of the world were 'at the same instant under our view'. For those living at the heart of Britain's burgeoning empire, like Burke, it seemed that 'the great map of mankind is unroll'd at once'.[1] This extraordinary efflorescence was no coincidence, however. Burke was writing at the same time as James Cook and his men were resting and recuperating at Tonga (the 'Friendly Islands'), on Cook's third, and final, voyage to the Pacific Ocean. As Kathleen Wilson has powerfully demonstrated, Cook's voyages initiated a 'Pacific craze' in Britain.[2] This chapter attempts to show how physical artefacts – two-dimensional print and images, as well as three-dimensional material culture – contributed to that phenomenon by exhibiting exploration and empire to people in Britain at the time. The great voyages of scientific exploration – or more precisely their various results in the form of objects, images and even people brought back from the Pacific, as well as the cultural products they inspired – provided crucial conduits for presenting this global engagement to people in late eighteenth-century Britain. This relationship with the wider world, as this chapter seeks to demonstrate, was mediated through cultures of display and exhibition that linked travel, exploration and empire.

The history of exploration, in the British context in particular, is deeply entwined with the history of empire. As many commentators have observed, James Cook's instructions from the Admiralty, as he prepared to embark on his first voyage, did not provide a coherent blueprint for empire, and it is anachronistic to interpret Britain's later imperial history through the lens of Enlightenment voyages of exploration.[3] Nevertheless, these expeditions convey the ambiguities and frequently blurred boundary between disinterested scientific exploration and more self-interested, strategically motivated forms of social and political interaction. As the Admiralty's instructions to Cook made clear, 'the making of Discoverys of Countries hitherto unknown … will redound greatly to the Honour of this nation as a maritime power, as well as to the dignity of the Crown of Great Britain, and may tend greatly to the advancement of the Trade and Navigation thereof'.[4] The Swiss historian Urs Bitterli has remarked that, 'despite their pretence of disinterested scholarship, eighteenth-century explorers were chiefly concerned with the enhancement of national prestige'.[5] And P.J. Marshall and Glyndwr Williams similarly caution that:

> The motives for the Pacific expeditions after 1763 were not simply, nor even primarily, scientific. This second New World promised resources of such potential that its discovery and control might tip the commercial balance of power in Europe – for Britain confirm the overseas superiority brought by the wartime conquest, for France redress the humiliations of an unsuccessful war.[6]

As a consequence, therefore, exhibiting exploration could never be a straightforward display of travel routes, scientific research and personal encounters; it was necessarily bound up in complex ways with Britain's expanding global role in the late eighteenth century.

The voyages of scientific exploration undertaken in the second half of the eighteenth century have inspired a panoply of literature on a range of themes across many disciplines, from anthropology to zoology, art history to taxonomy.[7] This chapter attempts to build on much of that valuable scholarship. It considers not just the information, knowledge and attendant material culture brought back to Europe by Cook and his colleagues but also the ways in which this was exhibited and displayed to the wider public in such diverse contexts as printed publications, art exhibitions and object displays. As a result of the collecting activities of various voyages, and the subsequent exhibition of the fruits of their endeavours, the British public had the opportunity to see, at first hand, the material cultures of various Pacific Island, American and Australasian societies. These 'numerous specimens of the ingenuity of our newly discovered friends', as John Douglas (the editor of one of Cook's voyage accounts) termed them, were accompanied by a variety of other media that exhibited exploration to the public. And all of these offered 'real matter for important reflection' on the nature of Britain's place in the world, the status of the societies encountered on these voyages, and the relative merits of each.[8] The paintings of voyage artists, such as William Hodges and John Webber, adorned the walls of influential art exhibitions. Lavishly illustrated official travel narratives and cheaper, more popular accounts were eagerly anticipated by the reading public, at the same time as audiences were exposed to narratives of exploration in theatres, panoramas and music halls. The presence of indigenous people in the imperial metropolis powerfully confirmed that exploration literally brought the world back to Britain, while missionary societies displayed their proselytising activities using the material culture of indigenous religious practices.[9] And with objects such as the hand-held terrestrial globes that were so fashionable, it was even possible to carry the story of exploration and Britain's maritime engagement with the wider world in one's pocket.[10] One particular example, a papier-mâché and plaster globe made by John Cary in 1791 and 'agreeable to the latest Discoveries', depicts the route of Cook's three voyages and carefully records his place of death. But it also incorporates the track of Constantine Phipps's voyage towards the North Pole in 1773 and includes Mackenzie's explorations in Canada of 1789, thereby setting the exhibition of Pacific exploration in a broader chronological and geographical context. This object, one that could be displayed in the palm of one's hand, reinforced the idea of exploration as a distinctly British activity and one connected to rising imperial ambitions.[11]

This chapter seeks to demonstrate the various ways in which visual and material information relating to eighteenth-century voyages of exploration – principally those of James Cook – circulated among the general public in Britain. Second, the chapter sets out to show how the display and exhibition of material culture helped to shape public discourse about the purpose, value and results of these expeditions.[12] In doing so, it is hoped that it will assist us better to locate the place of exploration in the creation and development of empire and its systems of knowledge. As David Clayton has pointed out, a whole welter of practices, such as mapping, charting, depicting, recording and describing, have been reinterpreted in the context of a complex, and increasingly entangled, web of power and knowledge.[13] The discussion contributes to this scholarly reappraisal by considering 'display' as part of that process. It suggests that by interrogating the collecting and display of images and objects, as well as their production and widespread distribution, we can gain a greater understanding of the British public's engagements with exploration and empire.

Text, image and the exhibition of exploration

The mid-eighteenth century brought a new engagement with the world beyond Britain. John Campbell remarked that Arthur Dobbs's expedition to discover the North-west Passage in the 1740s was 'the topic of common discourse, and of almost universal expectation'.[14] In 1772, the year in which Cook set off on his second voyage to the South Seas, Johann Reinhold Forster commented that 'circumnavigations of the globe have been of late the universal topics of all companies'.[15] One of the foremost ways in which these endeavours were exhibited to the British public (or rather 'publics') was through the publication of travel accounts. In *The Complete English Gentleman*, first published in 1730, Daniel Defoe reflected that, such was the penchant for travel literature:

> [A man] may take a tour of the world in books, he may make a master of the geography of the universe in maps, atlases and measurements of our mathematicians. He may travel by land with the historians, by sea with the navigators. He may go round the globe with Dampier and Rogers, and kno' a thousand times more doing it than all those illiterate sailors.[16]

Whatever their status as accurate accounts, Charles Batten reminds us that we should not underestimate the importance of travel accounts for well-educated people in the eighteenth century.[17] The writing, publishing and circulation of travel accounts were, in the words of Kathleen Wilson, 'very real weapons in the wars for empire'.[18] Others have argued that these publications provided crucial support for the 'myth that an island kingdom through sea power and administrative genius could impose a Pax Britannica on a major portion of the world'.[19] At the very least, the publication of travel and exploration literature successfully displayed the expanding boundaries of Britain's global endeavours to an ever-increasing reading public. Thomas Bankes, in the preface to his *Universal Geography* (1784), remarked that the 'latest discoveries appear to engross conversation from the politest circles and throughout every class of the Kingdom'.[20] An indication of this may be found by considering the information about the South Pacific available in the *Encyclopaedia Britannica*. This swelled from a meagre seven lines in the first edition to an impressive forty double-column pages by the third edition of 1788/89.[21]

A key measure of the success of any scientific expedition was whether its results were published, and how popular the account proved to be with the public. The scope and success of Cook's voyages followed a pattern that characterised the eighteenth-century publishing world. William Dampier's *New Voyage around the World* was an instant bestseller, going into five editions in six years; fifty years later, the *Voyage* of Admiral George Anson (1748) went through five editions in seven months and had over 1,800 pre-publication subscribers.[22] Even before the 1748 authorised version of Anson's account became a bestseller, five unofficial versions of the voyage had already been published.[23] Indeed, a copy was taken on board the *Endeavour*, as both Cook and Banks refer to it.[24] Perhaps unsurprisingly then, these publications became a model for the narratives of the great explorations after 1764.

Publication added gravitas and the imprimatur of authenticity to exploration accounts that often recounted tall tales of travel in distant lands, with European explorers surrounded by unusual people and strange customs.[25] These texts were contributions, however partial and incomplete, to the 'imperial archive' of information being steadily accumulated throughout the eighteenth century.[26] Debates about the nature of knowledge and the authenticity of facts put a significant premium on the 'truthfulness' of such accounts. At the end of his first voyage, Cook urged that it should be 'published by authority to fix the prior right of discovery beyond dispute'.[27] Conversely, the absence of a published account could do untold damage to reputations and the perceived veracity of exploration voyages. The importance of publication as a guarantee of accuracy is borne out by the controversy surrounding Vitus Bering's voyage of 1741 (the Second Kamchatka or Great Northern Expedition). Doubts about its significance surfaced partially because the Russian authorities failed to publish any proper account of the voyage until 1758.[28] And Alessandro Malaspina's achievements in the same region of the north Pacific are still relatively unknown because, for a whole host of complex political reasons, his account lay unpublished for almost one hundred years.[29]

Publication, and subsequent distribution and consumption, offered a forum for exploration endeavours to enter public consciousness. James Cook's expeditions were particularly important in bringing exploration to a wider public audience, and the published accounts derived from them offer strong evidence of the interest in exploration at all levels of society. Within three years of Cook's return from his first expedition, as David McKitterick puts it, western Europe was 'intoxicated' by illustrated accounts of the voyage.[30] Official and unofficial accounts proliferated: more than one hundred editions and impressions of these voyages were published between 1770 and 1800.[31] Even before they appeared in print, public interest in the publications was high, as Horace Walpole remarked wryly in May 1773: 'at present our ears listen and our eyes are expecting East Indian affairs, and Mr Banks's voyage'. Walpole expected that the publishers, who had paid a huge advance for the account of Cook's first voyage, would 'take due care that we shall read nothing else till they meet with such another pennyworth'.[32] John Hawkesworth was selected to chronicle this expedition (as well as those of Wallis and Byron undertaken in the previous decade). On the recommendation of Charles Burney, supported by David Garrick, he was appointed by Lord Sandwich, First Lord of the Admiralty, to compile the official account of the voyages to the south Pacific, based on the journals kept by Cook and others. He was given exclusive access to the voyage journals by the Admiralty and given free rein to strike a deal with a publisher. Hawkesworth proved to be as much a sleek businessman as a literary talent. Recognising the huge public appetite for such accounts, Strahan and Cadell gave him the enormous sum of £6,000 for his text, which was lavishly illustrated with plates from the work of the late Sydney Parkinson, or otherwise concocted (as no artists accompanied the Byron or Wallis expeditions).[33] Written in the first person, Hawkesworth's narrative of the voyages of Byron, Carteret, Wallis and Cook appeared in 1773 and was rapidly reprinted; a second edition appeared the same year. Although expensive, and aimed at an educated and elite audience, Hawkesworth's *Voyages* quickly aroused widespread interest in the Pacific and its contents reached a wide section of the British public.[34] As Paul Kaufman has shown, it was the most popular title in the Bristol Library from 1773 to 1784, being borrowed 115 times between 1773 and 1775, and 201 times over the whole period.[35] By the end of 1773, a second English edition and a New York edition had appeared; it was translated into French, German, Spanish and Italian, and excerpts were widely published in the periodical press.[36] And it also came out in shilling parts entitled *Genuine Voyages to the South Seas, published in sixty weekly numbers.*[37]

Cook's second voyage produced three accounts, partially owing to the falling out between the Forsters and Cook. Cook, with the full support of the Admiralty, published a two-volume work in May 1777. *Voyage to the South Pole* included twelve charts and fifty-one monochrome engravings of places, people and artefacts mainly based on originals produced by the official voyage artist, William Hodges. When he returned to Britain, Hodges had been employed by the Admiralty at £250 per annum to complete the paintings and drawings he had brought home with him in preparation for the publication of the voyage.[38] The first edition sold out in just one day. A second edition appeared the same year and, by 1784, the book was in its fourth edition. The success of the publication was even more remarkable, given the competition it faced. Six weeks before the official account appeared, George Forster had published a two-volume account. His father, Johann Reinhold Forster, who had also accompanied the expedition, published his single-volume observations on 'Physical Geography, Natural History and Ethnic Philosophy' in 1778. And, although neither this nor George's contained illustrations, the fact that they appeared at all gives a sense of the public's appetite for such material.[39]

The book describing Cook's last voyage to the Pacific – Cook and King's *Voyage to the Pacific Ocean* – appeared in June 1784 and sold at 4½ guineas. Although it was more the work of its editor, John Douglas, than that of Cook or King, in terms of presenting a view of

Britain's exploration activities for widespread public consumption it was an even more impressive operation.[40] The official voyage artist, John Webber, was engaged to illustrate the official account of voyage, again at a salary of £250 per annum. The project eventually incorporated sixty-three drawings as copper plates, which necessitated the help of twenty-five assistants. Perhaps unsurprisingly, it took two and a half years, rather than the eighteen months originally estimated by Webber.[41] The Admiralty assumed the production costs for the prints, including Webber's salary and the engravers' fees of about £1,000, thereby effectively subsidising the *Voyage*'s publication by about £2 per copy.[42] Despite the book's delayed appearance, and its relative costliness, results were impressive: it sold out within three days.[43] One London periodical noted:

> We remember not a circumstance like what has happened on this occasion. On the third day after publication, a copy was not to be met with in the hands of the bookseller; and to our certain knowledge, six, seven, eight and even ten guineas, have since been offered for a sett.[44]

The runaway success of Cook's voyages illustrates not only the 'craze for Cook' but the fact that media like published travel accounts could bring people closer to exploration and engagement with the wider world. And results were not just limited to the enlightenment and education of the armchair traveller. From his posting in India, James Strange (Henry Dundas's future son-in-law) decided to outfit a voyage to the Columbia River on the Pacific coast of America influenced by 'an attentive perusal of Captain Cook's last voyage'.[45]

Just as published descriptions brought exploration to people in Britain, so visual images also contributed to this expanding universe of knowledge. In some instances, as we have seen, official voyage artists played a crucial role in displaying the results of exploration, by contributing to voyage accounts, or by working up field sketches into finished works for public exhibition. In other cases, artists who had never been beyond the shores of Europe exploited this interest in exploration for their own commercial and artistic ends. In both cases, crucial cultural and artistic fora, such as the annual exhibition at the Royal Academy, displayed works that advertised Britain's increasingly global role.

William Hodges, the official voyage artist on the second of Cook's expeditions, sent pictures of Funchal, Port Praya and the Cape back to Britain for public display within months of setting out with Cook. Seven paintings by him were exhibited at the Free Society of Artists Exhibition of 1774, more than a year before the *Resolution* returned.[46] In 1776, the London public could see more works at the Royal Academy on what Douglas Fordham has called 'explicitly imperial themes' than on any other theme since its foundation.[47] Prominent among these themes was exploration: several of the oils painted by William Hodges for the Admiralty were exhibited at the Academy in this bumper year and the following one.[48] The critic of the *London Packet*, while generally unfavourable to the work of William Hodges that he saw on display in the Royal Academy exhibition of 1777, recognised the impact of the work of Hodges and his colleagues. The critic acknowledged the fact that 'the public are indebted to this artist for giving them some idea of scenes which before they knew little of'.[49] The artist on Cook's third voyage, John Webber, was particularly prolific. Over the course of his career, Webber exhibited some twenty-nine paintings based on his Cook voyage; the Royal Academy exhibition of 1784 had three paintings related to voyage.[50]

Many images were not only displayed in the culturally rarefied atmosphere of the academy but circulated more widely in the form of prints. The production of prints was a key means by which visual information about exploration endeavours reached a wider public. The forty-two prints published as part of Anson's *Voyage* could be bought separately at seven shillings a set.[51] Over the course of his career, John Webber utilised the storehouse of Cook images he had amassed on the third voyage. In 1788, he issued a series of plates of Pacific views, based on drawings and studies not included in the official account. By 1792, sixteen views were for sale by subscription.[52] In 1808, Boydell published a folio volume of *Views in the South Seas* based on Webber's drawings.[53] The impact of such prints in creating visual and cultural expectations can be gauged by the words of George Mortimer, a lieutenant on a later voyage to the Pacific North-west. In 1789, he described how 'in this and in every other particular [the natives of Oonalashka] exactly resemble the prints of them in Captain Cook's last voyage, taken from the elegant drawings of Mr Webber'.[54] So widespread and instantly recognisable had these products of exploration become that they themselves became a benchmark for assessing the people and places encountered by future expeditions.

Prints could sustain their own exhibitionary impulse, inspiring a range of different display contexts. For example, Thomas Pennant received a gift of the prints from Cook's third voyage and immediately hastened to have 'half a room hung with them'.[55] William Hodges's landscapes, derived from the second voyage, were so popular that they encouraged Matthew Boulton to buy depictions of Tahitian landscapes and have them reproduced using the new mechanical, copperplate method that imitated oil paintings.[56] Illustrations of Cook's voyages, based predominantly on Webber's drawings, provided basic information about the Pacific that was published in the great Italian and French costume books that appeared during the first third of the nineteenth century.[57] A series of wallpapers entitled 'Les Sauvages de la Mer Pacifique', designed in 1804–05 by Jean-Gabriel Charvet and printed by Josef Dufour at Maconin, provides striking evidence of the ways in which such images of exploration were redeployed for European consumers at the beginning of the nineteenth century. The wallpaper series included a four-page prospectus which offers an insight into why these various visual outcomes proved enduringly popular:

> We hoped that viewers would be pleased to see assembled in a convenient and vivid manner this multitude of peoples who are separated from us by vast oceans, arranged in such a way that, without leaving his apartment, a studious man reading the history of the voyages or the specific accounts of the explorers used in these decorations, might think himself, by casting his eyes around him, in the presence of the depicted peoples.[58]

The twenty panels – each about fifty centimetres wide – were arranged as a serried display of colourful panoramas which were sold as a set so that, without leaving home, 'the reader of the histories of travel can imagine himself among those nations ... and will become familiar with their costumes and the diversity of nature'.[59] The wallpaper gained a modicum of international recognition when it was shown at an exposition in 1806, and the series found its way into at least one English country house: Laxton Hall in Northamptonshire.[60]

One of the most striking ways in which exploration could be exhibited was through the display of people and personal experiences. The most famous example of this was Mai, a native of Raiatea in the Society Islands (or, as the British press described him, a 'wild Indian, that was taken on an island in the South Seas') who returned with Cook's expedition in late 1774.[61] However, this element of personal interaction could be vicariously achieved by putting 'exploration' on the stage. Theatre played a vital role in recycling, modifying and circulating the texts, images and objects derived from British voyages of exploration. In December 1785, a theatrical production of *Omai, or; A Trip around the World*, by John O'Keefe, incorporated some of the best-known themes and images from the Cook voyages. First performed on 20 December 1785, *Omai* was the Christmas pantomime show for the Theatre Royal in Covent Garden. One contemporary described it as 'the stage edition of Captain Cook's voyage'.[62] John Webber painted background landscape scenes and provided first-hand information on dress and accoutrements, as well as advising Philippe Jacques de Loutherbourg, who was in charge of costume and decor.[63] Many of the objects that were used as theatrical props were based on material culture that had been collected on various voyages. Such was the pervasive nature of exploration that, as Adrienne Kaeppler reminds us, Loutherbourg could simply have walked across Leicester Square to study the collections on display in Sir Ashton Lever's Holophusicon.[64] Like the images and travel narratives from which it was partially derived, the production proved to be a great success: it was repeated fifty times during the season, once by Royal Command. In autumn 1786, it was revived for another eight performances, and for yet another eight in the spring of 1788.[65] It effectively displayed, according to *The Times*'s critic, 'all the productions of nature in the animal and vegetable worlds' that European explorers were likely to encounter on expeditions. The same critic went on to make a direct comparison with the published account of such voyages, highlighting the visual nature of public engagement with exploration:

> It may be considered a beautiful illustration of *Cook's Voyages* – an illustration of importance to the mature mind of an adult, and delightful to the tender capacity of an infant. The scenery is infinitely beyond any design or paintings the stage has ever displayed. To the rational mind what can be more entertaining than to contemplate prospects of countries in their natural colours and tints – to bring into living action, the customs and manners of distant nations! To see exact representations of their buildings, marine vessels, arms, manufactures, sacrifices and dresses?[66]

As the success and popularity of *Omai* proved, the texts and images derived from voyages of exploration – especially those of James Cook in the Pacific Ocean – found a ready and varied audience in Britain. From those in a social and financial position to pay for luxury publications and to view art exhibitions, to those who saw prints of the voyages in printsellers' shops in St Paul's Churchyard or on stage in Covent Garden, these expeditions percolated widely into the cultural consciousness of people in eighteenth-century Britain.

Objects, museums and exhibitions

If texts and images formed a key part of exhibiting empire through exploration, then tangible objects and material culture were equally as important in presenting the voyages of Cook and his colleagues to audiences in Britain. If publication could increase the aura of such truth, then the evidence of the object was even more incontrovertible.[67] Such artefacts were collected as part of the process of exchange and transaction that occurred as European ships sailed from place to place, providing tangible confirmation of these encounters and offering material proof of the ways of life of the people encountered by European travellers, and of the resources and the environments in which they lived.[68]

The collecting of 'curiosities' was a pastime equally as popular among those who sailed with Cook as with connoisseurs back in Europe. George Forster makes repeated reference to the eagerness with which all members of the ship's company acquired specimens as 'targets without number were bought by almost every sailor'. He notes that 'not less than ten' of the elaborate mourning dresses of Tahiti 'were purchased by different persons on board and brought back to England'. Officers and sailors built up huge collections of material on their travels, partially because of their desirability in Europe. These objects found a willing market among museums and collectors: one mourning dress brought back to England by a seaman on Cook's second voyage was sold for the sum of 'five and twenty guineas'.[69] Similarly, David Samwell, the assistant surgeon on the third voyage, auctioned off his collection in 248 lots in 1781. Over two thousand items related to the voyages were known at the end of the nineteenth century.[70] And these objects could be distributed far and wide. When Cook's ships arrived back in Europe, the dealer George Humphrey obtained shells that he subsequently sold to purchasers such as the Duchess of Portland and the Literary and Philosophical Society of Danzig.[71] The most notable collector on Cook's voyages was Joseph Banks, who accompanied the first voyage. On his return to London, his home at 14 Burlington Street became 'an early "Museum of the South Seas"'. It provided a focus for those seeking information about Cook's voyages, much of which was gleaned from the arrangement and interpretation of objects. The reaction of one visitor to Banks's house in 1772 offers a glimpse of the sort of impact that material culture collected through voyages of exploration had on British views of the rest of the world. The Revd William Sheffield, Keeper of the Ashmolean Museum, could hardly be described as an average visitor. Yet he felt 'utmost astonishment' and could 'scarce credit my senses'.[72]

It was not just in the world of cultural and social ethnography that Cook's voyages brought back material of interest to those in Europe. Economic botany, of the kind championed by Banks, was also important. In this regard, for example, one might consider the small book produced by Alexander Shaw, which contains over thirty pieces of bark cloth (*tapa* or *kapa* in Polynesian languages) cut to size and sewn into the binding.[73] The first eight pages contain excerpts from the journals of William Anderson and the Forsters, while the book ends with two pages detailing pieces of cloth, listing the item number, the origin of the piece, its characteristics and how it was used.[74]

Ethnographic objects also satisfied an appetite for display and exhibition. Cook himself recognised the 'prevailing passion for curiosities'.[75] Such material was initially most in demand from educated and scientifically curious audiences, or those with a direct connection with the voyages. As early as 1773, William Falconer wrote to Joseph Banks expressing genuine interest and curiosity in the indigenous arts of the Pacific: 'I was highly entertained at Oxford with a sight of some curiosities you sent from Otahieta and new Zealand [*sic*].'[76] In 1780, the London-based merchant and collector George Humphrey auctioned his museum, which included 182 'artificial curiosities' from the South Seas. The items for sale from his collection represented the types of objects that could convey the ways of life of these newly explored Pacific spaces: 'the best and most extensive collection of cloths, garments, ornaments, weapons of war, fishing tackle and other singular inventions of the natives of Otaheite, New Zealand and other new discovered islands in the South Seas'.[77] In negotiating his place on the second voyage, which he later abrogated, Johan Zoffany asked for £1,000 and 'a third of all curiosities'.[78] John Webber returned from the third voyage with over one hundred items, many of which he bequeathed to the museum in Berne, the town of his birth. When Fanny Burney visited Webber's house 'to see his south Sea drawings' in March 1781, she instead spent the morning inspecting the 'curiosities' with which he had returned. The author had a personal connection with Cook's voyages as her brother, James Burney, had accompanied the second and third voyages. When Webber and Captain King explained the objects and their significance to her, Burney proclaimed them 'extremely well worth seeing'.[79]

But the interest in such material – and the impulse to put it on public display for general audiences – went beyond those directly connected with the voyages. Cook's first biographer, Andrew Kippis, acknowledged that 'the curiosities which have been brought from the discovered islands, and which enrich the British Museum and the late Sir Ashton Lever's (now Mr Parkinson's) repository, may be considered as a valuable acquisition to this country, as supplying no small fund of information and entertainment'.[80] Several donations of Cook voyage material were made to the British Museum at regular intervals. In February 1770, Philip Stephen, Secretary to the Admiralty, wrote to the trustees of the British Museum with the 'offer of several Curiosities from the late discovered Islands' in the Pacific.[81] On 3 February 1775, the Lords of the Admiralty wrote to the British Museum to consign 'a collection from New Zealand and Amsterdam in the South Seas, consisting of 18 articles, Domestic and Military, brought by Captain Furneaux'. On 24 November 1780, the museum's 'Book of Presents' records a gift of 'several artificial curiosities from the South Sea from Captain Williamson, Mr John Webber, Mr Cleveley, Mr William Collett, and Mr Alexander Hogg'.[82]

Joseph Banks, who made donations in 1778 and 1780, described the 'several cart loads' of 'arms and curiosities from the South Sea' that he had sent to the museum, which had 'engaged to fit up a room for the sole purpose of receiving such things'.[83] A 'South Seas Room' was planned at the British Museum as early as 1775. In April 1776, the carpenter was reprimanded for his tardiness and instructed to complete the arrangements as a matter of urgency. By March 1778, the room was being papered in a 'neat mosaic pattern'.[84] The display subsequently became a major public attraction. It was the first occasion that the museum had organised a display with specific geographical and cultural references.[85] Daniel Solander, together with some assistants, arranged and labelled everything.[86] In doing so, they had to 'intirely renew the arrangement'. On 10 August 1781, Solander reported that the display was opened to visitors.[87] When Sophie von la Roche visited the museum in the summer of 1786, she was intrigued by the objects ('all the pots, weapons and clothes from the South Sea islands just recently discovered'), which were 'just as they are shown in the prints illustrating the description of [Cook's] voyage: crowns, helmets and war-masks, state uniforms and mourning'. And, even at this stage, the material was inextricably linked to the personal story of Cook: Sophie described the room as being 'devoted to Captain Cook, that luckless, excellent man'.[88] In the early nineteenth century, the 'Otaheite and South Sea Rooms' of the British Museum were described as among the great sights of London for visitors. James Malcolm described the sight in *London Redivivum*:

> The researches of Captain Cook are well known to the publick; and perhaps no age or country were ever more happy in the choice of a Navigator, and his companions in science and perseverance. The visitor will find in this room the result of years of labour and danger: a fund of information, supported by undoubted authenticity; and a source for poignant regret, that our possession of these treasures led to the unhappy end of this illustrious seaman.[89]

Of course, the exhibition of exploration did not just happen in London. Many other public institutions in Britain and across Europe acquired and displayed objects and material culture derived from these voyages of exploration. John Webber donated objects to Berne, Johan Reinhold Forster presented some of his collection to the University of Oxford, while Anders Sparrman left material to the Academy of Sciences in Stockholm.[90] In October 1771, only two months after Cook had transmitted 'the bulk of the Curiosity's' collected on the first voyage to the Admiralty, Lord Sandwich presented Trinity College, Cambridge, with 'a great number of curiosities brought from the newly discovered islands in the south seas'.[91] From the evidence of contemporary guidebooks, it created considerable interest among visitors to the Wren Library.[92] William Hunter, the great Scottish collector, was another who acquired a variety of 'First Contact' pieces from Cook's voyages. These were initially exhibited in his museum in Great Windmill Street, Soho. But, by the early nineteenth century, the entire collection was on display in Glasgow.[93] Both James Patten, surgeon on the *Resolution*, and James King, second lieutenant on the *Resolution* on the third voyage and later commander of the *Discovery*, left large collections to Trinity College, Dublin. Patten's donation even led to the consideration of display conditions for the material by the College Board, and how best to exhibit this collection. The Board Minutes for 22 July 1777 record the resolution:

> That a room be prepared for a Museum, and that Dr Wilson receive under his care the curiosities collected in the South Sea by Dr Patten, and presented by him to the College. Ordered also that the College Architect give his opinion whether the great room over the gate be fit for that purpose, and, if he shall find it fit, that he shall give in plans of glass cases for it.[94]

The Board's resolution had been enacted by 1810. In that year, in *An Historical Guide to Dublin*, the Revd G.N. Wright described the museum containing the 'very curious collection brought from the South Sea Islands, and presented to the University by Dr Patten'.[95]

Sir Ashton Lever's Holophusicon was one of the most remarkable public display phenomena of the period. Initially opened in Lever's home, Alkrington Hall near Manchester, it was subsequently moved to Leicester House (which dominated the north side of what became Leicester Square) in London.[96] Objects collected on Cook's second voyage were on public display in the Otaheite Room and Club Room. By 1784, when Lever was in the process of disposing of his collection, he had 1,859 Pacific objects, the majority of which must have been derived from Cook's voyages.[97] On 16 July 1778, Susan Burney wrote to her sister, the author Fanny, about a visit to the Holophusicon, where there 'were a great many things from Otaheite' already on display.[98] The Sandwich Room, named after the First Lord of the Admiralty, later opened to accommodate material from third voyage.[99] In a public announcement dated 31 January 1781, Lever acknowledged 'the patronage and liberality of Lord Sandwich, the particular friendship of Mrs Cook, and the generosity of the officers of the voyage, particularly

Captain King and Captain Williamson' in endowing his establishment. He hastened to add that he had made 'many considerable purchases himself', and that he was 'now in possession of the most capital part of the curiosities brought over by the Resolution and Discovery in the last voyage'. Lever's collection was 'displayed for public inspection: one room, particularly, contains magnificent dresses, helmets, idols, ornaments, instruments, utensils, etc. etc. of those islands never before discovered, which proved so fatal to that able navigator, Captain Cook, whose loss can never be too much regretted'.[100] John Feltham's *Picture of London*, a series of guidebooks to the capital which were updated almost annually, provided information about the Leverian Museum, the successor to the Holosphusicon. By this time, the collection was now in the possession of James Parkinson, who had moved it to a house located to the south of Blackfriars Bridge. Nevertheless, it was still recommended as one of 'the most instructive objects of curiosity in the metropolis'.[101] A later edition of the same guidebook pointed out the remarkable nature of a museum that offered visitors 'the completest and most interesting collection of natural curiosities in the metropolis ... exhibiting, in one grand assemblage, the beauties, perfections, prodigies and irregularities of nature'.[102]

The public reception of the display of this material may be partially gauged from a description of Lever's collection that appeared in *The European Magazine and London Review* of 1790, when it was still on display in Leicester House. The author of the piece was in no doubt that 'of all the spectacles contained in this opulent and extensive city, there is not one more worthy the attention of a curious and intelligent person than the Holosphusicon'.[103] As well as providing information on the arrangement of the material on public display, the article also gives an insight into the ways in which these objects were interpreted for visitors:

> 15. The next is the Otaheite Room, where are numerous dresses, ornaments, idols, domestic utensils, &c. of the people in the newly discovered islands, which, to an active imagination, convey a forcible idea of them and their manners.
> 16. In the Club Room are the warlike weapons of the several savage nations of America. The clubs are many of them curiously carved, and some require prodigious strength to be able to wield with agility.
> 17. The Sandwich Islands Room is a continuation of the subjects in the Otaheite Room, being full of curious Indian dresses, idols, ornaments, bows, &c. which express very strongly the character of the people.[104]

Objects provide 'a forcible idea' of the strange nations and 'express very strongly the character of the people' and 'their manners'. The very materiality of the objects on display (the 'curiously carved' clubs which 'require prodigious strength') became a key interpretative device for conveying ideas about the results of British exploration in the Pacific. The Sandwich Room was described in John Feltham's *Picture of London for 1806*:

> The arched passage leading from the hall to the Sandwich Room is ornamented on the sides with flaxen mantles from Nootka, or King George's Sound, and New Zealand, made by the people to whom the use of a loom is totally unknown; above which are the war-clubs, adzes, and paddles, of New Caledonia, Otaheite and the Friendly Islands ... Here also are several beautiful specimens of matting from the Sandwich Islands, which, in strength, firmness, and beauty, excel the similar productions of the world; daggers, in shape like to that which afterwards put a period to Captain Cook's existence; cava bowls; feathered and other necklaces; cordage; adzes; chissels; hand-weapons; fishing-hooks and lines; helmets, with wicker linings; feathered cloaks; drums; models of canoes; idols; and innumerable other rarities.

The specimens here 'excel the similar productions of the world'. The very fact of their presence in London and their public display was highlighted as crucial in conveying a sense of the people and places represented here. The material culture gave 'a clearer conception of the people who make and use them, than can ever be obtained from descriptions'.[105] A similar way of presenting and interpreting material derived from exploration was incorporated in the Dublin guidebooks that were so closely modelled on the London prototypes. *The Picture of Dublin for 1811* described the display space in Trinity College, Dublin, in glowing terms:

> The Museum is a beautiful room 60 feet by 40 feet, furnished with a collection of Irish fossils and a variety of curious and exotic natural and artificial productions among which is a very good collection of curiosities from the South Pacific Ocean and the North-West Coast of America, presented by Dr. Patten and Captain King, which make a very conspicuous figure. A chief mourner's dress of Otaheite displays much taste mingled with barbarity, and the one of the naval warrior merits attention. There is also a quantity of the various cloths made from the barks of trees in the different islands of the South Seas and fishing nets well executed. The rich cloaks and feathers with the war-like weapons and drums and other instruments of music will not be passed by un-noticed.[106]

There was no charge for visiting the museum, which was 'open to the public every day, (Sundays and Holidays excepted,) from one to two o'clock'.[107]

Interest in collecting and displaying objects derived from exploration extended beyond metropolitan centres. Samuel Rush Meyrick's collection at Goodrich Court, Herefordshire, had a South Sea Room.

In the account of a 'Tour of a German Prince', the room is described as being 'filled with the rude weapons, feathered cloaks, etc., of the islanders of the Pacific Ocean. Among these is a war cloak made from the plumage of the tropic bird, brought from the Sandwich Isles by Captain Cooke, and presented by the late Sarah Napier, and a cap with the representation of the whale fishery upon it, from Nootka Sound, engraved in the plates to his third voyage, and formerly in the Leverian Museum.'[108] As late as 1865, the museum of the Bedfordshire Architectural and Archaeological Society contained, among other things, 'two paddles from Owhyhee, curiously carved ... a war club from Tahiti, brought over by Captain Cook – a chieftain's cloak from one of the South-sea islands'.[109]

The display of material culture was undertaken for a variety of reasons, and with a number of motives in mind. Sir Ashton Lever clearly considered that objects demonstrated the ingenuity of the individuals who made them. The *Companion to the Museum* (1790) was published to assist the 'many persons of the most distinguished learning and abilities, admirers of the works of nature, in its almost infinite variety of forms and properties' by highlighting and explaining 'those curious works of art, which display the inventive genius as well as of the untutored Indian, as of the more polished European or Asiatic'.[110] Lever's collection achieved a modicum of success in shaping public opinion and increasing public knowledge. In the preface to the official account of the third voyage, John Douglas contended: 'If the curiosities of Sir Ashton's Sandwich-room alone, were the only acquisition gained by our visits to the Pacific Ocean, who that has the taste to admire, or even the eyes to behold, could hesitate to pronounce, that Captain Cook had not sailed in vain?'[111]

Objects associated with exploration continued to be of display interest into the nineteenth century. In his *Treatise on the Art of Preserving Objects of Natural History* (1818), William Bullock used naval associations and narratives of Britain's maritime history in order to advertise and promote his activities. His collections embraced the 'most interesting articles brought from the South Seas during the Voyages of Discovery of Captain Cook. They include the identical idols, weapons and other domestic and military implements engraved in the History of these Voyages.'[112] But objects from the Pacific were also increasingly displayed to commemorate Captain Cook, who died on the third voyage. By the time it became Parkinson's Museum, or the 'Leverian Museum' at the Rotunda on the south side of Blackfriars Bridge, the 'Sandwich Room' was 'dedicated to the immortal memory of Captain Cook', and contained 'the admirable and curious articles he collected in his third, and unhappily last, voyage'.[113] Feltham's description here owed a lot to the official 'Companion' to the museum which reminded visitors that 'on entering this apartment, the first thing that meets the eye is the following inscription: "To the immortal memory of Captain Cook." Being the same inscription that the public have seen at Leicester-house.'[114]

Conclusion

After James Cook's death on the third voyage, the presentation of voyage material became increasingly refracted through his commemoration. As Lissant Bolton argues, Cook is 'more trope than history', and his 'popular fame today is partly constructed through and by museums, and through the collections made on his voyages'.[115] Kathleen Wilson has demonstrated how late eighteenth-century thinking about national identity was articulated and refined through representations of Cook and the South Pacific.[116] Monuments erected by Sir Hugh Palliser near Chalfont St Giles and the Earl Temple at Stowe illustrate the widespread impact of Cook, and his developing mythic status. And later, as Jillian Robertson has shown, monuments, memorials and markers that commemorated Cook were employed by a range of interested groups for a variety of political ends.[117]

The contemporary collecting, exhibiting and interpreting of information and objects derived from eighteenth-century voyages of exploration occurred at a time when British responses to the rest of the world were being rapidly forged and reshaped.[118] The enduring appeal of objects, exhibitions and displays relating to Cook, up to the present day, demonstrates the long-lasting impact of these voyages.[119] By the early nineteenth century, the British Museum's collection formed 'one of the most conspicuous parts' of that museum.[120] And the history of these voyages, the objects associated with them and their public display continue to play a crucial role in exhibiting the history of exploration.

Notes

1 Edmund Burke to Dr Robertson, 10 June 1777, in Charles William, Earl Fitzwilliam, and Sir Richard Bourke (eds), *Correspondence of the Right Honourable Edmund Burke*, 4 vols (London: Francis and John Rivington, 1844), vol. 2, p. 163.
2 Kathleen Wilson, *The Island Race: Englishness, Empire and Gender in the Eighteenth Century* (London: Routledge, 2003), p. 59.
3 See Dan O'Sullivan, *In Search of Captain Cook: Exploring the Man through His Own Words* (London: I.B. Tauris, 2008), p. 250, n. 9, and Daniel A. Baugh, 'Seapower and Science: The Motives for Pacific Exploration', in Derek Howse (ed.), *Background to Discovery: Pacific Exploration from Dampier to Cook* (Berkeley, CA: University of California Press, 1990), pp. 1–55.

4 J.C. Beaglehole (ed.), *The Journals of Captain James Cook on His Voyages of Discovery. Vol. I: The Voyage of the 'Endeavour', 1768–1771* (Cambridge: Cambridge University Press, 1955), p. cclxxxii.

5 Urs Bitterli, *Cultures in Conflict: Encounters between European and Non-European Cultures, 1492–1800*, trans. Richie Robertson (Cambridge: Polity, 1989), p. 162.

6 P.J. Marshall and Glyndwr Williams, *The Great Map of Mankind: British Perceptions of the World in the Age of Enlightenment* (London: Dent, 1982), p. 259.

7 See M.K. Beddie, *Bibliography of Captain James Cook*, 2nd edn (Sydney: State Library of New South Wales, 1970).

8 John Douglas, 'Introduction', in James Cook and James King, *A Voyage to the Pacific Ocean ... for Making Discoveries in the Northern Hemisphere, in the Years 1776, 1777, 1778, 1779, and 1780*, 3 vols (London: G. Nicol and T. Cadell, 1784), vol. 1, p. lxix.

9 For more on the collecting and display of material culture as a result of missionary activities, see Sujit Sivasundaram, *Nature and the Godly Empire: Science and Evangelical Mission in the Pacific, 1795–1850* (Cambridge: Cambridge University Press, 2005), and Chris Wingfield, 'The Moving Objects of the London Missionary Society: An Experiment in Symmetrical Anthropology', unpublished PhD thesis, University of Birmingham, 2012.

10 For further information, see Katie Taylor, 'Pocket-Sized Globes', *Explore Whipple Collections*, Whipple Museum of the History of Science, University of Cambridge, 2009 (www.hps.cam.ac.uk/whipple/explore/globes/pocketsizedglobes/) (accessed 5 July 2013).

11 National Maritime Museum, Greenwich, GLB0001. For further information, see http://collections.rmg.co.uk/collections/objects/19688.html (accessed 5 July 2013).

12 The public reception of images and objects is a notoriously difficult area to research, and all conclusions need to be read in this context. For more on the problematic nature of audience reception, see Sarah Longair and John McAleer, 'Curating Empire: Museums and the British Imperial Experience', in Sarah Longair and John McAleer (eds), *Curating Empire: Museums and the British Imperial Experience* (Manchester: Manchester University Press, 2012), pp. 1–16 (pp. 11–13).

13 Daniel Clayton, 'Captain Cook's Command of Knowledge and Space: Chronicles from Nootka Sound', in Glyndwr Williams (ed.), *Captain Cook: Explorations and Reassessments* (Woodbridge: Boydell, 2004), pp. 110–33 (p. 112).

14 Quoted in Glyn Williams, *Voyages of Delusion: The Search for the Northwest Passage in the Age of Reason* (London: HarperCollins, 2003), p. 140.

15 Johann Reinhold Forster, 'The Translator's Preface', in Lewis [sic] de Bougainville, *A Voyage round the World* (London, 1772), p. v. Quoted in Alan Frost, 'New Geographical Perspectives and the Emergence of the Romantic Imagination', in Robin Fisher and Hugh Johnston (eds), *Captain Cook and His Times* (Vancouver: Douglas and McIntyre, 1979), pp. 5–19 (p. 6).

16 Quoted in Brian W. Richardson, *Longitude and Empire: How Captain Cook's Voyages Changed the World* (Vancouver: University of British Colombia Press, 2005), p. 146.

17 Charles L. Batten, *Pleasurable Instruction: Form and Convention in Eighteenth-Century Travel Literature* (Berkeley, CA: University of California Press, 1978), p. 3.

18 Wilson, *The Island Race*, p. 58.

19 John L. Abbott, *John Hawkesworth: Eighteenth-Century Man of Letters* (Madison, WI: University of Wisconsin Press, 1982), p. 185.

20 Quoted in Bernard Smith, *European Vision and the South Pacific* (New Haven, CT: Yale University Press, 1985), p. 114.

21 Wilson, *The Island Race*, p. 59.

22 O.H.K. Spate, 'Seamen and Scientists: The Literature of the Pacific, 1697–1798', in Roy MacLeod and Philip F. Rehbock (eds), *Nature in its Greatest Extent: Western Science in the Pacific* (Honolulu: University of Hawaii Press, 1988), pp. 13–26 (pp. 14, 15).

23 Williams, *Voyages of Delusion*, p. 147.

24 Bernard Smith, *Imagining the Pacific: In the Wake of the Cook Voyages* (Carlton, Victoria: Melbourne University Press, 1992), p. 53.

25 For further discussion of explorers' claims for the truthfulness of their accounts, see Dorinda Outram, 'On Being Perseus: New Knowledge, Dislocation, and Enlightenment Exploration', in David N. Livingstone and Charles W.J. Withers (eds), *Geography and Enlightenment* (Chicago: University of Chicago Press, 1999), pp. 281–94, esp. p. 283. See also Barbara Maria Stafford, *Voyage into Substance: Art, Science, Nature, and the Illustrated Travel Account, 1760–1840* (Cambridge, MA: MIT Press, 1984).

26 See Thomas Richards, *The Imperial Archive: Knowledge and the Fantasy of Empire* (London: Verso, 1993).

27 Williams, *Voyages of Delusion*, p. 354.

28 Ibid., p. 247.

29 Robin Inglis, 'Successors and Rivals to Cook: The French and the Spaniards', in Glyndwr Williams (ed.), *Captain Cook: Explorations and Reassessments* (Woodbridge: Boydell, 2004), pp. 161–78 (p. 177).

30 David McKitterick (ed.), *The Making of the Wren Library, Trinity College, Cambridge* (Cambridge: Cambridge University Press, 1995), p. 105.

31 Frost, 'New Geographical Perspectives', pp. 6–7.

32 Quoted in Helen Wallis, 'Publication of Cook's Journals: Some New Sources and Assessments', *Pacific Studies* 1 (1978), pp. 163–94 (p. 165).

33 See Nicholas Thomas, *Discoveries: The Voyages of Captain Cook* (London: Penguin, 2004), p. 152.

34 Smith, *European Vision*, p. 46.

35 Paul Kaufman, *Borrowings from the Bristol Library: 1773–1784* (Charlottesville, VA: Bibliographical Society of the University of Virginia, 1960), p. 122.

36 Wilson, *The Island Race*, p. 59.

37 Wallis, 'Publication of Cook's Journals', p. 165.

38 Smith, *European Vision*, p. 62.

39 See Tony Rice, *Voyages of Discovery* (London: Natural History Museum, 2008), p. 176.

40 For a discussion of the impact of Douglas's editorship, see I.S. MacLaren, 'Exploration/Travel Literature and the Evolution of the Author', *International Journal of Canadian Studies* 5 (1992), pp. 39–68 (p. 43).

41 William Hauptman, *Captain Cook's Painter, John Webber, 1751–1793: Pacific Voyager and Landscape Artist* (Bern: Kunstmuseum, 1996), p. 48.

42 John E. Crowley, *Imperial Landscapes: Britain's Global Visual Culture, 1745–1820* (New Haven, CT: Yale University Press, 2011), p. 105.

43 Frost, 'New Geographical Perspectives', pp. 6–7.

44 Quoted in Williams, *Voyages of Delusion*, pp. 336–8.

45 James R. Fichter, *So Great a Profitt: How the East Indies Trade Transformed Anglo-American Capitalism* (Cambridge, MA: Harvard University Press, 2010), p. 214.

46 Smith, *Imagining the Pacific*, p. 118.

47 Douglas Fordham, *British Art and the Seven Years' War: Allegiance and Autonomy* (Philadelphia: University of Pennsylvania Press, 2010), p. 247. RA catalogues reveal the following statistics for works of art directly related to the Americas, Asia and South Pacific: seven (1769); five (1770); one (1771); three (1772); two (1773); one (1774); three (1775); eleven (1776). See Fordham, *British Art and the Seven Years' War*, p. 291, n. 136.

48 Smith, *European Vision*, p. 62.

49 *London Packet or Lloyd's New Evening Post*, 25 April 1777.

50 Hauptman, *Captain Cook's Painter, John Webber*, p. 48.

51 Crowley, *Imperial Landscapes*, p. 79.

52 Hauptman, *Captain Cook's Painter, John Webber*, p. 52.

53 Smith, *European Vision*, p. 346, n. 11.

54 Quoted in Richardson, *Longitude and Empire*, pp. 94–5.

55 Wallis, 'Publication of Cook's Journals', p. 185.

56 Crowley, *Imperial Landscapes*, p. 92.

57 See Rüdiger Joppien, 'The Artistic Bequest of Captain Cook's Voyages: Popular Imagery in European Costume Books of the Late Eighteenth and Early Nineteenth

[61]

Centuries', in Robin Fisher and Hugh Johnston (eds), *Captain Cook and His Times* (Seattle, WA: University of Washington Press, 1979), pp. 187–210.

58 Quoted in Crowley, *Imperial Landscapes*, p. 230.

59 Quoted in Smith, *European Vision*, p. 113.

60 Adrienne L. Kaeppler, *Holophusicon: The Leverian Museum. An Eighteenth-Century English Institution of Science, Curiosity and Art* (Altenstadt: ZKF Publishers, 2011), p. 94.

61 Richard Altick, *The Shows of London* (Cambridge, MA: Harvard University Press, 1978), p. 48. The case of Mai has inspired much recent scholarship and the literature is prodigious and growing. The classic biography is still E.H. McCormick, *Omai: Pacific Envoy* (Auckland: Auckland University Press, 1977).

62 Quoted in Wilson, The Island Race, p. 63.

63 Hauptman, *Captain Cook's Painter, John Webber*, p. 48. See also Rüdiger Joppien, 'Philippe Jacques de Loutherbourg's Pantomime "Omai, or a trip round the world" and the Artists of Captain Cook's Voyages', in T.C. Mitchell (ed.), *Captain Cook and the South Pacific* (London: British Museum, 1979), pp. 81–136; David Worrall, *Harlequin Empire: Race, Ethnicity and the Drama of the Popular Entertainment* (London: Pickering and Chatto, 2007), chapter 6.

64 Kaeppler, *Holophusicon*, p. 40.

65 Smith, *European Vision*, pp. 114–16.

66 *The Times*, 26 December 1785.

67 Nick Thomas, 'William Hodges as Anthropologist and Historian', in Ricardo Roque and Kim A. Wagner (eds), *Engaging Colonial Knowledge: Reading European Archives in World History* (Basingstoke: Palgrave, 2011), pp. 235–53 (p. 235).

68 Howard Morphy and Michelle Hetherington, 'Introduction: Encountering Cook's Collections', in Michelle Hetherington and Howard Morphy (eds), *Discovering Cook's Collections* (Canberra: National Museum of Australia Press, 2009), pp. 1–10, p. 5.

69 George Forster, *A Voyage Round the World in His Britannic Majesty's Sloop Resolution commanded by Capt. James Cook, during the years 1772, 3, 4, and 5*, 2 vols (London: B. White, 1777), vol. 2, pp. 71, 72, 75.

70 Hauptman, *Captain Cook's Painter, John Webber*, pp. 80, 109, n. 10.

71 Neil Chambers, *Joseph Banks and the British Museum: The World of Collecting, 1770–1830* (London: Pickering and Chatto, 2007), p. 21.

72 Chambers, *Joseph Banks and the British Museum*, p. 9.

73 Alexander Shaw, *A Catalogue of the Different Specimens of Cloth collected in the Three Voyages of Captain Cook* (London: Alexander Shaw, 1787).

74 Richardson, *Longitude and Empire*, p. 138.

75 Quoted in Lissant Bolton, 'Brushed with Fame: Museological Investments in the Cook Voyage Collections', in Michelle Hetherington and Howard Morphy (eds), *Discovering Cook's Collections* (Canberra: National Museum of Australia Press, 2009), pp. 78–91 (p. 87).

76 Smith, *European Vision*, p. 123.

77 Hauptman, *Captain Cook's Painter, John Webber*, p. 83.

78 Smith, *European Vision*, p. 123.

79 Hauptman, *Captain Cook's Painter, John Webber*, p. 50.

80 Andrew Kippis, *The Life of Captain James Cook* (London: G. Nicol, 1788), p. 498.

81 Chambers, *Joseph Banks and the British Museum*, p. 11.

82 Kaeppler, *Holophusicon*, pp. 33, 39.

83 Chambers, *Joseph Banks and the British Museum*, p. 11.

84 Jenny Newell, 'Revisiting Cook at the British Museum', *Journal of Museum Ethnography*, forthcoming. I am grateful to Dr Newell for allowing me to read her article in advance of publication.

85 See Bolton, 'Brushed with Fame', p. 88.

86 Chambers, *Joseph Banks and the British Museum*, p. 12.

87 Newell, 'Revisiting Cook at the British Museum'.

88 Clare Williams (ed.), *Sophie in London, 1786: Being the Diary of Sophie von la Roche* (London: Jonathan Cape, 1933), p. 109.

89 James Peller Malcolm, *Londinium Redivivum, or An Ancient History and Modern Description of London*, 4 vols (London: John Nichols, 1802–7), vol. 2 (1803), p. 520.
90 Forster, *A Voyage Round the World*, vol. 2, p. 72.
91 Beaglehole (ed.), *The Journals of Captain James Cook on His Voyages of Discovery. Vol. I*, p. 638; *Cantabrigia Depicta: A Concise and Accurate Description of the University, Town and County of Cambridge* (Cambridge: J. & J. Merrill, 1790), pp. 89–90. See also Wilfred Shawcross, 'The Cambridge University Collection of Maori Artefacts, made on Captain Cook's First Voyage', *Journal of the Polynesian Society* 79 (1970), pp. 305–48 (p. 305); and Peter Gathercole, 'Lord Sandwich's Collection of Polynesian Artefacts', in Margarette Lincoln (ed.), *Science and Exploration in the Pacific: European Voyages to the Southern Oceans in the Eighteenth Century* (Woodbridge: Boydell, 2001), pp. 103–15.
92 McKitterick (ed.), *The Making of the Wren Library*, p. 107.
93 See Lawrence Keppie, *William Hunter and the Hunterian Museum in Glasgow, 1807–2007* (Edinburgh: Edinburgh University Press, 2007), pp. 24–5, 27. I am grateful to John MacKenzie for this reference. See also Euan W. MacKie, 'William Hunter and Captain Cook: The 18th Century Ethnographical Collection in the Hunterian Museum', *Glasgow Archaeological Journal* 12 (1985), pp. 1–18.
94 J.D. Freeman, 'Polynesian Collection of Trinity College, Dublin; and the National Museum of Ireland', *Journal of the Polynesian Society* 58 (1949), pp. 1–18 (p. 3).
95 Quoted in Freeman, 'Polynesian Collection of Trinity College, Dublin', p. 5.
96 See Altick, *The Shows of London*, pp. 28–9.
97 Kaeppler, *Holophusicon*, p. 10.
98 Susan Burney to Fanny Burney, 16 July 1778, in A.R. Ellis (ed.), *The Early Diary of Frances Burney, 1768–1778*, 2 vols (London: George Bell, 1889), vol. 2, p. 249.
99 Kaeppler, *Holophusicon*, p. 6.
100 Quoted in Kaeppler, *Holophusicon*, p. 83.
101 [John Feltham], *The Picture of London for 1802* (London: Richard Philips, 1802), p. 187.
102 [John Feltham], *The Picture of London for 1806* (London: Richard Philips, 1806), p. 281.
103 'A Description of the Holophusicon, or, Sir Ashton Lever's Museum', *The European Magazine and London Review* 1 (1782), pp. 17–21 (p. 17).
104 'A Description of the Holophusicon', pp. 20–1.
105 [Feltham], *The Picture of London for 1806*, p. 282.
106 [W. Gregory], *The Picture of Dublin for 1811* (Dublin: J. and J. Carrick, 1811), p. 91.
107 Ibid., pp. 91–2.
108 Kaeppler, *Holophusicon*, p. 265.
109 Charles Longuet Higgins, 'A Few Plain Remarks on Local Museums', *Bedfordshire Architectural and Archaeological Society* 8 (1865), pp. 321–9 (p. 323).
110 *A Companion to the Museum (Late Sir Ashton Lever's) removed to Albion Street, the Surry End of Black Friars Bridge* (London, 1790), preface.
111 Cook and King, *A Voyage to the Pacific Ocean*, vol. 1, p. lxix.
112 Quoted in Robert D. Aguirre, *Informal Empire: Mexico and Central America in Victorian Culture* (Minneapolis, MN: University of Minnesota Press, 2005), p. 14.
113 [Feltham], *The Picture of London for 1806*, p. 282.
114 *A Companion to the Museum (Late Sir Ashton Lever's)*, p. 6
115 Bolton, 'Brushed with Fame', pp. 82, 83.
116 Wilson, *The Island Race*, pp. 54–91.
117 See Jillian Robertson, *The Captain Cook Myth* (London: Angus & Robertson Publishers, 1981).
118 Kaeppler, *Holophusicon*, p. 91.
119 Bernard Smith, 'Cook's Posthumous Reputation', in Robin Fisher and Hugh Johnston (eds), *Captain Cook and His Times* (Seattle, WA: University of Washington Press, 1979), pp. 159–85.
120 British Museum, *Synopsis of the Contents of the British Museum* (London, 1808), pp. xxiv–xxv, quoted in Chambers, *Joseph Banks and the British Museum*, p. 17.

CHAPTER THREE

Satirical peace prints and the cartographic unconscious

Douglas Fordham

Image reproduction in the eighteenth century was dominated by the single-sheet intaglio print, which could take the form of etching, engraving, aquatint, mezzotint or some combination of these intaglio techniques. Even for those with access to original works of art, the preponderance of imagery relating to Britain's overseas interests would have come to them through the mediation of prints. For eighteenth-century Britons we can speak quite literally of 'impressions of empire'. Scholars have documented the exponential growth of imperial knowledge in the eighteenth century and the dissemination of this knowledge through printed maps, botanical illustrations, costume studies and topographic views. But alongside this insatiable curiosity came a palpable insouciance about its lessons. The exhibition of empire, typically associated with ambition, pride and expertise, also included an unruly genre that I shall describe here as the satirical peace print.

The ostensible aim of satirical peace prints was to promote and extend Great Britain's military might and imperial reach. In the second half of the eighteenth century the genre burst to life any time the King or Court made any gesture (real or perceived) towards peace. Nearly always faulting the administration in power, satirical peace prints attacked those who were deputised to make the King's peace. While most of the graphic satire produced in London focused on Westminster politics and metropolitan society, satirical peace prints engaged directly with imperial themes and debates.[1] It had been possible, of course, to catch glimpses of Algonquin Indians, Hindu carvings and religious ceremonies in China through intaglio prints of the seventeenth and early eighteenth centuries, but these typically appeared in expensive folio volumes and as fine art reproductions.[2] It was with the satirical peace print that imperial subject matter moved into the less expensive and more demotic register of English graphic satire.

While the bulk of imperial visual culture in Georgian London was celebratory and optimistic in tone, satirical peace prints traded in dire warnings and apocalyptic prognostications. Indeed, many satirical peace prints expressed condescension, and even distaste, for the colonies and territories that were the object of the expansionist's desiring gaze. In a provocative and now-canonical essay, W.J.T. Mitchell described Western traditions of landscape as 'something like the "dreamwork" of imperialism', loosely invoking Freudian metaphors of repression, displacement and condensation in cultural production.[3] To fully appreciate the satirical peace print we must also look below the primary level of signification to a series of contradictory meanings and iconographic residues that may not have been entirely apparent to the satirists or those who laughed at their prints.

If landscape painting expressed the dream of empire, then satirical peace prints presented Britons with a recurring imperial nightmare. James Gillray's *A Phantasmagoria: Scene Conjuring up an Armed Skeleton*, published in early 1803, counter-intuitively juxtaposed peace with death (Figure 3.1). Based on the famous witches scene in Shakespeare's *Macbeth*, the intaglio print poses three politicians in the guise of the weird sisters who conjure from their cauldron an armed skeleton of Britannia. Etched into the smoke above her head is the word 'PEACE' in an elegant script. The complex iconography of this print depended upon the public's familiarity with the satirical peace print as a genre, which I will establish below before returning to an analysis of *A Phantasmagoria*. But at the simplest level, Gillray's print deploys the genre's basic refrain that a hasty peace produced national decline and even death.

Rather than dreams, however, the operative Freudian framework in graphic satire is that of the joke. In many of the satires examined in this chapter, humour exceeded, and even ran counter to, the prints' stated political aims. The overt, conscious claim made by satirical peace prints was that Britain's greatness depended on the maintenance and extension of its overseas colonies. A number of prints made this point by representing the colonies as a vital part of the body politic. To cede Gibraltar to the French or Spanish would be like cutting off one of Britannia's limbs (see Figure 3.2). This straightforward metaphor reinforced the print's political claims. Quite a few peace prints, however, offered more ambivalent metaphors. Politicians either devouring distant colonies or expelling them as excrement were common (Figures 3.3, 3.4 and 3.7). Ostensibly arguing for the preservation of Britain's Empire, the humour of these prints derives, at least in part, from an indecorous treatment of those very same colonies. Tensions between a satire's immediate geopolitical claims (protecting and extending Britain's territorial holdings) and visual metaphors that

Figure 3.1 James Gillray, *A Phantasmagoria: Scene – Conjuring up an Armed Skeleton*, 5 January 1803, hand-coloured etching and aquatint, 350 mm x 255 mm

work against those claims constitute a puzzling phenomenon that I will term the cartographic unconscious. Many of the prints examined here exhibit a complete disregard for the location, strategic value or anything else that the public might know about distant territories from the imperial knowledge industry. While knowledge was power, satire could be bliss. And the public's desire to deny or misconstrue imperial knowledge offers an important caveat to the ways in which empire was exhibited and consumed in Georgian Britain.

The autonomy of British art relative to a market economy and the consolidation of the fiscal-military state have been important loci of recent art-historical debate. This debate has been sharpened by a growing literature on the relationship between art and empire, which claims that exploration, colonisation and military conquest were central to the development of British art.[4] Relatively little, however, has been written about the significance of peacemaking and diplomacy to visual form.[5] Perhaps because peacemaking was an uncommon subject for fine art, or because it belonged to the formal and bureaucratic (rather than the informal and cultural) dimensions of the British state, it has largely escaped art-historical analysis. It might come as a surprise, therefore, that peacemaking constituted a major theme in English print culture. Between 1762 and 1815, the definitive period for this chapter, peace appeared in roughly the same proportion as war in English graphic satire.[6] This chapter offers some possible reasons for the emergence of peace as a major satirical theme, including but not limited to the rise of politics 'out of doors', a growing populist militarism and a shift in perceptions regarding international diplomacy. Popular debates over peace treaties became a crucible into which a potent brew of Parliamentary politics, territorial acquisition and European alliances could be stirred together to invoke ever-shifting phantasms of the fiscal-military state.

Timothy Hampton has traced the link between early modern diplomacy and artistic form in the realm of literature. Arguing that early modern diplomacy shaped both the form and content of certain types of fiction writing, Hampton observes that 'diplomacy is the *symbolic* political act par excellence. It is a form of action that is eminently political, but that is also, in its very essence, semiotic, carried out through the exchange of signs.'[7] Satirical peace prints, like Gillray's *A Phantasmagoria*, gave visual form to the airy nothingness upon which European peace terms seemed to rest. Contrary to prevailing notions about the British public sphere as a rational, well-informed cultural space, satirical peace prints rollicked on a rhetorical sea of hyperbole and false cognates. True to the conventions of the satirical peace print, *A Phantasmagoria* represents imperial holdings by nothing more than scraps of paper. The words 'Malta', 'Cape', 'Ireland', 'Dominion of the Sea' and 'Gibralter' [*sic*] are written on bits of paper that stand ambiguously for the written treaty, for formal deeds or possibly for newspaper text. The only principle ordering this geographic chaos is a Manichaean worldview in which might is right and more is always better.

As a genre, the satirical peace print has a discernible beginning and end, which is to say, it fulfilled important cultural and political functions during a specific historical period. While a number of intaglio prints responded to the Treaty of Utrecht in 1713, for example, those prints do not belong to the genre that would ultimately inspire Gillray. Satirical prints dealing with the Treaty of Utrecht tend to represent peacemaking as a contest between nations, effectively presenting allegories or emblematic figures of respective nations as coextensive with those speaking on its behalf. Many of the extant prints in this vein are of Dutch or German origin, and they circulated internationally.[8] A rare British print relating to the Treaty of Utrecht comes from a deck of playing cards commemorating the Duke of Marlborough's victories. Louis XIV stands waist deep in water between the rocks of Peace and Unity as he tries to cut a cord that binds them. An angelic Queen Anne swoops in to thwart the cruel blade. A verse from the card reads, 'In vain the gallick Tyrant strives to be / An enemy to Peace and Unity'.[9] In legislative practice, the British Parliament was deeply divided over a European peace between 1711 and 1713, and in a bid to conclude the war the ministry even removed Marlborough from office. The visual record, however, does not contain substantial evidence of these divisions.

Most of the prints relating to peace from the late seventeenth and early eighteenth centuries invoke the 'internationalist' focus of early modern writing on diplomacy, which 'stressed the role of the ambassador as an agent of international concord, as a promoter of peace among nations and the establishment of a unified *res publica christiana*'.[10] This view came to be challenged by a 'nationalist' conception of the diplomat's role, particularly in Britain, which emphasised the fraught place of the diplomat in state building and national consolidation. Timothy Hampton notes that this contest began as early as the late sixteenth century in fictional and non-fictional representations of the diplomat.[11] It is not surprising then that prints relating to the Treaty of Utrecht already show a fraying of internationalist rhetoric. Satirical peace prints that emerged around the mid-eighteenth century, however, mark a fairly decisive break from internationalist hopes. Unlike the Treaty of Utrecht prints, satirical peace prints viewed diplomacy as *consistently* detrimental to state interests. Satirical peace prints worked from a general presumption that Britain would prevail on the battlefield and the high seas, while continental (and particularly French) diplomats would snatch victory from the jaws of defeat. These satires take the nationalist conception of diplomacy to its logical conclusion by denouncing the administration in power for engaging in any peace process at all.

A distinctive feature of the satirical peace print emerged in 1748 at the conclusion of the War of Austrian Succession: peace came to be represented as a form of ministerial betrayal. To be sure, older visual conventions persisted. A print titled *The Congress of the Brutes at Aix-la-Chapelle, 1748* represents the Prussian wolf, Gallic cock and Dutch boar, among other emblematic animals, bargaining around a table as they respectively argue their own nation's strategic interests.[12] The British lion says 'Pray accept of Cape Breton' acknowledging one of the treaty's more controversial concessions. There is no obvious sense of ministerial malfeasance, however, because the one-to-one equation between nation and animal does not allow for enough symbolic distance to distinguish between a nation's diplomacy and its interests. George Bickham's *Conduct of the Two B[rothe]rs* (Figure 3.2), on the other hand, emphasises domestic tensions that the peace process catalysed in Britain, and it is with this etching that the satirical peace print comes of age. The Duke of Newcastle and his brother Henry Pelham, who were largely in control of the ministerial agenda in 1749, gruesomely vivisect Britannia whose attributes lie at her feet. Both of her arms have been amputated and bear the words 'Cape Breton' and 'Gibralter' respectively. The former is inscribed for its cession and the latter for its near-cession in the Treaty of Aix-la-Chapelle. A Hanoverian horse licks up Britannia's blood, which is inscribed 'all The Blood & Treasure of ye Nation this Animal Devours yearly'. With a publication date of 1749, the print attacks the Pelhams more vigorously than peace. It nonetheless imagines diplomatic concessions in Nova Scotia and the tip of Spain as a violation of Britannia and the body politic. Mark Hallett noted that the satire reinterprets a seventeenth-century etching of *The Martyrdom of St Erasmus*. Bickham's translation of Christian martyr into national allegory is conceptually problematic and visually awkward.[13] But it reveals a dawning recognition that oppositional satirists could turn peace treaties into effective visual weapons. The older iconography of emblematic nations bargaining around a table gives way to an internecine battle between British factions over the composition of the body politic. Just as importantly, the health and shape of the nation is directly related to the retention or loss of overseas colonies.

While Bickham's *Conduct of the Brothers* was prescient, it remained something of a visual and conceptual outlier.[14] That would change

Figure 3.2 [George Bickham the younger] *The Conduct of the Two B[rothe]rs*, 1749, etching, 325 mm x 199 mm

dramatically in 1762 with a swarm of prints relating to the Preliminaries then under debate for the Peace of Paris, which concluded a global conflict that would come to be known as the Seven Years War (1756–63). It was during the heated public debate over the Peace of Paris that satirical peace prints became a fixture in the London print trade with a strong repertoire of metaphors and symbols.

In response to rumours of a potential peace in the summer of 1762, John Wilkes, the brilliant opposition MP, published a potent brew of xenophobia and populist imperialism in the *North Briton.* His primary target was the de facto prime minister, and King's 'favourite', John, third Earl of Bute. Attacking the Scottish-born Bute as a foreign usurper, the 'Wilkes and Liberty' movement in London gave voice to literate middle classes longing for a more active political presence. Of the hundreds of oppositional prints produced in London in 1762 and 1763, a great many could be described as satirical peace prints, which is to say they explicitly targeted the administration's desire for peace with France and Spain.[15] There is a strong correspondence between the rise of politics 'out-of-doors' during the 1760s and the popularity of satirical peace prints, which tells us much about the purpose and logic of the latter.[16] Like the larger body of Wilkesite satire from the 1760s, satirical peace prints sought to organise the forces of opposition and pressure the administration in power. Even the most popular prints in this period had a relatively modest print run, with William Hogarth's notorious caricature of John Wilkes from 1763 not exceeding four thousand single-sheet prints.[17] Unless or until we learn more about the distribution and reception of these prints outside London, the primary audience appears to have been those in the immediate vicinity of Westminster.[18]

Henry Howard's satirical songsheet *The Peace-Soup-Makers, Or, A New Mess at the Bedford Head* (Figure 3.3) typifies the genre's thematic concerns, while pioneering a new iconographic trope. Arguing that Lord Bute was incapable of cooking up a hearty peace in 1762, the song declares:

> No longer let Bunglers in Cook'ry pretend
> To poison their Tastes for their own private Ends:
> Insipid Soup Meagre, or Crowdy, or Sallad,
> Are not strong enough for Englishmen's Palate ...
> Let your Soup, if you have it, be lasting and strong,
> To stick to the ribs of the Old and the Young:
> High season'd and rich, it will add to your Vigour,
> And give you fresh Courage to draw Sword or Trigger.

If we must have peace, the song suggests, it should be without territorial concessions, and it should provide a basis for subsequent imperial

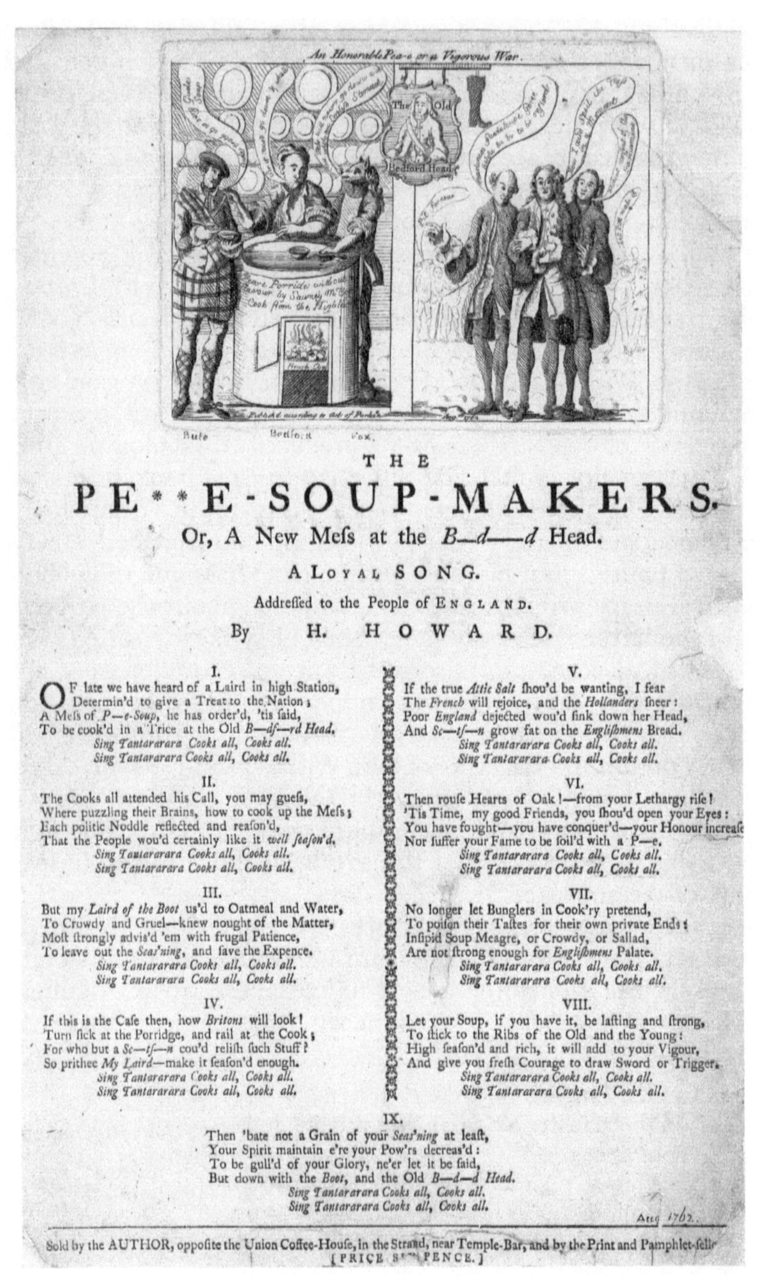

Figure 3.3 Anon. for Henry Howard (publisher), *The Peace-Soup-Makers. Or, A New Mess at the Bedford Head*, 1762, etching and letter press, 372 mm x 215 mm (full printed area)

[72]

conquests. This print marks the earliest instance that I have found of the 'peace soup' motif that would recur intermittently for the next fifty years. The obvious verbal pun on 'pea soup', also worked on a metaphorical level, evoking a cheap and often unsatisfying recipe.[19] The ingredients for this soup are enumerated by one of Lord Bute's chefs in the Bedford Head kitchen: 'Martinico Guadaloupe Goree Belisle &c &c to be restored [i.e. returned to the French and Spanish]', to which another adds 'Without consent of the Parliament'. As the British envoy to Paris, the Duke of Bedford negotiated the preliminary treaty, which Parliament ultimately ratified.

Peace soup provided an adaptable recipe that enabled satirists to throw any and every colony into a single pot and stir it around. There was no need to establish where the colonies are, how much they are worth or whether their populations are Protestant, Catholic or pagan. This was also true if you reversed the metaphor, and showed Britannia retching out her colonies. In December 1762, Mary Darly published an anonymous satire titled *The Evacuations; or an Emetic for Old England Glorys* (Figure 3.4). Britannia is clearly not feeling well as George III's ministers force her to take an emetic. British possessions including Cuba and the slave trading port of Goree are purged into a bowl held by Louis Baboon, a recursion to the emblematic form of peace prints. Represented as his namesake animal, Henry Fox is armed with a giant clyster. A lyric below the image laments, 'Oh disgrace view our Treasures our Conquests thrown up.' The actual peace treaty is represented as 'A Bubble. An Empty exchange for men, money and trouble.' The only supporters of the peace, according to this satire, are those in the background who were bought off with state pensions, while London merchants see their business in Newfoundland cod, West Indian sugar and Chinese tea taken over by foreign countries. As the print suggests, the Seven Years War was profitable and distant for a rising class of British merchants and tradesmen. The Peace of Paris with its closed-door negotiations and potential for 'secret terms' was a potent satirical target.

The attitude that colonies should be devoured in as great a number as possible encounters a bit of iconographic resistance, however, in *The Evacuations*. The satirical conceit of the emetic, the clyster and the evacuation was fairly common in British graphic satire of the eighteenth century, where it was frequently deployed against ministers who were viewed as greedy or corrupt. Vic Gatrell notes that 'between the 1720s and 1750s something odd happened in the history of English publication. Bookshops were hit then by a small boom in excretion-obsessed pamphlets and verses; thereafter they mysteriously died out. It was Swift's scatology – in *Gulliver's Travels* particularly (1726) –

Figure 3.4 Anon. for Mary Darly (publisher), *The Evacuations; or an Emetic for Old England Glorys*, December 1762, etching, 305 mm x 202 mm

Figure 3.5 Anon., *The Political Vomit for the Ease of Britain*, 1742, etching, 226 mm x 314 mm

that activated this taste.'[20] A good example of this ribald taste can be found in *The Political Vomit for the Ease of Britain* published in 1742, which depicts Robert Walpole being purged (from both ends) of all the patronage associated with the prime minister's position that he had just vacated (Figure 3.5). Beneath the title is a quotation from the Book of Job: 'He hath swallowed down Riches and he shall Vomit them up again; God shall cast them out of his Belly.'

By the time *The Evacuations* was published in 1762, this kind of imagery had become increasingly rare in literary texts. According to Gatrell, 'after mid-century the relative decorum of the written text is striking, not least because it throws the continuing scatology of graphic satires into much sharper relief. Clearly, things could be said in images that in texts were tabooed.'[21] Gatrell suggests that this shift was due to a growing female readership, which compelled authors to clean up their imagery. Why this decorum did not extend to graphic satire is unclear, particularly in this case where 'evacuations' are described in the song lyrics and Mary Darly proudly appended her name as the print's publisher. Iconographically, satirical peace prints attempted to recast evacuation as undesirable. It was the expulsion of colonies, rather than a greedy consumption, that constituted failure and corruption.

The attempt to recode expulsion as detrimental to the body politic may not have been entirely successful. The visual rhetoric of expulsions, enemas and emetics, which was born out of a critique of ministerial corruption, was awkwardly applied to the forced evacuation of colonies by peace treaty. William Hogarth hints at this in *The Times, Plate 1*, published in September of 1762 (Figure 3.6). This print is largely unprecedented in the tradition of satirical peace prints because it *endorses* the administration's desire for peace. In the third state of the print, shown here, William Pitt fans the flames on a street sign of 'the globe' as London burns in the distance. *The Times, Plate 1* ridiculed William Pitt's demagoguery, and the City's insatiable demand for conquests and profits. Less clear is whether the print constituted an endorsement of Lord Bute, who wears a kilt and fetches water for the fireman who attempts to extinguish the flames of war. Certainly the opposition interpreted it this way and vigorously attacked Hogarth for producing ministerial propaganda.[22]

In one of the print's more curious episodes, three gentlemen, two in a garret and one in a first floor window of the 'Temple Coffee House', attempt to dislodge the fireman with clysters. The London public quickly identified these figures as Lord Temple, an influential leader of the Pittite opposition, and two of his hired guns, John Wilkes and the poet Charles Churchill. One of the most striking aspects of Hogarth's print is that he brings the war home, so to speak. *The Times, Plate 1* represents the metropolis as a welter of competing interests. In place of the traditional litany of colonial names (Gibraltar, Minorca, Cape Breton and so on), Hogarth includes a single reference to the colonial world: a street sign on the left is labelled 'Alive from America'. Parodying the public's interest in Native American 'ambassadors' who arrived in London that year, the allegorised Indian on this sign wears moneybags around his waist. As in *The Political Vomit* (Figure 3.5), money corrupts, although this time it is the middling sorts who have been corrupted by imperial profits and delusions of grandeur. Unheeded in the smoke-filled air is a dove of peace. The efflorescence of satirical peace prints provoked Hogarth to produce one of the darkest, most cynical visions of the city that he loved.

In the long run, satirical peace prints made greater use of metaphors of eating and excreting than they did of physical embodiment. Pennsylvania's agent in London, Benjamin Franklin, offers a telling exception. He represented the Stamp Act as a blow to Britannia that was equivalent to the loss of her limbs. *Magna Britannia: Her Colonies Reduc'd* was produced by Franklin for personal use as a calling card in late 1765 or early 1766 and it represented Virginia, Pennsylvania, New York and New England as Britannia's four severed limbs. The print was reprinted in London's *Public Register* on 3 December 1768 where it was paired with a new engraving, *Its Companion*, which also denounced the Stamp Act, although it represented the American colonies as a Native American.[23] Even Englishmen who were sympathetic to repeal baulked at the idea that the American colonies were the very limbs of Britannia.

The actual loss of American colonies in 1783 only reinforced this perspective. Responding to the Treaty of Paris, *The General P—s, or peace* represents an Englishman, a Dutchman, a Spaniard, a Frenchman and a Native American urinating into a pot.[24] The Englishman says, 'Say what they will, I call this an honourable P--,' and the Native American says, 'I call this a free and Independent P--'. Once again America appears as an emblematic savage. This had become a fairly conventional insult by this date, and it reflects a general condescension towards the colonies. As Benjamin Franklin complained to Henry Home, Lord Kames, in 1767: 'Every man in England seems to consider himself as a Piece of a

Figure 3.6 William Hogarth, *The Times, Pl. 1*, 7 September 1762, etching, third state, 247 mm x 307 mm

Sovereign over America; seems to jostle himself into the Throne with the King, and talks of OUR *Subjects in the Colonies.*'[25] Satirical peace prints largely reflect this ethos, presenting their perspective as a kind of 'shadow government' in which foreign policy, long the preserve of diplomats, could be debated in the public realm.

There were never any fears that an emblematic Native American might be confused with the real thing. Satirical peace prints rarely, if ever, represented peace treaties between Britain and non-Western powers. This was despite the fact that Britain, and tributary arms such as the East India Company, concluded a great many treaties with Native American tribes, Mughal Indian rulers and other non-Western powers during the eighteenth century. The representation of peace treaties with these sovereigns would have attributed agency to precisely those peoples and regions that satirical peace prints were intent on denying anything other than a place name on a scrap of paper. If the condescension of London satirists towards the American colonies was palpable, towards the non-Western world it was absolute.[26]

Following the Seven Years War satirical peace prints became a regular staple in the London print trade, recurring each time a new treaty was announced to the public, including the Treaty of Paris of 1783 and the Anglo-French Commercial Treaty of 1786. Unprecedented developments in Revolutionary France placed significant pressure on the conventions of the satirical peace print in the 1790s. Rather than a discrete set of declared and concluded wars, Revolutionary France opened up the possibility of an ongoing ideological conflict that verged on perpetual war, a possibility that Immanuel Kant met with a proposal *Toward Perpetual Peace* (1795). That 'philosophical sketch' borrowed its title, curiously enough, from a satirical street sign:

> "To Perpetual Peace"
> We can leave open the question whether this satirical caption to the picture of a graveyard, which was painted on the sign of a Dutch innkeeper, applies to *human beings* in general, or specifically to the heads of state, who can never get enough of war, or even just to philosophers who dream the sweet dream of perpetual peace.[27]

In this altered political environment, graphic satirists began to view peace in the 1790s and the early 1800s as at least potentially desirable, if perpetually out of reach. Satirical prints also began to integrate peace and diplomacy into a broader range of thematic contexts, which is to say they produced peace prints that were less immediately related to specific treaties and Parliamentary debates.[28] To take one example, the 1790s witnessed a new kind of satire in which the public's reception of peace became the principal subject. A satire titled 'Peace' from

1790 depicts a well-fed government pensioner on one side of a table debating with a thin and uncouth member of the revolution society on the other. On the walls and tables around them are a chaotic assemblage of maps, prints and pamphlets that helped to precipitate their argument. In this meta-image of popular political culture we catch a glimpse of the satirical peace print's place in national debate.[29]

While satirical peace prints had typically reflected a Whiggish, expansionist and oppositional perspective, prints with a more elitist and conservative bent also began to appear in the 1790s. One print titled *Deep Politicians* represents a gentleman with a 'Gazette' in his pocket with a headline reading 'Peace'. He faces another gentleman and asks 'Who brought it about?' To which the second gentleman responds, 'I don't know!!'[30] A print from a decade later represents the 'peace opinions' of eight different citizens, including a woman who hopes to 'pick and choose' a suitor from the returning military officers. All eight Englishmen and women are seated, five around a table, which further domesticates earlier themes of ingestion and negotiation.[31] Whereas peace treaties had been a rallying point for political opposition, they were now shown to elicit highly subjective opinions. Once a formidable weapon in the opposition's arsenal, peace treaties were losing their ability to unite either the public or the opposition.

In 1806, David Wilkie exhibited a modestly sized painting of *Village Politicians* to an enthusiastic Royal Academy audience in London. In terms of both theme and tone, the painting shares much with prints like *Deep Politicians* from the 1790s. In an incisive analysis of Wilkie's painting, David Solkin noted that the scene is set in a Scottish interior where locals argue over an article from the radical Edinburgh newspaper the *Gazetteer*. Published between 1792 and 1794, the *Gazetteer* locates Wilkie's genre scene one decade earlier at a fraught political moment. For Solkin, the painting's appeal lay in an 'awareness that the private lives of all Britain's citizens, including newspaper readers of every rank and geographical location, had now to be seen as inseparably bound up with the great public events unfolding within and even beyond the country's borders'. This 'time-space compression' was unique to turn-of-the-century Britain, Solkin argues, owing to improvements in transport, the distribution of news via expanded print outlets, improved mail coaches and the psychic shock of the French Revolution.[32]

Satirical peace prints had concerned themselves with great public events beyond Britain's borders since at least the Seven Years War, as we have seen. But Solkin's description of heightened time-space compression around 1800 provides an interesting gloss on the peace print's fate. While it is notoriously difficult to quantify the distribution and reception of graphic satire outside of London, it is certainly the case that transport improved, circulation expanded and even Scottish villagers joined the national dialogue on war and peace by the early nineteenth century. We know, for example, that Gillray's print of *A Phantasmagoria* was reproduced as an etching for *London und Paris*, and that it circulated throughout the German-speaking states just months after it had been published in London.[33] As previously noted, satirical peace prints initially appear to have been directed at those in the immediate vicinity of Westminster. By 1800, these prints had garnered a national and even an international audience. The satirical peace print lost much of its political force and focus in this expanded field, and it failed to signify within its own generic terms. *London und Paris* denounced Gillray as a 'warmonger' for his print of *A Phantasmagoria*, but praised him as an 'inspired artist and talented arranger of characters'.[34] This interpretation misses much of the irony, scepticism and self-referentiality of Gillray's print. But how could it be otherwise? The genre depended upon an assumption of insular metropolitan superiority. This had always been a fantasy, of course, which helped to produce a psychic dissonance fundamental to the cartographic unconscious.

These assumptions, and this anxious humour, began to break down in post-Revolutionary Britain. The satirical peace print depended on a broadening of the body politic, but only within certain limits. There came a point when the body politic became too large for the peace print's humour to signify properly. For one thing, the expansion of a politically engaged public, gently chastised by *Deep Politicians* and *Village Politicians*, helped to catalyse and mobilise a significant technological change. By the first third of the nineteenth century single-sheet intaglio prints gave way to woodcuts, lithographs and other forms of illustration capable of much larger print runs.[35]

In retrospect, graphic satires concerning the Treaty of Amiens marked the climax, and inaugurated the decline, of the satirical peace print tradition. When the Treaty of Amiens was signed on 25 March 1802, it was apparent to many that it would not offer a lasting peace between Britain and Napoleonic France. Gillray's best satires on the peace came in early 1803 as the treaty's terms became increasingly tenuous, eventually imploding in May of that year. The *Evacuation of Malta* (Figure 3.7) was published on 9 February 1803, and it recycled the central motif of *The Evacuations* (Figure 3.4). Gillray caricatures the Prime Minister, Henry Addington, who expels the territories of Malta, St Domingo, Egypt, Cape of Good Hope, Guadaloup (*sic*) and Martinique. Addington was the son of a physician, and the opposition had dubbed him 'the Doctor' for his prosaic background

Figure 3.7 James Gillray, *Evacuation of Malta*, 9 February 1803, hand-coloured etching and aquatint, 255 mm x 357 mm

and uninspired leadership. In Gillray's print the doctor becomes the patient as Bonaparte encourages a complete purge.[36] The print's hand-colouring makes it clear that the colonies are to be viewed not just as faeces but also as brightly coloured map pieces. Bonaparte demands 'All! All!' colonial holdings, while Addington splutters: 'Pray do not insist upon Malta! – I shall certainly be turned out! And I have got a great many Cousins and Uncles & Aunts, to provide for, yet!' The colonies are pawns in a diplomatic game, the satire implies, involving fragile egos and nepotistic patronage. Evacuation is once again associated with a corrupt ministry, but unlike *The Political Vomit* (Figure 3.5), Addington is encouraged to hold it all in. The cartographic unconscious would seem to culminate in this print with a debased analogy between colonial map pieces and excrement. But how aware was Gillray of the iconographic succession traced in this chapter? Does this print repress and displace a colonial antipathy, as we have seen in numerous satirical peace prints, or does it bring the cartographic unconscious fully to light? Is Gillray playing doctor or patient?

I am inclined to view Gillray's manipulations as deliberate or, at the very least, as visually and conceptually informed. The ironic self-consciousness of Gillray's vision becomes particularly clear in *A Phantasmagoria* (Figure 3.1). Published one month before the *Evacuation of Malta*, it also features Addington, who came into office in 1801, promising to broker a peace with France. The other two witches are caricatures of Lord Hawkesbury, the Foreign Secretary, and Charles James Fox. All three bear tricolour ribbons. When viewed within the tradition of satirical peace prints, *A Phantasmagoria* can be seen as a clever manipulation of the 'peace soup' motif. The main ingredients of peace soup had been Britain's colonies, while Gillray reverses this logic by sacrificing Great Britain itself, in the form of an emblematic lion. Addington ladles coins into the cauldron from a bag that reads 'to make the gruel thick and slab', a line borrowed from *Macbeth* (IV.1). The tenor of Gillray's satire can be found in lines chanted by Shakespeare's Third Witch:

> Scale of dragon, tooth of wolf,
> Witches' mummy, maw and gulf
> Of the ravin'd salt-sea shark,
> Root of hemlock digg'd i' the dark,
> Liver of blaspheming Jew,
> Gall of goat, and slips of yew
> Silver'd in the moon's eclipse,
> Nose of Turk and Tartar's lips,
> Finger of birth-strangled babe
> Ditch-deliver'd by a drab,
> Make the gruel thick and slab:
> Add thereto a tiger's chaudron,
> For the ingredients of our cauldron.

This list of exotic and repulsive objects stirred into a single pot is employed brilliantly by Gillray to parody 'peace soup' recipes. Britannia's exotic territorial holdings were a sordid, magical incantation to the British public, albeit a powerful one. In Gillray's print the witches feed territorial names into the fire, rather than feeding them into the cauldron. It is a rhetorical move that resonates with *The Times, Plate 1* (Figure 3.6), where William Pitt fans the flames of war. In front of the cauldron, William Wilberforce kneels down in monkish robes where he sings a 'Hymn of Peace'. Despite his best efforts, Wilberforce failed to compel Addington to include the abolition of slavery in the final terms for the Treaty of Amiens. In this unflattering caricature, Wilberforce sacrifices Britain's good for the liberation of slaves, a desire that Gillray equates with black magic. It is a disturbing claim and it resonates with one of Gillray's most brutal and perplexing caricatures from a decade earlier. *Barbarities in the West Indias* (1791) represents an 'English Negro Driver' stirring an ailing black slave into a massive copper cauldron of boiling sugar juice.[37] The slave's arms and legs protrude from the cauldron, like the lion's paw in *A Phantasmagoria*.

The principal target of both prints appears to be hyperbolic political rhetoric rather than a specific political claim or ideology. It is well known that Gillray's poison pen was for sale, and that he failed to espouse a consistent political viewpoint. Scholarship still tends to assume, however, that *individual prints* were politically didactic; that a given print must have espoused a single, consistent political orientation. The intention of individual prints, in other words, must have been to persuade.[38] While this is true in some cases, a close examination of individual satires (and *A Phantasmagoria* is not unique in this regard) reveals a surprising degree of ambivalence. It is often difficult to know whether we are looking at a devastating political critique, or a satire of what others thought was a devastating critique. Gillray excelled at turning off-hand metaphors and figures of speech, particularly those propounded in Parliament, into etched lines and aquatinted surfaces.[39] His satires on the Treaty of Amiens, for example, offer no obvious political alignment and nothing like a critical assessment of the treaty's geopolitical significance. What they offer instead are visions of diplomacy as '*symbolic* political acts par excellence' in which politicians and public alike were prone to terrific flights of fancy.

A Phantasmagoria is explicit about peace as a mediated projection. The print's title refers to a recently invented device that produced optical illusions with the aid of a projecting lantern. The curious oval format of Gillray's scene turns out to be a projection on to a dark stone wall. So whose projection is this? Who is entertaining whom, and to what end? Generally interpreted as a critique of Addington's administration, the print could just as plausibly be viewed as the projection of a paranoid opposition or the frantic dream of a militant public. Rather than a polemical critique of the Treaty of Amiens, *A Phantasmagoria* begins to look like a meta-picture of the satirical peace print. It pokes around at the genre's expectations and biases.

More than half a century ago, E.H. Gombrich described *A Phantasmagoria* as a print that belonged to 'the congenial climate of the Romantic era' in which 'the weirdest combinations of symbols, the most grotesque conglomerations of images, were no longer merely tolerated as the pardonable licence of a low medium of illustration. They could be attuned to the taste of the time if they were presented as phantoms, nightmares, and apparitions.'[40] More recently, Finbarr Barry Flood has noted the prevalence of optical metaphors in satires by Gillray and others, particularly in their response to the Warren Hastings trial of the 1780s and 1790s.[41] Many of these prints questioned the documentary status of visual art at the very moment that new technologies promised to render visual representation scientific and faithful. Representations of distant territories, such as India, 'amplified contemporary assertions and aporias regarding the documentary status of the image, which recourse to optical technologies sometimes attempted to bolster'.[42] This marked an important shift in the status of imperial knowledge. Satirical prints from the Seven Years War playfully referenced imperial knowledge, but rarely if ever questioned the truthfulness or validity of its source material. Indeed, a shared confidence in the imperial knowledge industry enabled printmakers to score easy, humorous reversals. The 'phantasmagoric spirit' of the Romantic era, to use Gombrich's phrase, rendered imperial knowledge intrinsically subjective and distorted.[43] What had once belonged to the cartographic unconscious now emerged as latent subject matter.

Both of these analyses help to locate the power and significance of *A Phantasmagoria* in a nested set of social relations. Gombrich's analysis is the broadest, locating the print in a 'Romantic era' with predilections for magic and mystery. Flood describes an obsession with illusion catalysed by imperial and technological developments. More narrowly still, Frans De Bruyn notes that Shakespeare's *Macbeth* was a touchstone for Britons in the 1790s, given its 'riveting portrayal of regicide … On the stage it was surpassed only by *Hamlet* in popularity, seeing sixty-nine performances to *Hamlet*'s seventy-five' in that decade.[44]

The witches scene in *Macbeth* had long teetered between tragedy and farce. Sir William Davenant produced a Restoration version of *Macbeth* that thrilled audiences with singing, dancing and vaudevillian male comic witches. By the eighteenth century it was common for comic male leads to riotously play the witches scene. Horace Walpole published a political parody of *Macbeth* in 1743 in which the weird sisters chant, 'Double, double, Toil and Trouble / parties burn and Nonsense bubble'.[45] These lines are equally applicable to Gillray's parody of *Macbeth* and the Treaty of Amiens. Neither political propaganda nor fine art, Gillray's print comes closest to Restoration farce, and even pantomime. Once a potent oppositional weapon, satirical peace prints had devolved into a ridiculous, hilarious bit of theatre.

It would be convenient at this point to describe *A Phantasmagoria* as a radically ambivalent document that condensed (unconsciously, the term suggests) some of the era's greatest cultural preoccupations. But as a response to the satirical peace print tradition, and as an expression of Gillray's own creative agency, the print deserves a more pointed analysis. One possibility is that *A Phantasmagoria* offered the British public a tragic view of nationalist diplomacy. Rather than commenting on the Treaty of Amiens's virtues or failures, the print raised a more terrifying spectre; that peace with France could never be anything more than an apparition. Britannia was not just the personification of a place; she was also the personification of a process. She was conquest, occasional concession and force. Only the inertia of peace could destroy her. Or so nationalist diplomatic thinking might suggest. *A Phantasmagoria* projected the tragedy of nationalist diplomacy and the farce of populist imperialism on to the edifice of British state power. In a volume dedicated to the 'exhibition of empire' it is worth pausing on the very conjunction of Britain's global war with France and the 'Scottish play'. The public's insatiable appetite for imperial spectacle descends, in Gillray's dystopian vision, into 'a tale told by an idiot, full of sound and fury, signifying nothing' (*Macbeth*, V.v.26–8).

Gillray died on 1 June 1815, in the very same month that the Allies defeated Napoleon at the Battle of Waterloo. The satirical peace print would not survive him by long. While the Congress of Vienna of 1814–15 did its best to roll back the clock to 1793, the historical forces that had given the satirical peace print its potency had dissipated. A print from 1832 with many of the same iconographic elements as *A Phantasmagoria* makes this shift particularly clear. 'The Genius of Britain' stands at the left 'and waves the olive branch of peace in

Figure 3.8 Anon., *Designed for a transparency exhibited at No 14 Catherine Street, Strand, on occasion of the general illumination to celebrate the passing of the Reform Bill - 1832*, 1832, etching, aquatint image printed on a letterpress page, 245 mm x 488 mm
(© Trustees of the British Museum)

[85]

her right hand; with her left she points to a slave, in the fore-ground, endeavouring to break off his chains, to whose oppressed race she is rising on the wing with the message of freedom'. On the other side of William IV's throne stands a skeleton with 'the great military, legal, and clerical array which so long obstructed Reform' (Figure 3.8). The print claims to reproduce a transparency that had been illuminated in London to celebrate the passage of the 1832 Reform Act. A dramatically expanded electorate ensures peace, the print suggested, while the machinations of a recalcitrant elite passes away. The very premise of the satirical peace print – that an Ancien Régime diplomacy thwarted the will of the people and the good of the nation – is reconceptualised in the wake of electoral reform. Peace and abolition now mark the 'Genius of Britain', which constitutes a nearly perfect reversal of the peace print tradition.

Notes

1 See Diana Donald, *The Age of Caricature: Satirical Prints in the Reign of George III* (New Haven, CT: Yale University Press, 1996), and Mark Hallett, *The Spectacle of Difference: Graphic Satire in the Age of Hogarth* (New Haven, CT: Yale University Press, 1999).

2 I have chosen these examples based on superb art-historical analyses by Michael Gaudio, *Engraving the Savage: The New World and Techniques of Civilization* (Minneapolis, MN: University of Minnesota Press, 2008), Partha Mitter, *Much Maligned Monsters: A History of European Reactions to Indian Art* (Oxford: Clarendon Press, 1997), and Lynn Hunt, Margaret Jacob and Wijnand Mijnhardt (eds), *Bernard Picart and the First Global Vision of Religion* (Los Angeles: Getty Publications, 2010).

3 W.J.T. Mitchell, 'Imperial Landscape', in W.J.T. Mitchell (ed.), *Landscape and Power* (Chicago: University of Chicago Press, 2002), p. 10. This argument is particularly compelling in regard to picturesque landscapes of British imperial territories, which have been interpreted as a means of homogenising the empire. See Jeffrey Auerbach, 'The Picturesque and the Homogenisation of Empire', *The British Art Journal* 5 (2004), pp. 47–54, and John E. Crowley, *Imperial Landscapes: Britain's Global Visual Culture, 1745–1820* (New Haven, CT: Yale University Press, 2011).

4 For a historiographical overview of these developments, see Douglas Fordham, 'State, Nation, and Empire in the History of Georgian Art', *Perspective: La revue de l'INHA* 1 (2012), pp. 115–35.

5 A notable exception is Benjamin West's *William Penn's Treaty with the Indians* (exhibited 1772), which takes a seventeenth-century treaty as its subject. See Anne Cannon Palumbo, 'Averting "Present Commotions": History as Politics in Penn's Treaty', *American Art* 9 (1995), pp. 28–55.

6 The British Museum's online catalogue provides a schematic sense for the scope of this material. English satirical prints in the British Museum's holdings published between 1762 and 1815 include roughly 550 prints which include war as a principal search term, and 425 that deal with peace and treaties as principal search terms, factoring out prints that prioritise all three terms. This tells us little, except that war and peace were major themes in satirical print culture of the period. That peace was a major theme for English graphic satirists has gone largely unobserved and it controverts twenty-first-century notions of peace as consensual and desirable.

7 Timothy Hampton, *Fictions of Embassy: Literature and Diplomacy in Early Modern Europe* (Ithaca, NY: Cornell University Press, 2009), p. 5.

8   For prints directly related to the Treaty of Utrecht, see Frederick George Stephens and
    Mary Dorothy George (eds), *Catalogue of Political and Personal Satires Preserved
    in the Department of Prints and Drawings in the British Museum*, 12 vols (London:
    British Museum Publications, 1870–1954), vols 3–9. This will subsequently be refer-
    enced as BMC followed by the relevant catalogue number.
9   BMC 1585.
10 Hampton, *Fictions of Embassy*, p. 138.
11 Ibid., pp. 138–9.
12 BMC 3009.
13 Hallett notes that the print strains against sexual type, with St Erasmus being trans-
    formed into an awkward female figure of Britannia. See Hallett, *The Spectacle of
    Difference*, pp. 228–32.
14 While the Treaty of Aix-la-Chapelle inspired a number of graphic satires in 1748
    and 1749, these prints ridiculed celebrations following the peace at least as much as
    they attacked the treaty's official terms. There are satires relating to the fireworks
    display in St James's Park on 27 April 1749 and the accidental conflagration that it
    started on one of the triumphal arches erected for the celebration. There are at least
    four extant prints responding to the scandalously thin dress that Miss Elizabeth
    Chudleigh, future Duchess of Kingston, wore in the guise of Iphigenia to a celebra-
    tory masquerade at Ranelagh Gardens. For more on Miss Chudleigh, see Vic Gatrell,
    City of Laughter: Sex and Satire in Eighteenth-Century London (London: Atlantic
    Books, 2006), pp. 207–8.
15 In the introduction to BMC, vol. 4, Frederick George Stephens notes that 'The Peace
    of Paris, 1763, one of the most attractive subjects for the satirists of that period, is
    distinguished by many entries in this catalogue' (p. xcv). There is no indication,
    however, of how or why this occurred.
16 For a more extensive account of the impact of the Seven Years War on the London
    art world, including the work of graphic satirists, see Douglas Fordham, *British Art
    and the Seven Years' War: Allegiance and Autonomy* (Philadelphia: University of
    Pennsylvania Press, 2010).
17 For more on the complex reception of Hogarth's print, see Shearer West, 'Wilkes's
    Squint: Synecdochic Physiognomy and Political Identity in Eighteenth-Century
    Print Culture', *Eighteenth-Century Studies* 33 (1999), pp. 65–84.
18 Studies dealing with the political role of graphic satire overwhelmingly focus on
    London and Westminster, including Eirwen E.C. Nicholson, 'Consumers and Specta-
    tors: The Public of the Political Print in Eighteenth-Century England', *History* 81
    (1996), pp. 5–21, and my own *British Art and the Seven Years' War*.
19 For one example, see Anon., *The Lady's Assistant for Regulating and Supplying her
    Table* … (London, 1773), written by 'a professed housekeeper who had upwards of
    thirty years' experience in families of the first fashion', which includes a recipe for
    pea soup simply titled 'A cheap soup', p. 178.
20 Gatrell, *City of Laughter*, p. 185.
21 Ibid., p. 189.
22 For a more extensive analysis of Hogarth's print and his declining artistic influence,
    see Fordham, *British Art and the Seven Years' War*, pp. 91–102.
23 Lester C. Olson notes that Darly's version of the print blamed Britannia's dismem-
    berment on 'HER ENEMIES' rather than unfair taxation. Olson also suggests that
    Magna Britannia sought to appease a colonial audience who suspected Franklin of
    complicity in Stamp Act legislation. The print may have also been used to persuade
    British MPs to vote for repeal, although the probable publication date of late 1765 or
    early 1766 made the print politically safe in Britain given the Rockingham adminis-
    tration's push for repeal. See Lester C. Olson, *Benjamin Franklin's Vision of Ameri-
    can Community: A Study in Rhetorical Iconology* (Columbia, SC: University of
    South Carolina Press, 2004), pp. 77–111.
24 Anon., *The General P—s, or peace*, published 16 June 1783 by J. Barrow, New York
    Public Library, Horace Walpole Collection.
25 Quoted in Olson, *Benjamin Franklin's Vision of American Community*, p. 106.

26 Caricatures of non-Western rulers are rare in eighteenth-century satire, with James Gillray's representation of Tipu, Sultan of Mysore, and the Chinese Emperor, Chi'en Lung, in the 1790s as notable exceptions. These prints do not belong to the satirical peace print tradition, but they do create an interesting dialogue with it. See Douglas Fordham, 'On Bended Knee: James Gillray's Global View of Courtly Encounter', in Todd Porterfield (ed.), *The Efflorescence of Caricature* (Burlington, VT: Ashgate, 2011), pp. 61–78.

27 Immanuel Kant, *Toward Perpetual Peace and Other Writings on Politics, Peace, and History*, ed. Pauline Kleingeld, trans. David L. Colclasure (New Haven, CT: Yale University Press, 2006), p. 67.

28 See, for example, Gillray's complex rendering of war and peace as described by Harriet Guest, '"The Consequences of War" in the Winter of 1794–95', in Geoff Quilley and John Bonehill (eds), *William Hodges, 1744–1797: The Art of Exploration* (New Haven, CT: Yale University Press, 2004), pp. 67–9.

29 *Peace*, from the *Attic Miscellany*, 1 December 1790, drawn by Collins, etched by Barlow.

30 *Deep Politicians*, 20 November 1790, drawn by G.M. Woodward, published by S.W. Fores (not recorded in the BMC). Location: Satires British Supplement 1790, Unmounted Roy. This print can be seen as a sharpening of a print from 1783, *Intelligence on the Peace* (BMC 6351) in which the Treaty of Paris is received with differing emotions.

31 *Peace Opinions Contrasted*, 1801, published by William Holland (not recorded in the BMC). Location: Satires British Supplement 1801, Unmounted Roy.

32 David Solkin, *Painting out of the Ordinary: Modernity and the Art of Everyday Life in Early Nineteenth-Century Britain* (New Haven, CT: Yale University Press, 2008), pp. 7–36.

33 See Christian Deuling, 'Aesthetics and Politics in the Journal *London und Paris* (1798–1815)', in Maike Oergel (ed.), *(Re-)Writing the Radical: Enlightenment, Revolution and Cultural Transfer in 1790s Germany, Britain, and France* (Berlin and Boston: De Gruyter, 2012), pp. 102–18, p. 107.

34 Ibid.

35 Timothy Clayton concludes his monumental survey of *The English Print 1688–1802* (New Haven, CT: Yale University Press, 1997), pp. 283–6, with an epilogue entitled 'The Peace of Amiens and After', which notes a divergence between art and commerce as it had been previously structured around the single-sheet intaglio print.

36 The Pittite MP George Canning apparently coined 'The Doctor' as a nickname. Gillray depicted Addington as 'the Doctor' in *Britannia between Death and the Doctor's*, published on 20 May 1804. See Draper Hill (ed.), *The Satirical Etchings of James Gillray* (New York: Dover Publications, 1976), pp. 126–7.

37 For an analysis of the print's ambiguities, see Kay Dian Kriz, *Slavery, Sugar, and the Culture of Refinement* (New Haven, CT: Yale University Press, 2008), pp. 113–15.

38 Amelia Rauser challenges this assumption by arguing that caricature emerged as a foil to modern conceptions of subjectivity and interiority, and that one of its functions was to plumb tensions between surface and depth. See Amelia Rauser, *Caricature Unmasked: Irony, Authenticity and Individualism in Eighteenth-Century English Prints* (Newark, DE: University of Delaware Press, 2008). This question is also examined in Mike Goode, 'The Public and the Limits of Persuasion in the Age of Caricature', in Todd Porterfield (ed.), *The Efflorescence of Caricature, 1759–1838* (Farnham: Ashgate, 2011), pp. 117–26, although he draws an unnecessarily stark dichotomy between novelistic depth and satirical superficiality.

39 For Gillray's deployment of Parliamentary debates and metaphors, see Christopher Reid, *Imprison'd Wranglers: The Rhetorical Culture of the House of Commons, 1760–1800* (Oxford: Oxford University Press, 2012), pp. 97–112.

40 E.H. Gombrich, 'Imagery and Art in the Romantic Period' (1949), republished in Richard Woodfield (ed.), *The Essential Gombrich: Selected Writings on Art and Culture* (London: Phaidon, 1996), p. 533. Gombrich claims that *A Phantasmagoria*

was 'picked almost at random from the last volume' of Mary Dorothy George's British Museum catalogue (BMC) (p. 530).

41 Finbarr Barry Flood, 'Correct Delineations and Promiscuous Outlines: Envisioning India at the Trial of Warren Hastings', *Art History* 29 (2006), pp. 47–78.

42 Ibid., p. 72.

43 The phrase comes from Gombrich, 'Imagery and Art in the Romantic Period', p. 531.

44 Frans de Bruyn, 'Shakespeare and the French Revolution', in Fiona Ritchie and Peter Sabor (eds), *Shakespeare in the Eighteenth Century* (Cambridge: Cambridge University Press, 2012), pp. 297–313 (p. 310).

45 The published title of the work was *The Dear Witches: An Interlude; being a Parody on some Scenes of Macbeth*, published in *Old England; or, The Constitutional Journal* of Saturday 18 June 1743. An analysis of Walpole's parody and the staging and reception of *Macbeth* in the eighteenth century can be found in Catherine M.S. Alexander, '*The Dear Witches*: Horace Walpole's *Macbeth*', *The Review of English Studies* 49 (1998), pp. 131–44.

CHAPTER FOUR

Sanguinary engagements: Exhibiting the naval battles of the French Revolutionary and Napoleonic Wars

Eleanor Hughes

Wartime becomes modern as it becomes spectacle; and because modern war is spectacle it is always to some extent a cold war, conducted by means of strategic representations of remote conflict and waged at home on behalf of some citizens and against others.[1]

On seeing Mr. Clevely's [*sic*] two paintings of Lord Howe's action with the French Fleet, on the 1st of June, 1794, now exhibiting at Mr. Pozzi's, Bond-Street:

> By love of Country lur'd – by Conquest! – Fame!
> The Hero like a Devil fought…
> Yet, many a Briton could have done the same:
> But such, could only sea-bred Clevely paint![2]

Visitors to London in the spring of 1795 encountered a city peppered with representations of the ongoing conflict between Britain and revolutionary France. The first large-scale naval battle of the French Revolutionary War had taken place on 1 June 1794. At Orme's gallery in Old Bond Street, Mather Brown's painting *Lord Howe on the Deck of the Queen Charlotte, 1 June 1794* began showing on 1 January 1795.[3] On 21 February, a pair of paintings depicting the battle by the marine painter Robert Cleveley went on display nearby, at Poggi's New Room, No. 91 New Bond Street.[4] Two weeks later, on 2 March, at the Historic Gallery in Pall Mall, less than half a mile from Orme's and Poggi's galleries, Philippe Jacques de Loutherbourg's enormous painting of the battle, painted as a sequel to his *The Grand Attack on Valenciennes*, was first exhibited. When the annual exhibition of the Royal Academy opened at Somerset House on 4 May, paintings of the battle by the marine painters Robert Dodd and Robert Cleveley – as well as seascapes by William Anderson, Nicholas Pocock, Thomas Whitcombe and Samuel Atkins – were displayed alongside views by Pocock and Dodd of celebrated skirmishes between individual frigates, such as those between *La Nymphe* and *Cleopatra*, and Anderson's *Capture of Fort Royal, Martinico*. In early June, Robert Barker's panorama in Leicester Square, in only the fourth display since it had opened a year earlier, followed its inaugural view of the Grand Fleet at Spithead with 'an exact representation of every ship in the English and French fleets, as they appeared at one o'clock P.M. of the first of June, 1794'.[5]

The Glorious First of June, as the battle came to be known, had been a qualified success – the British had taken six French ships of the line and sunk one, but the French fleet realised its strategic goal, protecting the passage of a grain convoy bound from North America – and as such continued to form the focus of contention not only between the French and British, who disputed its outcome, but also among factions in Britain who wished to claim the significance of the battle in validating their own political strategies.[6] In the immediate aftermath of the battle, the government conceived the battle as the first victory of the war after a year of embarrassing failures and thus as validating ministerial military strategy, while the opposition saw success at sea as proof of the undesirability of a land war on the continent: 'The sea is our protecting element, and as long as Britannia rules the waves, nothing can hurt us. A victory at sea must ever give us more heart-felt pleasure than twenty victories on the Continent.'[7] The battle's second anniversary saw renewed struggle over its meaning during the Westminster election of May–June 1796, when Admiral Alan Gardner, who had commanded the *Queen* under Lord Howe at the First of June, stood as the government candidate against the Whig incumbent Charles James Fox and the radical John Horne Tooke.[8]

Similarly, a competition was playing out in the exhibition spaces of the metropolis, between competing artists and forms of representation. The first opportunity for artists to depict a contemporary, full-scale naval engagement since the War of American Independence had ended a decade earlier, the battle also coincided with explorations of new ways to depict and exhibit naval triumph, including contemporary history painting, 'romantic' modes of depiction and the emergence of new media, most notably the panorama. The First of June also signalled a shift away from the Royal Academy as the primary site for exhibiting scenes of national triumph. During the War of American Independence, marine paintings had been exhibited at the Academy in unprecedented numbers, peaking in 1783 and 1784. The number of naval actions exhibited at the Royal Academy between 1789 and 1794, having dropped off to between four and six per year in the later 1780s, was at the most three per year, and none at all in 1790. Although the commencement of hostilities with France triggered a new spate of such exhibits, only a handful of paintings of the First of June were exhibited at the Royal Academy throughout the wars.[9] In the early 1790s, the Royal Academy underwent the most contentious and factional period in its history. Following the death of Dominic Serres, the marine painter and a founding member of the Academy, in 1792, a number of artists – among them Cleveley, Brown and de Loutherbourg – adopted the strategies initiated by John Singleton Copley with his first solo exhibition of *The Death of the Earl of Chatham* in 1781 and culminating in *The Siege of Gibraltar* in 1791: working with publishers and the press to market engravings by exhibiting paintings in solo exhibitions.[10] It would be fair to say, then, that at the beginning of the wars the Royal Academy was not the site of national and imperial self-imaging that it had been a decade earlier.

The French Revolutionary and Napoleonic Wars (although this could not have been anticipated in 1795) would result in the eclipse of the French, Spanish and Holy Roman Empires, and Britain's emergence as a 'global, naval, commercial, and imperial superpower', a status achieved and maintained – vitally – as much through the idea of naval supremacy in the cultural imagination as in fact.[11] An imperial conflict waged as much at sea as on land, through blockades, disruption of trade and seizure of colonial possessions, it was the major naval battles that seized the popular imagination and served as opportunities for the formation and expression of ideologies that would endure well into the nineteenth century. The ultimate importance of the First of June, then, as a tactical victory that neither served imperial aspirations towards strategically important territories (like the Battle of the Nile, 1798) nor resulted in the decisive defeat of Britain's naval competitors (like Trafalgar, 1805), may lie in its role as a catalyst for cultural responses that would become imperial tropes.

This chapter will focus on the visual responses to the First of June as a case study for the ways in which Britain's identity as an imperial nation began to be shaped through visual culture in new ways at the end of the eighteenth century. Through a synoptic examination of the competition among artists, publishers and exhibitors, I will argue that the unprecedented array of visual responses to the First of June set the stage for a battle of representational modes and aesthetic strategies that would play out over the course of the Revolutionary and Napoleonic Wars.[12] While such responses have tended to be treated monographically (in the case of paintings and prints, whether by painters of contemporary history or marine painters and exhibited in solo or group exhibitions) or in the context of literary, landscape and theatrical histories (as with panoramas and especially naumachia, or mock sea battles), a number of recent studies have brought together categories of representation traditionally separated into spectacle and art, particularly in the context of the modern metropolis. For example, John Brewer has suggested that a shift in the 'scale and nature of cultural presentation ... most obvious in the case of exhibitions of all sorts' – including art exhibitions and 'one-picture shows', scientific demonstrations, venues for theatrical and musical entertainment, and panoramas – took place 'about the time of the American War'.[13] Geoff Quilley has noted the alignment of Brown's and Loutherbourg's paintings of the First of June with the theatrical performances that formed part of the spectacular response to the victory, as part of 'the pandemic, multimedia celebration of British naval victory in London theatres and exhibition spaces' and 'a distinct move ... in the sphere of popular culture, towards an inculcation of a nationalist cult of the maritime'.[14] And Ann Bermingham, writing on the aesthetic impact of the panorama and diorama on the exhibition landscape in the early nineteenth century, has argued that 'the fertile cross-pollination between the exhibition landscape and the popular landscape entertainments of the period needs to be understood in the context of metropolitan modernity'.[15]

Taking as its parameters the territory marked out by these studies, this chapter aims to refine an approach to the nexus of art, spectacle and maritime concerns in several ways. First, and experimentally, by attending to time: in terms of the intervals both between events and representations thereof, and between representations produced over time that tend, as in the studies cited above, to be collapsed through 'the analytical eye of hindsight'.[16] The passage of time over which events took place also was an obdurate feature for which artists had to find representational solutions. In a more general sense, representations of war, whether textual, graphic, theatrical or sculptural, have a distinct and complex relationship to time. In his discussion of 'wartime', Jerome Christensen has described the 'episodic structure' acquired by the reporting of incidents of conflict that 'effectively implicates the noncombatant auditor or reader in its narrative unfolding'.[17] While this is true of immediate responses to a victory – including illuminations, theatrical interludes and press reportage – the necessarily delayed responses comprised by prints, paintings, panoramas and sculpted monuments, which took longer to produce, complicate this linear structure, introducing a repetitive and ideologically productive cycle of commemoration that was further complicated by a tendency in times of war for the commissioning and exhibiting of past victories.[18] Finally, and in part through resisting the tendency to collapse events and representations produced over time, this chapter aims to resituate the quintessentially metropolitan phenomenon of the panorama, the subject of a burgeoning literature that has tended to focus on its landscape subjects to the exclusion of the naval subjects that made up half of the displays in the period, in the context of a tradition of maritime imagery that inflected it in every way.

In the spring of 1794, the population of Paris was facing starvation due to a failed grain harvest exacerbated by political disturbance. French envoys had been able to purchase grain in America and, by December 1793, 117 ships containing grain and stores were gathered in the Chesapeake, to be escorted across the Atlantic by four French ships of the line. The main French fleet under Admiral Villaret de Joyeuse was to sail out from Brest and provide cover for the convoy as it neared the coast of France. The French Republic had declared war on Britain the previous February, Jacobin extremists announcing their intention of planting '50,000 Trees of Liberty' in England. Lord Howe, commander-in-chief of the Home Fleet and the Western Approaches, had been issued instructions to 'protect the trade of the King's subjects' and 'to molest the ships of war and trade of the enemy'.[19] Howe sailed from Spithead, arriving off Brest on 5 May with twenty-six ships in order to intercept the convoy as it approached France. Villaret de Joyeuse had not yet sailed, and so Howe headed south-west, hoping to put himself between the grain ships and the French fleet. There ensued two weeks of unsuccessful searching and, on 19 May, Howe's frigates reported Brest empty; Villaret de Joyeuse and the French fleet had sailed three days earlier, passing close to Howe. On 28 May, the French fleet was sighted to windward, sailing ahead of the grain convoy. The two fleets converged but did not engage. For three days the French alternately drew the English fleet away from the grain ships and drifted around in a heavy fog, with some fighting but no large-scale engagement. On 1 June, the fog lifted and, at about 10 o'clock in the morning, Howe broke the French line, and the battle became a general mêlée, which lasted about an hour and a half.[20] By the end of the day the British had taken six of the French ships and sunk one without the loss of a single British ship. The grain convoy reached France unharmed.

When news of the battle reached London on the evening of 10 June, theatrical performances were interrupted for announcements of the victory, and spontaneous celebrations took place on stage. *The Times* reported the celebrations the next day, noting that at Covent Garden:

> The communication was peculiarly apropos – for it succeeded the technical narration of a sea-fight, so animatedly told by Fawcett. The colours were brought on the stage, and the House, as if inspired by one sentiment, joined in those noblest of all choruses, 'Rule Britannia' – 'Britons Strike Home' – and 'God save the King.'
>
> ...

> But the triumph of a happy people did not end with the night; the succeeding day bore witness to their loyal exultations – the bells pealed merrily during the whole of the morning – constant discharges of ship guns were heard – and every flag ... [was] hoisted in compliment to Lord Howe.[21]

Illuminations were general throughout London; *The Times* noted that 'all the Public Offices were illuminated, particularly the ADMIRALTY, which look beautifully; and not a lane or passage but put forth its lights'.[22] On 12 June, the theatre at Covent Garden announced the addition of a 'Loyal Effusion' to its playlist; Drury Lane followed suit on the 20th, announcing 'a new and appropriate Entertainment, commemorating, and founded on, the glorious Naval Victory of the 1st of June'.[23] The pleasure gardens at Ranelagh and Vauxhall marked the occasion with a fireworks display and a 'naval gala', respectively.[24] The arrival in Portsmouth of the British fleet triggered a mass exodus from London to view the French prizes, particularly at the time of the Royal Review of the fleet, which took place on 26 June.[25] Among those who travelled to Portsmouth were the artists Robert Cleveley, James Gillray, Philippe de Loutherbourg, Mather Brown, John Thomas Serres and Nicholas Pocock, and the print publishers Robert Bowyer and Valentine Green.

Even before they were produced, some of the artistic responses to the battle were the subject of a public and self-conscious competition in the press, characterised by an insistence on the credentials of the artists and the lengths to which they were going to achieve accuracy in their representations. Shortly after the fleet reached Portsmouth, for example, it was announced that Philippe de Loutherbourg, aided by Gillray and in the company of Green, 'had submitted to His Majesty at Windsor the plan' of the picture of the First of June on which they proposed to collaborate, intended as a sequel to his *The Grand Attack on Valenciennes* (1794, collection of Lord Hesketh). Having met with the King's approval and agreement of patronage, Loutherbourg set off 'immediately for Portsmouth, that every particular in this picture may be correctly represented by an appeal to the objects themselves'.[26] Referring to *The Grand Attack on Valenciennes*, the *Oracle* remarked that 'with the animating assurance of having already succeeded beyond the reach of competition on land, we anticipate the brilliancy and the certainty of his complete success on sea'.[27] A day later and yet more to the point, the same paper reported that 'the Communications from *Portsmouth* from the Corps of Observation, led on by Loutherbourg, give us to expect as brilliant an *Expedition* as ever was planned or executed by the Arts'.[28]

Competition was offered by the publisher A.C. Poggi, who 'engaged Robert Cleveley of the Royal Navy, Marine painter to the Prince of

Wales and Marine Draughtsman to His Royal Highness, the Duke of Clarence'. The *Oracle* reported that:

> on the arrival of Lord Howe's Fleet, Mr R. Cleveley immediately went to Portsmouth, for the express purpose of taking Portraits of the different ships of the British fleet, and of the six captured Line of Battle ships, and has collected from the best authority a plan of the two fleets, at the different points of time in which he is to represent them, and every other information requisite for the elucidation of so extensive a subject.[29]

While 'puffing' Cleveley's work, this report beautifully serves as a précis of the methods by which marine painters gathered the materials needed to construct their depictions of highly complex events that occurred over time and at a distance. Its mention of the taking of 'portraits' of the ships both British and French, and securing a plan of the action, is typical and also borne out in sketches made by Nicholas Pocock (Figure 4.1). Predating any proof of artistic merit, then, the advance marketing of images depended on – one might say deployed as ammunition – claims to accuracy and to social approbation, and on making these claims in the same organs that were reporting on the wars and thereby binding the citizenry into the 'great public events unfolding within and even beyond the country's borders'.[30] The specific claims about accuracy are coeval with the reception of marine paintings exhibited at the Royal Academy, which invariably commented on the 'correctness' and 'accuracy' of the representations, in turn reflecting the production of such images for the naval patron who 'scrupulously directs the artist in everything that relates to the situation of his vessel, as well in regard to those with whom, as to those against whom he fought'.[31] In the speculative, monographic and public exhibition, then, this distinguishing feature of transactions between naval patrons and marine painters became a source of authority.

The mention of Cleveley securing information 'from the best authority' is also significant. Other artists and publishers likewise made the best use of their connections, most tellingly revealed through the diary of Joseph Farington, the Royal Academician and chronicler of the intersecting spheres of art and politics in the later eighteenth century. Farington served as an intermediary between artists and naval officers, particularly his second cousin Admiral Gardner, who had commanded the *Queen* at the battle and stood for Parliament the following year. On 16 July 1794, Farington breakfasted with Gardner and 'mentioned to the Admiral [Robert] Smirke['s] and [Robert] Bowyer[']s proposal to publish a Print on the subject of the late engagement and desired His portrait. This he readily granted, and assisted me in making out a list of the Captains with their directions, in order to get their portraits.'[32] Farington also introduced Gardner to the portrait painter Nathaniel Dance-Holland and 'explained Dance's scheme of portraits of distinguished characters of the present age, solicited the Admiral to sit for him'. Dance, noted Farington, was 'happy to have this line of professional men opened to him'. In turn, Gardner promised to get Howe to sit for Dance.[33] Marine painters likewise made use of Farington's connections. On the same day that Farington breakfasted with Gardner, '[John Thomas] Serres came there with some designs to represent the naval engagement, Viz: the ships breaking the line; and the state of the Fleet, including prizes after the engagement'.[34] Two days later Farington visited Serres,

> who showed me his 4 sketches, one of the action & one after it, on the first of June … He has applied by letter to Admiral Gardner to get him a commission from the Admiralty to paint them, or for their sanction that He may make Prints of them. I told him I [would] speak my opinion to the Admiral of his sketches, which I much approved of, and would learn if I could, whether either of his requests [could] be complied with.[35]

Robert Cleveley was also working on his compositions, to be engraved and published by Anthony Poggi. In early August, Farington called on Poggi, who 'desired me to give him an introduction to Admiral Gardner, that He might shew him Cleveley's designs – accordingly I gave him a

Figure 4.1 Nicholas Pocock, *The Battle of the Glorious First of June, 1794; stern views of the captured French ships* L'America *and* La Juste, 1794, ink and graphite on paper

[97]

Figure 4.2 Mather Brown, *Lord Howe on the Deck of the* Queen Charlotte, *1 June 1794*, 1795, oil on canvas

letter'.[36] When the exhibition of Cleveley's pictures opened at Poggi's on 21 February 1795, Poggi called again on Farington's connections by asking him to speak to John Boydell, the leading publisher and merchant printseller, 'to induce them to come there & hoped they [would] take in subscriptions for him'.[37] Publishers, none of whom was immune to the impact of the war on the print trade, clearly depended on these speculative projects – Poggi told Farington that if Cleveley's prints were not a success he would be ruined.[38]

Later advertising for the monographic exhibitions, while clearly puffing the works, also attempt to shape their reception in advance of their being shown:

> LOUTHERBOURG'S picture of Earl HOWE'S victory will shortly be ready for public view. Those who have seen it speak of it in the highest terms, as being treated in a manner entirely new and with all the fire and animation which the event requires. It will form an excellent companion to the Grand Attack on Valenciennes, now exhibiting at the Historic Gallery, Pall Mall.[39]

Poggi's and Cleveley's advertisers responded:

Figure 4.3 B.T. Pouncy, after Robert Cleveley, *To the Right Honourable Earl Howe Commander in Chief Admirals Thos Graves & Sir Alex Hood K.B. Rear Admirals Bowyer, Caldwell, Gardner & Pasley ... This Plate Representing the Morning of The Glorious First of June 1794, Is Dedicated*, 1795, engraving and etching

> Nothing has yet been said of the Pictures painting by CLEVELEY, respecting the glorious Action of the 1st of June, though too much cannot be advanced in their praise. The Public, who are already well acquainted with the merits of this ingenious Artist, want nothing to increase their opinion of them; but his fine talents were never so well employed as in commemorating an action that will to remotest ages excite the admiration of the world. One of the Pictures is finished, the other nearly so, and one of the Plates is considerably advanced. The Public at large will be anxious for their completion.[40]

Once the paintings were on exhibition, this language both intensified and diverged. Advertisements for Cleveley's pictures focused on their accuracy, 'a faithful and most CORRECT representation of that glorious action'.[41] Loutherbourg's publicity in the same newspaper reiterated earlier claims: 'universally acknowledged to be the most complete representation of a Naval Engagement that has ever been offered to public inspection, it is treated in a manner so perfectly new and interesting, that it excites the highest admiration in the numerous visitors who daily resort to that exhibition'.[42] Orme likewise made

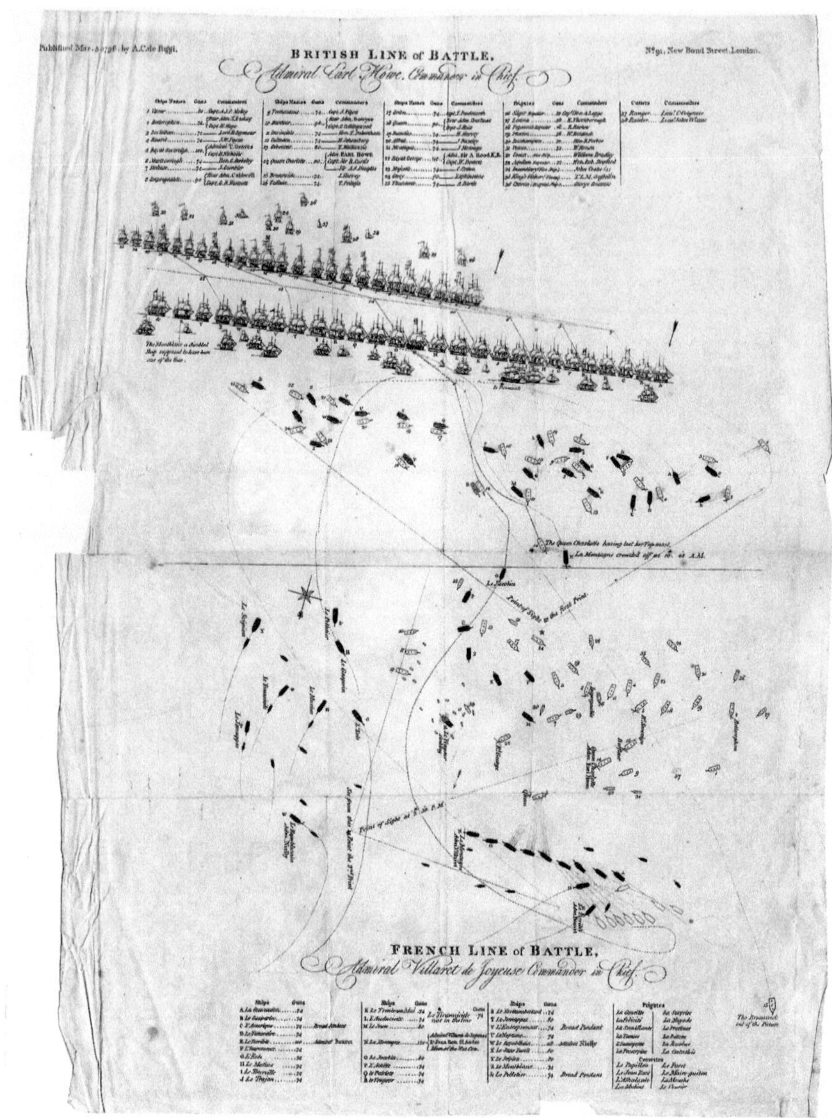

Figure 4.4 *Diagram showing the positions of the British and French fleets at the start of the action and in the course of the engagement on 1st June 1794, 1796, published by Antonio Cesare Poggi, engraving*

the case that Mather Brown's *Lord Howe* (Figure 4.2) was 'treated in a Manner entirely *Novel*, and perfectly distinct from any other Nautical Engagement, hitherto executed'.

What is it about Loutherbourg's and Brown's pictures that is 'new' and 'novel', 'perfectly distinct from any other nautical engagement'? Cleveley's publicists made no such claims, and indeed his pictures (Figure 4.3) were fairly generic, broad views of the battle at two stages in the action, each showing 'at one view, the whole of the Engagement'.[43] Although the location of the paintings is now unknown, they were later engraved by B.T. Pouncy and published by Poggi accompanied by a key showing the lines of battle, the positions of the ships at the beginning and end of the day and, using dotted lines, their interim movements (Figure 4.4). The plan also includes an indication of the point of view taken in each print, and the times of each view. Multiple perspectives are thus made available to the viewer. The prints show the paintings to have been of a type consistent with British views of naval engagements. Whereas seventeenth-century Dutch naval battles tended to be shown in bird's-eye views, eighteenth-century British marine painters generally adopted a low horizon and showed the combatants arrayed parallel to the horizon. Other conventions of landscape painting are also employed: in the absence of topographical features, the separation of the viewer from the action by a band of water, usually in shadow, and alternating patches of light and shade articulate the recession of space.[44]

Brown and Loutherbourg, on the other hand, approached the depiction of a naval subject from other arenas of artistic practice. Brown, the American portrait painter, had for the previous five years been attempting to establish himself as a history painter.[45] Inspired by the success of Copley's *Siege of Gibraltar* (1791, Guildhall, London) as well as Benjamin West's *Death of General Wolfe*, Brown turned from medieval subjects to contemporary history in the early 1790s, foregrounding portraits of the main figures, based on sketches made from life or from engraved portraits, posed in arranged masses and communicating emotional responses to the central action of the picture. The novelty of Brown's painting of the Glorious First of June, then, derives from the same treatment being applied to a naval subject:

> There has never yet been *even* attempted the Introduction of Portraits into a Naval Picture, and the Mode of thus Marking the Resemblance of our Gallant Officers and the View of the Awful Conflict, has been thought by our first Connoisseurs to be a singular and fortunate Combination.[46]

The claims made for the portrait likenesses slip easily into those made for nautical accuracy: the published 'Description' of the painting notes that 'Earl Howe has sat to him *expressly* for this picture and most of the Admirals of the Fleet have given their Advice and Assistance'. While at Portsmouth, Brown not only painted the portraits of principal officers 'in Earl Howe's own state cabin' but 'had the singular opportunity of *actually residing* on board the Queen Charlotte at Spithead', where he took 'measurements of the different parts of the ship, and obtain[ed] the first sources of documentary information'.[47] While introducing a new subgenre, that of 'Naval Pictures', Brown's painting belongs to the trend begun by West and Copley. As Linda Colley has observed, pictures of British heroes of a certain class dying at the moment of victory, although generally popular by 1800, were particularly influential for the polite (male) classes, the consumers as well as the subjects of such representations, schooled in the classical rhetoric of heroic sacrifice.[48]

Loutherbourg's painting (Figure 4.5) focuses not on the commanding figures in the action but rather on establishing national character-types in the service of the picture's ideological message, which, as the description accompanying the print makes clear, derives from the comparison made in every quarter between the English and French forces: 'every minute attention has been paid to the difference of the rigging of the English and French ships; to the general forms of their construction; and to a faithful representation of the national characters of the sailors'.[49] On the foredeck of the *Queen Charlotte* (the left-hand ship), troops are drawn up in orderly lines despite the chaos surrounding them. The figure of Sir Andrew Douglas, silhouetted against the smoke, is visibly ordering five sailors to clear away the spritsail, whose list has just been shot away. Mirroring him on the deck of *La Montagne*, the French captain raises his hand against his own sailors, 'forcing the men to their duty'. The five British sailors perform their precarious task with an air of expertise: meanwhile, two French sailors from *La Montagne* have just fallen overboard. Heroism has been located in the figures not of the captains but of the ordinary sailors:

> In the foreground of the composition, several English men of war's boats, with their crews, are represented saving their drowning enemies. To the left, some French sailors are seen clinging to the wreck of a cross-tree, to whose aid an English boat is making way. On the right, others on part of a main mast, whom the English are endeavouring to save ... These form but a small portion of the traits of that noblest of sympathies, humanity, the active exertions of which so highly dignified the character of the British sailors in this most important and splendid victory. The *Alfred*, Captain Bazley, saved 230 French sailors from inevitable destruction; the English, not content with the ordinary means of preserving them from perishing, stripped themselves, and plunged into the sea.[50]

Figure 4.5 Philippe de Loutherbourg, *Lord Howe's Action, or the Glorious First of June, 1794*, 1795, oil on canvas

However, it is in the extraordinary backdrop of this scene that Loutherbourg, as has recently been acknowledged, 'executed a tableau that clearly broke with the pictorial tradition of naval battles, however firmly established in England since the days of the Van de Veldes'.[51] The middle ground of Loutherbourg's painting depicts the *Queen Charlotte* breaking the French line and engaging with both the French flagship, *La Montagne*, and the French admiral's 'second', the *Jacobin*, about an hour into the fighting. Although the *Queen Charlotte*'s foretopmast was shot away, the British ship fought so fiercely that both the French ships disengaged and ran to leeward.[52] The failure of the French ships to press their advantage over the disabled *Queen Charlotte*, and the *Queen Charlotte*'s willingness to engage both ships, were predictably seen as proof of both French cowardice and British bravery. At the same time, they reiterated a treasured national myth, that of the outnumbered and outgunned British 'band of brothers' prevailing over a stronger enemy, a trope that had been part of British imperial mythology at least since the early 1740s following Admiral Vernon's capture of Porto Bello with 'six ships only' and that would persist in relation to the acquisition of large tracts of the empire in subsequent centuries.[53] Loutherbourg's ships, towering over and plunging toward the viewer, are in a state of highly aestheticised chaos, sails billowing in taut curves, and damaged rigging describing arabesques in the air. Even the holes in the canvas sails have their own kind of visual interest, rendered three-dimensional by the play of light at their edges. The dramatic impact of the image is heightened by the exaggeration of the ships' size and the water-level perspective from which the scene is viewed. Chaos is rendered legible, however, partly through the graphic technique used in the painting, where Gillray's hand is apparent. The figures are all delineated in brown, the figures in shadow are in monochrome, and highlights are more drawn than painted. This showy technique, graphically legible and reminiscent of a theatrical backcloth, was perhaps the effect objected to by Joseph Farington when he visited the exhibition with Hoppner the day after it opened, on 3 March 1795:

> We thought the picture ill coloured & I think not so ingeneously [*sic*] designed as I should have expected from Loutherbourg. The picture of Valenciennes appeared to me much worse than I thought it the last year – when the novelty is over these pictures appear very deficient.[54]

Brown's and Loutherbourg's pictures of the First of June restaged an earlier rivalry between the two painters. The previous year, Brown had exhibited at Orme's Gallery *The Attack on Famar*, a depiction of an attack led by the Duke of York (a patron of Brown's) near Valenciennes. At the same time, Loutherbourg was exhibiting his own *Grand Attack on Valenciennes* at Boydell's Historic Gallery. However, it was with Cleveley's two paintings that Anthony Pasquin compared de Loutherbourg:

> Since the demise of Mr Serres, this branch of the polite arts has been evidently on the decline; the most prominent efforts towards its restoration, are those which have recently been exhibited by Mr Loutherbourg, and Mr Cleveley, upon the glorious incident which occurred upon the first of June, 1794; of whom it is but justice to aver, that Mr Cleveley has been the more perfect. Mr Loutherbourg's picture on this popular subject is too licentious in the points of historic fact to please any nautical observer.
>
> Mr Cleveley's performance did not impress me instantaneously, with so much pleasure as did Mr Loutherbourg's; but it had this very desirable effect, that my satisfaction was strengthened in proportion as I viewed it. It is evident that this Artist has a far deeper knowledge of his subject than his compeer, and has not violated authenticity upon any material point; he has not painted to amaze but to satisfy: he has grouped both his pictures with an admirable taste; all the minutiae of the marine are rigorously preserved, and the effect of his atmosphere at morning and evening is strictly compatible with truth and harmony.[55]

The 'licentiousness' is usually taken to refer to the inclusion of two episodes in the battle which happened eight hours apart, the breaking of the French line and the sinking of the *Vengeur*, which took place much later, no doubt in order to be able to include the desperation of the *Vengeur*'s crew and the 'nobility' of the British sailors who rescued them. However, marine painters frequently compressed the narrative of a battle taking place over many hours, or divided the narrative between two or more canvases, often showing the beginning and end of an action, as did Cleveley and John Thomas Serres.

The foregoing detailed account of the marketing of, and response to, the paintings shown in 'one-picture' exhibitions provides the context into which Robert Barker's panorama of the First of June made its entrance. It was surely with the presence of these representations in mind that Barker advertised his panorama in April 1795, although it would not open until early June – the fourth panorama (and the second naval subject) to be displayed at the permanent premises that Barker had opened in Leicester Square the previous year:

> A Painting in the Panorama is shortly to be brought forward, which will give an exact representation of every ship in the English and French fleets, as they appeared at one o'clock P.M. of the first of June, 1794. Taken from the most correct observations made by Captain Barlow of the Pegasus, Lord Howe's repeating frigate; and by Captain Seymour, who was signal officer at that time with Captain Barlow. The Pegasus being near the centre, the observers may suppose themselves on the open sea, and have the fleets scattered round them in every direction, as they really were at that time; the fire commencing on the Queen by nine French ships of the line.[56]

Barker's advertisement at once establishes a continuum between the panorama and other representations of naval engagements, and marks its difference. As with marine paintings, the authority of the panoramic representation depended on the correctness of its observations ('an exact representation') and derived its accuracy from knowledgeable sources (Captains Barlow and Seymour), including eyewitnesses. Like the monographic exhibitions, also operating outside the legitimating confines of the Royal Academy, panoramas made claims to social approbation, most famously the widely reported visit by George III and Queen Charlotte to Barker's first panorama in Leicester Square, *The View of the Grand Fleet at Spithead*. Like marine paintings, they depended on a range of sources – equivalents of which were made available to the public in order to decode the representation – in the form of narrative descriptions, plans and listings of lines of battle. Barker sold visitors a key to the panorama, now the only evidence of its appearance, that included a line of battle as it appeared at 9 a.m., identifying the ships.

To judge by Barker's keys, the compositional structure of the naval panorama mimicked that of the eighteenth-century marine painting and a related form, the topographical coastline view, depending on a low horizon, the action arrayed across it. In response to Stephen Oetterman's argument that the panorama depended on the experience of the horizon as a 'new aesthetic experience of the eighteenth century', Oliver Grau has noted the long history of other premodern forms that depend on the horizon, including 'town- and city-scapes, coastal panoramas, and overview maps'.[57] The topographical coastline view persisted in an official capacity into the late eighteenth century. These forms of imperial mapping, 'conventional' marine painting and panorama come together most notably in the oeuvre of the marine painter John Thomas Serres, son of Dominic Serres and the artist noted by Farington as having made sketches of the First of June representing the beginning and end of the action. Serres, who was commissioned to create a series of topographical profiles of the coast of France for the Admiralty in 1799, also produced a panorama in 1805: a view of Boulogne showing the fleet amassed for Napoleon's planned invasion of England, for which Serres joined the British Fleet to make sketches of Napoleon's forces and the town's fortifications, recording his eyewitnessing in the panorama itself by including his own figure sketching from a boat.[58]

The unique features of the panorama derived from its 360-degree format and the extent of the image above and below a viewing platform, which combined with highly illusionistic facture to create 'a calculated confusion about the literal location of the painted surface as a way of enhancing its illusions of presence and distance'.[59] Or, as Barker put it, 'the observers may suppose themselves at sea'. It is this that marks the fundamental difference of the panorama from marine painting and which has caused eighteenth-century marine paintings to be held in hindsight to be carrying out a function they were never intended to fulfil – again in Barker's words, 'to make observers ... feel as if really on the very spot'.[60] Rather, images of naval engagements served the retelling of narratives as part of an array of 'actualities' including texts, plans and other genres (including portraiture), from which a comprehension of the event was constructed. By including the sinking of the *Vengeur* in the panorama and giving the line of battle as it appeared at 9 a.m. in the key, Barker gestures at the strategies used by marine artists. But these are secondary considerations here: the key functions in the service of the viewer's orientation within the field of representation, rather than as one element among an array through which the battle is meant to be constructed.

During the French Revolutionary War (1793–1802), according to Denise Oleksijczuk, scenes involving the British fleet made up half of the panoramic subjects exhibited in London. Barker's received up to 40,000 visitors a year during the period, for example. During the Napoleonic War (1803–15), moreover, 'nearly every image shown at the Panorama had to do with the movements of the Royal Navy or British army'.[61] In addition to views of naval and military engagements, a large proportion of the panoramas on display in Leicester Square depicted sites crucial to imperial naval strategy, such as Gibraltar, Malta and Portsmouth; together these made the panorama arguably the most influential confluence of cultural and imperial concerns prior to the Great Exhibition of 1851. Oleksijczuk's study focuses on the early panoramas as precursors of what would, in the nineteenth century, become a metaphor for 'the social reality of the British empire', contending that their 'increasingly imperialist subject matter' enlisted spectators to the imperial cause.[62] While in her argument the naval panoramas were instrumental in legitimising the British Empire's use of force 'by presenting it as a rousing competition between England and its rival, France', they do not play a proportional role in her discussion.[63]

Indeed, in general, discussions of panorama as depicting naval topics have tended to shy away from direct engagement with their subject matter, instead focusing on the spatial/optical and semiotic meanings of panoramic viewing. Other strands of the literature on panoramas have focused on the status of, and audiences for, the panorama in relation to those of 'high' art.[64] The occlusion of the naval panorama's relationship to marine painting is no doubt due to the peripheral status to which maritime visual culture has been relegated in relation to mainstream art history. Geoff Quilley has adeptly highlighted the conundrum posed by the 'post-Napoleonic truism that British national identity was naturally and empirically tied to the sea' and the 'low position occupied by marine art both in the academic hierarchy and in the discipline of art history'.[65] If, as I have suggested here, the roots of the naval panorama can be recognised to lie in the British eighteenth-century tradition of marine painting, then it is through the panorama that the tradition retained a relevance into the nineteenth century; as part of the 'global imperial landscape' developed and defined through the visual culture of the metropolis.[66]

A few weeks after Barker's First of June panorama opened in early June 1795, news of fleet actions against the French off L'Orient by Lord Bridport and Admiral Cornwallis reached London. By May 1796, Barker was displaying simultaneously panoramas of both engagements; at the same time, following the success of his inaugural foray into maritime subject matter with the First of June, Loutherbourg exhibited a large canvas depicting the defeat of the Spanish Armada at Boydell's Historic Gallery.[67] Nicholas Pocock's grim evocation of the bloodiest encounter of the First of June, *His Majesty's ship the Brunswick engaging the Vengeur on the 1st of June*, was exhibited at the Royal Academy in the same year, alongside J.M.W. Turner's debut in oils, *Fishermen at Sea*.[68] This pattern of exhibition would continue to be replicated in response to the major engagements of the wars, with immediate spectacular responses (illuminations, theatrical displays) followed by depictions in painting, print and panorama, exhibited in monographic exhibitions and at exhibiting societies. In wartime, then, the metropolitan artistic sphere, fraught with its own internal politics and rivalries, was drawn into engagement with the remote conflicts through which the Empire was being formed, an engagement that would transform the modes of depiction and display by which these conflicts were represented and understood.

Notes

1 Jerome Christensen, *Romanticism at the End of History* (Baltimore, MD: Johns Hopkins University Press, 2000), p. 4.
2 'J. B.', *Oracle and Public Advertiser*, 4 April 1795.
3 Dorinda Evans, *Mather Brown: Early American Artist in England* (Middletown, CT: Wesleyan University Press, 1982) p. 128.
4 Kenneth Garlick and Angus Macintyre (eds), *Diary of Joseph Farington*, 17 vols (New Haven, CT: Yale University Press, 1978–84), vol. 1, p. 307.
5 *Oracle and Public Advertiser*, 30 April 1795.
6 See Timothy Jenks, *Naval Engagements: Patriotism, Cultural Politics and the Royal Navy, 1793–1815* (Oxford: Oxford University Press, 2006), pp. 27–36.
7 *St James's Chronicle*, 12–14 June 1794; cited in Jenks, *Naval Engagements*, p. 27.
8 Jenks, *Naval Engagements*, pp. 58–74.
9 See Eleanor Hughes, 'Ships of the "Line": Marine Painting at the Royal Academy Exhibition of 1784', in Tim Barringer, Geoff Quilley and Douglas Fordham (eds), *Art and the British Empire* (Manchester: Manchester University Press, 2007), pp. 139–52.
10 While monographic exhibitions were not without precedent, they underwent an 'unprecedented development' in the 1790s, characterised not only by their frequency but also by the collaboration with printmakers and unabashed marketing in the press. See Olivier Lefeuvre, *Philippe-Jacques de Loutherbourg, 1740–1812* (Paris: Arthena, 2012), p. 170; Emily Ballew Neff and Kaylin H. Weber, 'Laying Siege: West, Copley, and the Battle of History Painting', in Emily Ballew Neff and Kaylin H. Weber (eds), *American Adversaries: West and Copley in a Transatlantic World* (New Haven, CT: Yale University Press, 2013), pp. 208–35.
11 See Holger Hoock, *Empires of the Imagination: Politics, War, and the Arts in the British World, 1750–1850* (London: Profile, 2010), p. 3.
12 See also Pieter van der Merwe, 'The Glorious First of June, a Battle of Art and Theatre', in Michael Duffy and Roger Morriss (eds), *The Glorious First of June 1794: A Naval Battle and its Aftermath* (Exeter: University of Exeter Press, 2001), pp. 132–58 (pp. 133–4).
13 John Brewer, 'Sensibility and the Urban Panorama', *Huntington Library Quarterly* 70 (2007), pp. 229–49 (p. 230). While many of these spectacles may have emerged during the 1780s, it was, significantly, with the advent of the Revolutionary Wars,

to which the panorama truly belongs, that they fully flowered. Robert Barker's panorama was first exhibited in Edinburgh in 1789 and in London in 1792.

14 Geoff Quilley, *Empire to Nation: Art, History, and the Visualization of Maritime Britain, 1768–1829* (New Haven, CT: Yale University Press, 2011), pp. 196–7.

15 Ann Bermingham, 'Landscape-O-Rama: The Exhibition Landscape at Somerset House and the Rise of Popular Landscape Entertainments', in David Solkin (ed.), *Art on the Line: The Royal Academy Exhibitions at Somerset House, 1780–1836* (New Haven, CT: Yale University Press, 2001), pp. 127–44 (p. 127).

16 See Jennifer L. Roberts, 'Copley's Cargo: *Boy with a Squirrel* and the Dilemma of Transit', *American Art* 21 (2007), pp. 20–41, a response to Pierre Bourdieu's charge to the historian to '"reintroduce time, with its rhythm, its orientation, its irreversibility" into the analysis of cultural production'. See Pierre Bourdieu, *Outline of a Theory of Practice* (Cambridge: Cambridge University Press, 1977), p. 6, cited in Roberts, 'Copley's Cargo', p. 22.

17 Christensen, *Romanticism at the End of History*, p. 5.

18 To choose just one example among many: prompted by the success of his first venture in maritime subject matter, Loutherbourg exhibited *The Defeat of the Spanish Armada* at the Historic Gallery in 1797. See Hughes, 'Ships of the "Line"', p. 147.

19 Oliver Warner, *The Glorious First of June* (London: Batsford, 1961), p. 20.

20 The principle of breaking the line involved a fleet's running through the enemy line of ships while firing broadsides and rounding up with each ship to the leeward of its opponent. The enemy line would be unable to manoeuvre or break off action. David Davies, *Fighting Ships: Ships of the Line, 1793–1815* (London: Constable, 1996), p. 69; see also William Laird Clowes, *The Royal Navy: A History*, 7 vols (London: Sampson, Low, Marston, 1897–1903), vol. 4, pp. 227–8.

21 *The Times*, 12 June 1794.

22 *The Times*, 14 June 1794.

23 *Morning Chronicle*, 18 June, 1794

24 *Morning Post*, 16 June, 1794

25 The excursion to Portsmouth to view the prizes became the subject of theatrical entertainments: a one-act interlude on the subject was produced on 20 August at the Theatre Royal, Haymarket, entitled *Britain's Glory; or, A Trip to Portsmouth*. The characters in another, *Rule Britannia*, join the crowds going from London to Portsmouth and fall victim to the opportunism of the town's innkeepers.

26 National Art Library, V&A Museum, London (NAL), V&A Press Cuttings, III, 675.

27 *Oracle and Public Advertiser*, 1 July 1794.

28 *Oracle and Public Advertiser*, 2 July 1794.

29 *Morning Chronicle*, 14 July 1794.

30 David H. Solkin, *Painting out of the Ordinary: Modernity and the Art of Everyday Life in Early Nineteenth-Century Britain* (New Haven, CT: Yale University Press, 2008), p. 16.

31 Jean Andre Rouquet, *The Present State of the Arts in England* (London: J. Nourse, 1755), pp. 60–1.

32 Garlick and Macintyre (eds), *Diary of Joseph Farington*, vol. 1, p. 214.

33 Ibid., p. 215. The schemes of Bowyer and Dance should be seen in the context of the ongoing craze for portrait collecting and the demand for portraits of British heroes; see Timothy Clayton, *The English Print 1688–1802* (New Haven, CT: Yale University Press, 1997), p. 244; also Marcia Pointon, *Hanging the Head: Portraiture and Social Formation in Eighteenth-Century England* (New Haven, CT: Yale University Press, 1993), pp. 53–62.

34 Garlick and Macintyre (eds), *Diary of Joseph Farington*, vol. 1, p. 214.

35 Ibid., p. 217.

36 Ibid., p. 225.

37 Ibid., p. 307.

38 Ibid., vol. 2, p. 339.

39 NAL, V&A Press Cuttings, III, 666.

40 *True Briton*, 30 December 1794.
41 *True Briton*, 5 March 1795.
42 *True Briton*, 21 March 1795.
43 *True Briton*, 5 March 1795.
44 See Hughes, 'Ships of the "Line"', pp. 146–7.
45 Evans, *Mather Brown*, p. 102.
46 *True Briton*, 2 February 1795.
47 Ibid.
48 Linda Colley, *Britons: Forging the Nation, 1707–1837* (New Haven, CT: Yale University Press, 1992), p. 195.
49 Description accompanying print engraved by James Fittler, published by Robert Cribb for Valentine and R. Green on 1 January 1799. On the reverse of the description is a key to the ships in the painting and a listing of the British and French lines of battle. As with more conventional forms of marine painting, multiple views are made available for the viewer to construct the narrative. British Museum, Department of Prints and Drawings, 1917, 1208.1230.
50 Ibid.
51 Loutherbourg 'a executé un tableau qui tranche nettement avec la tradition pictural des batailles navales, pourtant établie en Angleterre depuis le séjour des Van de Velde'. Lefeuvre, *Philippe-Jacques de Loutherbourg*, p. 292.
52 Andrew C.F. David, 'The Glorious First of June: An Account of the Battle by Peter Heywood', *Mariner's Mirror* 64 (1978), pp. 361–6 (p. 364).
53 See Eleanor Hughes, 'Guns in the Gardens: Peter Monamy's Paintings for Vauxhall', in Jonathan Conlin (ed.), *The Pleasure Garden, from Vauxhall to Coney Island* (Philadelphia, PA: University of Pennsylvania Press, 2013), pp. 78–99 (pp. 80–6); Kathleen Wilson, *The Sense of the People: Politics, Culture, and Imperialism in England, 1715–1785* (Cambridge: Cambridge University Press, 1998), pp. 140–65.
54 Garlick and Macintyre (eds), *Diary of Joseph Farington*, vol. 11, p. 312.
55 Anthony Pasquin [pseud.], *Memoirs of the Royal Academicians: Being an Attempt to Improve the National Taste* (London: H.D. Symonds, 1796), p. 109.
56 *Oracle and Public Advertiser*, 30 April 1795. For the early history of the panorama, see Richard Altick, *The Shows of London* (Cambridge, MA: Harvard University Press, 1978), pp. 128–40; Denise Oleksijczuk, *The First Panoramas: Visions of British Imperialism* (Minneapolis, MN: University of Minnesota Press, 2011).
57 Oliver Grau, *Virtual Art from Illusion to Immersion* (Cambridge, MA: MIT Press, 2003), p. 62.
58 M.K. Barrett, *Eyes of the Admiralty. J.T. Serres: An Artist in the Channel Fleet* (London: National Maritime Museum, 2008); Altick, *The Shows of London*, p. 136.
59 Jonathan Crary, 'Géricault, the Panorama, and Sites of Reality in the Early Nineteenth Century', *Grey Room* 9 (2002), pp. 6–25 (p. 19).
60 British Patent No. 1612, 19 June 1787, reprinted in Robert Barker, 'Specification of the Patent Granted to Mr. Robert Barker', in *The Repertory of Arts and Manufactures* (1796), p. 167.
61 Oleksijczuk, *The First Panoramas*, p. 6.
62 Ibid., pp. 3–4.
63 Ibid., pp. 145–54.
64 See Scott B. Wilcox, 'Unlimiting the Bounds of Painting', in Ralph Hyde (ed.), *Panoramania! The Art and Entertainment of the All-Embracing View* (London: Trefoil, 1988), pp. 13–44; Grau, *Virtual Art from Illusion to Immersion*, pp. 62–5. Oleksijczuk provides an excellent overview of the literature, pp. 8–10.
65 Geoff Quilley, 'Missing the Boat: The Place of the Maritime in the History of British Visual Culture', *Visual Culture in Britain* 1 (2000), pp. 79–92 (p. 81).
66 Hoock, *Empires of the Imagination*, p. 6.
67 *Oracle and Public Advertiser*, 19 May 1796; *True Briton*, 19 March 1796.
68 See Eleanor Hughes, 'The Battle of the Pictures', in Christine Riding and Richard Johns (eds), *Turner and the Sea* (London: Thames & Hudson, 2013), pp. 52–4.

CHAPTER FIVE

Empire under glass: The British Empire and the Crystal Palace, 1851–1911

Jeffrey Auerbach

The Great Exhibition of 1851, held in London's Hyde Park, has long served as a symbol not only of Britain's industrial development but also of its burgeoning Empire. Numerous scholars in recent years have noted the centrality of the Indian exhibits in the Crystal Palace and emphasised the exhibition's role in promoting commodities from Britain's colonies.[1] Yet in retrospect one of the most remarkable features of this first world's fair was how limited a role the Empire played. In fact, it was not until 1886 that the Empire received top billing at a British exhibition, at the 'Colonial and Indian Exhibition' held in South Kensington. And it was not until 1911 that Britain's colonies predominated at the Crystal Palace. The Empire, therefore, rose to prominence in British exhibitions very slowly during the second half of the nineteenth century.

Tracing the history of imperial displays at the Crystal Palace suggests that, in 1851, 'empire' was still an amorphous and infrequently used concept in Britain. For many commentators the most meaningful distinctions were national and global, not imperial, either between themselves and continental Europeans, or between Europeans and non-Europeans. The enlarged Sydenham Crystal Palace was the successor to the Hyde Park building, and it remained standing in south London from 1854 to 1936. Its displays illustrate how the British increasingly began to view themselves as heirs to the great ancient empires such as Egypt and Assyria. But they were also mindful that, just as those once dominant empires had collapsed, so too might their own. Nonetheless, by the time of the 1886 Colonial and Indian Exhibition, the Empire had grown and sufficiently coalesced to merit its own exhibition. This in turn helped pave the way for the 1911 Festival of Empire, the apex of imperial display at the Crystal Palace – an event clearly designed not just to celebrate the Empire but also to fortify already tenuous links between Britain and its dominions.

Woven into this history of imperial display is the increasing use of human exhibits. There were no people on display at the Hyde Park Crystal Palace in 1851, nor did the Royal Commission that planned and organised the Great Exhibition ever discuss having such a display. But foreigners – from both Europe and elsewhere, including regions that were part of Britain's Empire – were ubiquitous in the ephemeral literature that was published at the time of the event, and there were a few wax models on display as well. The Sydenham Crystal Palace, with its increased emphasis on natural history, included an ethnological 'museum of man' that featured plaster-cast models of supposedly representative Africans, American Indians, Aboriginal Australians and Pacific Islanders. On the one hand, it suggested that all human beings were descended from common ancestors; in this respect, it constituted an important intervention in the vibrant contemporary debate over monogenesis and polygenesis. On the other hand, even though the exhibits emphasised human unity, they also promoted and reinforced the belief that humanity could be divided between civilised and savage, Christian and heathen, hunter-gather and commercial, European and Other.[2] By the end of the century, when a Somali kraal was reconstructed inside the glass palace, living people would themselves be put on display, as they would to an even greater extent at the Festival of Empire in 1911, when entire native villages were recreated.[3] The Crystal Palace, therefore, played a significant role both in imperial politics and in the politics of display, and it charts the rise, efflorescence and fraying of imperial ties from the mid-nineteenth century to the early twentieth century.

The Hyde Park Crystal Palace, 1851

The Empire occupied only a relatively small place at the Great Exhibition of 1851. The early discussions of the exhibition's organisers contain scarcely any references to the Empire, and the inclusion of Archibald Galloway, Chairman of the East India Company, on the Royal Commission was as much an obligatory nod as a reflection of commitment.[4] Three highly publicised London Mansion House speeches promoting the exhibition likewise made no mention of how the exhibition might boost trade or foster closer ties with the Empire.[5] Only a single meeting in Woolwich in June 1850, where the principal speaker was David Williams Wire, under-sheriff (and later Lord Mayor) of London, highlighted Britain's imperial connections. Wire presented a rosy vision of the Empire as an institution of mercantile exchange that was driving not only the British but also the entire world economy. Every time there had been a threat to British commerce, he boasted, the

British had found new routes and new markets by 'sending their sons to distant lands'. As a result, Britain was 'becoming the emporium of the commercial, and the mistress of the entire world'. Characterising the Empire as a central British institution, he argued that by 'civilising' foreign lands and peoples, the British were creating new markets for their goods, a process that would be furthered by the exhibition.[6]

Despite Wire's rousing defence of imperial commerce, when it came to soliciting exhibits and generating enthusiasm for the exhibition, the organisers' focus was overwhelmingly on the British Isles and continental Europe.[7] The vast majority of the hundred thousand objects on display were European, even among the raw materials and manufactures, the only two classes of exhibits in which there was any significant imperial participation. In fact, among the prizewinning exhibits, virtually none came from the Empire.[8] Although the press provided some coverage to Britain's colonies, they were rarely singled out.[9] The *Illustrated London News*, for example, devoted hundreds of pages to the construction of the Crystal Palace and the opening of the exhibition, and eagerly noted the arrival of the French goods – and the paucity of American goods – perhaps because Britain's economic and commercial rivalry with those nations was, in 1851, far more significant than its still nascent colonial trade.[10] The paper provided less coverage of the East Indian Courts than Prince Albert's model working-class houses, only a few of which were ever built.[11] It is also telling that, in its coverage of the opening ceremony, the *Illustrated London News* referred to the event as 'the Great *National* Exhibition of 1851' (italics added).[12]

Nevertheless, inside the Crystal Palace, the exhibits from India and the other regions of the Empire were given a prime location near the intersection of the nave and the transept, at the very centre of the exhibition building. But so too were the contributions from Turkey, China, Tunis, Persia and Egypt, suggesting an Orientalist zone as much as an imperial grouping.[13] Moreover, the colonial displays were so enmeshed within the dizzying panoply of goods that they are barely visible in most of the widely reproduced engravings of the nave.[14] The three-volume *Official Catalogue* offered a different but hardly more imperial vision, with its embossed cover showing Britannia crowning Asia and Europe with Africa and America looking on, suggesting a global, more than an imperial, hegemony.[15]

The most prominent imperial display in 1851 was the Indian Court (Figure 5.1). Henry Cole's plan, ably implemented by the Indian-born British botanist and professor John Forbes Royle, was to present India, and by extension the Empire, as a vast treasure-trove of untapped wealth and resources.[16] Although the Court was stocked with fine finished products, including a 'rich variety' of Indian shawls, especially cashmere, that were highlighted by the *Illustrated London News* just before the close of the exhibition, the underlying purpose of the display was to introduce manufacturers to raw materials.[17] As Royle wrote in his introduction to the Indian section of the *Official Catalogue*, the goal of the Indian exhibits was 'at once to interest the public and to give such confidence to the manufacturer as to induce him to submit them to trial'.[18] He continued: 'The peculiar products' of the colonies would be of interest to 'the merchant seeking a new source for known materials'.[19] For Royle, it was axiomatic that the exhibition would benefit all countries with 'little-known products possessed of valuable properties, and procurable in large quantities at a cheap rate, if a demand could be created for them'.[20] The *Illustrated London News* reinforced his point soon after the opening of the exhibition by reminding its readers that India was one of Britain's 'best markets, either to buy produce or sell British manufactures', even though it was 'scarcely known to a very large part' of the 'educated public'.[21]

The most famous Indian exhibit – and one of the highlights of the exhibition, according to *The Times* – was the Koh-i-Noor diamond, which had been confiscated from the Sikh Empire by the East India Company in 1850. Valued at more than £2 million, the gem was exhib-

Figure 5.1 John Nash, 'Stuffed Elephant and Howdah'

ited by the Queen herself, with its own display case which took the form of a large gold cage with an ingenious mechanism designed to lower the diamond into the pedestal at night for greater security.[22] In one of its articles, *The Illustrated London News* described the diamond as 'gigantic but somewhat rough and unhewn', clearly a metaphor for India itself.[23] The paper claimed that Indian rulers were so enamoured of 'rich and lavish magnificence' that they had appreciated the diamond solely on the basis of its striking 'magnitude'. Only a reduction in size by a European jeweller, the writer opined – seemingly forgetting that the stone had originally been cut not by an Indian but by a Venetian who was subsequently fined and executed for having performed his task in an 'unartist-like manner' – would render its 'beauty' visible and increase its value. As Lara Kriegel has observed: 'The koh-i-noor offers the most striking instance of the practice of miniaturising the "vast" continent for the purposes of entertainment, consumption and rule at mid-century.'[24]

India was not the only colony relegated to the role of supplier of raw materials. Canada sent in two 'trophies' – tribute, in effect – one constructed of timber (Figure 5.2), the other consisting of furs organised by the Hudson's Bay Company.[25] And yet the *Illustrated London News* deemed the Canadian contributions so unimportant

Figure 5.2 'Canadian Timber Trophy', *Illustrated London News* (21 June 1851)

that it covered the Timber Trophy alongside the Russian Court and the horological section.[26] In the West Indies stand, the most prominent objects on display included a case of artificial fruits and flowers, and several articles made from the leaves of palm trees.[27]

The scale and scope of the exhibits from Australasia – New South Wales, South Australia and Van Diemen's Land (Tasmania) – was similarly limited. Delays and controversies hindered the timely arrival of the Australian exhibits; the first edition of the *Official Catalogue* included only 'about twenty exhibitors' from New South Wales and half that number from South Australia.[28] According to one popular guidebook, Britain's Australasian possessions 'had nothing very new or very showy'.[29] Still, the organisers presented an optimistic vision of Australia transformed from a penal colony into an economically vital component of the Empire.[30] The *Official Catalogue* promoted Australia as 'the most extensive wool-producing country in the world', and proudly noted the growing value of its exports to Britain.[31] Likewise, the *Illustrated London News* raved about the 'superb specimens' of the 'well-known and remarkable mines of South Australia', including the famous Burra Burra copper mines, which were already making a dent in world trade.[32] The London organisers actively encouraged the submission of raw materials, and the Australian local commissioners complied by sending unusual flora and fauna, such as wombats and black swans, as well as wool, wood, coal and beef that were part of the fledgling colony's effort to expand its overseas markets in Europe and North America.

There were some Australian manufactured goods on display. Not surprisingly, many of the motifs which embellished them derived from the early experiences of travellers, scientists, navigators and settlers.[33] Among these, the emu and the kangaroo were highlighted as distinctive inhabitants of the Australian colonies and reproduced extensively, suggesting, iconographically, a high level of integration between metropole and periphery. A Tasmanian furniture maker, for example, exhibited a chair, on the back of which was a shield supported by a kangaroo and an emu surmounted by an English rose. On one side was a Scottish thistle, on the other an Irish shamrock.[34] In objects such as these, far-flung territories became integrated – and integrated themselves – into a Greater Britain, helping to domesticate the Empire.

The 1851 exhibition also promoted the Empire by introducing British men and women – producers and consumers, and most importantly future supporters and defenders of the idea of empire – to the diversity and fascinating otherness of imperial territories. One indication of this was the highly publicised visit of a group of 240 would-be emigrants sponsored by the Colonization Loan Society, who were scheduled to depart to Australia just a few days after the exhibition opened when the price of admission was still £1. They petitioned the commissioners for reduced admission to 1s, arguing that they were engaged in 'the rugged work of colonization' and that a visit to the exhibition would enable them to take with them 'their country's spirit of improvement'.[35] Visitors to the Crystal Palace learned about the British world through maps and charts as well as objects and dioramas.[36] The colonial exhibits familiarised British men and women with Britain's newly acquired and distant outposts, metaphorically taking British men and women to places they had never seen and, in all likelihood, would never be able to see. At the exhibition, British men and women could tour a recreated Mughal throne room or admire a howdah on an elephant, as well as exotic goods from Turkey, symbol of the 'East'.[37] For the many Britons who still had little connection with the Empire, the exhibition made clear that it was an important and growing component of British wealth, power and prestige. As one observer enthused, the East India Company exhibits had the effect of 'impressing every visitor with the importance of such possessions to Great Britain'.[38] The very language used by the organisers – 'British possessions' – suggested a degree of control and coherence that was still lacking at the administrative level.[39]

Unlike at many subsequent exhibitions, however, there were no people from the colonies on display in 1851, although the Tunisian Court featured an 'extremely picturesque and obliging native custodian' who, being a 'good-natured Turk [*sic*]', handed out sweetmeats and guided visitors around articles of 'rudest description', but which were, according to the *Illustrated London News*, 'admirably calculated to afford illustration of the *ménage* and *convenances* of the North African tribes'.[40] His presence was in addition to the models of foreign people that were on display: the Indian Court featured a collection of more than sixty groups of figurines designed to showcase the various Hindu castes, and the Fine Arts court included wax models of North and South American peasants clothed in traditional costumes and arranged in tableaux illustrating their respective customs.[41] There were also statues, such as Peter Stephenson's *The Wounded American Indian* (1848–50), poignantly symbolising the noble savagery of Native Americans, who were being conveniently erased from Britain's imperial past by virtue of their association with America's imperial present.[42]

Representations of colonial people, however, were omnipresent in the ephemeral literature that proliferated at the time of the exhibition. In 'The Happy Family in Hyde Park' (Figure 5.3), which John Tenniel drew for the humorous magazine *Punch*, there is a clear demarcation between the Europeans, who, alongside Mr Punch and the royal family,

Figure 5.3 John Tenniel, 'The Happy Family in Hyde Park',
Punch (19 July 1851)

are standing outside the Crystal Palace, and the foreigners, including a Chinese man, a Native American Indian, a turbaned Turk and a hairy Cossack, all of whom are inside, under glass and virtually behind bars. It is as if they are exotic specimens in a colossal greenhouse – which was how the design for the Crystal Palace developed, from Joseph Paxton's work as landscape architect for the Duke of Devonshire. As if to underscore the point, the smartly dressed gentleman on the right, whose visage bears a remarkable resemblance to Prince Albert, the guiding force behind the 1851 exhibition, is using his walking stick to point out an especially interesting figure. Inside, the foreigners are not examining the exhibits but instead performing national dances as if they were themselves on display. These elements undermine the image of a happy family, and instead highlight a separation between European and Other, between the British and their Empire.

Figure 5.4 Thomas Onwhyn, 'Cannibal Islanders', in *Mr and Mrs John Brown's Visit to London to see the Great Exhibition of All Nations* (London: Ackerman, [1851])

Many of these images had clearly racist undertones. In *Mr and Mrs Brown's Visit to London to see the Great Exhibition of All Nations*, by the draughtsman and engraver Thomas Onwhyn, the Browns encounter a menacing Russian carrying a long sword, some Bedouin with spears and a Turk with a dagger. Most threatening of all, though, are the 'Cannibal Islanders' (Figure 5.4) who are sitting at the same picnic table at the restaurant as the Browns, beneath a sign that reads 'Soup a la Hottentot'. They have dark skin, bare feet and monkey-like faces; one of them is holding a knife, and is threatening to eat the Browns' boy, Johnny. They are depicted as cannibalistic savages.[43]

Although imagined, these illustrations had a profound effect, especially given how few actual foreigners were in London during the summer of 1851.[44] *The Times*, for example, complained of a 'dearth of Turks and Turbans' at the opening of the exhibition.[45] Nonetheless, the artist Henrietta Ward recalled:

> From every part of the globe came representatives, many gorgeous in oriental robes. Dusky Indian princes with turbans and jewels on their foreheads; sallow-faced Chinese Mandarins in silken embroidered dress; sedate little Japanese potentates with inscrutable faces; broad-faced, woolly-headed African Chiefs wearing bright colours; travellers from America, Australia, Canada other countries mingling with Russians, Poles, Frenchmen, Italians and Austrians.[46]

Ward's phrasing illustrates how undifferentiated the Empire was in the mid-nineteenth century, and that, with the possible exception of India, colonial people were lumped together with every other sort of foreigner.

Although Britain's Empire was featured much more prominently at the Great Exhibition than it had ever been before, when compared to subsequent exhibitions the imperial presence was actually quite limited. Jamaica, for centuries one of Britain's most important colonies, was represented by only one exhibitor – from Manchester, no less – who sent in 'artificial flowers in imitation of the gorgeous productions of the Tropics'. The various catalogues of the exhibition make this point as well. The *Art Journal Illustrated Catalogue*, which comprised more than three hundred pages and included some fifteen hundred illustrations, contained only one item, an 'Oriental Tabletop', which reflected Britain's overseas interests.[47] Likewise, Tallis's three-volume *History and Description of the Crystal Palace* offered only a few chapters and plates devoted to imperial objects. The Empire was clearly only a very small part of a much larger exhibition, and lacking coherence and cohesiveness.

The Sydenham Crystal Palace, 1854–86

Six months after the Great Exhibition closed, Joseph Paxton, architect of the Crystal Palace, raised £500,000 in capital by selling shares in a newly formed corporation to purchase the iron and glass structure and relocate it to the south London suburb of Sydenham, where it stood until 1936.[48] The rebuilt Crystal Palace, which opened in 1854 to strains of 'God Save the Queen' and Handel's 'Hallelujah Chorus', was for several decades one of London's most popular attractions, and a place of amusement, recreation and instruction for the middle and lower classes. Although the venue lost some of its appeal over the years – both Fyodor Dostoevsky and Hippolyte Taine mocked it when they visited in the 1860s – George Gissing's reference to the building in his novel *The Nether World* (1888) as a place where 'the slaves of industrialization' could go on their day off and stare at 'a wooden model of the treacherous Afghan or the base African' suggests that it nonetheless functioned as a locus of imperialist sentiments. Indeed, the Sydenham Crystal Palace depicted Britain's Empire as the successor to the great ancient empires of Egypt, Greece, Rome, Assyria and Byzantium, and also served as the site of Benjamin Disraeli's famous speech in which he sought to unite all classes under the banner of monarchy and empire. And yet there was very little on display about Britain's contemporary empire.

Aside from the model dinosaurs nestled into the terraced grounds, the most original features of the enlarged Crystal Palace were its ten 'courts' illustrating the art and architecture of iconic historical periods and styles including Greek, Roman, Medieval, Byzantine and Renaissance.[49] The idea of dedicated courts had begun with the Hyde Park Crystal Palace: the term was first used to describe the rectangular sections of the building in the central area that were divided from each other but open to the arcaded glass roof. These included, in 1851, the East Indian, Tunis and Canadian Courts. After Sydenham, the term came to mean the central open space of a museum or atrium surrounded by arcades and galleries. Most of the Sydenham courts were meticulously designed 'living reconstructions' and 'restorations' of defunct empires such as Egypt and Assyria.[50] As many contemporary guidebooks made clear, they were designed to be interpreted in sequence, to provide an overview of civilisation, 'of a vast panorama of extinct life, of vanished institutions, of habits and usages long since passed away, of decayed forms of polytheism, and of superseded arts'.[51]

While none of the courts focused on regions that were part of the British Empire – Britain would not conquer Egypt until 1882, and Nineveh, near Mosul, would not become a British-ruled territory until after the First World War – many of them carried imperial resonances. Collectively, they produced a politics and morality of empire: the fall of once proud, wealthy and powerful civilisations which provided a warning to those in Britain about what might happen to their own rapidly expanding imperium. In the official *Guide to the Palace*, the journalist Samuel Phillips encouraged his readers to trace the course of art in order to gain 'an idea of the successive stages of civilizations rising and falling', until 'overturned by the aggression of barbarians or the no less destructive agency of a sensual and degraded luxury'.[52] Owen Jones, who helped design the courts, had spent months drawing and measuring in Egypt and the Alhambra, where he claimed to have made tracings and casts of numerous decorative details. In one of his lectures he spoke about the fresco on the walls of the Egyptian Court depicting 'the greatest of the Pharaohs' in which 'the conqueror ... crushes beneath the wheels of his chariot crowds of the enemy', perhaps a veiled allusion to recent British wars in Afghanistan, the Punjab, China and elsewhere, including Crimea, where the famous Charge of the Light Brigade during the Battle of Balaclava proved disastrous and humiliating.[53]

The Nineveh Court (also called the Assyrian Court or Nineveh Palace), which offered a similar message, was designed with the co-operation of Henry Layard, who had excavated the originals on the banks of the Tigris a decade earlier. It was a monument to imperial power and pride, and to the architecture of the conqueror, showing subject peoples slaughtered in battle. It may have been with Britain's own Crystal Palace in mind that the official guide described the court as a place of 'great public ceremonies, national triumphs or religious worship'.[54] And yet, for the educated observer, the warning could not have been clearer: For all its pride, Nineveh fell in a day. Similarly, it took only an hour for Pompeii – the subject of one of the other courts – to be buried in ash. According to *The Crystal Palace Expositor*: 'He who only gazes with curiosity and admiration at its recovered treasures can never appreciate the moral lesson which its catastrophe is so well calculated to teach.'[55] As one historian has observed, Nineveh stood as a 'beckoning prototype' for the grandiose New Delhi that the famed architect Edwin Lutyens would build in India, as well as a 'prophetic *memento mori*' of the possible demise of Britain's Empire.[56]

As instruments of display, the courts were quite controversial. Critics claimed they were inconsistent in scale, too conjectural and inaccurate in that they combined elements of different originals.[57] Owen Jones's polychromatic colour schemes, which he applied to all the courts, and not only his own Alhambra display, were subjected to special ridicule. In promoting polychromatism, Jones was implying that, although English painters had long been regarded as colourists, the English lagged behind 'in employment and appreciation of colour' in interior and exterior decoration.[58] He would work out these ideas more fully and influentially in *The Grammar of Ornament* (1856), in which he sought to establish basic principles for the colour combinations that would be in vogue for decades to come.[59] Although the colouring of the courts seemed garish to many visitors, at least one guidebook offered the reminder that Jones's bright colours were from 'Eastern' countries with intense sunshine.[60] The colouring scheme certainly added to the theatrical excitement of the displays.[61] This was in marked contrast to the Hyde Park building, which also employed colour – though to lesser effect – but where the sections of the exhibition had temporary partitions constructed or hung between them. In many respects then, the fine arts courts at the Sydenham Crystal Palace had a crucial influence on museums and on the display of architecture, sculpture and natural history. As the Revd Charles Boutell wrote in his series of articles on the courts in the *Art Journal*, what the 'Sydenham Museum' – as he termed it – taught was 'clear, expressive, and easy to understand'.[62]

Owen Jones's Egyptian Court was also criticised. It reflected his many years studying Egyptian antiquities, but he designed the pavilion as a composite memorial not as a scale model or replica of one particular monument. Certainly its reduced size was incongruous – and even misleading – when compared to full-size reproductions such as the ancient Pompeian House. This was particularly evident with the reproduction of the Hall of Columns from the Temple of Carnac, which the antiquary and auctioneer Samuel Leigh Sotheby, a major Crystal Palace shareholder, groused was 'Lilliputian' and 'most uninteresting'. Nonetheless, it must have been thrilling to turn from the nave of the Crystal Palace on to the side avenue that was flanked by eight lions cast from a pair brought from Egypt by the Duke of Northumberland, which led up to the giant entrance portal. The highlight of the Egyptian exhibits was the full-size reproductions of two colossal seated figures from the great temple of Abu Simbel in Nubia (Figure 5.5).[63] They occupied a prominent position at the north end of the vaulted glass transept: visitors approached them along an avenue of sphinxes, formed of twenty statues cast from an original in the Louvre. The promenade, which stretches a mile long in Egypt, had been reduced to less than 300 feet, symbolically encapsulating Britain's ability to envelop and contain even the greatest of ancient empires – at least for a while. Both the colossal figures and the Nineveh Court were destroyed in a fire in 1886.

The Nineveh Court also illustrated Britain's taming of empire. Henry Layard, who excavated the buildings on which the court was

Figure 5.5 'North Transept, Sydenham', in Matthew Digby Wyatt, *Views of the Crystal Palace and Park, Sydenham* (London: s.n., 1854)

modelled and whose bestselling book about the excavations, *Nineveh and Its Remains*, was published in 1848, had said that 'a small packing case' could contain 'all that Europe knew or possessed' of Assyria.[64] Yet the Nineveh Court was about 20 per cent larger than the other courts. It was bounded on one side by the Abu Simbel figures, and faced the tropical department with its great palms and wild botanical flourishes, creating a kind of hybridised zone of imperial exoticism. Nineveh had numerous contemporary associations. Assyria was the most ancient of the cultures recalled by the Sydenham courts, the location of the origin of civilisation and associated with the rise and fall of a powerful monarchy. Nineveh was also featured in the biblical Book of Kings and the prophecies of Isaiah and Jeremiah about desolation. Byron had written about Sardanapalus and the fall of Sennacherib, and Alexander's sack of Persepolis was part of the history curriculum. The court, therefore, had historical, biblical and literary associations, all of which Layard romanticised with his brightly coloured accents. Although Dante Gabriel Rossetti wrote a poem, 'The Burden of Nineveh', about the arrival of Assyrian antiquities – the 'winged beasts' – at the British Museum that evinces a great dislike for imperial culture, and although his brother William Michael Rossetti hated the Nineveh Court, which he called an oppressive 'nightmare life in death', the link between the modern British and ancient Assyrian empires could not have been clearer.[65]

However, there was an uneasy relationship between the fine arts courts, with their imperial resonances, and the more strictly imperial displays, especially those from China and India. In July 1852, the *Athenaeum* reported that an Indian palace and Chinese court were being planned, although they never came to fulfilment.[66] Then in 1856, the Crystal Palace Company announced that an exhibition of Indian manufactures would be on view 'in a specially appropriated Court or compartment' with facsimiles of the famed Ajanta frescos, to be overseen by James Fergusson, one of the foremost mid-nineteenth-century experts on Indian art and architecture.[67] But when the display opened, reviews were lacklustre: *The Athenaeum* called it 'small' and 'incongruous' with too many 'showy goods'. Fergusson's wooden models of temples and mosques, which were surrounded by a hodgepodge of garments and musical instruments, simply could not compare to the more grandiose courts.[68] Additionally, the Indian and Chinese displays were located in the galleries above the Egyptian and Greek Courts, well off the main walkway. *The Crystal Palace Herald* reported in 1855 that these minor courts were 'hardly known and seldom discovered'.[69]

Alongside the prehistoric dinosaurs and the ancient civilisations, the Sydenham Crystal Palace, which was conceived as 'a three-dimensional encyclopaedia of ... nature and art' that combined edification and entertainment in the hope of turning a profit for its shareholders, also featured a 'museum of man' that sought to offer something of an ethnological education.[70] Designed by the physician and philologist Robert Gordon Latham, a follower of James Prichard whose taxonomy of human variation was among the first to assign all races to a single species, the natural history department greeted visitors with life-sized groupings of stuffed animals, living plants and wax models of human beings, carefully placed in front of painted backdrops. The New World displays were located on the west side and the Old World exhibits were in the east, as if viewers were themselves circumnavigating the globe. These dioramas constituted a major change in techniques of display, and built on the increasing popularity of human exhibits during the first half of the nineteenth century.[71] They certainly represented a shift from highlighting colonial products, which had characterised the Great Exhibition of 1851, to focusing on colonial people, though in terms of classification the two were treated in remarkably similar ways.

The most extensive tableau was devoted to Africa. In addition to representative animals such as the hippopotamus, giraffe and lion, there were examples of people from the Niger River area, Sierra Leone

Figure 5.6 Henry Negretti and Joseph Zambra, 'Models of the San at the Crystal Palace, Sydenham, including Flora and Martinus', *c.* 1862

and South Africa, including the San and Zulu. The human models were arranged into visual narratives that Latham deemed representative of their ethnic traits. The adult male in the San family, for example, stood on high ground and was gazing out towards the horizon, an allusion to the reputed visual acuity of the San, who were frequently described in travel literature as having astonishing long-range vision that was particularly useful when hunting (Figure 5.6).[72] The guide-book to the natural history court, co-authored by Latham and Edward Forbes, Professor of Botany at King's College, London, was designed to help viewers interpret the displays with details about ethnolog-ical characteristics and descriptions of manners and customs.[73] By intermingling humans, animals and plants, the court promoted the classification of the various people that inhabited British territories as natural history specimens. And, as Sadiah Qureshi has noted, "The substitution of visitors for specimens of British types neatly encour-aged visitors to compare themselves with the peoples on display and note their progress from … [their] relatively lowly states of social

[126]

Figure 5.7 John Leech, 'Crystal Palace – Some Varieties of the Human Race', *Punch* 28 (1855): xxiii

organization and moral purpose.'[74] This is particularly evident in a John Leech cartoon for *Punch* (Figure 5.7), which extends some of the themes Tenniel explored in his earlier sketch. It depicts two young women sitting at a bistro table enjoying some refreshments; behind them a dark-skinned Bushman – or perhaps a Maori – holds a shield and is about to throw his spear. The caption, 'Crystal Palace – Varieties of the Human Race', certainly implies that the well-dressed women were themselves to be thought of as part of the display. In any event, until the colonial models burned down in the 1860s, they, like the nearby arts courts, helped encode Britain's imperial standing, implicitly positioning it at the apex of historical development.

The Sydenham Crystal Palace and the modern British Empire were not fully yoked togethe, however, until 1872, when Benjamin Disraeli used the site to give a landmark speech in which he declared that the Empire was central to the Conservative Party as well as to the British nation. Disraeli's speech ushered in a radical realignment in British politics. As Chancellor of the Exchequer, Disraeli had derided the colonies as a 'millstone 'round our necks' and as 'dead-weights'. Now he attacked a succession of Liberal governments for attempting to dismember the Empire by the progressive granting of colonial self-rule. His subject was especially topical, coinciding with Henry Morton Stanley's search for the Scottish missionary David Livingstone, and with a renewed debate over state-assisted emigration. Disraeli, as always, captured the public mood, in this case in favour of imperial consolidation and development.[75] Sydenham, therefore, would be remembered as an imperial site, but more for the imperial past and future that served as Britain's inspiration than for the imperial present.

The Festival of Empire, 1911

The Crystal Palace reached its apogee as an imperial site with the 1911 Festival of Empire, also known as the Coronation Exhibition. The festival had been planned for 1910, but was postponed because of Edward VII's death. It served as the first public function attended by George V, who, along with Queen Mary, opened the exhibition to rapturous applause. Highlights included a ceremonial greeting from some Maori warriors, described in the *Illustrated London News* as 'New Zealand's primitive inhabitants', as well as a thunderous performance of Elgar's arrangement of the national anthem by a 400-voice choir accompanied by the London Symphony Orchestra, the Festival of Empire Brass Band and thousands of enthusiastic observers in attendance.[76] *The Times* patriotically proclaimed it 'the most elaborate advertisement of the resources of the British Empire that has ever been devised', and an official brochure confidently asserted that 'The Gospel of Empire will be the dominant note at the Festival'.[77]

But the organisers seem to have had a slightly different concept in mind.[78] According to one souvenir pamphlet, the primary objective of the exhibition was 'the firmer welding of those invisible bonds which hold together the greatest empire the world has ever known'.[79]

This may explain in part why the opening programme included the London-born Anglo-Canadian composer Charles Harriss's *Empire of the Sea*, which he conducted himself. Described as 'an Imperial greeting chorus and orchestra', and dedicated to Earl Grey, Governor General of Canada, it celebrated Anglo-Canadian unity:

> Hail! Sons of the race, from afar!
> Joyous kings of the wind and the star,
> We daughter of Britain's glad Isles,
> Warmly welcome you home with our smiles ...
> Come, from your far fields of foam!
> Farewell to sadness,
> Waken to gladness,
> Welcome to Britain, your home ...
> Come, then, come to our own, in the Empire of the sea
> Might and joy never ending await the brave and the free.[80]

At a time when doubts were beginning to surface about the future of the Empire, the 1911 exhibition and the associated pageant sought to strengthen the ties between the metropole and the colonies.

The roots of the 1911 festival lay in the many attempts to revive the declining fortunes and popularity of the Crystal Palace in the late nineteenth century, as well as the influence and popularity of the Colonial and Indian Exhibition of 1886, which was held in South Kensington, not far from the site of the original Crystal Palace. Organised largely by J. Forbes Watson, Keeper of the Indian Collection at the South Kensington Museum, the Colonial and Indian Exhibition was designed to highlight the growing importance of Britain's Empire.[81] As Watson pointed out, commerce between Britain and its colonies was growing faster than trade between Britain and other independent countries: in 1874, India and the colonies accounted for 30 per cent of British exports, more than the United States, Germany and France combined. He also reminded potential doubters that India and the colonies were important repositories for British investment capital.[82]

Opened by Queen Victoria, recently crowned Empress of India, to a newly composed Arthur Sullivan ode, the 1886 exhibition brought together Britain's dominions and colonies for the first time. It was the product of a much greater effort on the part of both imperial and colonial organisers to include and fully represent the colonies.[83] The notion of a Greater Britain was symbolised by the figure of Britannia surmounting five giant clocks over the entrance to the central annexe, which showed the local time in Greenwich, Ottawa, Cape Town, Calcutta and Sydney.[84] Beneath them was a 700-foot canvas map, on which British possessions were coloured a bright scarlet. Considered as a whole, the entrance display mapped the British Empire in time and space.

The 1886 Colonial and Indian Exhibition was also the first major British exhibition to put on display the people of the Empire. South Asian artisans were assigned to shops in the forecourt of the purpose-built Indian palace, to illustrate how they would ply their trade in a local setting, and six 'natives' from British Guiana were employed to weave hammocks and make jewellery from beads and twine in what was claimed to be a traditional dwelling.[85] Other displays – such as the Australian colonies – featured models arranged in such a way as to demonstrate the progress of civilisation, from nomadic Aboriginals attired in kangaroo skins who carried clubs and were positioned as if they were walking through the forest in complete harmony with the fauna surrounding them, to a bushman's hut hewn from rough timber and thatched bark. The *Illustrated London News* likened the latter to the nostalgic reminiscence of a successful old man looking back on his youthful adventures and years of solitary isolation with a sense of idyllic satisfaction.[86] That the 'primitive' huts belonged to the present while the pioneer's hut was a temporary abode that resided in the past made clear the effects of 'civilisation' and reinforced a hierarchical view of humankind that simultaneously underpinned and was reinforced by Britain's economic, political and military strength.

As for rehabilitating the Crystal Palace, although Henry Cole boasted in 1884 that the Sydenham site had attracted 'millions of gratified visitors', attendances began to fall precipitously in the 1870s. By the end of the century the building had become severely dilapidated.[87] Efforts to revive the site's popularity included musical festivals as well as other forms of entertainment such as balloon flights, firework displays and demonstrations of moving pictures.[88] Several small colonial exhibitions were also held there. The African Exhibition of 1895 featured some two hundred African animals, birds and reptiles, but the featured attraction was a group of eighty Somalis wearing animal skins with red mud in their hair who performed traditional dances. An entire kraal had been reconstructed for the exhibition, where the Somalis slept at night and ate their meals.[89] But when they walked around working-class South London they were hooted and whistled at, and even threatened with fisticuffs.[90]

The 1905 Colonial and Indian Exhibition, also held at the Crystal Palace and the most direct forerunner of the 1911 Festival of Empire, was considerably larger and more popular than the African Exhibition. Its goal was 'to offer to the people of the United Kingdom an object lesson which would demonstrate that the British Empire produces all the necessaries and luxuries of life in quantities large enough to supply the wants of all its inhabitants'. The hope was that it would also boost 'inter-Imperial trading', a point the organisers emphasised in order to differentiate it from the many international exhibitions that had been held during the previous three decades. Whereas the Great Exhibition had been promoted at least partly on the grounds that it would benefit world trade, the focus had now shifted to imperial commerce. The organisers' decision that there was 'no better site … for this Imperial undertaking than the vast house of glass constructed for the epoch-making exhibition of 1851' reinforced the ever-tightening links between the Crystal Palace and the Empire.[91]

The 1911 Festival of Empire, which ran from 12 May to 28 October and featured representative and iconic scenes and structures from the British Empire in miniature, was the grandest imperial celebration ever held in the Crystal Palace. Among its most eye-catching and popular attractions were the three-quarter-sized replicas of the parliament houses of Ottawa, Melbourne, Wellington, Cape Town and St John's, Newfoundland, one of several ways the festival attempted to foster ties with the dominions. These specially constructed buildings, which dotted the terraces and grounds adjacent to the glass palace, housed displays of indigenous manufactures and produce (Figure 5.8). The South African building, for example, contained uncut diamonds worth £2 million, loaned by the De Beers Company. A miniature railway, the 'All-Red Route', one and a half miles long, linked these pavilions with other contemporary imperial scenes including a Malay village on stilts, a Jamaican sugar plantation, an Australian sheep farm, an

Figure 5.8 Postcard showing 'General View of the Crystal Palace and Canadian Building', 1911

[131]

Indian tea plantation and jungle 'well stocked with wild beasts' and a Maori village.[92]

Patriotic music was omnipresent, especially from the Band of the Coldstream Guards, which offered repeated performances of Edward Elgar's *Pomp and Circumstance March No. 1* ('Land of Hope and Glory'). There was also the 400-voice Empire Choir, which gave weekly imperial concerts, each devoted to a different country (Canada, England, Australia, Scotland, Ireland, Wales, New Zealand and South Africa, the latter conducted by the black British composer Samuel Coleridge-Taylor).[93] Inside the Crystal Palace, many of the statues and early Victorian relics had been put into storage and replaced by an 'All-British Exhibition of Arts and Industries'. It featured important developments in mining, engineering, transportation and chemistry, as well as arts and crafts, photography, 'British and Colonial Agriculture', forestry and 'Imperial Industries'.

Building on the success of the 1908 London Olympics held just three years earlier, the festival also included an Inter-Empire sports championship – although only dominion countries could participate – in which teams from Australasia (a combined team from Australia and New Zealand), Canada, South Africa and the United Kingdom competed in five athletics events (100 yards, 220 yards, 880 yards, 1 mile and 120 yards hurdles), two swimming events (100 yards and 1 mile), heavyweight boxing and middleweight wrestling. This was the first-ever sporting competition between teams representing Britain and its dominions, and is generally regarded as a forerunner of the British Empire (now Commonwealth) Games, which began in 1930.[94]

Another attraction was the series of forty historical tableaux, many of them with imperial themes. South Africa, for example, was represented by the Great Trek, Stanley's meeting with Livingstone, Cecil Rhodes negotiating with the natives and the opening of the Union Parliament by the Duke of Connaught. The Duke himself loaned a selection of animals he had shot during his recent East African tour, including a lion, a buffalo and an impala, which formed part of a display of big game trophies, 'probably the most representative of its kind that has been held in this country'. Although it was limited to 'sporting animals killed within the British Empire', the King loaned two 'fine specimens of Newfoundland caribou', the head of a musk ox and an Indian markhor (a large species of long-haired wild goat with majestic corkscrewing horns). Other big-game hunters lending trophies included the Duke of Westminster, Lord Kitchener and the Crown Prince of Bhopal.[95]

The India Section was again the centrepiece of the imperial display, as it had been sixty years earlier at the Great Exhibition of 1851. The emphasis had shifted, however, to showing the progress India had made under British rule since 1857, symbolised by a model of the new railway station at Howrah. The Indian exhibits also featured a series of twelve miniature historical tableaux, 'carefully prepared by English artists, as far as possible from drawings by Indians, so as to represent native ideas'. Scenes included the enthronement of Rama and Sita from the *Ramayana*, along with more contemporary events such as the 1858 reading of Queen Victoria's proclamation in Calcutta. These tableaux reflected the emerging Indian nationalist movement, and represent a move towards an Indo-, rather than Anglo-centric view of India.[96]

There were other hints of the fragility of imperial integration and the possibility of imperial decline. According to Winston Churchill, many people at the time feared the Empire was so rickety that 'a single violent shock would bring it clattering down and lay it low for ever'.[97] At the opening ceremony, in addition to the national anthem, those in attendance heard a performance of Rudyard Kipling's 'Recessional', with its reminder that those who rule must be guided by the injunction in the Book of Common Prayer for 'an humble and contrite heart'. The couplet in the poem about 'All our pomp of yesterday is one with Nineveh and Tyre', against the backdrop of the decaying and cracked statues of the Assyrian Court, surely reinforced the message.

Amidst this imperial celebration, the festival clearly had commercial intentions as well. Although one of the many souvenir publications declared that the Crystal Palace and its grounds were 'an ideal place for a striking display of our commercial supremacy',[98] the organisers, again, saw things differently. According to the *Official Guide*, the festival would 'demonstrate to the somewhat casual, often times unobservant British public the real significance of our great self-governing Dominions, to make us familiar with their products, their ever-increasing resources, their illimitable possibilities'.[99] An 'International Rubber Exhibition' at the Agricultural Hall, for example, highlighted the recent growth of the rubber industry, but, just as importantly for *The Times*, demonstrated that, although Brazil occupied a 'a prominent position', it did not 'stand alone in the development of plantation rubber'. The exhibition, continued the paper, made it 'quite clear' that the British Dominions would 'play an important role in the future of the industry'.[100] The start of the 'All-British Shopping Week' six weeks before the exhibition underscored the economic imperatives at stake. According to *The Times*, there were many who took 'a limited and pessimistic view of the range of British arts and crafts' or who were 'obsessed by constant depreciation of home manufactures and insistence on the supposed supremacy of their competitors'.[101] In this respect, the 1911 Festival of Empire shared a fundamental similarity with the Great Exhibition of 1851, in that both were organised to remedy perceived economic weaknesses, but were typically celebrated in the popular press for demonstrating Britain's superiority. In any event, two acres of the Sydenham grounds were laid out with live farm animals, and representatives of various agricultural societies staffed information bureaux in order to offer farmers tips and techniques. There were also traditional amusements such as the TopsyTurvy, Hiram Maxim's Flying Machine, Joy Wheels, River Caves and the Coaster, which provided visitors with exhilarating rides throughout the season.

The Festival of Empire was also integrated with the adjacent Pageant of London, a four-part, forty-scene event staged over three days by fifteen thousand volunteers. The Pageant, which owed much to the imperial vision of Frank Lascelles, the long-time British diplomat known in the popular press as 'the man who staged the Empire', had originally been planned to recall London's central role in the history of Britain, with performers drawn from the various London boroughs, but, in view of the coronation and the general emphasis on the Empire, it was decided to add a fourth part, performed entirely by men and women of colonial birth, 'with the exception of the characters representative of the dark-skinned races'.[102] It told the 'living story' of London 'from the dawn of British history', concluding with an elaborate 'Masque Imperial' that doubled as 'An Allegory of the Advantages of Empire'.[103] The 'dramatic thrust' of the pageant, therefore, which began with the discovery of Newfoundland and took its audience through the proclamation of Queen Victoria as Empress of India in 1877, 'was to suggest that the whole of the previous 2000 years of British history had been leading up inevitably to the glories and grandeur of the British Empire'.[104] There was, however, a certain irony to the pageant's implicit claim that London was not just an imperial city but the heart of the Empire, given that the Pageant took place at the Crystal Palace which – unlike its Hyde Park predecessor – was now located not in central London but in the suburbs, on the outskirts of the city.[105] Still, in blending theatre, dance and dialogue against the backdrop of the Crystal Palace, and with its parade of exotic animals including elephants, camels and zebus, the pageant was an extraordinary spectacle, and represented an enormous leap in modalities of display.

No amount of imperial pomp, however, could restore the fortunes of the Crystal Palace Company. The Crystal Palace was put on the market immediately after the 1911 festival, with the preface to the luxuriously illustrated sale catalogue expressing the hope that the idea of empire might once again be crystallised at the Sydenham Palace.[106]

Just over two decades later, however, the Sydenham Palace burned down, an event which newspapers at the time saw as a portent, and which in retrospect seems an apt metaphor for the fortunes of the increasingly fraying Empire.

Conclusion

There would be other imperial festivals, though not at the Crystal Palace. The most famous was at Wembley in 1924–25, which drew a record twenty-seven million people and was designed to reinforce imperial economic ties after the First World War.[107] In 1938, a second Empire Exhibition was held in Glasgow, the 'second city of the empire', attracting millions of visitors who shared the organisers' hope that the Empire would help revive the city's and the nation's depression-ravaged economies.[108] But by the time the Festival of Britain took place in 1951, in the aftermath of the Second World War and fifteen years after the Crystal Palace itself had burned down, the Empire was in disarray. India, where Britain had beat a 'shameful flight', had been granted its independence; Palestine had been ignominiously turned over to the United Nations and, like India, partitioned amidst unanticipated and unimaginable violence.[109] The Festival of Britain, national rather than imperial in scope, relegated the imperial and Commonwealth exhibits to a secondary location, away from the main exhibition site on the South Bank.[110]

The Crystal Palace, therefore, illuminates the changing place of the Empire in British society and culture during the second half of the nineteenth century and the first decade of the twentieth. From 1851, when industry and manufactures were the focus and the term 'empire' was barely even in use; to the 1850s and 1860s, when the British started to see themselves as heirs to the great ancient empires; to the 1890s, when the Crystal Palace began to display the people of the Empire, as colonial peoples themselves were increasingly making their way to the imperial metropolis; to 1911, when the British Empire was portrayed as a family but where the first stirrings of colonial nationalism were evident.[111] Beneath the surface, a continuing process of contestation and negotiation took place, as organisers, visitors and commentators, both in Britain and in its colonies, struggled to articulate and refine the relationship between Britain and its Empire.

But the imperial exhibits at the Crystal Palace from 1851 to 1911 also illustrate changing techniques of display. Between these years, the imperial presence at the Crystal Palace grew in size, as a portion of the overall collection of goods being exhibited, as well as in height (the Abu Simbel figures in Sydenham) and scale (the recreated parliament buildings and villages at the 1911 Empire exhibition). The exhibitions also became more lifelike and theatrical, increasingly seeking to entertain and amuse, and not simply to educate. They became spectacles, bridging high and popular culture, moving inexorably away from raw materials and manufactured goods to living simulacra that not only took on a freak-show quality that bolstered Britain's sense of superiority but blurred the lines between metropole and periphery by bringing the recreated and miniaturised empire to the imperial centre.[112] In this respect, the imperial exhibitions that were held 'under glass' between 1851 and 1911 encapsulate British efforts to control and contain the Empire. Yet by 1911, it had become clear that the Empire had grown far too large to be enclosed in glass, but was now spilling over on to the adjacent grounds, just as it was beginning to burst the bonds that had held it together for so long.[113]

Notes

1 Jeffrey A. Auerbach, *The Great Exhibition of 1851: A Nation on Display* (New Haven, CT: Yale University Press, 1999), pp. 100–2; Jeffrey A. Auerbach, 'The Great Exhibition and Historical Memory', *Journal of Victorian Culture* 6 (2001), pp. 89–112; Paul Greenhalgh, *Ephemeral Vistas: The Expositions Universelles, Great Exhibitions and World's Fairs, 1851–1939* (Manchester: Manchester University Press, 1988), pp. 52–9; Peter H. Hoffenberg, *An Empire on Display: English, Indian, and Australian Exhibitions from the Crystal Palace to the Great War* (Berkeley, CA: University of California Press, 2001), p. 8; Thomas Richards, *The Commodity Culture of Victorian Britain: Advertising and Spectacle, 1851–1914* (Stanford, CA: Stanford University Press, 1990), p. 40; Tim Barringer, 'Imperial Visions', in John M. MacKenzie (ed.), *The Victorian Vision: Inventing New Britain* (London: V&A Publications, 2001), p. 321; P.J. Marshall (ed.), *The Cambridge Illustrated History of the British Empire* (Cambridge: Cambridge University Press, 1996), pp. 14–15; Carol Breckenridge, 'The Aesthetics and Politics of Colonial Collecting: India at World Fairs', *Comparative Studies in Society and History* 31 (1989), pp. 195–216.
2 Sadiah Qureshi, *Peoples on Parade: Exhibitions, Empire, and Anthropology in Nineteenth-Century Britain* (Chicago: University of Chicago Press, 2011), pp. 199–201.
3 For a broad overview of these 'human showcases', see Greenhalgh, *Ephemeral Vistas*, pp. 82–111.
4 Auerbach, *The Great Exhibition of 1851*, pp. 23–4, 27–31.
5 *The Times*, 18 October 1849, 26 January 1850, 22 March 1850; *Illustrated London News*, 28 June 1851.
6 *Collection of Printed Documents and Forms used in carrying on the Business of the Exhibition of 1851*, 8 vols (London: Victoria and Albert Museum, 1853), vol. 2, p. 283.
7 Auerbach, *The Great Exhibition of 1851*, pp. 54–88.
8 *Illustrated London News*, 18–25 October and 6 December 1851.
9 *Illustrated London News*, 3 May 1851.
10 *Illustrated London News*, 8 March 1851, 22 March 1851.
11 *Illustrated London News*, 10 May 1851, 14 June 1851.
12 *Illustrated London News*, 3 May 1851.
13 See Edward Said, *Orientalism* (New York: Vintage Books, 1978), and, more generally, James Buzard, 'Conflicting Cartographies: Globalism, Nationalism, and the Crystal Palace Floor Plan', in James Buzard, Joseph W. Childers and Eileen Gillo-

oly (eds), *Victorian Prism: Refractions of the Crystal Palace* (Charlottesville, VA: University of Virginia Press, 2007), pp. 40–50.

14 *Dickinsons' Comprehensive Pictures of the Great Exhibition of 1851* (London: Dickinson Brothers, 1854), II(1), Frontispiece.

15 *Official Descriptive and Illustrated Catalogue*, 3 vols (London: Spicer Brothers, 1851).

16 See David Arnold, *The Tropics and the Traveling Gaze: India, Landscape, and Science, 1800–1856* (Seattle, WA: University of Washington Press, 2006), pp. 162–6, for an interesting discussion of how Forbes's personal commitment to botany fitted with his East India Company service. More broadly, see Richard Drayton, *Nature's Government: Science, Imperial Britain, and the 'Improvement' of the World* (New Haven, CT: Yale University Press, 2000). On Orientalism and nineteenth-century exhibitions, see Timothy Mitchell, 'The World as Exhibition', *Comparative Studies in Society and History* 31 (1989), pp. 217–36.

17 *Illustrated London News*, 4 October 1851. See also Hoffenberg, *An Empire on Display*, p. 159.

18 *Official Descriptive and Illustrated Catalogue*, pp. 857–937

19 Ibid., p. 988.

20 Ibid., p. 857. See also J. Forbes Royle, *On the Culture and Commerce of Cotton in India* (London: Smith, Elder & Co., 1851); British Library, India Office Records, E/4/803, India and Bengal Dispatches, 7 January 1850; Ray Desmond, *The India Museum* (London: HMSO, 1982).

21 *Illustrated London News*, 10 May 1851; Bernard Porter, *The Absent-Minded Imperialists* (Oxford: Oxford University Press, 2004).

22 The display was depicted in the *Illustrated London News*, 31 May 1851, though without the gold cage.

23 Ibid., 17 May 1851. James Tennant, in his lecture on gems and precious stones at the Society of Arts on 24 March 1852, similarly concluded that the diamond 'disappointed' many of those who saw it. See 'On Gems and Precious Stones', in *Lectures on the Results of the Great Exhibition of 1851 delivered before the Society of Arts, Manufactures, and Commerce*, second series (London: David Bogue, 1853), p. 80.

24 Lara Kriegel, 'Narrating the Subcontinent in 1851: India at the Crystal Palace', in Louise Purbrick (ed.), *The Great Exhibition of 1851: New Interdisciplinary Essays* (Manchester: Manchester University Press, 2001), p. 168.

25 'A Few Words upon Canada', *Illustrated London News*, 21 June 1851.

26 *Illustrated London News*, 21 June 1851.

27 *Dickinsons' Comprehensive Pictures*, 'West Indies'.

28 *Official Descriptive and Illustrated Catalogue*, pp. 988–92. For New Zealand, see Amiria J.M. Henare, *Museums, Anthropology and Imperial Exchange* (Cambridge: Cambridge University Press, 2005), pp. 148–53.

29 John Tallis, *Tallis's History and Description of the Crystal Palace and the Exhibition of the World's Industry in 1851*, 2 vols (London: John Tallis & Co., 1852), vol. 1, p. 53.

30 Ibid.; Hoffenberg, *An Empire on Display*, pp. 129–65.

31 *Official Descriptive and Illustrated Catalogue*, pp. 998–9.

32 *Illustrated London News*, 24 May 1851.

33 See Bernard Smith, *European Vision and the South Pacific*, 2nd edn (New Haven, CT: Yale University Press, 1983), and Bernard Smith, *Imagining the Pacific: In the Wake of Cook's Voyages* (Carlton, Victoria: Melbourne University Press, 1993).

34 *Official Descriptive and Illustrated Catalogue*, p. 992.

35 *Illustrated London News*, 10 May 1851.

36 Niall Ferguson, *Empire: The Rise and Demise of the British World Order and the Lessons for Global Power* (New York: Basic Books, 2004); John Darwin, *The Empire Project: The Rise and Fall of the British World-System, 1830–1970* (Cambridge: Cambridge University Press, 2011); Carl Bridge and Kent Fedorowich (eds), *The British World: Diaspora, Culture and Identity* (London: Routledge, 2003).

37 *Dickinsons' Comprehensive Pictures*, India No. 1, India No. 4, Turkey No. 2.

38 *Art Union* 29 (1851), p. 1845.
39 The difficulties the British had governing their Empire are legendary. For a suggestive overview, see Ged Martin, 'Was There a British Empire?', *Historical Journal* 15 (1972), pp. 562–9; Thomas Richards, *The Imperial Archive: Knowledge and the Fantasy of Empire* (London: Verso, 1993), pp. 1–9.
40 *Illustrated London News*, 31 May 1851.
41 Edward Ziter, *The Orient on the Victorian Stage* (Cambridge: Cambridge University Press, 2003), p. 110.
42 Kate Flint, 'Exhibiting America: The Native American and the Crystal Palace', in James Buzard, Joseph W. Childers and Eileen Gillooly (eds), *Victorian Prism: Refractions of the Crystal Palace* (Charlottesville, VA: University of Virginia Press, 2007), pp. 171–85.
43 Thomas Onwhyn, *Mr and Mrs John Brown's Visit to London to see the Great Exhibition of All Nations* (London: Ackerman, [1851]).
44 The Royal Commission estimated that 60,000 foreigners came to London in 1851, approximately half of them from France. See Auerbach, *The Great Exhibition of 1851*, pp. 185–6; Royal Commission for the Exhibition of the Works of Industry of All Nations, *First Report* (London: William Clowes & Sons for HMSO, 1852), pp. 112–14.
45 *The Times*, 2 May 1851.
46 Henrietta Ward, *Memories of Ninety Years* (New York: H. Holt, 1925), p. 63.
47 *Art Journal Illustrated Catalogue* (London: George Virtue, 1851), p. 85.
48 On the early finances of the Crystal Palace Company, see Henry Atmore, 'Utopia Limited: The Crystal Palace Company and Joint-Stock Politics, 1854–1856', *Journal of Victorian Culture* 9 (2004), pp. 189–215.
49 For contrasting reviews of the arts courts, see Harriet Martineau, 'The Crystal Palace', *Westminster Review* 62 (1854), pp. 534–50, and Elizabeth Eastlake, 'The Crystal Palace', *Quarterly Review* 96 (1855), pp. 303–54, both of which focus on the nature of aesthetics and the need for aesthetic elevation through civic training and educational reform.
50 J.R. Piggott, *Palace of the People: The Crystal Palace at Sydenham 1854–1936* (London: Hurst & Company, 2004), p. 67.
51 *The Crystal Palace Exhibitor* (London: James S. Vertue, 1854), p. 143.
52 Samuel Phillips, *Guide to the Crystal Palace and Park* (London: Crystal Palace Library and Bradbury and Evans, 1854), p. 39.
53 Owen Jones, 'On the Influence of Religion', in *Lectures on Architecture and the Decorate Arts* (London: Strangeways & Walden, 1863), p. 7.
54 Phillips, *Guide to the Crystal Palace*, p. 52.
55 *The Crystal Palace Expositor*, p. 6.
56 Piggott, *Palace of the People*, p. 75. For an analysis of the Nineveh Court in relation to Baudrillard's theories about simulation, see Shawn Malley, *From Archaeology to Spectacle in Victorian Britain: The Case of Assyria, 1845–1854* (Farnham: Ashgate, 2012), pp. 127–60.
57 William Michael Rossetti, 'The Epochs of Art as Represented in the Crystal Palace (from *The Spectator*, 1854)', in *Fine Art, Chiefly Contemporary: Notes Re-Printed with Revisions* (London: Macmillan, 1867), p. 53. See also Natasha Eaton, *Colour, Art and Empire: Visual Culture and the Nomadism of Representation* (London: I.B. Taurus, 2013), pp. 77–94.
58 Owen Jones, 'On the Decorations Proposed for the Exhibition Building in Hyde Park', in *Lectures*, p. 4.
59 In 1887, Lewis F. Day wrote that *The Grammar of Ornament* marked 'a turning point in the history of English ornament'. See *British Art: Art Journal Royal Jubilee Number* (London: Virtue, 1887), pp. 187–8.
60 *Guide to the Ten Chief Courts of the Sydenham Palace* (London: Routledge, 1854), p. 25.
61 Ibid., p. 116.
62 *Art Journal* 3 (1 March 1857), p. 95.

63 Samuel Leigh Sotheby, *A Few Words by way of a Letter Addressed to the Directors of the Crystal Palace Company* (London: John Russell Smith, 1855), p. 20.

64 James Fergusson, *The Palaces of Nineveh and Persepolis Restored* (London: John Murray, 1851, p. 6.

65 Rossetti, 'The Epochs of Art', p. 80.

66 *Athanaeum*, 10 July 1852, p. 751.

67 Piggott, *Palace of the People*, p. 77.

68 *Athenaeum*, 10 July 1852, pp. 814–15.

69 *Crystal Palace Herald*, November 1855, p. 100.

70 Piggott, *Palace of the People*, p. v.

71 See Richard D. Altick, *The Shows of London: A Panoramic History of Exhibitions, 1600–1862* (Cambridge, MA: Harvard University Press, 1978); Qureshi, *Peoples on Parade*; Coco Fusco, 'The Other History of Intercultural Performance', in Coco Fusco, *English Is Broken Here: Notes on Cultural Fusion in the Americas* (New York: New Press, 1995), pp. 41–3.

72 See, for example, Henry Lichtenstein, *Travels in Southern Africa, in the Years 1803, 1804, 1805, and 1806*, trans. Anne Plumtre, 2 vols (London: Henry Colburn, 1812), p. 196. On Latham and the Crystal Palace ethnological display, see Qureshi, *People on Parade*, pp. 194–221; Sadiah Qureshi, 'Robert Gordon Latham, Displayed Peoples and the Natural History of Race, 1854–1866', *Historical Journal* 54 (2011), pp. 143–66; Efram Sera-Shriar, 'Ethnology in the Metropole: Robert Knox, Robert Gordon Latham and Local Sites of Observational Training', *Studies in History and Philosophy of Biological and Biomedical Sciences* 42 (2011), pp. 486–96.

73 R.G. Latham and E. Forbes, *A Hand Book to the Courts of Natural History* (London: Bradbury and Evans, 1854); *Punch* 27 (1854), pp. 8–9.

74 Qureshi, *Peoples on Parade*, p. 201.

75 Paul Smith, *Disraeli* (Cambridge: Cambridge University Press, 1996), pp. 163–4.

76 *Illustrated London News*, 20 May 1911.

77 *The Times*, 5 May 1911; *Festival of Empire Imperial Exhibition Pageant of London 1911* (Crystal Palace, 1911), p. 7.

78 *The Times*, 12–13 May 1911. Lord Plymouth conveyed to *The Times* that he had 'some doubt as to whether the aims and intentions of those of who worked for the success of the Festival of Empire and the Pageant of London are fully understood'.

79 *Souvenir of Royal Visit to the Festival of Empire, Imperial Exhibition and Pageant of London Crystal Palace, Coronation Year 1911* (London: Bemrose, 1911), p. 5; Piers Brendon, *The Decline and Fall of the British Empire 1781–1997* (New York: Random House, 2007), p. 256.

80 Jeffrey Richards, *Imperialism and Music: Britain, 1876–1953* (Manchester: Manchester University Press), pp. 181–2.

81 J. Forbes Watson, *The Imperial Museum for India and the Colonies* (London: Wm H. Allen, 1876); Watson, letter to *The Times*, 9 June 1874. On the relative lack of interest in empire, see Porter, *The Absent-Minded Imperialists*. The 1886 exhibition also built on the successes of the 1879 Sydney Exhibition, which was held at a large, purpose-built exhibition building called The Garden Palace that was a reworking of London's Crystal Palace (although it was comprised predominantly of wood, brick and iron), and the 1880 Melbourne International Exhibition, which heralded the city's emergence as an industrial metropolis and Australia's move towards self-rule government and federation.

82 Watson, *The Imperial Museum*, pp. 8–10.

83 The best discussion of the colonial role in exhibitions is Hoffenberg, *An Empire on Display*.

84 *The Art Journal, Colonial and Indian Exhibition Supplement* (1886).

85 Frank Cundall (ed.), *Reminiscences of the Colonial and Indian Exhibition* (London: William Clowes and Sons, 1886), pp. 26, 81.

86 *Illustrated London News*, 29 May 1886, p. 586. See also 'The Queen's Visit to the South Australian Court', *Illustrated London News*, 29 May 1886, p. 575.

87 *The Times*, 21 July 1872, 25 July 1908.

88 Auerbach, *The Great Exhibition of 1851*, pp. 202–3.
89 *Illustrated London News*, 15 June 1895; Carl Hagenbeck, *East African Village and Great Display of Natives of Somaliland* (Sydenham: Crystal Palace Company, 1895); Qureshi, *Peoples on Parade*, p. 116. Carl Hagenbeck (1844–1913) was a German merchant of wild animals who supplied many European zoos, as well as P.T. Barnum. He helped create the modern zoo by designing animal enclosures without bars that resembled the animals' natural habitats. He was also a pioneer in displaying humans. On the display of Africans in late nineteenth-century Britain, see Annie E. Coombes, *Reinventing Africa: Museums, Material Culture and Popular Imagination in Late Victorian and Edwardian England* (New Haven, CT: Yale University Press, 1994), esp. pp. 85–97.
90 Neil Parsons, *King Khama, Empire Joe, and the Great White Queen: Victorian Britain through African Eyes* (Chicago: University of Chicago Press, 1998), p. 28.
91 *The Times*, 12 October 1904.
92 John M. MacKenzie, *Propaganda and Empire* (Manchester: Manchester University Press, 1984), pp. 106–7.
93 Michael Musgrave, *The Musical Life of the Crystal Palace* (Cambridge: Cambridge University Press, 2005), p. 212; Richards, *Imperialism and Music*, pp. 186–7.
94 Nigel Burton, 'Festival of Empire', *History Today* 52 (2002), pp. 2–3.
95 Richards, *Imperialism and Music*, pp. 180–1.
96 *Indian Court: Festival of Empire 1911: Guide Book and Catalogue* (London: Bemrose and Sons, [1911]).
97 Robert Rhodes James (ed.), *Winston S. Churchill: His Complete Speeches, 1897–1963*, 8 vols (London: Bowker, 1974), vol. 7, p. 6920.
98 *Souvenir of Royal Visit to the Festival of Empire*, p. 5.
99 *Festival of Empire Imperial Exhibition Pageant of London 1911*, p. 7. On this point see Porter, *The Absent-Minded Imperialists*.
100 *The Times*, 7 July 1911.
101 *The Times*, 28 March 1911.
102 Deborah S. Ryan, 'The Pageant of London, 1911', in Felix Driver and David Gilbert (eds), *Imperial Cities: Landscape, Display and Identity* (Manchester: Manchester University Press, 1999), pp. 119, 124; Richards, *Imperialism and Music*, p. 188. See also H.V. Nelles, *The Art of Nation-Building: Pageantry and Spectacle at Quebec's Tercentenary* (Toronto: University of Toronto Press, 1999), esp. pp. 141–97.
103 M. Baxter, 'An Imperial Triumph', in Earl of Darnley (ed.), *Frank Lascelles: Our Modern Orpheus* (London: Oxford University Press, 1932), p. 50.
104 *Festival of Empire: The Pageant of London, May to October, 1911: Pageant Programme* (London: Bemrose, 1911), Parts I–IV; Richards, *Imperialism and Music*, p. 188; Daniel Gorman, *The Emergence of International Society in the 1920s* (Cambridge: Cambridge University Press, 2012), pp. 151–3.
105 Ryan, 'The Pageant of London, 1911', pp. 117, 127–8. On London as the 'heart of empire', see Jonathan Schneer, *London 1900: The Imperial Metropolis* (New Haven, CT: Yale University Press, 1999); Antoinette Burton, *At the Heart of Empire: Indians and the Colonial Encounter in Late-Victorian Britain* (Berkeley, CA: University of California Press, 1998); Angela Woollacott, *To Try Her Fortune in London: Australian Women, Colonialism, and Modernity* (Oxford: Oxford University Press, 2001). The term was also widely used in the decade before the exhibition. See Charles Masterman, *The Heart of the Empire: Discussions of Problems of Modern City Life in England* (London: T. Fisher Unwin, 1901).
106 Piggott, *Palace of the People*, p. 178.
107 See Daniel Stephen, *The Empire of Progress: West Africans, Indians, and Britons at the British Empire Exhibition, 1924–25* (London: Palgrave Macmillan, 2013).
108 Ian Johnstone (ed.), *Glasgow's Greatest Exhibition: Recreating the 1938 Empire Exhibition* (Edinburgh: RIAS, 2008); Perilla and Juliet Kinchin, *Glasgow's Great Exhibitions, 1888, 1901, 1911, 1938, 1988* (Wendlebury: White Cockade, 1988); John M. MacKenzie, 'The Second City of the Empire: Glasgow – Imperial Municipality', in Felix Driver and David Gilbert (eds), *Imperial Cities: Landscape, Display and*

Identity (Manchester: Manchester University Press, 1999), pp. 215–37.

109 Stanley Wolpert, *Shameful Flight: The Last Years of the British Empire in India* (Oxford: Oxford University Press, 2006); Michael J. Cohen, *Palestine: Retreat from Mandate: The Making of British Policy 1936–45* (London: Paul Elek, 1978).

110 Auerbach, *The Great Exhibition of 1851*, pp. 220–7; Becky Conekin, *The Autobiography of a Nation: The 1951 Festival of Britain* (Manchester: Manchester University Press, 2003).

111 See Schneer, *London 1900*, and Burton, *At the Heart of Empire*.

112 According to the postmodernist French theorist Jean Baudrillard, a simulacrum is not a copy of the real, but becomes truth in its own right. See *Jean Baudrillard, Selected Writings*, ed. Mark Poster (Stanford, CA: Stanford University Press, 1988), pp. 166–84.

113 For a Foucauldian analysis of the relationship between exhibition and confinement, containment and control, see Tony Bennett, 'The Exhibitionary Complex', *New Formations* 4 (1988), pp. 73–102.

CHAPTER SIX

Ephemera and the British Empire

Ashley Jackson and David Tomkins

Historians have long been aware of the significance of imperial themes in British culture, and of their visual representation as experienced by ordinary people in a variety of conscious and subconscious forms. Images conveying ideas and messages about empire, the non-European world and the relationship between Britons and non-Europeans appeared on a diverse range of media encountered in the course of everyday life in a variety of ways. This could occur during the pursuit of defined leisure activities, such as going to the cinema, visiting an exhibition or attending a concert, or in the pursuit of everyday tasks such as grocery shopping or lighting a cigarette. Often the media employed were intended to last for a long time, such as the statuary that populated the streets and squares of British and colonial towns and cities, oil paintings in art galleries, books or prints and souvenirs designed to adorn mantelpieces and living-room walls. But arguably the most powerful purveyors of imperial ideas and images were to be found in the realm of 'ephemera'; 'things of short-lived interest' as the *Oxford English Dictionary* defines the word. Items of ephemera included tracts, paper bags, posters, food packaging, advertisements, matchboxes and labels. Their power lay in the fact that they were frequently encountered in the quotidian experience of people of every age and of all classes.

In a volume devoted to examples of the exhibition of the British Empire, this chapter seeks to achieve a number of things and to develop a niche in the ever-expanding literature relating to imperialism, society and culture. Most importantly, it concentrates on the subject of ephemera as a concept of display, more firmly embedding ephemera studies into the literature relating to the British Empire and popular culture than has been the case to date. In so doing, it examines the Bodleian Library's John Johnson Collection of Printed Ephemera and the manner in which its material can be used to investigate imperial themes. Secondly, and leading logically on from this primary aim, the chapter investigates the *means* by which imperial themes were encountered and key aspects of the manner in which the Empire was displayed through printed ephemera. It registers the important fact that, while ephemera were typically visual media, they were also in many cases textual. A third main area of focus is ephemera studies – a distinct field of scholarship that has its own research centres and publications. Though ephemera were one of the most important media that introduced ideas about empire and the wider world to the public, the field of ephemera studies has not been sufficiently integrated into the study of the British Empire's engagement with popular culture. Finally, the chapter offers insights into the types of imperial and wider world themes encountered in different types of ephemeral material.

The chapter's main historiographical contribution is to highlight the importance of ephemera as a hitherto overlooked medium vital for the dissemination of information regarding the imperial and wider world. It was a major factor in the very 'everydayness' of empire and imperial ideas that some authors have touched upon, but one that, perhaps by its very nature, has not been widely recognised. While this chapter seeks to stake this claim regarding ephemera in the specialist literature, it must be noted that John MacKenzie – almost inevitably! – was first in the field. His landmark work of 1984, *Propaganda and Empire: The Manipulation of British Public Opinion, 1880–1960*, made numerous references to the significance of ephemera in disseminating ideas and images related to the British Empire and, more generally, overseas lands and peoples, and Britain's position vis-à-vis them. Indeed, in the book's opening chapter, appropriately titled 'The Vehicles of Imperial Propaganda', MacKenzie stated that the

> provision of ephemera and popular literature of all sorts will be an underlying theme in what follows, for many of the agencies described in subsequent chapters made assiduous use of the public interest in such material and the collecting activities associated with it.[1]

Defining ephemera, ephemera studies and 'the visual'

The word 'ephemera' was employed in medieval times in a medical context to describe a fever lasting only one day, and ultimately derives from the Greek 'ephemeros', meaning to last for a day. The mayfly belongs to the Ephemeroptera order of insects because of its short lifespan, and the term 'ephemeron' has been used to describe a plant which lives for only one day or which causes death within a day, or more generally a short-lived person, institution or production. In more recent times, 'ephemera' has most commonly been used to describe material which has been produced only to last for a finite period before being discarded, though the unqualifiable nature of the word 'finite' renders this definition somewhat less than definitive. In its printed form, however, the meaning bestowed upon 'ephemera' by the late Maurice Rickards, compiler of *The Encyclopaedia of Ephemera*, can largely be considered fit for purpose.[2] He described ephemera as 'the minor transient documents of everyday life'.[3]

Given this definition, printed material created with the intention of lasting permanently or for a considerable period of time – books, journals or photographs, for example – should not be considered 'ephemeral', while a sweet wrapper or a cigarette packet can usually be deemed redundant once its contents have been consumed. Yet material which was produced specifically to be discarded once its purpose was served can assume new value when it is collected over a period of time. Items which were intended to be 'throwaway' become indispensable when they can be used as documentary evidence concerning our social and cultural past. As Marina Warner puts it, 'The point of ephemera is to reveal the ordinary texture of existence – not its exceptional moments. Ephemera aren't sacred relics, just accidental traces.'[4]

Private collectors of such evidence are far more numerous than public ones, and remarkably few libraries or museums pursue an active policy of collecting ephemera.[5] And when displayed, such material is more often than not the supporting act rather than the star attraction. Nevertheless, this type of material is increasingly being recognised as a primary source for academic historical research and for providing a more conscious understanding of the past as it was actually experienced by those who inhabited it. Furthermore, those who specialise in the study of ephemera have in recent decades taken measures to mobilise themselves; indeed, it was the aforementioned Rickards who 'identified the need to elevate the study of ephemera into an academic discipline and, moreover, to bring together people who held in common a passionate interest in the forgotten byways of history'.[6] He and seven like-minded individuals founded the Ephemera Society in London in 1975, an organisation which has since grown into an internationally recognised authority in the field with its own quarterly journal, *The Ephemerist*. The Ephemera Society of America was established five years later. The study of ephemera was firmly recognised as an academic discipline in 1992 with the inauguration of the Centre for Ephemera Studies – the first of its kind in the world – in the Department of Typography & Graphic Communication at the University of Reading, patronised by Asa, Lord Briggs, and championed by Rickards among others.[7] The Centre aims to promote the study of ephemera, and its activities include the publication of research tools for ephemerists, courses on various aspects of ephemera, and the compilation of a register of ephemera collections publicly available in Britain.[8]

Although ephemera often comprise both images and the written word, their visuality is arguably their most distinctive characteristic. It is difficult to underestimate the importance of the visual: as Raphael Samuel puts it, the visual provides us with our stock figures, our subliminal points of reference, our unspoken points of address.[9] In her powerful study of the employment of images of non-European people in British advertising, Anandi Ramamurthy contends that '[i]mages are historical documents':

> They do not simply reflect the ideological perspectives of an era, but form part of the process through which these ideologies are produced ... racist representations continually developed and shifted through the nineteenth and twentieth centuries, depending on the particular political and economic interests of the producers of these images.[10]

The study of ephemera involves the history of design and of printing dating back to the Renaissance, and in later times colour printing, which led to a flowering of ornate and vivid ephemera in the nineteenth century. Colonial printers and engravers imported British equipment and used the same manuals as those 'back home', a significant element in extending the range of printed ephemera into the colonial world itself. As such, ephemera which survive from the eighteenth to the twentieth centuries allow us to examine social and cultural aspects of imperial history through the study of original printed material produced throughout the period of the British Empire. Whilst the vast bulk of Empire-related and wider-world-related ephemera was produced after the printing boom of the mid-nineteenth century, it is important to remember that it did exist before then, and that it could still be found even in the distinctly post-imperial late twentieth century.

Patricia Anderson writes of the manner in which the printed image transformed British culture as a 'modern mass culture' developed in the early nineteenth century.[11] Between 1790 and 1860 the widening dissemination of print led to the unprecedented expansion of popular cultural experience, and from the centre of this there emerged a mass culture. The new culture's hallmark was its pictorial character. Illustrated magazines, broadsides and other artefacts played a significant part in the mass dissemination of imagery – as did the range of imagery conveyed in ephemeral items. Indeed, a recurring theme in Anderson's work is the declining role of art reproduction in people's otherwise expanded pictorial experience. John MacKenzie emphasised the link between advances in printing technology, the 'new mass medium of the printed word and the visual image' and the production of ephemera relating to empire, the wider world and Britain's place in it:

> [T]he growth of 'jobbing' printing led to a great increase in the publication of leaflets, pamphlets, booklets, programmes, and other small ephemeral items which could be distributed free as advertising and propaganda or sold for a few pence each. Such material was used by all forms of entertainment, by the exhibitions, the armed forces, and missionary societies. Much of it must indeed have been ephemeral, but some was sufficiently attractive to be collected, and contemporary agencies and advertisers certainly saw these cheap pieces of printed paper as an effective way of purveying their ideas or their wares.[12]

While we acknowledge the importance of the visual in British popular culture relating to empire and the non-European world, and the role of ephemera in delivering visual images, printed ephemera also contained textual information, a fact that should not be overlooked. This could take the form of succinct statements, such as the motif on the Diamond Match Company's 'Empire' matchbox – 'We Hold a Vaster Empire than Has Been'[13] – or references to the imperial landscape and interracial relations, such as the Guinness 'Safari So Good!' advertisement, featuring a pith-helmeted white man and grinning 'native' bearers carrying his supplies.[14] But items of ephemera could contain much lengthier tracts of text. For example, a poster advertising an exhibition on the 'Polar Regions' at the Ducrow's Theatre in Aberdeen in 1833 contained about four hundred words describing the geographical zone in question.[15] The advertisement for a circa 1850 'Diorama of the Ganges', shown at the Portland Gallery, Langham Place, Regent Street, offered copious reviews drawn from the newspapers describing the visions of the Orient that it conjured.[16] Similarly, an 1841 advertisement for a Madame Tussaud's waxwork exhibition depicted Commissioner Lin (known to the public because of the recent opium war) and 'his favourite consort', the pair 'modelled from life with magnificent dresses actually worn by them'. Lin was billed as 'the author of the Chinese war' and 'the Destroyer of £2,500,000 of British property'.[17] As well as presenting a biased British perspective on the nature of the war and the justifications for military intervention, the text below the images provided a lengthy description of Madame Tussaud's work, the specifics of the exhibition, and the manner in which the waxworks had been prepared. It was also quite common for certain items of ephemera to contain pithy snapshots relating to episodes in imperial history. A trade card from about 1910 for Price's Night Lights, for instance, showed a scene from the Battle of Plassey, providing on the reverse side a laconic account of the battle in which it was stated that it was conducted in order to avenge the 'black hole of Calcutta' massacre. The battle, the card claimed, set down the 'foundation of the Empire of England in the East'. This was a typical bite-sized, didactic representation of an episode in the British national and imperial story, inaccurately and uncritically rendered for easy public consumption and purveyed through an item of ephemera.[18]

The John Johnson Collection of Printed Ephemera

The Bodleian Library's John Johnson Collection of Printed Ephemera has been mined on numerous occasions by scholars examining imperial themes.[19] While it pertains to printed ephemera of all kinds and was certainly not intended to reflect imperialism per se, the collection nevertheless contains a range of different types of items that relate, on the one hand, specifically to the British Empire and, on the other, more generally to depictions of the non-European world. Indeed, the fact that a collection which was assembled without any imperial agenda nonetheless yields so much material pertinent to the study of empire reinforces the extent to which an underlying imperial theme pervaded much of the ephemera produced during the period in which the British Empire prevailed. Items include programmes, postcards, tickets, posters, playbills, paper bags, cigarette cards, food labels, shippers' tickets and advertisements. Sometimes representations of imperial events in such material will have been consciously generated in order to market produce or appeal to a certain type of audience, while other references to imperial themes would have been more incidental, almost accidentally expressing some association with empire or projecting an image of non-European people. Either way, such ephemera cannot help but reflect the era in which they were created and, by extension, the society for which they were produced.

The John Johnson Collection was assembled by John de Monins Johnson, Printer to Oxford University from 1925, who began collecting printed ephemera between the wars (continuing to do so until his death in 1956) and who envisaged the collection as 'the museum of what is commonly thrown away ... all the ordinary printed paraphernalia of our day-to-day lives in size from the large broadside to the humble calling card, and varying in splendour from the magnificent invitations to coronations of Kings to the humblest piece of street literature sold for a penny or less'.[20] Collecting ephemera was Johnson's hobby rather than his profession, and while most such collectors were relatively specific with regard to the nature of the material they gathered – be it beer mats or cigarette cards or firework labels, but rarely all three together – Johnson retrospectively collected every conceivable type of ephemeral printing, eventually amassing over a million items. While some material in the collection dates from as long ago as 1508, its strengths are generally acknowledged to lie in the eighteenth, nineteenth and early twentieth centuries, when the British Empire was at its height. And although neither Johnson nor successive custodians of the collection actively sought to select material which was indicative of an imperial theme, it is inevitable that much of the ephemera of this period reflect a perception of Britain as being at the heart of an empire.

While the John Johnson Collection is now recognised as a significant resource for academic research, maintained (and indeed expanded) by one of the world's foremost research libraries since its transfer from Oxford University Press to the Bodleian in 1968, it should be understood that its assembly began as a largely recreational activity. As such, the material in it was not subject to rigorous classification, but was simply divided into categories. There are some seven hundred categories in total, grouped into twenty-two broader themes; 'railways', 'motor cars' and 'airlines' are grouped under 'transport', for example. Even the categories themselves reveal the arbitrary nature of the collection; while many headings refer to subjects, ranging from the general ('museums' or 'authors, various') to the specific ('National Maritime Museum' or 'Du Maurier'), others refer to types of ephemera ('paper bags' or 'receipts'). Each of these categories represents a single box or folder of material, or numerous boxes and folders (five boxes and one folder in the 'colonies' category, for instance, or as many as fifty-two boxes in the 'education' category). Indexes provide a guide to the contents of many of the boxes in the collection (available online in PDF format)[21] and, in many cases, the arrangement of material within them, and a number of digitisation initiatives of varying scale have allowed for online delivery of images for some categories or selections within categories.[22] However, less than 10 per cent of the collection can be searched at item-level in the online catalogue, and so searching is invariably a somewhat serendipitous activity whereby researchers simply order boxes and folders in a given category to the reading room and manually sift through all the material within them.

The current authors' initial approach when conducting research for their 2011 book *Illustrating Empire* was to select some of the boxes most likely to contain relevant material, and to use keyword searches for the parts of the collection that have been digitised. So, of the seven hundred categories, the initial sift targeted thirty-six: 'air', 'airlines', 'banking', 'beer', 'Boy Scouts', 'campaigns and protest groups', 'Canada and East India companies', 'Canada and New Zealand companies', 'cigarette cards', 'cocoa, chocolate, and confectionery', 'colonies', 'exhibitions', 'exhibition catalogues', 'exploration', 'free trade and protection', 'Gladstone', 'harbours, docks, and piers', 'hats', 'Kipling', 'match boxes', 'men's clothes', 'missionary societies', 'monarchy and the House of Lords', 'naval', 'Nelson', 'nigger minstrels', 'postal collection', 'shipping', 'shipping lines', 'slavery', 'soap', 'South Sea Company', 'tea and coffee', 'tobacco', 'travel' and 'war'. These were deemed to be categories likely to have material relating to empire and the non-European world. But this was not exhaustive, and did not reflect a belief that all the other categories would be unlikely to furnish relevant information. What it indicated was the fact that these categories, together with material drawn more widely from the digitised portion of the collection, yielded sufficient material for our publication purposes (*Illustrating Empire* contains around 150 colour images drawn from the collection).

While some categories were regarded as unlikely to provide much or any relevant material – 'Arber and Grosart reprints', for instance, or 'beauty parlour', 'Christmas cards', 'duty stamps' or 'German presses' – the element of 'you never know' was always present (the twenty-two boxes of Christmas cards, for example, might well have revealed a snowy scene from the hill-station of Simla, where enough snow fell for British residents, missing home, to produce traditional seasonal cards showing wintry views of the town and the surrounding Himalayan foothills). Furthermore, there were many other categories which almost certainly would have yielded relevant material but which were not investigated, such as 'Bible societies', 'book jackets', 'burghers', 'cigar bands', 'education', 'Queen Victoria', 'South African War', 'street ballads', 'tourist agencies', 'travel agencies' and 'wireless'.

Types and themes

A far from exhaustive list of some of the different types of printed ephemera contained in the collection offers an impression of the breadth of material encountered by British people which contained references to empire and the non-European world. In the course of a single afternoon's research, the authors handled invitations and menu cards relating to luncheons and dinners such as the inauguration of the Jinja Municipal Council in Uganda in 1956, the Royal Albert Hall banquet for 'His Majesty's Ministers of the Self-Governing Colonies' in 1907 and the inaugural luncheon of the Kipling Society at the Princes Restaurant in Jermyn Street in 1927.[23] We looked at official forms, such as those signed by eighteenth-century recruits to the East India Company's army and those of the Government Emigration Office on Park Street, Westminster, completed by aspiring emigrants in the mid-nineteenth century.[24] There were numerous postcards, such as those produced for Empire Day bearing images of the king and depictions of the 'mother country' and her settler colony 'offspring', as well as unusual examples such as that showing 2,600 Sheffield boys spelling out in 'living letters' the words 'God Bless our Empire'.[25] There were also postcards produced for the 1911 Festival of Empire exhibition at the Crystal Palace and the 1924–25 British Empire Exhibition.[26] Regarding this particular type of ephemera, and the latter exhibition held at Wembley, John MacKenzie writes: 'The production of ephemera of all sorts was staggering in its scope'. More than 150 different official postcards were produced, as well as hundreds more relating to the exhibition produced by commercial companies, as well as large quantities of handbills, leaflets, programmes, maps and posters.[27] MacKenzie contends that the 'democratization of the visual image was undertaken by the postcard and it must be seen as a central element in the ephemera book of the period'.[28]

The John Johnson Collection contains unusual items of ephemera, including a paper bag from a tea dealer in 'Newcastle-on-Tyne' that in the 1850s produced bags bearing images of exotic animals. Animal number three was the elephant, the illustration accompanied by a detailed caption on the life and habits of the beast.[29] A typical discovery in the authors' research for *Illustrating Empire* was an illustrated calendar called 'The Nigerian Year 1938', which featured monthly sketches of Nigerian scenes by Captain R.R. Oakley accompanied by sonnets by C.A Woodhouse, late Resident, Northern Provinces, Lagos.[30] There was also a Christmas souvenir from 1897 in which a verse from 'God Save the Queen' was rendered in fifty different languages spoken within the Empire.[31]

There are many ways of approaching the theme of 'imperial ephemera' because there were numerous *types* of ephemera, and they addressed a variety of *themes* relating to empire and the wider world. To illustrate this, the following subsections examine some of the types of ephemera encountered in the John Johnson Collection (such as bolt labels and food packaging), and some of the Empire-related and wider-world-related themes that they addressed (such as emigration, the veneration of 'heroes' and the representation of non-Europeans as servants or labourers for Europeans). In considering types of ephemera and common themes relating to empire, the section deliberately focuses on a summary sample, rather than providing an in-depth analysis of individual items.

The veneration of prominent figures

Lord Roberts was widely considered to be one of the most successful military figures of the middle to late Victorian period, serving with distinction in Abyssinia, Afghanistan and India as well as in the Transvaal and the Orange Free State during the Second Boer War. His image was adopted as a marketing device for a range of products and used to endorse political and national activities. A political poster showed the map of South Africa shaded British red, the outline of Roberts's face appearing on the map. Under the title 'All Red Now Joey', pictures of Queen Victoria, Joseph Chamberlain (the belligerent Colonial Secretary) and Robert Baden-Powell surround the map.[32] Roberts's face was used by James Fortt of Bath to promote Bath Oliver Biscuits with the byline 'On what does Bobs fight?' (Bobs was a moniker for Roberts used in the British press). Before leaving for South Africa, the Field Marshal had visited his sister in Bath, where he procured some of the biscuits which then accompanied him to South Africa, from where he later sent back for further supplies (see Figures 6.1 and 6.2).[33] Advertisements for Wilson's Horehound beer (or 'stomach tonic' as it was also, rather inventively, described) showed the product next to a picture of Roberts beneath the banner 'Two Great Leaders'. Tom Stedman sold boots with the aid of a puzzle picture in which Roberts holds the enemy by the scruff of the neck, with the caption 'Bobs – Destroy the mines would you? Not this time, sonny' (a reference to potential Boer sabotage of the lucrative South African diamond and gold mines).[34] And Roberts also appeared on a colourful Indian cotton bale label of the late nineteenth century in which various illustrious officers of the army and navy are depicted posing before a flag-bedecked statue of Queen Victoria.[35] Indeed, for a time Roberts's image was used to advertise just about anything: he appeared on a calendar issued by George Blackburn of Halifax, 'Given Away with One Pound 2/- Tea'; on the cover of the sheet music to Theo Bonheur's 'Siege of Ladysmith, Grand Divertimento'; on the lid of 'With Bobs in the Transvaal', the 'Up to Date War Game'; on the tin containing Field's Khaki Toilet Soap; on a commemorative tin bearing the words 'Hilton's Boots are Like Our Generals – Famous for Endurance'; on the packaging for Wills 'United Service' cigarettes; and on a bookmark issued with soap, which bore the legend 'Dr Lovelace's Soap Commands Respect', clearly associating the respect demanded by the soap with that commanded by Lord Roberts.[36]

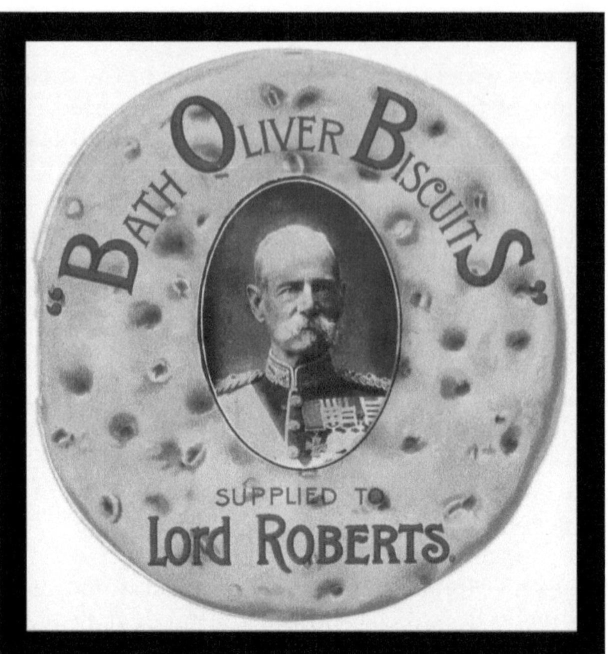

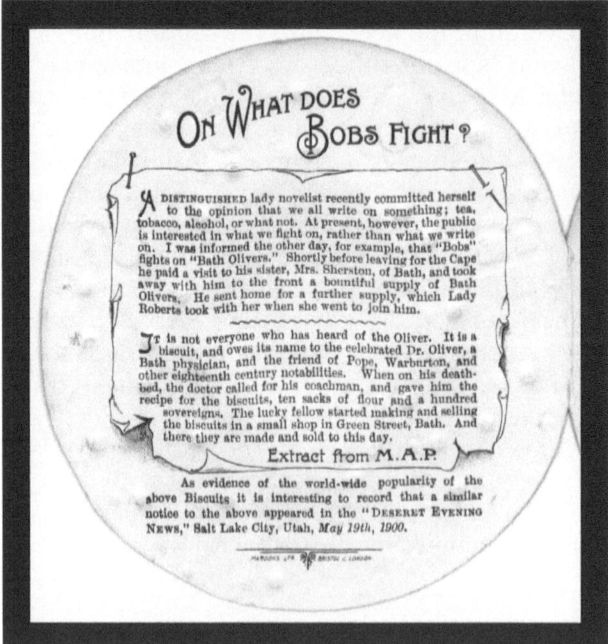
ON WHAT DOES BOBS FIGHT?

A DISTINGUISHED lady novelist recently committed herself to the opinion that we all write on something; tea, tobacco, alcohol, or what not. At present, however, the public is interested in what we fight on, rather than what we write on. I was informed the other day, for example, that "Bobs" fights on "Bath Olivers." Shortly before leaving for the Cape he paid a visit to his sister, Mrs. Sherston, of Bath, and took away with him to the front a bountiful supply of Bath Olivers. He sent home for a further supply, which Lady Roberts took with her when she went to join him.

IT is not everyone who has heard of the Oliver. It is a biscuit, and owes its name to the celebrated Dr. Oliver, a Bath physician, and the friend of Pope, Warburton, and other eighteenth century notabilities. When on his death-bed, the doctor called for his coachman, and gave him the recipe for the biscuits, ten sacks of flour and a hundred sovereigns. The lucky fellow started making and selling the biscuits in a small shop in Green Street, Bath. And there they are made and sold to this day.

Extract from M.A.P.

As evidence of the world-wide popularity of the above Biscuits it is interesting to record that a similar notice to the above appeared in the "DESERET EVENING NEWS," Salt Lake City, Utah, *May 19th, 1900.*

Figures 6.1 & 6.2 'Bath Oliver Biscuits supplied to Lord Roberts'

Bolt labels

Bale labels, also known as bolt labels or shippers' tickets, were attached to the ends of cotton bolts exported from British mills around the world. One of the earliest references to the labelling of cloth is mentioned in Wadsworth and De Lacy Mann's *The Cotton Trade and Industrial Lancashire, 1600–1780*.[37] Describing the textile trade with Africa in the late seventeenth century, the authors talk of fabric 'packed in a stiff paper cover with a gaudy picture of an elephant, the device of the Royal Africa Company on the outside'.[38] Adrian Wilson writes that the labels were used 'on the "faceplate" (front) of fabric pieces sent around the world. They were used in conjunction with water soluble ink trade-marks to identify the brand, type and length of fabric in the piece.'[39]

Each label was designed specifically for the market to which it was sent. The ticket was supposed to catch the eye of the purchaser, and often employed various symbols which today can be baffling at first glance.[40] Colour coding and recognisable symbols were a part of the bolt label design, signalling details about the product to the Oriental merchants at whom the labels were often targeted, and 'the florid and often exuberant and exaggerated designs [were] frequently responsible for the sale of the fabrics, particularly in the Bazaars of India, China and Japan where the colour scheme is of supreme importance'.[41]

Sria Chatterjee used an example of a bolt label produced at the beginning of the twentieth century to suggest that such ephemera represent the locus of colonial experience. She described a label, framed at each corner by the crown of St Edward, depicting an Indian elephant being hoisted on to a naval ship and destined for the Regent's Park Zoological Gardens in London, one of four such 'gifts' to the Prince of Wales (and heir to the throne – the words 'For the King' are spelt out retroactively on the elephant's harness) following his 1875–76 state visit to India (see Figure 6.3).[42] Interpreting the elephant as a symbol of both a wild, untamed India and Royal Imperial India, and identifying the naval ship as a signifier of both military protection and military possession, she argues:

> This illustrated description becomes the coloniser's construct of truth, or what I would like to term 'an imagined reality'... [and] that the cotton bale label, read in the context of colonial advertising, becomes a tool that furthered this construct by selling to the viewer-consumer not only the commodity but also the culture of Imperialism.[43]

Chatterjee further suggests that 'in the context of the printed image in Victorian and early Edwardian Britain, there emerges a visual rhetoric, drawing from a similarly constructed visual vocabulary, resulting in ... a British Imperial iconography'.[44]

Emigration

Another distinct and sizeable category, scattered throughout the John Johnson Collection, comprises material related to the emigration of Britons to the settler colonies. Within this category, there are numerous journals and newsletters relating to the business of emigration, with titles including the *British and Colonial Traveller*, *The British Emigrant*, *The Empire Review*, *The Imperial Colonist*, *The Imperial and Colonial Magazine and Review*, *Britannia: A Monthly Magazine for the Promotion of the Closer Union between Home Country and Colonies*, the pamphlets and magazine advertisements of the *British Women's Emigration Association* and a handbook for

Figure 6.3 'Bale label with illustration of an Indian elephant being hoisted onto a naval ship'

would-be emigrants published by a shipping line.[45]

In a slightly different direction, in 1823 a new monthly journal was launched called *Oriental Herald and Colonial Advocate*. Its 'mission statement' reflected contemporary beliefs in the 'civilising mission' and faith in the capacity of Western science and technology to improve the world, the journal's purpose being the maintenance of

> A constant interchange of useful and interesting Communications between Great Britain and her Eastern and Western Dependencies; for encouraging throughout Europe every effort towards ameliorating the condition of British India in particular, and the colonies in Asia, Africa, and America, in general; – and for diffusing over every portion of those distant lands, the lights of British science and intelligence, by the powerful influence of which, the ends of the earth may be united in the bonds of mutual benefit, and learn to cultivate together the arts of industry and peace.[46]

The John Johnson Collection also contains numerous one-off items relating to emigration, including political tracts and posters (such as an early nineteenth-century example warning of the 'horrors' of emigration) and cartoons (including a satirical print showing African women being imported to make up for the emigration of British women).[47] There were then numerous pamphlets published by colonial and dominion governments, including Manitoba, New Zealand and Southern Rhodesia, attempting to attract and inform would-be migrants from the 'mother country'.

Indigenes as servants, labourers and producers

An example of a common theme encountered in ephemeral material is that of the native porter, servant or labourer and the white leader or overseer. This type of image was often used in printed ephemera and can only have reinforced, in the minds of some people at least, impressions of white superiority and dominance and non-white inferiority and servility.[48] Ramamurthy notes that one of the main perspectives employed by scholars in analysing images such as those under consideration here has been *stereotyping*, a form of representation that 'essentialises, naturalises, and fixes difference [and] ... operates effectively through a general level of consent'.[49] Stereotyping through advertising reinforced, and was reinforced by, 'unthinking Eurocentrism'.[50] It was reflected in countless colonial-era images showing non-Europeans involved in the process of collecting raw materials that had become part of Western consumer culture, such as cocoa, palm-oil products, tea and tobacco, or acting as servants and porters. Europeans, meanwhile, were universally portrayed in superior roles, often quite subtly. But the significance and power of such images, Ramamurthy argues, went beyond 'merely' stereotyping. They were also part of the process of the *production* of definitions, not simply reflective of pre-existing ideas: 'In the late nineteenth and early twentieth centuries colonialism provided a political logic for capitalism and almost all of the images of black people in advertising gave expression to the ways in which we [non-white people] were dehumanised, diminished and naturalised as servants and inferior beings.'[51] She observes that visual imagery in advertising was 'a new and powerful weapon with which to express a company's outlook on the world'.[52] In advertisements for colonial-produced consumer goods, 'black representations were employed more strategically ... to represent company interests in specific colonial ideologies and policies'.[53] By the late nineteenth century, for example,

> It was not just the exoticism of black people and their skin which was depicted in cocoa advertisements and images. A dominant image of Africans on cocoa and other advertising during this period was of labourers working tropical plantations, producing raw materials for European consumption.[54]

These advertisements almost universally conveyed the idea of abundant natural produce, of the willing participation of non-European people in harvesting it, and the beneficence of European and non-European relationships. Western technological superiority and industrial and economic progress were seen to have a role in 'civilising' the natives.

Images such as these displayed surprising longevity, from early modern woodcuts to twenty-first-century advertisements for tea. A woodcut from around 1700, used as a package label for Virginian tobacco, showed settlers seated at their ease around a table, drinking and smoking pipes, while African slaves laboured in the tobacco field behind them. A cotton bolt label from the early nineteenth century bears the words 'Mofussil Court Ticket' ('mofussil' being a contemporary word used to describe rural regions of India beyond the presidency settlements of Bombay, Calcutta and Madras). It shows a European magistrate at a large desk, Indian court clerks at lower desks arranged around the European's desk, Indian guards for an Indian prisoner and an Indian punkah-wallah standing behind the European official.[55] This type of image also appeared on food labels, such as 'Penang-Pineapple', a tinned product from the late nineteenth century which bore on its label two pictures, one showing native people harvesting pineapples on a neat plantation in the tropics, the other showing two elegantly attired women in a European drawing room enjoying the fruit at table, the fruit prominently displayed on a pineapple pedestal (see

Figure 6.4 'Swan Brand Penang-Pineapple'

Figure 6.4).[56] An Edwardian-era advertisement for Colman's Starch showed a European man and woman at leisure on the deck of a ship and dressed in resplendent white garments, greeting a non-European woman and her child as they walk past carrying a large basket full of white garments that have been laundered and are about to be starched.[57]

Advertisements for lime cordial and cocoa showed native peoples harvesting the crops, often supervised by a white figure and juxtaposing a background of tropical vegetation with the neat lines of a modern processing plant. Indigenous people were associated with labour and production for European consumers, in an ordered yet still exotic environment. Advertisements for Lipton's cocoa and a variety of soft drinks or products such as Black & White whisky all showed images of indigenous people labouring under white supervision or serving Europeans. A series of advertisements for Huntley & Palmer biscuits depicted various imperial themes, including 'Stanley's Expedition to Relieve Emin Pasha', which showed African porters carrying head loads (including boxes of the advertised product) across a river, with Stanley standing on the foreground bank in a supervisory capacity, hand on hip, and a fellow European performing the same role on the far bank.[58] Another advertisement in this series, 'An Ascent of the Himalayas', showed tweed-clad Europeans on the ascent with uniformed native porters carrying the precious biscuits. 'India – Fort on the Indus' showed Indians unloading boxes of Huntley & Palmer biscuits from an elephant, supervised by a European checking off the delivered goods in a log book (see Figure 6.5).[59]

Collectable items were sometimes issued with particular products, such as Cadbury's trade cards, and these often depicted similar scenes of native porterage or service to Europeans. A Cadbury series on transport issued in the 1930s showed aircraft, trains and motor cars, with Africans making an appearance as porters bearing head loads in the

Figure 6.5 'India – fort on the Indus'

Gold Coast.[60] The drawing for the month of June in the 'Nigerian Year' calendar for 1938 showed a mounted European wearing a pith-helmet followed by three Africans on foot, two of them bearing head loads containing bottles and a bedroll.[61]

Consumer branding

Labels and advertisements for food and consumer goods often bore images and text relating to the Empire and the wider world. These included labels for Indian curry powder, Stower's lime cordial, Bovril, Mogul or real 'chetna' sauce produced by John Burgess of the Strand, bearing an image of a turbaned Asian male, 'genuine Indian arrowroot' showing an 'Oriental' scene, and 'Pride of Empire' sliced peaches bearing the Union Jack and the flag of Australia. Colman's starch advertisements featured a whole series of images of the Prince of Wales's visit to India and Ceylon in the mid-1870s, depicting him tiger-hunting, investing Indian princes with knighthoods and companionships from the Star of India order of chivalry, and holding a durbar. Indeed, Indian themes were very popular; Johnston's corn flour employed images of

Figure 6.6 'Australia in London'

Indian cavalry soldiers on its advertisements and labels in the 1890s, as did the collectable cards issued with Pascall's mints in the interwar years.[62] Images of uniformed native troops were relatively common in this form of material (including a John Player cigarette card series of 1938 entitled 'Military Uniforms of the British Empire Overseas'). The 'loyal' native was a favourite imperial trope, suggestive of British imperial strength and the willing submissiveness of the Empire's subject peoples, while uniformed native troops also conveyed an impression of imperial splendour.

The manufacturers of Bovril were inveterate employers of imperial and imperial-military themes in their product advertisements.[63] So too were medicinal companies: a popular cough mixture label depicted British soldiers in South Africa under the banner 'Our Defenders', Dr Rooke's 'Oriental Pills and Solar Elixir' showed a caravan of balsam merchants 'of the oriental regions', while a brand of 'cure-all bile beans' displayed their Australian origin through a far-fetched picture of Parliament Square and the Houses of Parliament beset by gum trees and wallabies (see Figure 6.6).[64]

Affirming a British world

Ephemeral material could affirm the existence of a distinctly British world and British possession of overseas territories and produce. Two ways in which this occurred were the use of words and the use of maps. Words such as 'empire', 'imperial' and 'colonial' were regularly used, particularly in advertising. There was, for example, Ogden's St Julien Empire Blend tobacco and Three Nuns Empire Blend tobacco. In a pamphlet on how to make coffee, consumers were exhorted to use Indian coffee which was 'Empire Grown'.[65] The fruiterer E.T. Moore, whose business was based at Empire House, Ripston, printed the words 'Finest English and Colonial Fruit' on his paper bags (see Figure 6.7).[66] The appeal to imperial sentiment, or reference to imperial ties, was deliberately employed and suggests a widespread public awareness. Emu Wines, for instance, offered a 'testing cabinet', a sampler selection of the company's wares. 'This invitation', their publicity leaflets claimed, 'is made to help Empire Trade.' Mundane items, such as blank postcards, could contain such references – a packet of 'Ten British Empire Three-penny Postcards', for instance.[67] So, too, could material more specifically targeted, such as the New Zealand Meat Producers Board's lamb recipe card, which labelled New Zealand as 'The Empire's Sunny Sheep Farm'.[68] The word 'Empire', or the term 'British Empire', were often employed because of their association with the stability that the British Empire was widely thought to generate and epitomise, or because of a desire to invoke patriotic sentiment, or both. It also seems possible to conclude that the word and the term were used by some companies or government agencies (such as the Empire Marketing Board) to encourage the British people to regard the Empire as a mutually interdependent economic community.[69]

Maps were also an important form of representing the British Empire and illustrating themes connected to empire and the wider world, and of creating the impression of a distinctly British world.

In particular, they contributed to proprietorial attitudes towards colonised spaces and the ownership of sources of supply. In 1934, for instance, the Ceylon Tea Propaganda Board published a colour map of Ceylon, 'showing its tea industry'.[70] In the same decade, the Coffee Board of Kenya produced a brochure entitled 'Kenya Coffee and How to Make It' (see Figure 6.8).[71] One of its pages showed a map of the British Isles and the African continent. Under the heading 'From one country to another', a direct line joined the East African colony of Kenya with Britain. An advertisement in the *Investor's Chronicle* of 1953 showed businessmen in a London office, the office window looking out on to Trafalgar Square. On the wall hung a map of Malaya and Singapore, which the men were studying, one indicating the peninsula with a pointing stick.[72]

Figure 6.7 'E. T. Moore, fruiterer, &c.'

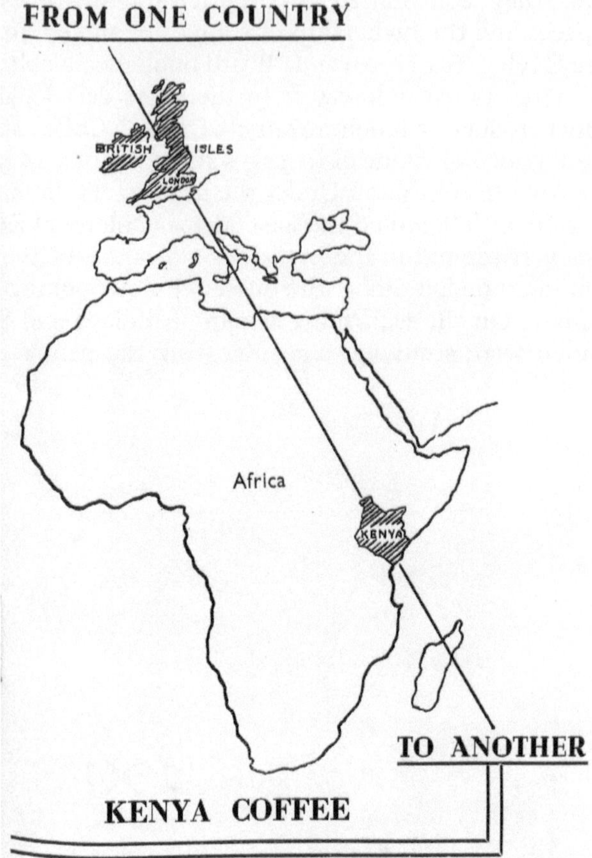

Figure 6.8 Inside page from 'Kenya Coffee and how to make it'

Conclusion

Ephemera fostered a sense of the existence of a British world, from the iconic map shaded in red to the 'Empire Christmas Pudding' showing ingredients drawn from British colonies, and advertisements connecting British people with distant places.[73] A magazine advertisement for Barneys tobacco, for instance, proclaimed that 'From Croydon to the Cape, across India to Port Darwin: Along the Air Routes of the Empire Barneys is Always Factory-Fresh'. The advertisement featured a pilot 'spontaneously' attesting to the tobacco's vaunted 'EverFreshness' under 'almost every condition of climate – from the arid dryness of the African deserts to the steaming heat of Singapore'.[74] A British Industries Fair leaflet for a trade fair at London's Olympia in 1935 showed an aerial picture of London with a heart-shaped inset containing a Caribbean scene, the title reading 'Visit Jamaica in the Heart of London'.[75]

This material enhanced public awareness of the British Empire, of the non-European world, and of the relationships between European and non-European people. It sharpened the identity of Britons vis-à-vis non-Britons, supported common assumptions about the 'civilising mission' and increased awareness of the non-European origins of a range of consumer products that British people had become dependent upon and to which, by virtue of the Empire, they enjoyed proprietorial rights, just as they did to the labour that acquired them.

Aligning this chapter with themes addressed in this volume's introduction and John MacKenzie's chapter on Delhi durbars, it is clear that ephemera were an important variable in the construction and operation of the 'imperial archive'. Ephemera were significant media in the 'exhibition' of imperial and wider world themes, impinging on the lives and imaginations of millions of people. They reinforced key imperial ideas and fantastical notions, such as the beneficence of British influence and presence overseas and the popular acceptance of British cultural and racial superiority. Empire-related and wider-world-related ephemeral material widened and deepened prevailing imperial ideas and ways of seeing the world, such as the fantasy of an ordered British world, of global governance, of a universal and omnipresent monarchy, and of the inevitability and moral appropriateness of British rule. Ephemeral items often featured the 'exotic', the allure of travel and adventure, representatives of the imperial state, and reinforced a worldview heavily shaped by British proprietorship and non-European servility.

As is well known, making assumptions about what people thought of the images and the ideas they potentially conveyed is difficult. Partially for this reason, we are careful to talk about ideas relating to empire *and* the non-European world, for while some images might directly convey a message about the British Empire or British superiority, others might convey nothing more than basic information about the flora and fauna found in overseas countries, or the impression that foreign people dressed differently. Nevertheless, cultural norms and depictions are powerful influences upon the way in which people construct a view of the world around them. They were able, for example, to make some colonial peoples feel that they were culturally British in certain ways. Conversely, as late as the 1970s, golliwogs on the labels of jam jars and the branding of aniseed-flavoured chews (together with television shows and racist jokes widely considered to be acceptable) continued to act as powerful conveyors of ideas (and contributors to constructions) of whiteness and its antithesis.[76] Ephemera are a form of 'cultural display' and therefore a reflection of, or hangover from, the imperial culture which produced them. As Graham Hudson maintains, ephemera, 'produced to meet the needs of the passing day', are 'wholly part of the culture in which they are created'.[77] And the culture which produced much of the ephemera of the last three centuries was undeniably imperial.

Notes

1 John M. MacKenzie, *Propaganda and Empire: The Manipulation of British Public Opinion, 1880–1960* (Manchester: Manchester University Press, 1984).

2 Maurice Rickards, *The Encyclopaedia of Ephemera: A Guide to the Fragmentary Documents of Everyday Life for the Collector, Curator and Historian* (London: British Library, 2000).

3 Maurice Rickards, *Collecting Printed Ephemera* (Oxford: Phaidon, 1988), p. 7.

4 Marina Warner, 'Imagining the Orient', Writers' Responses, The John Johnson Collection: An Archive of Printed Ephemera, 2009, at http://johnjohnson.chadwyck.co.uk/search/displayEssayByID.do?ItemID=66666666666666mw (accessed 15 August 2013).

5 The Robert Opie Collection is an interesting example of a large body of such material which was compiled by a 'private' collector but which fulfils a 'public' role through its display at the Museum of Brands, Packaging and Advertising in London's Notting Hill. See www.robertopiecollection.com/Application/corporate/about3GB.asp (accessed 1 October 2013).

6 Patrick Hickman Robertson, 'Obituary: Maurice Rickards', *The Independent*, 20 February 1998, at www.independent.co.uk/news/obituaries/obituary-maurice-rickards-1145817.html (accessed 15 August 2013).

7 See www.reading.ac.uk/typography/research/typ-researchcentres.aspx (accessed 15 August 2013).

8 University of Reading, Centre for Ephemera Studies, *Register of Ephemera Collections in the United Kingdom: Excluding Those in the Major National Institutions and Others Not Normally Available to the Public* (Reading: University of Reading, 2003).

9 Carlo Ginzburg, '"Your Country Needs You": A Case Study in Political Iconography', *History Workshop Journal* 52 (2001), p. 1, quoting Raphael Samuel's 'Theatres of Memory'.

10 Anandi Ramamurthy, *Imperial Persuaders: Images of Africa and Asia in British Advertising* (Manchester: Manchester University Press, 2003), p. 1.

11 Patricia Anderson, *The Printed Image and the Transformation of Popular Culture, 1790–1860* (Oxford: Clarendon Press, 1994).

12 MacKenzie, *Propaganda and Empire*, p. 19.

13 Bodleian Library, University of Oxford: John Johnson Collection: Labels, 12 (30a).

14 The Guinness advertisement shows a European wearing a pith-helmet, on top of which is a can of the product, and with a rifle slung over his shoulder. Walking behind him are three African porters, each carrying a case of Guinness on his head. See Ashley Jackson, *Mad Dogs and Englishmen: A Grand Tour of the British Empire at Its Height* (London: Quercus, 2009), p. 190.

15 Bodleian Library, University of Oxford: John Johnson Collection: Exploration box.

16 Bodleian Library, University of Oxford: John Johnson Collection: Dioramas 1 (16).

17 Bodleian Library, University of Oxford: John Johnson Collection: Waxworks 1 (55).

18 Bodleian Library, University of Oxford: John Johnson Collection: Oil and Candles 1 (84).

19 The current authors' work has been based on the John Johnson Collection, leading to the publications *Illustrating Empire: A Visual History of British Imperialism*

(Oxford: Bodleian Library, 2011), and 'Branding Empire: Imperial Associations in British Advertising', *Bodleian Library Record* 25 (2012). Most, though not all, of the images discussed in this chapter are drawn from the John Johnson Collection. Other authors who have used the collection while pursuing research on aspects of the representation of imperial themes in British culture include Ramamurthy in *Imperial Persuaders*. On the same theme, see also David Ciarlo, *Advertising Empire: Race and Visual Culture in Imperial Germany* (Cambridge, MA: Harvard University Press, 2011).

20 Charles Batey, 'Johnson, John de Monins (1882–1956)', rev. Julie Anne Lambert, *Oxford Dictionary of National Biography*, Oxford University Press (2004), www.oxforddnb.com/view/article/34203 (accessed 14 August 2014).

21 See www.bodleian.ox.ac.uk/johnson/search/indexes (accessed 14 August 2014)

22 Parts of the collection have been digitised (see www.bodleian.ox.ac.uk/johnson). The online collection contains 9,000 images, a 2007–09 collaborative JISC-funded project resulted in around 175,000 images, and in the mid-1990s the Toyota City Imaging Project digitised motoring material in the collection and 1,000 samples from other transport-related boxes and folders.

23 Bodleian Library, University of Oxford: John Johnson Collection: Empire and Colonies Box 5; Empire and Colonies Box 2; Kipling (Rudyard) Box.

24 Bodleian Library, University of Oxford: John Johnson Collection: East India Company Box 1.

25 Bodleian Library, University of Oxford: John Johnson Collection: John Fraser Collection: GB (3).

26 Bodleian Library, University of Oxford: John Johnson Collection: Exhibition Catalogues Box 20; Bodleian Library, University of Oxford: John Johnson Collection: Postcards.

27 MacKenzie, *Propaganda and Empire*, p. 109.

28 Ibid., p. 21.

29 Bodleian Library, University of Oxford: John Johnson Collection: Paper Bags 1 (6).

30 Bodleian Library, University of Oxford: John Johnson Collection: Empire and Colonies Box 4.

31 Bodleian Library, University of Oxford: John Johnson Collection: Ceremonial Box 3.

32 Bodleian Library, University of Oxford: John Johnson Collection: Empire and Colonies Folder.

33 Bodleian Library, University of Oxford: John Johnson Collection: Food 5 (51).

34 Bodleian Library, University of Oxford: John Johnson Collection: Boots and Shoes 1 (24).

35 Bodleian Library, University of Oxford: John Johnson Collection: Labels 17 (20).

36 Most of these items are illustrated in Robert Opie, *Remember When: A Nostalgic Trip through the Consumer Era* (London: Bounty Books, 2006), while the final two items appear in Robert Opie, *Rule Britannia: Trading on the British Image* (London: Viking, 1985).

37 Alfred Wadsworth and Julia De Lacy Mann, *The Cotton Trade and Industrial Lancashire, 1600–1780* (Manchester: Manchester University Press, 1931).

38 Ken Gibb, 'Exporting the Empire: Labels of the British Cotton Trade', Curator's Choice: Selections from the John Johnson Collection of Printed Ephemera, 2009, at http://johnjohnson.wordpress.com/2009/04/30/exporting-to-the-empire-labels-of-the-cotton-trade/ (accessed 15 August 2013).

39 See Adrian Wilson's bale labels website: www.textiletrademarks.com/ (accessed 15 August 2013).

40 See www.boltonmuseums.org.uk/collections/local-history/work-and-industry/bleaching/ (accessed 15 August 2013).

41 On 18 January 1928, the Chadwick Museum curator Thomas Midgley, who was seeking to add bolt labels to the museum's collection, received this reply from someone he had contacted for advice. See 'Bleaching – Bolt Stamps and Labels', Bolton Museum and Archive Service, www.boltonmuseums.org.uk/collections/local-history/work-and-industry/bleaching/ (accessed 15 August 2013).

42 Oxford, Bodleian Library, John Johnson Collection of Printed Ephemera, Labels 17 (10). This retroactive use of the word 'king' is interesting and occurs elsewhere: Colman's starch advertisements from around 1900 (see 'food labels' section) also referred to 'the king' – tiger hunting or conferring honours or holding a durbar – even though at the time depicted (1875–76) he was not king but Prince of Wales. It is likely that the companies involved thought it respectful to do this.

43 Sria Chatterjee, 'Empire for Sale: A Nineteenth-Century Cotton Bale Label in the John Johnson Collection of Printed Ephemera', extended essay for BA History of Art, University of Oxford, 2010, p. 3.

44 Ibid., p. 15.

45 Bodleian Library, University of Oxford: John Johnson Collection: Travel Box; Emigration Box 1; Prospectuses of Journals Boxes.

46 Bodleian Library, University of Oxford: John Johnson Collection: Prospectuses of Journals 40 (32a).

47 Bodleian Library, University of Oxford: John Johnson Collection: Emigration Box 1 and Emigration folder.

48 There were other contributory factors responsible for creating a socio-cultural milieu in which it was possible for British people to feel superior to 'foreigners' of various stripes, and to believe that the British were an elect nation with a duty to enlighten the world and to shoulder the burden of governing much of it. The music of George Frideric Handel (a naturalised Briton), for example, reflected the growing national and imperial pride and pomposity of eighteenth-century Britain.

49 Ramamurthy, *Imperial Persuaders*, p. 6.

50 Ibid., p. 8.

51 Ibid., p. 214.

52 Ibid., p. 215.

53 Ibid., p. 9.

54 Ibid., p. 65.

55 See Adrian Wilson's bale labels website: www.textiletrademarks.com/ (accessed 15 August 2013).

56 Bodleian Library, University of Oxford: John Johnson Collection: Labels 5 (103). Pineapple dishes and pedestals, manufactured from silver or ceramic by companies such as Spode, were a distinct type of tableware produced in the nineteenth century. They indicated the luxury status of pineapples, which were often consumed in order to display wealth.

57 Opie, *Remember When*, p. 31.

58 We use the word 'European' here (and throughout the text) to mean a person of European descent, thereby encompassing, for example, Americans or Australians. Henry Morton Stanley is a case in point: born in Wales, he moved to America when he was eighteen and was regarded as Anglo-American. In the image under discussion here, Stanley is flanked by both the Union Flag and the Stars and Stripes.

59 Bodleian Library, University of Oxford: John Johnson Collection: Food 5 (71a, 71b, and 72c).

60 Bodleian Library, University of Oxford: John Johnson Collection: M. L. Horn Collection, Transport album 3.

61 Oxford, Bodleian Library, University of Oxford: John Johnson Collection: Empire and Colonies Box 4.

62 Bodleian Library, University of Oxford: John Johnson Collection: Cocoa, Chocolate and Confectionery 4 (10e); Food 4 (16).

63 Two of Bovril's imperial-military advertisements are examined and reproduced in Jackson and Tomkins, 'Branding Empire'. Another Bovril advertisement used the map boundaries of dozens of British colonies to spell the word 'Bovril'. Associating the product with British patriotism, monarchy, and the military was also a common Bovril tactic. One advert had the product name spelled out in Union Flag letters and bore the legend 'By Royal Warrant to the King'; a showcard of 1903 showed naval ratings being served Bovril on board a warship, 'splicing the main brace' with the beef drink rather than the usual rum tot. For these last two, see Opie, *Rule*

Britannia, pp. 52 and 59. Other Bovril advertisements showed John Bull dispensing the drink to people representing the Empire's multi-ethnic population, and a Boer War soldier opening cases of Bovril above the legend 'A factor in our Empire's strength'.

64 Bodleian Library, University of Oxford: John Johnson Collection: Patent Medicines 12 (3a); Patent Medicines 8 (24).

65 Bodleian Library, University of Oxford: John Johnson Collection: Tea and Coffee 6 (23a).

66 Bodleian Library, University of Oxford: John Johnson Collection: Paper Bags 4 (23).

67 Bodleian Library, University of Oxford: John Johnson Collection: Labels 15 (101c).

68 Bodleian Library, University of Oxford: John Johnson Collection: Food 11 (15a).

69 For the Empire Marketing Board, see Stephen Constantine, *Buy and Build: The Advertising Posters of the Empire Marketing Board* (London: HMSO, 1986), and Stephen Constantine, 'Bringing the Empire Alive: The Empire Marketing Board and Imperial Propaganda', in John M. MacKenzie (ed.), *Imperialism and Popular Culture* (Manchester: Manchester University Press, 1986), pp. 192–231.

70 Bodleian Library, University of Oxford: John Johnson Collection: Tea and Coffee 5 (37).

71 Bodleian Library, University of Oxford: John Johnson Collection: Tea and Coffee 6 (24a).

72 Bodleian Library, University of Oxford: John Johnson Collection: Empire and Colonies Box 1.

73 See Jackson, *Mad Dogs and Englishmen*, p. 170.

74 Bodleian Library, University of Oxford: John Johnson Collection: Empire and Colonies Box 1.

75 Bodleian Library, University of Oxford: John Johnson Collection: Exhibition Catalogues Box 24.

76 See Bill Schwartz, *The White Man's World* (Oxford: Oxford University Press, 2011).

77 Graham Hudson, *The Design and Printing of Ephemera in Britain and America, 1720–1920* (London: British Library, 2008), p. 7.

The authors have deposited colour versions of the images presented in this chapter in the Oxford Research Archive for Data (ORA-Data) with the following DOI: http://dx.doi.org/10.5287/bodleian:xp68kg235

Exhibiting the Empire in print: The press, the publishing world and the promotion of 'Greater Britain'

Berny Sèbe

How were imperial themes exhibited in the rapidly expanding printed output of the nineteenth and early twentieth centuries? At a time when the Industrial Revolution allowed the mass media to reach an ever-expanding reading public, the place of the Empire in the printed material offered to the British market is a key indicator of the extent to which an 'imperial mindset' developed over the period, against the backdrop of a renewed steeplechase for colonies which pitted European powers against each other.[1]

The presence of imperial material in the publishing output generated as a result of the technical improvements brought about by the Industrial Revolution has been noted from a qualitative perspective, but rarely has it been approached from a quantitative angle. This is the approach which this chapter intends to develop, in order to establish the extent to which books played the role of a 'shop window' of British imperial feelings at home, offering a glossy perspective on the Empire to an increasing number of consumers. It has been noted quite rightly that 'the coming of the book, and its subsequent spread to mass markets, has brought entertainment, education, political change, and spiritual or intellectual development to millions of people over the centuries'.[2] The purpose of this chapter is to evaluate how the Empire featured in this movement, as it accompanied the development of the British nation, and its expression in public opinion at a time when popular sentiment became more important than ever. The conjunction of 'print-capitalism' and 'banal nationalism' had an unprecedented effect on nation building over the period, and the hypothesis of the present work is that it had an impact on popular attachment to the Empire too.[3] What role did authors, publishers and, naturally, their books, play in the development of what this chapter calls 'imperialism in print'?

Front covers, illustrations and the contents of the books themselves were all key elements in familiarising the British public with territories which became part of the British Empire, popularising at the same time the imperial idea.[4] Traditional book history projects have placed the emphasis on the publishing of major authors, such as Charles Kingsley, Alfred Tennyson or Thomas Hardy in the case of Macmillan, for instance, but they have rarely analysed the place of imperial material in the ever-growing output of the period.[5] Either such material did not exist or it has not been looked at. Based on the latter hypothesis, this chapter investigates the evolution of levels of popularity of the imperial idea in British publishing: it considers the extent to which books about the Empire were present in major publishers' catalogues, and whether they were successful (and if so, whether there was a specific period when they proved more popular).

Sociologists have argued that book production is one of the fields where power relations are at play and ideological struggles operate.[6] I intend to analyse the power of the imperial idea as it appeared in books, but I will also seek to establish whether books which conveyed this idea found buyers, since the economics of cultural production should not be overlooked. We can reasonably infer that book buyers read their purchases, or allowed someone else to read them, and therefore the success of any given title led to a greater spread of the ideas contained in it. Besides, with the development of lending libraries (sometimes thanks to philanthropic initiatives or clubs), up to several thousands of copies were actually read by dozens of people or more throughout their lifetime.

Though books and the periodical press (i.e. serials) could be studied together to give an overview of 'imperialism in print' in the largest possible sense, books have been used as the main source of information for the purpose of this predominantly quantitative study, on the grounds that serials usually featured more than one article, and it is therefore more difficult to ascertain exactly the origin of a sale performance.[7] By contrast, book print runs allow historians to establish confidently the popularity of the 'imperial mindset', in a way that newspapers or magazines, dealing with a variety of topics as they did, were clearly unable to match. In addition, reactions to imperialism have often been analysed through the press, but much more rarely through books.[8] Thus a study of working-class reactions to the South African war dedicated a lot of space to newspapers but hardly considered the case of books: in spite of an entire chapter on working-class clubs, it did not consider whether they had libraries, and if so which books populated them.[9] Through an examination of the place of empire books in British publishing output, this chapter redresses the imbalance between publishing and the press, and shows how the former was decisive in forging an imperial mindset in the nineteenth and twentieth centuries. It will do so by considering three major aspects dealt with by books published in the period: the 'imperial geographies', the 'imperial ethos' and the exhibition of the Empire in imperial territories through subsidiaries of major metropolitan publishers.

Imperial geographies

Possessing an empire appears as much about controlling populations as about knowing and administering territories. Awareness and familiarity with the geographical realities of spaces which were, or were about to become, parts of the Empire was an important aspect of the exhibition of empire.[10] This section will consider, in turn, books tackling exploration, atlases and travel guides which represent three modalities in the making of 'imperial geographies' which it may be argued placed the Empire in a privileged position in the British publishing output of the time.

The role of geography in acculturating British minds to the Empire took many shapes, ranging from fostering greater familiarity with far-flung territories to a vested interest in a set of issues (such as slavery) paving the way for formal conquest, advocated as a way of undertaking a much-glamorised 'civilising mission'. Such a role was rendered easier because the topic itself proved to be a popular one from the early nineteenth century: the category 'Geography, travel, history and biography' accounted for 17.3 per cent of titles of the *Bibliotheca Londinensis*, an index of books published in Britain between 1814 and 1846 (surpassed only by religion in the same period: 20.3 per cent). It remained popular throughout the century, with 12.4 per cent between 1870 and 1879 (suffering only relatively from the sharp rise of juvenile literature at the time).[11]

Some of these books endeavoured to describe territories of the British Empire minutely, such as William Hughes's *The Australian Colonies: Their Origin and Present Condition* (1852), which offered an exhaustive historical, geographical, geological, economic and human account of this island-continent. Though it was not a bestseller, it maintained a steady turnover with more than 3,000 copies of each of the two volumes sold in the year following their release, at a time when the average print run of a title at a major publishing house like Macmillan oscillated around 800 copies.[12]

The purely descriptive approach of Hughes's book was not likely to attract exceptionally wide readership. By contrast, books with a geographical angle associated with a humanitarian cause proved much more appealing to the general public. This was particularly true of the cause of anti-slavery in the early to mid-nineteenth century. It has been argued that the relationship between Britain and Africa was changed as a result of the abolition of the slave trade in 1807, because it validated another paradigm which bestowed a humanitarian duty upon Britain.[13] Though it was not openly imperial in intent, this duty carried heavily patriotic content which started to shape the British imagination and prepare it for actual conquests, or for the continued tutelage which the British Empire implemented around the world.[14] Such an ethos appeared clearly in the opening paragraphs of a collection of poems published in 1810 by James Montgomery under the title *West Indies*, which was a bestseller of the time with 7,750 copies printed between July 1810 and January 1828 (1,443 of which found buyers in the first five months following the book's launch) – an exceptional figure at a time when print runs were more likely to be in the hundreds:[15]

> 'Thy chains are broken, Africa, be free!'
> Thus saith the island-empress of the sea;
> Thus said Britannia. – O, ye winds and waves!
> Waft the glad tidings to the land of slaves;
> Proclaim on Guinea's coast, by Gambia's side,
> And far as Niger rolls his eastern tide,
> Through radiant realms, beneath the burning zone,
> Where Europe's curse is felt, her name unknown,
> Thus saith Britannia, empress of the sea,
> 'Thy chains are broken, African, be free!'[16]

Though the British Empire was not referred to directly, Britannia was mentioned eight times in the collection of poems, the appearance of which seemed a prelude to later literature which was openly imperialist while making its readers more aware of the wider world.

In 1856, a two-volume book conveying anti-slavery propaganda about the Niger region (by Thomas Hutchinson) was released, selling slightly more than 1,700 copies of each volume between 1856 and 1864.[17] Hutchinson often adopted a clearly pro-imperialist tone, especially towards the end of the work, when he called openly for the expansion of the British Empire in Africa:

> But if the government do not step in to put an end to the lawlessness of the Filatahs, all ideas of a successful trade with the Niger, Tshadda, and Binuë countries may be given up. There can be no neutrality on the subject. Independent of its character for unfurling the British banner as the aegis of civilisation and Christianity over the world, there still hangs a weighty debt on its shoulders to the vast continent of Africa. ... Let the government commence the work, and I have little doubt that in a few years hence private enterprise will do the rest. British influence will be extended; pillage shall cease; with its cessation will flow into central Africa all the blessings of civilization which otherwise centuries cannot

introduce; the trade will pay; and the industrial resources of the country will become at length developed to the peace and comfort of its inhabitants, and to the commercial prosperity of Great Britain.[18]

Profit, Bible and rifle appeared as close associates in such writings, making the idea of British imperial involvement in Africa more attractive from a religious, economic and even political perspective. Another example of the same period was David Livingstone's bestselling *Missionary Travels*, which appeared immediately as one of the most inspiring works stemming from exploration: from the outset, it was a 'publishing sensation', with a first print run of 12,000 copies, and the very swift sale of 30,000 copies of a 'guinea edition'.[19] Its intellectual impact on Britain appears even greater when considering that no fewer than 3,500 copies of the *Missionary Travels* were purchased by Charles Mudie's Select Library, therefore mechanically multiplying the readership of each copy sold.[20] Referring in its fifth chapter to the treaty between the Griqua chief Waterboer and 'the colonial government', Livingstone was pleased that 'not a single charge was ever brought against either him [Griqua] or his people', claiming on the contrary that 'his faithful adherence to the stipulated provisions elicited numerous expressions of approbation from successive governments'. He added that the Cape community should 'assert the right of choosing their own governors', before arguing that such an arrangement, coupled 'with colonial representation in the Imperial Parliament, in addition to the local self-government already so liberally conceded, would undoubtedly secure the perpetual union of the colony to the English crown', therefore offering a colonial plan which could easily be interpreted as a call for increased imperial involvement.[21]

The geographical discovery of the interior of Africa was also a potent way to bring to British audiences some insights into African lands which prepared public opinion for an imperial advance towards the interior of the continent. Recounting his explorations of the Nile, Samuel Baker regretted that 'although fertile', the 'heart of Africa' had become so 'shut out from civilization' that it had become 'an area for unbridled atrocities'. Though it seemed to him that missionaries would find their task 'difficult and almost impossible', he added a page later that 'an enormous extent of the country is opened to navigation, and Manchester goods and various other articles would find a ready market in exchange for ivory, at a prodigious profit, as in those newly-discovered regions ivory has a merely nominal value'.[22] Though no direct call for annexation was proffered, the potential profits which could be made from trading with the area, and the need to stabilise it in order to achieve this goal, paved the way for imperial intervention.

Table 7.1 Print runs of Samuel Baker, *The Albert N'Yanza, Great Basin of the Nile*

Date	Quantity	Price	Observations
May 1866	2000	28s	
May 1866	5000	28s	
February 1867	3000	16s	
December 1867			Two volumes made up as one
February 1869	500		
December 1869	2000	7s 6d	
February 1870	500	7s 6d	
March 1872	2000	6s	
December 1873	2000	6s	
March 1877	1000	6s	
December 1879	1000	6s	
January 1883	1000	6s	
March 1885	1000	6s	
March 1888	1000	6s	
February 1892	1000	6s	
November 1898	1000	6s	
July 1913	1000	6s	
Total	**25,000**		

(Source: British Library (BL), Macmillan papers, Deposit 10259, Index, p. 21)

Ten years after Baker wrote these lines, General Gordon was the governor of the province of Equatoria, and less than twenty years later an Anglo-Egyptian force occupied Khartoum, ultimately leading to a British retreat which legitimised the reconquest of the country in 1896–98, making the Anglo-Egyptian Sudan a prized member of the Empire until 1956.[23] Such books had steady sales throughout the period: 10,379 copies of John Hanning Speke's *Journal of the Discovery of the Source of the Nile* (sold at 21s) were printed between December 1863 and March 1864, with 75 per cent of the print run selling within two years after the launch of the book.[24] As is shown in Table 7.1, Baker's book was even more successful, thanks to several hardback and paperback versions which ensured a wide distribution of his work.

Baker produced other successful titles about regions which would fall within the sphere of influence of the British Empire: Egypt and the Sudan. Twelve thousand copies of *Ismaïlia* were printed between October 1874 and March 1895, whilst 6,250 copies of the *Nile*

Tributaries of Abyssinia were initially printed (original edition at 21*s*), to which were added 1,500 copies for the North American market (1867–69), 11,000 copies of a 6*s* edition between January 1871 and February 1894, and an extra print run of 1,000 copies at 3*s* 6*d* in January 1908.[25] Later in the period, Mary Kingsley's upmarket accounts of her *Travels in West Africa* was clearly successful among book buyers enjoying a comfortable purchasing power at 21*s* or a guinea. It was thus an expensive volume, but it found 4,500 customers between January and April 1897, and a further 4,500 copies at 7*s* 6*d* were released between September 1897 and May 1904.[26] Kingsley's links with Liverpudlian traders are well known, and, although she intended to provide a more flattering description of Africa and Africans than was usually the case, she also offered to the reader approving glimpses into what British, French and German imperialists were doing on the continent.

The British public became familiar with the geographies of territories which were later absorbed into the Empire thanks to exploratory accounts like the ones mentioned above. Their effectiveness was enhanced by their interaction with other forms of cultural production such as newspapers, illustrated magazines or public lectures. However, once these territories had ceased to be *terrae incognitae* by becoming imperial possessions, atlases proved to be a powerful means of 'exhibiting the Empire' too. The Macmillan print runs listed in Table 7.2 show that, taken together, a *Geography of India, Burma and Ceylon* and a *Geography of the British Colonies* published in the 1890s sold as many copies as a *Geography of the British Isles*. The potent carriers of imperial pride, these atlases were remarkably successful, exhibiting the Empire in a vivid manner.

The last category of books to promote an 'imperial geography' in the period was travel guides and narratives and physical descriptions of the British Empire. The former demonstrate the popularity of imperial destinations (as opposed to metropolitan or foreign ones) among British travellers, while the latter testify to the public's interest in their country's Empire.

The market for travel guides developed as soon as the end of the Napoleonic Wars allowed safe travel to resume. Imperial destinations appeared gradually among the guides and handbooks which catered for the needs of the wealthy travellers of the time. In the early nineteenth century, Ireland was an imperial destination of choice (though the imperial nature of British rule over this adjacent island needs to be considered carefully in comparison with later instances in India and Africa).[27] Thus, in 1819–20, the Greig's guide *Excursions in Ireland* was as popular as its equivalent titles on Essex, Norfolk and Suffolk, with 3,774 copies of the small-format edition and 2,044 copies of the

Table 7.2 Print runs of various books dedicated to the geography of Britain and the British Empire

Title	Author	Quantity	Date
An Elementary Geography of the British Isles	Archibald Geikie	2000	March 1888
		5000	October 1890
		5000	November 1893
		5000	February 1898
		3000	July 1904
		3000	April 1907
Total		**23,000**	
An Elementary Geography of India, Burma and Ceylon	Henry Francis Blanford	3000	September 1890
		3000	January 1894
		3000	November 1901
		3000	May 1904
Total		**12,000**	
An Elementary Geography of the British Colonies	George Dawson and Alexander Sutherland	3000	May 1892
		2000	September 1895
		2000	November 1898
		1000	July 1902
		2000	September 1904
		2000	April 1906
		2000	February 1908
Total		**14,000**	

(Source: BL, Macmillan papers, Deposit 10259, Index, pp. 203–4)

large-format edition sold between February and June 1820.[28] This was a very good print run at a time when book consumption was still limited, and overseas travel remained a privilege of the elites. With the combined effects of falling book prices and the development of more affordable means of travel, guidebook sales rocketed as the century drew to a close and more far-flung imperial territories joined the list of guidebooks which sold well. Thus Macmillan's guides on Palestine and Egypt sold around 10,000 copies between 1901 and 1918.[29] Arguably, interest in travelling to visit a territory under British rule could not be separated from feelings of curiosity towards the Empire itself.

Descriptions of imperial territories appear to have met with relative success throughout the period, attracting a growing readership. Immediately after the Napoleonic Wars, the *Sketches of India written by an Officer for Fire-side Travellers at Home* (1821) recounted the history of a British officer's discovery of India on the occasion of his posting in the late 1810s. No fewer than 631 copies were sold between its launch in May 1821 and June 1822, which was a very respectable result for the period.[30] Later, the former Governor General of Ceylon, J.E. Tennent, published *Ceylon, An Account of the Island: Physical, Historical and Topographical* in 1859, which sold 3,500 copies in the first six months, and remained on the sales ledgers of Longman publishers until 1882 (though the sales decreased sharply thereafter).[31]

Imperial ethos

Even more than the abovementioned 'geographies of empire', the imperial ethos appears as the primary tool which allows us to gauge the popularity of empire among the British public in the nineteenth and early twentieth centuries. It appeared under various guises, and this plasticity ensured it permeated British culture even more deeply. It could take the shape of the promotion of, or reflection on, imperial strategies, occasionally with an academic orientation. Often, it celebrated imperialism, through inspiring tales of conquest or administration involving imperial heroes. Lastly, it could appear in specific schoolbooks. Taken together, these various aspects contributed to sustain the development of an imperial mindset, the study of which is at the heart of the present volume.

Imperial theory cannot be expected to be a mainstream subject, and this was certainly the case of a variety of books which analysed the best forms of imperial government. One of them was Sir Edward Creasy's *The Imperial and Colonial Constitutions of the Empire* (1872) which never went beyond an initial print run of 1,000 copies: though 313 copies found a buyer in the first months, yearly figures quickly fell below fifty.[32] Equally difficult to sell were history, geography and political strategy relating to Canada: only 154 copies of C. Marshall's *The Canadian Dominion* were sold on the year of its release (1871), out of a single print run of 1,250 copies (understandably, the book was never reprinted).[33] In 1881, the sixty-five pages of reflections on the future of the British presence in South Africa by the politician Sir David Wedderburn, presented under the title *British Colonial Policy*, which was the fourth volume of the 'Practical Politics' series, never went beyond the 1,500 copies of its first print run.[34] However, such specialist titles managed to sell more steadily when they dealt with a topical subject, even more so as the century went on and average print runs increased. C.S. Roundell's *England and her Subject-races with Special Reference to Jamaica*, written in the wake of the Morant Bay rebellion, illustrates the first situation: 3,000 copies at sixpence were sold upon its release in December 1866.[35] As the 'Scramble for Africa' was unfolding and European rivalry for colonial control was raging, Edward John Payne's *History of European Colonies* met with relative success, with copies at 4s 6d printed in 1877–78 and an extra 2,000 released in 1889.[36] Reflecting the dominant beliefs of the time, Payne observed with a hint of satisfaction that 'the European peoples, though insignificant in numbers by the side of the countless millions of the non-European races, hold the keys of the earth, and only let in the non-European people as they please into its best parts' (p. 3). Many cases illustrate the gradual increase in print runs of books broaching the imperial question from a theoretical perspective. S. Nicholson's academic study of the economics of Empire 'with special reference to the ideas of Adam Smith' (*A Project of Empire*) was initially printed in 1,500 copies in August 1909, with a reprint of an extra 500 copies in August 1910.[37] An economist, Nicholson had become a fervent imperial apologist, and his work, though on an academic level, reflected his ideological belief in the Empire.[38] However, more nuanced views about the benefits of British imperialism also found echoes among British readers, especially after the Great War. Pramathanath Baner-jea's *Study of Indian Economics*, which had the ambition of staying 'free from political bias' (as stated in the preface) argued, nonetheless, that India had not much to gain from imperial preference. It proved to be a long-term seller. Following a first edition priced at 3s 6d and printed in 1,500 copies in August 1911, a new edition at 4s 6d was released in July 1915 with an initial print run of 1,000 copies. This was followed by a series of twelve reprints between February 1916 and February 1935, which totalled an extra 18,500 copies.[39] This title may have not been a bestseller, but it was certainly an established back-list title.

The bestseller of the period, which clearly outperformed all the other titles considered in this section, was John Robert Seeley's classic work *The Expansion of England*: it went through two editions and an exceptional twenty-four print runs, totalling 53,000 copies between its release in July 1883 and June 1931. As demonstrated by Table 7.3, *The Expansion of England* remained a popular title throughout the period. Though its sales understandably stalled during the Great War, it became popular again in the interwar years, which testifies to the appeal of triumphant imperialism in spite of the moral crisis brought about by the mass massacres of the war. Seeley's book appears as a steady bestseller of the time. Though it did not reach the popularity of Lewis Carroll's *Alice's Adventures in Wonderland* (85,000 copies of

Table 7.3 Print runs of John Robert Seeley's *The Expansion of England*, 1883–1931

Edition	Date	Quantity	Price
1st	July 1883	3000	4s 2d
	October 1883	3000	
	May 1884	2000	
	February 1885	2000	
	October 1886	2000	
	November 1888	2000	
	November 1891	2000	
	July 1894	2000	
2nd	April 1895	3000	5s
	October 1897	2000	
	September 1899	2000	
	January 1900	2000	
	July 1902	2000	
	August 1904	2000	
	April 1906	2000	
	December 1907	2000	
	October 1909	2000	
	November 1911	2000	
	April 1914	2000	
	March 1919	2000	
	January 1920	2000	
	December 1921	2000	
	January 1925	3000	3s
	June 1931	3000	
Total		53,000	

(Source: BL, Macmillan papers, Deposit 10259, Index, p. 465)

the 6s edition between August 1866 and March 1898), sales of 53,000 copies of this much more expensive book make Seeley's title among the top sellers of the publishing house.[40] *The Expansion of England* proved to be more successful than a lesser-known work by Seeley, *Our Colonial Expansion.* Influenced by the success of *The Expansion*, its first print run of 5,000 in April 1887 revealed high expectations on the part of the publisher. Though it was cheaper at only 1s, it proved to be less successful: the first print run took twelve years to be sold, and only 5,000 copies were subsequently reprinted until November 1913, making, however, an honourable – but not exceptional – total print run of 10,000 copies.[41]

The imperial ethos was also occasionally promoted in conjunction with the press. The future Lady Lugard, Dame Flora Shaw, published anonymously (as '*The Times* special correspondent') a selection of her colonial articles from *The Times* in 1893. The *Letters from South Africa* was printed in 20,000 copies in January 1893 (price 2s 6d), a performance which clearly outdid similar endeavours such as the *Letters from Donegal* (edited by Colonel Maurice in June 1884; 3,000 copies), and the *Letters from Queensland* (also by Flora Shaw, April 1893; 2,000 copies).[42]

Alongside these rigorous treatments of, or reflections upon, imperial theory, the 'imperial ethos' was also celebrated in fiction. Thus, C.J. Cutcliffe Hyne developed a vision of empire in his 1904 series of novellas relating to the 'atom of empire' (who, according to a *New York Times* review, was nothing else than the 'wandering Englishman'), in which he offered an ironic, yet highly imperialistic, view of the expansion of the British Empire.[43] Though its sales were not extraordinary, 4,000 copies of the first edition (at 6s) were printed, at the same time as a colonial edition had a print run of 5,000 copies, making it a relatively popular title.[44] The most enduring and powerful celebration of the imperial ethos was produced in a more literary form, especially through the works of Rudyard Kipling, the 'uncrowned laureate of the Empire'.[45] Kipling's work was deeply influenced by his own experience of imperialism, which makes him the epitome of the 'poet of empire'.[46] Though he came relatively late and he appeared to be strengthening an existing trend towards popular support of the empire, Kipling was one of the most successful literary champions of the 'imperial ethos'. His novel *Kim* was an immediate bestseller, with 35,000 copies of the British editions and 15,000 copies of the colonial edition printed in September 1901 alone. This was followed by an additional 25,000 copies of the British edition, and 5,000 copies of the colonial edition between October 1901 and April 1902.[47] The success of these books was durable (e.g. 39,500 copies of a pocket edition of *Kim* between March 1908 and May 1916), and public interest in them was kept up thanks to Macmillan's commercial inventiveness designed to develop a powerful 'selling machine' which, while fostering the interests of both the author and the publisher, also pushed the imperial agenda forward.[48] The multiplication of editions (for Sunday schools, soldiers, bibliophiles etc.) allowed Macmillan's to reach a wide readership with diverse socio-economic and cultural backgrounds whilst ensuring steady sales – for instance, 128,000 copies of the pocket editions of the *Jungle Book* were sold between 1894 and 1914.[49] Kipling's literary world conveyed an image of the British Empire which resembled a dream; 'almost a masterful dream-work of condensation, with its colonies, different from each other in history, culture and language, threaded together into one vision, solely by virtue of their belonging to the Empire'.[50] The aesthetic value of Kipling's fiction has been recognised (even by postcolonial critics, like Edward Said),[51] and this literary quality certainly augmented its influence on British visions of empire.[52] Besides Kipling, many lesser-known, but significant, literary figures also contributed to popularise the 'imperial ethos'. One of them was the *Daily Mail* correspondent G.W. Steevens, whose books about his imperial reporting registered steady sales, which were cut short only by their author's untimely death on the occasion of the South African war.[53] Though his best-selling title was *With Kitchener to Khartum*, which will be discussed below, his other imperial works did not remain unnoticed: 6,300 copies of the hardback edition at 4s of *In India* were sold in the six months following the release of the title in September 1899, and 32,769 copies of the 3s 6d edition of *Capetown to Ladysmith* between February and May 1900.[54] Indeed, it has been argued that 'no other author of the 1890s was as profitable' as Steevens. This financial profitability was all the more welcome as it matched Blackwood publishers' 'belief in Britain's imperial calling': as Laurence Davies observed, 'with a century's worth of hindsight, the distinction between the duty to serve an empire and the impulse to make money from it looks like a bad case of false consciousness'.[55]

Naturally, the ethos of empire was effectively celebrated in the printed material which was produced for imperial occasions. An obvious case of imperial sentiment being exhibited was the official account of what was called at the time a 'colonial tour' of the Duke and Duchess of Cornwall and York in 1901, which saw them visit Gibraltar, Malta, Egypt, Aden, Ceylon, Singapore, Australia, Mauritius, South Africa and Canada in an attempt to express how much they were 'in sympathy with the ever-increasing sentiments of mutual affection between the Colonies and the Mother Country'.[56] This 500-page account, which included 78 illustrations, was widely distributed in the wake of the official tour: 3,000 copies of the 21s (1 guinea) edition were printed in May 1902, followed by 30,000 copies of a sixpenny edition in April 1903, and 6,000 copies of an abridged version for schools.[57]

In the eyes of many contemporaries, the Empire gained at least part of its legitimacy from the processes by which it had been built: empire-building was the very proof of British superiority, sustaining a feeling of national self-confidence which fuelled imperial sentiment. As General Sir Arthur Thurlow Cunynghame put it at the time, writing about

South Africa, 'the country which is the subject of the following narra-tive is of considerable interest to Englishmen. The noble efforts to found colonies which have been made by England have been rewarded by results unequalled either in ancient or modern times.'[58] Given the emphasis placed on the circumstances and strong will which had made the Empire possible in the first place, tales of conquest or administra-tion are, understandably, a relevant category of books to analyse here.

Before the advent of the 'New Imperialism', the trend seems to have remained marginal. Thus, the *Letters written during the Siege of Delhi* by the commissioner and political agent H.H. Greathed, edited by his widow, received only an ephemeral welcome from the public: if 561 copies were sold in the first nine months, this respectable result was followed by a steep decline in the following years, to such an extent that the book never went beyond its first print run of 1,000 copies (October 1858).[59] However, in subsequent decades the public seems to have been more interested in the theme of imperial conquest. The already mentioned Cunynghame, lieutenant governor and commander of the (British) forces in South Africa, did well with *My Command in South Africa, 1874–1878, comprising experiences of travel in the colonies of South Africa and the independent states*, of which 3,250 copies were sold between February and September 1879.[60] The *Reminiscences of the Great Mutiny*, by Forbes-Mitchell, did much better than Greathed's posthumous work, with 2,000 copies at 8*s* 6*d* in 1893–94, 4,000 copies at 3*s* 6*d* between 1894 and 1904, and 10,000 copies at 1*s* produced in 1910.[61] At the same time, the notoriously unpopular Lord Curzon sold a limited number of his *In India* (1906), with only 1,000 copies printed in April 1906, and 2,000 copies of a colonial edition.[62] Another of the great administrators of the British Empire, the Earl of Cromer, proved to be a more popular writer: 10,000 copies of an edition at 24*s* of *Modern Egypt* were printed between February and March 1908, while 3,000 copies of a cheaper edition at 7*s* 6*d* were released in May 1911. This demonstrated that Cromer's views on Egypt were sought after, though it also indicated that most buyers with an interest in his writings enjoyed a high purchasing power and may not have been typical.[63] Overall, one of the bestselling titles of the genre in the period was Earl Roberts's *Forty One Years in India*, which appears as one of the most enduring successes in the field of 'tales of imperial conquest and administration'. Statistics for the title are incomplete, but on the basis of the title-page of the 1901 new edition in one volume, as well as the publisher's archival records, it appears that, by the time the title had reached its thirtieth edition, reprints of between 3,000 and 8,000 copies were routinely made, amounting to 30,000 copies between August 1898 and April 1911, which testifies the extent to which his work had become popular. Even an exceptionally expensive 36*s* edition found a thousand customers between 1900 and 1902.[64]

The sales of authors like Frederick Roberts were certainly helped by their popularity, which was deeply entrenched among the public at a time when exemplary figures were highly sought after. As they embodied triumphant nationalism and self-confidence, imperial heroes were among the defining cultural features of the Victorian and Edwardian ages, and they proved to be one of the longest-lasting ways of exhibiting the Empire.[65] In the first place, editions of their works (memoirs or letters) remained in the back-list often for several decades, perpetuating not only their memory but also the celebration of empire which their reputation enshrined. This was the case of the memoirs of a major figure of the British repression of the 1857 Indian revolt, Sir Henry Havelock. First published by his son, Sir Henry Marshman Havelock-Allan, in 1860, they remained available (through regular reprinting) until 1908, spanning an entire half century and totalling 11,000 copies.[66] Similarly, books by General Gordon remained in demand throughout the late nineteenth century. As Gordon was besieged in Khartoum and the object of sustained media interest as a result, his *Reflections in Palestine* were much in demand: 8,000 copies were printed between April and July 1884. Later on, his letters to his sister remained a steady sale, with 5,000 copies printed upon their release in 1888, and then subsequently 4,000 between February 1899 and January 1903. Naturally, books on (rather than *by*) imperial heroes were also a powerful channel of the 'imperial ethos', even if they often stemmed from dramatically adverse circumstances, as was the case with General Gordon. Thus 25,000 copies of *Charles George Gordon. A Sketch ... with facsimile letter* by Reginald Barnes and Charles Brown (106 pp., 1*s*) were printed in the months of March and April 1885, in the wake of the general's death in Khartoum.[67]

It has been observed that although 'biographical publishing was never a trade speciality, ... it formed a consistent part of the general output of print' and it should not be neglected when it comes to evaluating the way in which imperial material appeared in the British publishing market in the nineteenth century.[68] One of the most profitable books ever published by the famously pro-imperialist Blackwood publishers was G.W. Steevens's *With Kitchener to Khartum*, which, with 236,762 copies sold in two years, turned the Sirdar into one of the most successful and enduring heroic legends of the 'New Imperialism'. It was also an exceptionally profitable editorial venture for both publisher and author.[69] Indeed, profit was also a powerful rationale to promote the Empire, when it appeared that books dealing with this topic sold well. I have analysed elsewhere how Blackwood and Steevens devised a sophisticated strategy to ensure that Steevens's reporting in the trail of the Anglo-Egyptian expeditionary force would produce the best possible return on investment, while also establishing Kitchener's popular reputation.[70] Given the returns which could be expected from a book meeting the public's preoccupations of the moment, publishers were often ready to compete against each other to secure a contract for a book about an imperial hero. For instance, Thomas Norton Longman had offered Gordon's brother £5,000 to publish the 'Last Journals' of Gordon of Khartoum, only to be outbid by C. Kegan Paul in what Asa Briggs called a 'curious auction held in private' (Paul having offered seemingly 5,000 guineas).[71]

Though he is better known for his *History of England*, Thomas Babington Macaulay proved to be a prolific promoter of early imperial heroes in India, through his essays on Warren Hastings and Robert Clive, of which 23,193 and 20,690 copies respectively were sold by Longmans between 1851 and 1864 alone.[72] These works conveyed the imperial ethos with much dedication, as is shown by the penultimate paragraph of Macaulay's volume on Warren Hastings, in which he noted enthusiastically that 'not only had the poor orphan retrieved the fallen fortunes of his line – not only had he repurchased the old lands, and rebuilt the old dwelling – he had preserved and extended an empire. He had founded a polity.'[73] The *Essay on Lord Clive* was later taken over by Macmillan, which printed a further 28,000 copies between November 1905 and March 1935 (with 9,000 copies alone between November 1905 and November 1908). Macmillan also reprinted Macaulay's essay on Warren Hastings, producing 9,000 copies between April 1907 and May 1923.[74] This placed these early imperial heroes on a par with the most famous of Britain's exemplary men, Admiral Nelson. Robert Southey's *Life of Nelson*, first published in 1813, was reprinted with a new introduction by Macmillan in 1890, and 23,000 copies of a 3s 6d (later 2s 6d) edition were sold between August 1890 and August 1916, while a cheaper edition was released in February 1907, of which 21,000 extra copies were released by August 1937.[75]

The remarkably high sales figures of Macaulay's essays on early imperial heroes might explain why Macmillan included many later heroes of the British Empire in their 'English men of action' series, as is shown in Table 7.4. Macmillan's print runs demonstrate that imperial figures like General Gordon or David Livingstone could attract even more buyers than Nelson or Wellington. This is hardly surprising given David Livingstone's fame at the time, clearly demonstrated by the success of his writings from 1857 onwards.[76] The heroes of the development and maintenance of the British Empire in India,

Table 7.4 Print runs of various titles in the 'English men of action' series

Title	Author	Quantity	Period
Lord Clive	Charles William Wilson	16,500	1890–1913
		3000	1919–1937
Charles George Gordon	William Francis Butner	35,000	1889–1904
		20,000	1905–1922
Havelock	Archibald Forbes	13,000	1890–1908
		2000	1914–1924
Lord Lawrence	Richard Temple	16,000	1889–1928
David Livingstone	David Hughes	33,000	1899–1912
		2000	1921–1928
Sir Charles Napier	William Francis Butner	9000	1890–1911
Wolfe	Arthur Granville Napier	14,000	1895–1913
		3000	1914–1923
Nelson	John Knox Laughton	14,000	1895–1910
		2000	1910–1928
Wellington	George Hooper	27,000	1889–1911
		3000	1914–1923

(Source: BL, Macmillan papers, Deposit 10259, Index, pp. 161–5. All titles were sold at 2*s* 6*d*)

Clive, Havelock, Lawrence and Napier, did not reach the same levels of popularity, though their books performed honourably in this pantheon of national figures with print runs between 9000 and 19,500 copies over a twenty-year period.

If the resilience of the 'imperial ethos' was to be ensured, inter-generational transmission was crucial, and as a result schoolbooks provide an excellent source of information about the place of empire in the education of young British minds. It is not possible to provide a full quantitative survey of the place of empire in children's literature within the limits of this chapter, but the print runs of the famous Gleig's series of schoolbooks provide at least an idea of the relative importance of the Empire, in comparison with the metropole.[77] Table 7.5 compares the sales of titles in the Gleig's series in the 1850s, even before the peak of popular interest in imperialism towards the end of the century. Sales figures for the titles on the British colonies, British India and the British Empire reached, in most cases, at least two-thirds of the figures of the volumes on England, clearly making them popular

Table 7.5 Sales of Gleig's School Series, 1851–58, published by Longman

Title	June 1851 to June 1852	June 1852 to June 1853	June 1853 to June 1854	June 1854 to June 1855	June 1855 to June 1856	June 1856 to June 1857	June 1857 to June 1858	Total
Gleig's England – Part I	3667	5138	7153	7153	7623	7063	8586	**46,383**
Gleig's England – Part II	2861	3756	5625	5640	6490	5227	6584	**36,183**
Gleig's British Colonies	2065	2335	2145	3448	3018	3182	5272	**21,465**
History of British India	1609	1832	2996	3310	4537	3438	5692	**23,414**
Hughes's Geography of the British Empire	549	2444	2446	7311	3602	6379	4512	**27,243**
Hughes's General Geography	2970	3953	3394	6914	5070	4787	5377	**32,645**
History of France	—	416	244	1334	2785	1275	1693	**7747**

(Source: Reading University Library (RUL), Longman papers, MS 1393, Sales of books 1851–58)

topics. The contrast is particularly striking with the *History of France*, the sales figures of which were only 20 per cent of the first volume on England. Some of these textbooks might have been exported to the colonies, where they further propagated the 'imperial ethos', nurturing pride in imperial possessions which would sustain the birth of many 'Anglo worlds'.[78]

The Empire exhibited in the Empire

This spread of the 'imperial ethos' beyond the British Isles, cultivating a feeling of belonging to a common project, explains why this chapter also considers 'the Empire exhibited in the Empire'. *Exhibiting the Empire* intends to show the multiple ways in which the Empire was exhibited at home. Yet in the case of the publishing world, the Empire was also 'exhibited' in the Empire. At the time of the Industrial Revolution, when Britain systematically exported most of its goods, it is hardly surprising that it also spread its books and publishing practices, and especially the mass consumption of reading material. In the words of Frances Marion Crawford, writing to Macmillan in 1886, 'the cry in India is for cheap books, especially among the Eurasians'.[79]

The development of a print culture in the colonies often started with newspapers and official communication requirements, and book publishing came in their footsteps when colonial markets grew.[80] By the end of the nineteenth century, major metropolitan companies like Macmillan, Longmans or Oxford University Press (from 1886, 1890 and 1913 respectively) established branches around the British Empire – starting with India in many cases.[81] The process developed momentum, quickly encompassing the entire British Empire: for instance, Longmans established branches and subsidiaries in Australia, Canada, Hong Kong, India, Kenya, Malaysia, New Zealand, Nigeria, Pakistan, Rhodesia, South Africa, Zimbabwe, as well as the USA.[82] These subsidiaries sought to cater for burgeoning mass markets, producing 'Colonial libraries' which were not for sale in Britain (e.g. Macmillan's Colonial Library), or supplying textbooks and readers in large quantities. Indeed, it has been argued that 'modern British publishers owed much of their prosperity to imperial and other overseas markets'.[83] On the basis of the *Parliamentary Papers*, Alexis Weedon has demonstrated that British book exports to 'the most valuable colonial markets – Australasia, the East Indies, South Africa and North America – rose from a declared value of £35,841 in 1828 to £787,304 in 1898'.[84] Starting as an export trade, the Empire gradually became an area of book production in its own right thanks to the impetus of local branches of British publishers.[85]

A case in point was Macmillan, which became involved in the book trade in India (through the production of books specifically aimed at the Indian market) in the 1870s. In partnership with Professor Lethbridge, a local professor at Presidency College, Calcutta, Macmillan endeavoured to become the first provider of schoolbooks of the subcontinent.[86] Print runs demonstrate that the initiative was a highly successful one: the *Guide to Lethbridge's History of India* was printed in 15,000 copies between February 1901 and August 1902 alone.[87] By 1938, three and a half million copies of their 'First Reading Book' had been sold.[88] Alongside affordable literary works and popular editions of the Bible, education books were very important in the business model of colonial subsidiaries. These included some titles referring to the Empire. For instance, 25,867 copies of B.H. Kerr's *Growth of the British Empire* were sold between 1921 and 1935.[89] Titles dealing with the history of specific colonial territories were also a good opportunity to broach imperial themes. This was particularly evident in the case of J.C. Allen's *A Narrative of Indian History for High Schools*, published by Longmans in Bombay (Mumbai) and Calcutta (Kolkata), of which no fewer than 32,655 copies were sold between 1919 and 1935.[90]

Allen's *Narrative of Indian History* offers a revealing insight into the ways in which the Empire could be celebrated in books written specifically for young readers in the colonies. Apparently teaching the history of India, the book actually placed the emphasis on the history of *British* India, which was detailed through twelve chapters out of a total of twenty-six, in a volume meant to cover the history of the subcontinent since prehistory. Thus, the first 128 pages covered more than two millennia of Indian history up until Clive, whereas the remaining two centuries under British rule were covered in exactly the same number of pages. As the textbook progressed, the chapter breakdown became gradually articulated around the figures of successive governors general. The perspective on events was also clearly imperialist, implying full adherence to the 'imperial ethos'. Shortly after having described the Indian uprising, the author claimed that 'the terrible events of 1857 had roused the English nation to see the responsibilities of governing India' (p. 220). Lord Curzon's role as viceroy of India was summarised as being 'directed to the spread and improvement of the system of education, to the extension of irrigation and railways and the development of industries, and also to famine administration' (p. 238), which clearly downplayed the ravages of the famine of 1899–1900. The concluding sections of the book openly promoted a pro-imperialist vision of British action in India (pp. 260–2):

> The last conquerors of India were the British, who have kept the country at peace for the last hundred years. They are the first rulers who have not made their home in the country, and they therefore preserve the characteristics of a more vigorous climate. For this reason, the British government is as firm and strong today as it was when it was first established ...
>
> India is studded with ruins representing forgotten civilisations, the work of men whose skill has died with them. Kingly dynasties have died and been succeeded by new dynasties. Of continuity there was none until the British governed the land. Under a permanent government the half-erected irrigation works of these fallen dynasties have been completed. New irrigation works have been planned and steadily created. Means of quick communication have been provided. And for the first time the land has been governed in the interests of the people, and not of the rulers ... Prosperity among the people is only possible in times of peace. To preserve the country from invasion the Government keeps a trained army ... When crops fail a part of the revenue collected from the people is set aside. This is distributed over the famine area and

serves to save the people from starvation ... Famine is no longer the terrible thing it was.

Such an imperial stance in what was meant to be a historical textbook about India (and for Indian students) reveals the extent to which the 'imperial ethos' could be deeply embedded in books intended for colonial markets, even if their titles did not reflect any blatant commitment to imperialism. More research needs to be undertaken in this area, especially given the significant print runs registered for the period. In the *History Primers* series, *Indian History*, by W.J. Talboys and sold at one shilling, was released in a run of 27,000 copies between May 1890 and January 1906,[91] while 15,002 copies of *Heroes of Indian History* were sold between 1919 and 1935.[92] Among geographical titles, Sir David Wedderburn's *Burmese Geographies, First Lessons* sold 43,000 between May 1897 and November 1905, in addition to 50,000 copies of the *Elementary Geography of Burma*.[93] The potential impact of colonial book publishing was even more significant when considering that 'always the colonizers took with them the cultural institutions they had developed over the centuries, including libraries', and that this multiplied the number of potential readers for each book sold.[94]

Public libraries certainly instilled a taste for books among people who had not necessarily been accustomed to written cultures. However, they also brought with them an intellectual baggage which shaped colonial minds in favour of the imperial project because many of the narratives available to readers, 'far from casting doubt on the imperial undertaking, serve[d] to confirm and celebrate its success'.[95] The twentieth-century popularity in Ghana of Henry Rider Haggard, the 'literary darling of the empire' (in Robert Fraser's words), demonstrates the deep influence which such a pro-imperial writer could exert on African minds: his books came third in a survey of reading preferences in Accra undertaken on the eve of independence. His ideas were spread through many translations in vernacular languages (in the interwar and postwar years), and the appearance of his African tales in the form of language readers as well as illustrated 'classics'.[96]

Conclusion

The journey of 'imperialism in print' in the nineteenth and twentieth centuries started with geographical content coupled with colonial undertones, before moving towards a full imperial ethos openly laid out in a variety of books (ranging from academic studies to mainstream literature), which was also embedded in the physical and intellectual material exported to the colonies by British authors and publishers.

Using existing qualitative research which has shown the role of geographical knowledge in advancing imperialism, this chapter has quantified the extent to which explorers, anti-slavery campaigners and travel guide writers increased the familiarity of the British public with territories which had become, or were soon to become, parts of the Empire. The statistics used here have revealed the uninterrupted increase of the print runs of books dealing with the Empire, as the century went on. More generally, this chapter has also demonstrated the variety of channels through which an 'imperial ethos' was conveyed throughout the period, highlighting the need to consider 'popular imperialism' as a proteiform phenomenon requiring a careful analysis of its multiple expressions in metropolitan popular cultures. For the concept of popular imperialism to be entirely meaningful, it should not be systematically equated with active jingoism but rather with a permeation of metropolitan consciousness across class and time.[97] The archives around which this chapter revolves throw light upon the processes which contributed to shape an imperial frame of mind in Britain in the nineteenth century.

Histories of British publishing have left little space so far to the question of empire in their appraisal of the activity of nineteenth-century British publishers: in reality, the keyword is almost never listed in their indexes.[98] This appears a regrettable oversight given the importance of imperial territories or ideas in the case of a variety of books, the place of the Empire as an area of commercial expansion for the British publishing world and the archives available on the subject.[99] Though promising new research has started to use previously untapped archival sources, a lot of this historical territory remains to be explored.[100]

Notes

1 The concept of 'imperial mindset' was put forward by John MacKenzie in *European Empires and the People* (Manchester: Manchester University Press, 2011), in keeping with the idea of 'popular imperialism' which had crystallised in his earlier volume, *Propaganda and Empire* (Manchester: Manchester University Press, 1984).

2 David Pearson, *Books as History* (London: The British Library and Oak Knoll Press, 2008), p. 7.

3 On print-capitalism, see Benedict Anderson, *Imagined Communities* (Cambridge: Cambridge University Press, 1983). On banal nationalism, see Michael Billig, *Banal Nationalism* (London: Sage Publications, 1995).

4 In particular, the power of the visual element of material relating to the Empire, which was included in many of the books cited here, should not be underestimated. See, for instance, Tim Barringer, 'Fabricating Africa: Livingstone and the Visual Image, 1850–1874', in John M. MacKenzie (ed.), *David Livingstone and the Victorian Encounter with Africa* (London: National Portrait Gallery, 1996), pp. 169–200; James R. Ryan, *Picturing Empire: Photography and the Visualization of the British Empire* (Chicago: University of Chicago Press, 1998); Berny Sèbe, *Heroic Imperialists*

in Africa (Manchester: Manchester University Press, 2013), ch. 3; Leila Koivunen, *Visualizing Africa in Nineteenth-Century British Travel Accounts* (London: Routledge, 2008); Leila Koivunen, 'Africa on the Spot and from the Distance: David Livingstone's *Missionary Travels* and Nineteenth-Century Practices of Illustration', *Scottish Geographical Journal* 129 (2013), pp. 194–209.

5 See, for instance, Charles Morgan, *The House of Macmillan, 1843–1943* (London: Macmillan, 1944).

6 See, for instance, Raymond Williams, *The Long Revolution* (London: Penguin, 1965); Pierre Bourdieu, *The Field of Cultural Production* (Cambridge: Polity Press, 1993).

7 Laurel Brake, *Print in Transition, 1850–1910: Studies in Media and Book History* (Basingstoke: Palgrave, 2001), ch. 1.

8 For examples of imperial sentiment analysed through the prism of the press, see, for instance, Clare Pettitt, *Dr Livingstone, I Presume? Missionaries, Journalists, Explorers and Empire* (Cambridge, MA: Harvard University Press, 2007); Clare Pettitt, 'Exploration in Print: from the Miscellany to the Newspaper', in Dane Kennedy (ed.), *Reinterpreting Exploration: The West in the World* (Oxford: Oxford Unversity Press, 2013), pp. 80–108.

9 Richard Price, *An Imperial War and the Working Class* (London: Routledge & Kegan Paul, 1972).

10 This has been observed from a variety of angles – especially geography, history and postcolonial studies. See, for instance, Morag Bell, Robin Butlin and Michael Heffernan (eds), *Geography and Imperialism, 1820–1940* (Manchester: Manchester University Press, 1995); Felix Driver, *Geography Militant: Cultures of Exploration and Empire* (Oxford: Blackwell, 2001); Edward Said, *Culture & Imperialism* (London: Vintage Books, 1993), pp. 1–14.

11 Simon Eliot, *Some Patterns and Trends in British Publishing, 1800–1919* (London: Occasional Papers of the Bibliographical Society, 8, 1994), pp. 43–58.

12 Reading University Library (RUL), Longman papers, Sales of books 1851–58 (unpaginated). For the Macmillan figures, see Simon Eliot, '"To you in your vast business": Some Features of the Quantitative History of Macmillan, 1843–91', in Elizabeth James (ed.), *Macmillan: A Publishing Tradition* (Basingstoke: Palgrave, 2002), p. 23 (table 1.2).

13 Srividhya Swaminathan, *Debating the Slave Trade: Rhetoric of British National Identity, 1759–1815* (Farnham: Ashgate, 2009), pp. 211–14.

14 See, for instance, Catherine Hall, *Civilising Subjects: Metropole and Colony in the English Imagination, 1830–1867* (Cambridge: Polity Press, 2002).

15 RUL, Longman papers, Sales ledgers, A2 (p. 176), A3 (pp. 40 & 321) and A4 (p. 232).

16 James Montgomery, *The West Indies, and Other Poems* (London: Longman, 1823, 6th ed.), pp. 3–4.

17 Thomas J. Hutchinson, *Narrative of the Niger, Tshadda & Binuë exploration* (London, 1855). Sales figures: RUL, Longman papers, Sales of books 1851–58 (unpaginated).

18 Hutchinson, *Narrative of the Niger*, pp. 254–5.

19 Felix Driver, '*Missionary Travels*: Livingstone, Africa and the Book', *Scottish Geographical Journal* 129 (2013), pp. 164–78.

20 Guinevere L. Griest, 'A Victorian Leviathan: Mudie's Select Library', *Nineteenth-Century Fiction* 20 (1965), pp. 103–36, quoted in Louise C. Henderson, 'David Livingstone's *Missionary Travels* in Britain and America: Exploring the Wider Circulation of a Victorian Travel Narrative', *Scottish Geographical Journal* 129 (2013), pp. 179–93.

21 David Livingstone, *Missionary Travels and Researches in South Africa* (London: John Murray, 1857), ch. 5. David Livingstone's relationship with imperialism has remained a matter of controversy to this day, and seems to be open to interpretation: for a discussion of its multiple meanings, see John M. MacKenzie, 'David Livingstone – Prophet or Patron Saint of Imperialism in Africa: Myths and Misconceptions', *Scottish Geographical Journal* 129 (2013), pp. 277–91.

22 Samuel W. Baker, *The Albert N'Yanza, Great Basin of the Nile* (London: Macmillan,

1866), pp. 443–5.

23 On Gordon's role in the Equatoria province, see Alice Moore-Harrell, *Gordon and the Sudan: Prologue to the Mahdiyya, 1877–1880* (London: Frank Cass, 2001).

24 National Library of Scotland (NLS), MS 30860, Blackwood papers, Publication Ledger, 1861–1874, pp. 362–4.

25 British Library (BL), Macmillan papers, Deposit 10259, Index, pp. 21–2.

26 BL, Macmillan papers, Deposit 10259, Index, p. 771.

27 On the place of Ireland in the British Empire, and its specific status, see Stephen Howe, *Ireland and Empire* (Oxford: Oxford University Press, 2001), and Kevin Kenny (ed.), *Ireland and the British Empire* (Oxford: Oxford University Press, 2005).

28 RUL, Longman papers, MS1393, A3, Divide Ledger (1813–1866), pp. 62, 148.

29 BL, Macmillan papers, Deposit 10259, Index, p. 853.

30 RUL, Longman papers, MS1393, A3, Divide Ledger (1813–1866), p. 236.

31 RUL, Longman papers, MS 1393, A7, Divide Ledger, 1859–1881, p. 16 & A10, p. 23.

32 RUL, Longmans papers, MS1393, A11, Divide Ledger A11, pp. 297–8.

33 RUL, Longmans papers, MS 1393, A10, p. 275.

34 BL, Macmillan papers, Deposit 10259, Index, p. 430.

35 BL, Macmillan papers, Deposit 10259, Index, p. 462.

36 BL, Macmillan papers, Deposit 10259, Index, p. 251.

37 BL, Macmillan papers, Deposit 10259, Index, p. 667.

38 Robert H. Deans and Janet S. Deans, 'J. Shield Nicholson's Project of Empire: The Edinburgh Economist Evolved from a Free Trader into a Premier Apologist for Imperialism', *American Journal of Economics and Sociology* 46 (1987), pp. 319–40.

39 BL, Macmillan papers, Deposit 10259, Index, p. 23.

40 BL, Macmillan papers, Deposit 10259, Index, pp. 64–6.

41 BL, Macmillan papers, Deposit 10259, Index, p. 465.

42 BL, Macmillan papers, Deposit 10259, Index, pp. 313, 647, 654 & 647 d.

43 C.J. Cutcliffe Hyne, *Atoms of Empire* (London: Macmillan, 1904). *New York Times* review, 26 November 1904.

44 BL, Macmillan papers, Deposit 10259, Index, pp. 260.

45 Mark Paffard, *Kipling's Indian Fiction* (Basingstoke: Macmillan, 1989), p. 104.

46 Zohreh T. Sullivan, *Narratives of Empire: The Fictions of Rudyard Kipling* (Cambridge: Cambridge University Press, 1993), p. 179.

47 BL, Macmillan papers, Deposit 10259, Index, pp. 855, 942.

48 Morgan, *The House of Macmillan*, p. 151.

49 Charles Carrington, *Rudyard Kipling: His Life and Work* (Basingstoke: Macmillan, 1955), p. 624.

50 Kaori Nagai, *Empire of Analogies, Kipling, India and Ireland* (Cork: Cork University Press, 2006), p. 133.

51 Edward W. Said, 'Introduction', in Rudyard Kipling, *Kim* (London: Penguin, 1987 ed.), p. 37.

52 David Gilmour, *The Long Recessional: The Imperial Life of Rudyard Kipling* (London: John Murray, 2002).

53 On Steevens, see Sèbe, *Heroic Imperialists in Africa*, ch. 7, and Roger T. Stearn, 'G.W. Steevens and the Message of Empire', *Journal of Imperial and Commonwealth History* 17 (1989), pp. 210–31.

54 NLS, MS 30864, Blackwood papers, Publication ledger, 1895–1907, pp. 189, 193.

55 Laurence Davies, '"A sideways ending it all": G.W. Steevens, Blackwood and the *Daily Mail*', in David Finkelstein (ed.), *Print Culture and the Blackwood Tradition, 1805–1930* (Toronto: University of Toronto Press, 2006), pp. 226–58.

56 Donald Mackenzie Wallace, *The Web of Empire: A Diary of the Imperial Tour of their Royal Highnesses the Duke & Duchess of Cornwall & York in 1901* (London: Macmillan, 1902), p. 3.

57 BL, Macmillan papers, Deposit 10259, Index, p. 531.

58 Arthur T. Cunynghame, *My Command in South Africa, 1874–1878* (London: Macmillan, 1879), preface.

59 RUL, Longman Papers, Divide ledger, MS 1393, A6 (1853–1869), p. 679.

60 BL, Macmillan papers, Deposit 10259, Index, p. 109.
61 BL, Macmillan papers, Deposit 10259, Index, p. 666.
62 BL, Macmillan papers, Deposit 10259, Index, p. 109.
63 BL, Macmillan papers, Deposit 10259, Index, p. 108.
64 BL, Macmillan papers, Deposit 10259, Index, p. 789.
65 On the role of imperial heroes on the promotion of the imperial idea, see John M. MacKenzie, 'Heroic Myths of Empire', in J.M. MacKenzie (ed.), *Popular Imperialism and the Military* (Manchester: Manchester University Press, 1992), pp. 109–37; Edward Berenson, *Heroes of Empire* (Berkeley, CA: University of California Press, 2011); Sèbe, *Heroic Imperialists in Africa*.
66 RUL, Longman papers, Divide ledger, A7, pp. 96 & 484; A 10, pp. 149 & 539; A12, pp. 151 & 306; A14, pp. 333–4 & 703; A 18, pp. 391–2.
67 BL, Macmillan papers, Deposit 10259, Index, p. 230.
68 Robin Myers, Michael Harris and Giles Mandelbrote (eds), *Lives in Print: Biography and the Book Trade from the Middle Ages to the 21st Century* (London: Oak Knoll Press and The British Library, 2002), p. vii.
69 Sèbe, *Heroic Imperialists in Africa*, p. 72.
70 Ibid., ch. 7.
71 Asa Briggs, *A History of Longmans and their Books, 1724–1990* (London: The British Library and Oak Knoll Press, 2008), p. 324.
72 RUL, Longman papers, MS 1393, Sales of books 1851–1858.
73 Thomas Macaulay, *Warren Hastings* (London: Macmillan, 1851).
74 BL, Macmillan papers, Deposit 10259, Index, p. 896.
75 BL, Macmillan papers, Deposit 10259, Index, p. 155.
76 Henderson, 'David Livingstone's *Missionary Travels* in Britain and America'.
77 For a qualitative appraisal of the place of empire in literature for young people, see Jeffrey Richards (ed.), *Imperialism and Juvenile Literature* (Manchester: Manchester University Press, 1989).
78 Christopher Stray and Gillian Sutherland, 'Mass Markets: Education', in David McKitterick (ed.), *The Cambridge History of the Book in Britain: Volume 6, 1830–1914* (Cambridge: Cambridge University Press, 2009), pp. 359–81 and n. 66. On the rise of 'Anglo worlds', see James Belich, *Replenishing the Earth: The Settler Revolution and the Rise of the Anglo World* (Oxford: Oxford University Press, 2009).
79 F.M. Crawford to Macmillan, 8 January 1886, in Simon Nowell-Smith (ed.), *Letters to Macmillan* (London and New York: Macmillan, 1967), pp. 198–9.
80 David Finkelstein and Alistair McLeery, *An Introduction to Book History* (London: Routledge, 2013 (2nd ed.)), pp. 91–2.
81 Robert Fraser, *Book History through Postcolonial Eyes* (London: Routledge, 2008), p. 142.
82 Asa Briggs, *A History of Longmans and Their Books, 1724–1990* (London: The British Library and Oak Knoll Press, 2008).
83 Jonathan Rose, 'Britain, 1890–1970', in Simon Eliot and Jonathan Rose (eds), *A Companion to the History of the Book* (Oxford: Blackwell, 2007) p. 352.
84 Alexis Weedon, *Victorian Publishing* (Aldershot: Ashgate, 2003), p. 38.
85 John Feather, *A History of British Publishing* (London: Routledge, 1988), p. 186.
86 Rimi B. Chatterjee, 'Macmillan in India: A Short Account of the Company's Trade with the Sub-Continent', in Elizabeth James (ed.), *Macmillan: A Publishing Tradition* (Basingstoke: Palgrave Macmillan, 2002), pp. 153–69, p. 156.
87 BL, Macmillan papers, Deposit 10259, Index, p. 841.
88 Chatterjee, 'Macmillan in India', p. 156.
89 RUL, Indian Statement Book, p. 34.
90 RUL, Longman papers, MS1393, F4 (Indian Statement Book), p. 16.
91 BL, Macmillan papers, Deposit 10259, Index, p. 444.
92 RUL, Indian Statement Book, p. 16.
93 BL, Macmillan papers, Deposit 10259, Index, p. 374.
94 Wayne A. Wiegand, 'Libraries and the Invention of Information', in Simon Eliot and

Jonathan Rose (eds), A *Companion to the History of the Book* (Oxford: Blackwell, 2007), pp. 531–43, p. 535.

95 Edward Said, *Culture and Imperialism* (London: Vintage, 1993), p. 227.

96 Fraser, *Book History through Postcolonial Eyes*, p. 175.

97 On this question, see John M. MacKenzie, 'Introduction', in John M. MacKenzie (ed.), *European Empires and the People: Popular Responses to Imperialism in France, Britain, the Netherlands, Belgium, Germany and Italy* (Manchester: Manchester University Press, 2011), pp. 1–18.

98 There is no significant coverage of the Empire in general history of publishing, or even in the major histories of publishers of the time, such as Arthur Waugh, *A Hundred Years of Publishing, Being the Story of Chapman & Hall, Ltd.* (London: Chapman & Hall, 1930); Samuel Smiles, *A Publisher and His Friends: Memoir and Correspondence of the Late John Murray* (London: John Murray, 1891); John Attenborough, *A Living Memory: Hodder & Stoughton Publishers, 1868–1975* (London: Hodder & Stoughton, 1975).

99 Besides the sources used in this chapter, gathered in London (British Library: Macmillan), Edinburgh (National Library of Scotland: Blackwood) and Reading (University Library: Longmans), many more archival sources could be used to understand the reception of books which dealt with imperial or pre-imperial topics: see, for instance, on David Livingstone, Driver, *'Missionary Travels*: Livingstone, Africa and the Book'.

100 See, for instance, Rimi B. Chatterjee, *Empires of the Mind: A History of Oxford University Press in India under the Raj* (New Delhi and Oxford: Oxford University Press, 2006), and Louise C. Henderson, 'Geography, Travel and Publishing in Mid-Victorian Britain', unpublished PhD thesis, University of London, 2012.

CHAPTER EIGHT

Exhibiting empire at the Delhi Durbar of 1911: Imperial and cultural contexts

John M. MacKenzie

Empires cannot be self-effacing. Their rulers have always had a powerful need to exhibit themselves, to demonstrate the grandeur and power of their political creation, to overawe the populace (both the citizens at home and the subjects of conquered territories) as well as reveal to rivals just how significant they are and how dangerous it would be to tangle with them. Such exhibitions of authority were intended to display some central fantasies of sovereignty and empire which were designed to instil both self-confidence and reassurance, thereby justifying their existence and securing intellectual and ideological consolation. Their governmental and administrative elites fabricate such notions; their intellectuals, writers and educators develop and disseminate them; the populace, more or less, accept them as evidence of their superiority. Those who operate the economic networks of the imperial relationship – producers, merchants, shippers and industrialists – invariably see themselves as the vitally active components of these imperial ideas. They also provide a key justificatory foundation for the actions of the military and officials as they spread out and function within the imperial networks of power. Those who seek to bring down empires, whether by opposing them through violent confrontation or political agitation, need to gnaw away at such convictions, overthrowing them both by revealing the ludicrously overblown self-assessment of the imperialists and also by demonstrating the ultimate unreality and impracticality of their self-regarding conceptual fantasies.

The first of these imperial fantasies is the ambition for global government. Here, the British fantasy was based upon culturally specific concepts of 'freedom' and administrative and legal arrangements that supposedly set them apart as incomparably capable of world rule. The second fantasy is the notion of a uniquely superior civilisation, one so distanced from the empire's neighbours or, in modern times, overseas 'others', as to render rule both inevitable and morally appropriate. The corollary of this is the demarcation of all others as 'barbarians'. This was of course famously true of the self-assessments and attitudes of the Chinese. Even the Japanese, taking their cue from China, denoted visiting Europeans like Portuguese and Dutch as *nanban* or barbarians. The ancient Greeks devoted much attention to defining the nature of barbarism (for them language was one important criterion, as later for other empires) and the Romans adopted and developed such ideas. The migrating Arabs also applied them to peoples in North Africa, and 'Barbary' and 'Berbers' have survived as terms to this day. The British elite in turn, deeply influenced as they were by ancient Greece and Rome through their classical education, through travel (including the Grand Tour) and through their literary interests, adopted a similar binary between 'civilisation' and 'barbarism' – though barbarism could be attractive in its raw pre-industrialism. In many respects such a fundamental underpinning of the central ideology of imperialism was re-emphasised by the immense popularity of Edward Gibbon's multi-volume *Decline and Fall of the Roman Empire* (published between 1776 and 1788, important years for the emergence and transformation of the British Empire) which offered a full panoply of both parallels and warnings. Gibbon's concepts echoed down the nineteenth and early twentieth centuries. Indeed the whole fabric of historical allusion and alleged comparative insights was another of these several fantasies, all infused with visions of and lessons from the past.

Perhaps one of the greatest fantasies of empire was the notion that the allegedly superior standards and ideas of the rulers conferred freedoms and liberty upon subject peoples in ways that had been unknown before. These were duly transferred through the spread of intellectual and religious benefits by means of education and (in modern times) Christian missionary endeavour (often bound up together). By the later nineteenth and twentieth centuries, freedom and liberty were seen to have been enhanced by modern scientific, medical and technological ideas. Imperialists carried with them a portmanteau of disciplines, theories and practices (most of them only recently developed in the West) which included microbiology, germ theory, natural taxonomies in botany, zoology, entomology, geology and much else, related developments in chemical production, as well as the new technologies of steam, electro-magnetism, the telegraph and in the twentieth century electricity and all its related media developments. Linked to all of this was the fantasy of universal knowledge, the imperial archive as Richards called it, the notion that the natural phenomena and cultures and peoples of the world could be engrossed into a massive taxonomic project in which, ultimately, everything could be known.[1] Allied with this was the fantasy of what we may call comprehensive visualisation, that everything could be made available by new technologies like photography and, in the twentieth century, film.[2]

Yet another fantasy is that of free movement, of travel.[3] Like all the other fantasies, this tends to be class-specific and ethnically exclusive, though theoretically it contains within it the delusion of ready availability – not least for emigrants from the imperial metropole. This concept of free movement was invariably tied up with the provision of what were perceived as forms of good government and in modern times the two were seen to go inseparably together. Imperial rule offered unprecedented possibilities for movement, for officials, traders, the military, emigrants and even those seeking forms of pilgrimage and leisure. Again, ancient empires also flattered themselves as offering this fantasy of free movement.

The first delusionary ambition, that of global government, had as its corollary the fantasy of universal monarchy. Here global and universal are of course defined according to the worldview of the empire concerned: those of China and of imperial Rome are obvious examples. In early modern history, the Spanish and the French were seen as clear cases of aspirant universal monarchy and, for the first time, global really did seem to mean something approaching worldwide. But the British also indulged in the fantasy of global monarchy, evidenced by the raising of Queen Victoria's status to that of Empress (albeit theoretically solely in respect of India), the appearance of her material presence throughout the empire in statuary, on coinage (as in the case of Rome) and postage stamps, among other forms of visual imagery. And of course the fantasy of universal monarchy was inseparably associated with the notion of its assertion through display. A quiet, unassuming, bicycling modern Scandinavian-style monarchy would not suit the business of empire, for the mystique of the authority of an imperial monarchy was constantly asserted through lavish pageantry. Not even Victoria's withdrawal into her widow's 'weeds', her widowhood at Windsor, could stop such display in its tracks. If she was not available, then her statues had to be, as they undoubtedly were from the 1880s onwards. Everywhere in the Empire, her mystique was asserted by viceroys, governors, commissioners, mayors and others who saw themselves as her representatives. The grand show of monarchy remained possible without the monarch until she reappeared as the central figure of such magnificent displays in her jubilees of 1887 and 1897.

Thus, all imperial fantasies are encapsulated in the ritualistic display of power in ceremony, the regular exhibiting of empire. Ceremonial represents the public assertion of the ideologies and alleged successes of empire. If Ancient Rome had its triumphs and its circuses, modern empires had their ceremonies, their processions, grand openings, arrivals and departures, historical pageants[4] and regular commemorations. At all of these, both civilians and military could be exhibited to best advantage, dressed in formal attire, often mounted, their stylised movements and exchanges performed to the accompaniment of band music or the salutes of artillery. In such rituals, they became almost living statues, larger than life, self-conscious expressions of the heroic, virtually frozen in a moment of time. Roman triumphs incorporated the parading of the conquered, dominant and subordinate acting out their role in the demonstration of the might of Rome and the futility of resisting its power and authority. Modern empires were also concerned to include indigenous peoples, generally rulers, in the rituals of power, acting out their difference both through their dress and skin colour but also through their homage, their assimilation into the political, if not the social and cultural, processes of the ruling power. Rather than disguising politics as aesthetic entertainment, as it has been suggested, they were designed to expose political processes in a supposedly more appealing, 'user-friendly' form.[5]

In the British case, such displays occurred throughout the Empire, albeit in a great range of grandiloquent gestures from the truly spectacular to the vaguely ridiculous. In every colony, ritualised displays of power occurred with the arrival and departure of governors, with celebrations of the monarch's birthday, of special days in the calendar (in the twentieth century, often Empire Day), of royal coronations, jubilees or deaths and, as the means of transport became increasingly convenient – particularly from the 1870s or so – visits of members of an extended royal family. Such displays were meaningless without audiences. People turned out to be entertained and perhaps awed (in some cases, maybe alienated or simply rendered indifferent). They were encouraged to do so through holidays, through the participation of schoolchildren and through the appeal of music, uniforms, animals (elephants, horses, camels, military mascots) and processional displays. Moreover, in modern times, the audiences could be massively increased through various forms of photographic reproduction. Through these means, the displays of empire were indeed frozen in time, but they were also made much more widely available through their depiction in engravings – as in the *Illustrated London News* – through press photography once the technology was available from the 1890s, through the distribution of postcards[6] and eventually through the showing of films in informal, makeshift settings and eventually in the dedicated cinemas.

By the end of the nineteenth century and the beginning of the twentieth, royal jubilees and coronations had become the quintessential performances of such imperial power. If they represented the supreme metropolitan example, then the Indian durbars constituted the apex of such imperial displays in the Empire itself. There were three such durbars, in 1877, in 1903 and in 1911, although the word 'durbar' was avoided for the first. That of 1911 was genuinely climactic since it most clearly expressed the fantasies of empire, not least because of the presence of the King-Emperor and Queen-Empress. It aroused considerable worldwide interest promoted by advanced technologies of communications, printing, photography and film.[7] It came at the high point of imperialism before the great deluge of the First World War, enshrining the grand delusions of universal monarchy in its pageantry and displays, the fantasy of good government and its associations with peace and freedom, of uniquely advanced civilisation, of global knowledge including the anthropology of multiple 'peoples', of comprehensive visualisation and related technologies, of historical allusion and the appropriation of supposed traditions, as well as the fantasy of free travel both across the globe and within India. It was of course the last, although we know that George VI and his advisers hankered after another one in the late 1930s, doomed to be overwhelmed by the twin nemeses of nationalism and war. To contemporaries, it seemed like a great apotheosis in a continuing story. Moreover, one of its functions was to overwhelm – as some deluded imperialists imagined – the more extreme aspects of nationalism. It now has a very different flavour, of the last stand, the final imperial redoubt before the bastions fell in the face of the combined onslaughts of European war and nationalist activity in Ireland as well as in India. It also encapsulates an extraordinary paradox: in one sense it paraded the aspects of modernity that had made it possible, but in another it seemed hopelessly atavistic, a display of peoples and their clothing and accoutrements that were strikingly premodern.

It is well known in British Indian history that the word 'durbar' has Persian origins, that it was used in a variety of meanings, initially by the Viceroy Viscount Canning to secure the fealty of princes in the aftermath of the Indian revolt of 1857. As it developed from Lord Lytton's extravagant assemblage it was also closely connected with the rituals and performances of the imperial relationship, not least the creation of ever more complex hierarchies of honours, titles and gun salutes surveyed in the well-known article by Bernard Cohn.[8] But dramatic changes took place between Lytton's Imperial Assemblage of 1877 (Lytton shied away from the use of the word 'durbar' because he thought it would raise various problems of precedence), the notorious 'Curzonation', the great durbar of 1903, and the 1911 event.[9] These events displayed an impressively visual and mobile discourse of dominance, exhibiting empire in its most grandiloquent form.[10] It is true that they were spectacles of ceremony and ritual, which reaffirmed and sacralised hierarchy, but, more significantly, they symbolised hierarchical relationships in the service not only of power but also of propaganda.[11] Thus during this thirty-four-year period, metropolitan reactions to these changed dramatically, their imperial purpose was transformed, as was their contextualisation in imperial popular culture, for by the twentieth century the public penetration of news and images was revolutionised.

The Imperial Assemblage of 1877 was designed to announce the elevation of Queen Victoria to her role as Empress of India, the final stage in the transfer of India from Company to Crown rule. As Cohn described it, 1877 was the culmination of the processes initiated by the Queen's Proclamation of 1858, the creation of the hierarchies of princes in the 1860s, the visits of the Duke of Edinburgh in 1869 and the more celebrated one of the Prince of Wales in 1875–76.[12] In particular it was the apparent success of the latter that encouraged Disraeli in his desire to create an imperial throne. In his speech on the Royal Titles Bill, Disraeli laid out a succession of myths of British rule that were to remain standard through the succeeding two durbars.[13] The first of these was that India consisted of a whole range of princedoms requiring to be united in allegiance to a common emperor, as supposedly under the Mughals. Meanwhile, the vast regions ruled directly by the British were inhabited by nations (significantly plural) of Indians who were highly heterogeneous in ethnicities, cultures and religions. They were consequently incorrigibly disunited and achieved unity only through British rule. The Assemblage and later the durbars were required to emphasise that synthetic unity by producing through the symbols of overblown pageantry and display a materialisation of the administrative and monarchical pyramid that was the Indian empire: the assemblage or durbar supposedly dipped into the pyramid of Indian peoples to incorporate them into the powerful apex of rulers and representatives of the empress.[14] Lytton also hoped that his Assemblage would influence public opinion in Britain, by which he presumably meant mainly middle-class opinion, since the electorate had not yet been transformed by the extension of the franchise in the acts of 1884, 1918 and 1928.

There was, however, much that was farcical about the 1877 Assemblage. This parallels two other phenomena. It is often suggested that, if the British are expert at anything, it is the choreography of pageantry in the service of great national events. But that is a very recent perception. The coronations were frequently chaotic affairs until the twentieth century.[15] Moreover, there was something of a sea change between Victoria's Golden Jubilee in 1887 and the Diamond in

1897.[16] The first was rather more half-hearted at a time when republicanism was still active in Britain and when a good deal of opposition to the jubilee ceremonies was expressed. This was not the case in 1897 when republicanism seemed to be in its death throes and the imperial context of the Jubilee made it a great deal more consensual. Similarly, the Assemblage met with rather more opposition than the later durbars. If we look at the pages of one representative newspaper, *The Scotsman*, which regarded itself as Scotland's national newspaper, we find an intriguing combination of striking description and fierce opposition. The event was planned in 1876 and took place on New Year's Day 1877. The imperial proclamation was read out by the tallest military officer in India, whose elaborate uniform, it was reported, cost £200, and he was attended by six European and six 'native' trumpeters arrayed as heralds on grey horses. There were grand banquets, military reviews, a camp covering twenty square miles. The Assemblage was described as combining 'civilised solemnity' with 'barbaric splendour', bringing together the classic imperial dichotomy of civilisation and barbarism. It was a 'modern field of the Cloth of Gold', a scene of 'gorgeous brilliancy', with no fewer than '100 gorgeous standards' prepared for presentation to the chief princes, the banners designed by Dr Birdwood of the India Office. But all the solemnity was followed by the 'comic business' of 'races, balls, amusements'. It reflected Lord Beaconsfield's notion of 'the susceptibility of the Eastern mind to spectacular glitter and scenic display'.[17] No fewer than 16,000 prisoners were emancipated from the jails, a conscious following of a supposedly 'Oriental way of celebrating'.[18]

But all this was quickly racialised. 'Orientals' would be awed 'just as children at home are dazzled by the mock splendours of panto'.[19] While it was certainly of 'historical importance', press and politicians attacked the whole affair. The words 'gewgaws',[20] 'tomfoolery', 'farce' and pantomime frequently appeared in articles and speeches.[21] The 'natives', it was said were not greatly impressed; the attempt to overawe the Russians, threatening the North West frontier, was a failure, while Sir David Wedderburn, a proponent of Indian nationalism, viewed it as an 'expensive fiasco'.[22] It was seen as a brainchild of the Tory Party, opposed by senior administrators in India right up to the governors of Bombay and Madras who resented its pretentiousness, not to mention the consumption of much money, time and effort, at a time of famine. It was also held to be essentially un-British, like the Royal Style and Titles bill itself. It carried the taint of autocracy, unsuited to British democratic pretensions. Even its official artist, Val Prinsep, found it all horribly vulgar and lacking in taste.[23] Moreover, the actual organisation of camps and pageantry was far from perfect, with some of the ceremony marred by problems, particularly the notorious stampede of the elephants and horses stimulated by the noise of the *feux de joie*, which caused death and injury among onlookers.[24] One officer, Captain Clayton, died as a result of a polo accident and a soldier called O'Riley shot three colleagues at the Assemblage and was hanged in May.[25]

Thus, although huge numbers of people were involved, 84,000 by one count, the Assemblage was feudal and elitist in its overall thrust. It stimulated a good deal of opposition in the Indian press and among the educated elite of India who would shortly found the nationalist movement. Its impact upon popular culture in Britain may have been relatively slight, although it should be remembered that the tour of the Prince of Wales in India which preceded it did receive a good deal of press coverage: lavish supplements were published by the *Illustrated London News* and other papers. The Assemblage had its official historian, J. Talboys Wheeler, but his book *The History of the Imperial Assemblage at Delhi, held on 1st January 1877 to celebrate the Assumption of the Title of Empress of India by HM the Queen, including Historical Sketches of India and her Princes, Past and Present*, cannot have had more than elite circulation.[26] *The Scotsman* included it in its 'Christmas Books' review in December 1877, where it was described as 'elegant and excellent'.[27] It is hard, however, to imagine it finding its way into Christmas stockings with a title like that.

If the purpose of the Assemblage had been to confirm the authority of the Queen-Empress and set the seal to the many changes that had occurred since the 1857 revolt, the two durbars of the twentieth century had a rather different thrust. On the face of it they constituted the means whereby Victoria's successors could be proclaimed as King-Emperors, with George V uniquely present in 1911. But other forces were at work too. The durbars were supposedly designed to resolve the paradox of the twofold means by which the British ruled the subcontinent, that is through the princely states on the one hand and by direct administration in the presidencies and provinces on the other. But as in 1877 it was the pageantry of the princes, with their supposedly traditional and hugely opulent garments and jewels, as well as those of their retainers and followers, some with the now neutered accoutrements of war, which stole the show. Governors, lieutenant governors, commissioners and the vast numbers of British and Indian troops from the directly ruled parts of India found it hard to counter this luxuriant princely display. This was despite the fact that, according to the Indian Census of 1911, the so-called princely states accounted for just under 71 million of the population of the subcontinent, while British India accounted for over 244 million.[28] Such figures have to be treated with caution since enumeration was obviously so difficult, but the relative proportions are none the less reasonably clear. Moreover the durbars of 1903 and 1911 were designed to demonstrate the order the British were able to impose on such vast assemblages and by extension suggest that the Indian nationalist movement under middle-class leadership had little chance of creating the kind of unity that British rule allegedly produced. In addition, the two great 'boons' announced by George V in 1911 were intended to draw some of the sting of the nationalist movement. These were the revocation of the partition of Bengal and the move of the capital from Calcutta to the more traditional site of Delhi itself. That partition was the work of the creator of the 1903 durbar, Curzon himself. But it had seemed to stimulate the nationalist movement while Calcutta lay in what the British regarded as the most disaffected region of India, Bengal. In the event, for the nationalists, the two ultimately cancelled each other out. Curzon of course opposed those policies and cannot have been pleased when *The Times* described 1911 as an 'incomparably bigger and more majestic spectacle' than 1903.[29]

Thus, the imperial objectives of the durbars unquestionably changed over time, even if the location on the ridge above Delhi and the basic format did not: 'To the Eastern mind', a Press Association report averred 'Delhi is the only natural place to proclaim the Emperor'.[30] Moreover, it seems apparent that the intended audience for the durbars also significantly shifted. It may be said that the durbars were intended to impress several different audiences: in India there were the princely aristocrats, their retainers, followers and subjects; there was an Indian professional elite; and perhaps even the general populace. Similarly in Britain, there were the political classes, the elite and the public at large. In addition to these, there was also a global audience which can again be subdivided: there was the rest of the British Empire as well as a hoped-for international reception. There can be little doubt that the Assemblage of 1877 was directed at both Indian and British elites. Curzon's durbar was projected to politicians everywhere, with perhaps the main emphasis on the reception of the event in India, although Curzon was certainly adept at the manipulation of the press and paid considerable attention to its projection of the event in Britain.[31] The 1911 durbar was targeted much more precisely at the Indian nationalist movement and perhaps also at the public in Britain and the Empire with a possible spin-off into the international arena, all intended to enhance British prestige as well as justify Britain's imperial rule to Indians, the British, colonial populations and even peoples elsewhere.

The examination of press reactions also indicates that the two durbars were subject to far fewer criticisms than the 1877 Assemblage. There was even some rehabilitation of the earlier event. *The*

Scotsman proclaimed that, although it had ultimately cost £100,000, the 'sum was small in comparison with the political advantages it won for Britain'.[32] This new 1903 durbar would cost a good deal more, but an editorial suggested that it would celebrate not only the proclamation of Edward VII as the 'first Emperor' (presumably meaning white emperor) but also 'His Majesty's restoration to health, the end of the famine and ... the launching of India on a career of progress, peace and prosperity'.[33] Moreover, the suspicions that surrounded the 1877 event had now been allayed, while the new durbar would also carry with it real economic benefits.[34] Thus, in the weeks leading up to the durbar, there were generally favourable comments while the descriptions of the actual events (supplied by the Press Association, Reuters, and the special correspondents of various newspapers) were uniformly ecstatic.[35] 'All spectacles of our time fade into dullness by comparison' and this included the coronations both in London and in Moscow. If on the one hand, the Rajput cavalry swept by in their thousands wearing 'the armour of centuries ago – as though the trumpet of old romance were blown', the durbar also led to very modern infrastructural development. Railways were extended (with ten stations for the durbar camps alone), an electric light plant was created and telegraphic communications were created with Lahore, Bombay and Karachi.[36] British power appeared in a 'jewelled scabbard', the sword sheathed in favour of 'justice and beneficent rule', with the tributary princely states making progress in 'trade and wealth and the higher arts of civilisation'.[37] The durbar would be a great mingling of peoples from East and West, with quarter of a million present.[38]

Indian Empire was also exhibited through the great exhibition of art and manufactures organised by Dr George Watt, opened by Curzon.[39] Watt and his assistant had scoured the whole of India and Burma for the finest artistic works, while the gallery (a notably Orientalist structure with gardens) was decorated and furnished by the art schools of Burma, Lahore, Madras and Bombay. The Viceroy bemoaned the decline in Indian arts and expressed the hope that this exhibition would reverse the tendency, helping to keep Indian arts and crafts alive.[40] The Orientalist architecture and decoration of the amphitheatre in which the main ceremonies would take place was decorated by the 'eminent Indian artist Ram Singh', already famous for his work at Victoria's Osborne House.[41]

If the political objectives and the critical reception of the durbars changed, there was certainly a notable shifting in the centre of gravity of their intended reception, in both class and race terms. This was facilitated and conditioned by the development of new technologies and aspects of the media, providing them with a changing relationship with popular imperialism. If it may be said that the Assemblage probably produced little effect in Britain, the twentieth-century durbars turned out to be much more notable publishing events. The official historian of the 1903 durbar was none other than son of the chronicler of 1877, Stephen Wheeler, whose book, published by the celebrated publisher John Murray, matched the ponderous title of his father's, *A History of the Delhi Coronation Durbar held on the First of January 1903 to Celebrate the Coronation of His Majesty King Edward VII Emperor of India compiled from Official Papers*.[42] It was much criticised by Curzon himself and that was perhaps because it is as turgid as its title. But a number of other works celebrated the 'Curzonation', including at least two by women: Valentia Steer's *The Delhi Durbar 1902–3: A Concise Illustrated History* and another by Mrs Pearl Craigie (writing under the pseudonym of John Oliver Hobbes) who published *Imperial India: Letters from the East*. Their accounts were uniformly ecstatic. Steer saw the 'great gathering' as a grand 'living parable of India's loyalty and of Britain's might'. But this was 'no mere pageant' but a demonstration 'to ourselves our union [Britain and India]' 'and to the world our strength', an occasion bringing together the 'splendour of the East and the order of the West'.[43] Mrs Craigie, a rich American married to an English banker, was a friend of the Curzons and was their personal guest, so her enthusiasm is perhaps not surprising. For her, the durbar represented 'all that is best in Imperialism – the desire and aim to administer justice, to deliver the oppressed, to give freedom from anarchy, to dispense mercy in the hour of suffering'.[44]

The correspondent of *The Times*, the distinguished Lovat Fraser who wrote extensively about India, produced *At Delhi: An Account of the Delhi Durbar of 1903*, which was published in Bombay by *The Times* of India and had very little circulation in Britain.[45] Sir George Watt (knighted during the durbar) edited *Indian Art at Delhi, being the Official Catalogue of the Delhi Exhibition 1902–3*.[46] There were also a number of British artists present in 1903 and they published accounts, the most notable being Mortimer Menpes, who produced the lavishly illustrated *Durbar*.[47] Menpes's pictorial account is one of unalloyed enthusiasm both in aesthetic and in patriotic terms – although the text was written by Dorothy Menpes, it presumably reflected his sentiments. For them the durbar represented a massive wave of patriotic excitement, a necessary demonstration of power to both India and the world, justified by India's need for shows and ceremonies. They considered that the magnificent display revealed Britain's natural authority and therefore avenged the 1857 revolt, not least through the march of the Mutiny veterans, a central moment in Curzon's extravaganza. The Menpeses stressed – as Disraeli had done – the alleged great antiquity of Indian ruling families, much older than the British but incorporated by the durbar into the British royal traditions. For them, the brain could not fully take in the bewildering spectacle which was 'beyond description', representing the 'futility of the painter'. It all 'saturated' the onlookers with 'pride and loyalty', presenting a 'dream-like mystery' of 'unearthly beauty'. While the Mutiny was 'avenged', still it represented a 'picturesque old world in which chain-armoured people walked out of the Middle Ages' and 'a herald stepped out from an ancient page of British history'. Yet in all this purple prose and overpoweringly colourful illustrations, there is one very significant moment in the Menpeses' book: this is the description of the stillness and silence of the Indian crowds. In them, they wrote, the processions aroused no enthusiasm – 'it was not their show'.[48]

It is intriguing that at the next durbar in 1911, there was the same demonstration of silence among Indians viewing the ceremonies.[49] The official chronicler, John Fortescue, librarian of Windsor Castle and historian of the British army, wrote that the Indian crowds were entirely silent at the entry into Delhi of the King-Emperor. He attributed this to the fact that George V was on horseback and not riding an elephant as Curzon had done in 1903. The King, wrote Fortescue, looked like any of the other uniformed generals and field marshals in the procession and was therefore not recognised. The absence of the elephant was, he thought, a great mistake. During the durbar coronation itself, Fortescue again commented on the silence of the Indian crowds, while the Europeans cheered themselves hoarse. He now offered a different explanation – this was apparently because of the tradition of silent respect shown by Indians, which he considered to be much more tasteful than the exaggerated expressions of joy of the Europeans.[50] But can we see a certain pattern here? To what extent was this grand display, intended to impress Indians and demonstrate the might of the British and the futility of opposing them, actually an imported sight that moved them very little, particularly when the educated leadership was developing the nationalist movement as never before? Still *The Times* reports, obviously a biased source, emphasised the loyalty and reverence of Indians, particularly when the King and Queen showed themselves on the balcony of the Red Fort, when it was said that hundreds of thousands advanced and touched their foreheads.[51] Again, we must remember that this is *The Times*, itself reverently tugging its forelock. Moreover, Fortescue stressed that the British were the first to bring all the people of India under one imperial sovereignty and that the 'good Queen Victoria' 'looked upon all races as her children'.[52] Because he travelled on the P&O *Medina*, chartered as the royal yacht, Fortescue was also able to describe the

Figure 8.1 'Coronation Durbar, Delhi: The King Emperor
and Queen Empress', postcard, 1911

royal progress across the empire of the Mediterranean from Gibraltar
to Egypt and on to Bombay via Aden, calling at Malta on the way back.

So what about the public profile of these events in Britain? The 1903
durbar was attended by a number of newspaper special correspondents, and the early cinematographer Robert W. Paul produced a film.[53]
It may have been this film, or another, which seems to have been a
massive hit in Edinburgh (and presumably other cities too) in early
1903. As successive issues of *The Scotsman* indicate, it was shown in
the Waverley Market, in the Operetta House, the Queen Street Hall,
the Empire Palace Theatre and the Tivoli Theatre, while the Modern
Marvel Company had showings in a number of other venues in and
out of the city. These shows ran from January through to April and
May. Advertisements (clearly principally designed to 'puff' the event)
declared these pictures to be a 'phenomenal success', showing 'the
most brilliant pageant of our lifetime'. The Operetta House declared
that 'hundreds of patrons were turned away nightly' and later that the
film 'still continues to draw large audiences'. Interestingly, at the same
time a film about Canada was also being shown.[54]

More research might reveal even greater visibility of the 1903
durbar among the British public, although it certainly received
plenty of press coverage. Moreover, there is at least one fascinating
instance of an event linked with it. The South United Free Church

in Forfar in Scotland held a Delhi Durbar bazaar in the church hall, with decorations supposedly reminiscent of Delhi provided by a professional Liverpool company as well as various artistic representations of the durbar created by art masters in local schools. There were many stalls, including one entitled 'the grand shooting jungle', an art show, concerts, refreshments and so on. That shooting jungle clearly imitated in miniature the shooting expedition later pursued by George V and other royal visitors, supposedly conforming to another aspect of Mughal public display. There was even a performance of a farcical play, which somehow does not seem like the Free Church's style! The art show mirrored, on a tiny scale, the art shows that accompanied the 1877 Assemblage and the 1903 durbar or the exhibition of Indian artefacts in 1911, but they deserve separate studies. Of course the whole Forfar extravaganza was a fund-raising exercise, but it does seem to have been the event of the season in what was then the county town of Forfarshire. That it was linked to the durbar reveals some degree of public prominence. Moreover, it is hard to think that it was a lone instance. This enterprising Free Church produced a lavish Delhi Durbar Bazaar book, beautifully printed and illustrated, and there is a copy in the National Library of Scotland.[55] It may well be that there were others of a similar kind, but additional research is needed to hunt them down.

The 1911 durbar is better documented than the others, not least because its 400-page programme is readily available.[56] This gives a striking impression of the ways in which it followed precedent, but also capitalised on the presence of King-Emperor and Queen-Empress. It is intriguing that the well-known hierarchies of princes and processions were also reflected in the accompanying sporting events. Polo was a sport of the elite, though bringing together Indian aristocrats and British officers. Hockey was to be played by Indians, though some British officers were allowed to join teams. Football was the sport for European other ranks. The point-to-point races had a rule that the horses had to be owned by their riders, another elite restriction.[57] All of these sporting events charged entry fees for spectators, rising to a peak with the finals, so producing some income, but 1911 was also fiercely opposed, not least on financial grounds like its predecessors.

It was attacked at the Independent Labour Party conference, by Keir Hardie among others, to cries of 'shame' from some delegates, but the motion expressing sympathy with the Indian people and deprecating the cost was carried.[58] Curzon had tried to conceal the cost of 1903 with creative accounting and a suggestion that many items could be sold off. The 1911 durbar was staggeringly costly, but the presence of the King and Queen helped to blunt the attacks, at least of some. The durbar was also the subject of international comment, both in Europe and in Japan. French and Japanese newspapers were highly supportive, but perhaps that reflected the fact that they were in alliances with Britain at the time.[59]

But so far as popularisation is concerned, technology had moved on, particularly in the cinematography field and there can be no doubt that images of the King-Emperor's durbar were very widely distributed. In that year the popularisation of the grand pageantry in Delhi moved up a gear. It may be said that the London coronation of George V and also the Delhi Durbar helped to set the newsreels off in their dominant role in purveying news which they were to hold for forty years. Reeling forward, they were supplanted by television news in the 1950s, stimulated by the fillip provided by the 1953 Coronation of Elizabeth II to the purchase and ownership of television sets in Britain. At any rate, several cinematograph companies sent cameramen and representatives to Delhi, but none was so prominent as the American Charles Urban and the Kinemacolor Company, which for the first time brought efforts at colour filming (the colour applied to black and white film) to this strikingly colourful event. Unfortunately, very little of this film survives, but the small fragment that does gives a striking impression of the impact it must have had in Britain.[60] Charles Urban was appointed 'by the King', as it was formally stated, to record the durbar, and he sailed along with seven of his 'operators' (and many of the press corps, politicians and other visitors) on the P&O *Maloja*, sister ship of the *Medina*, which conveyed the King and Queen and their suites.[61] Urban and cameramen were all 'guests of the Indian Government'.[62] That means that they were paid for, so this was consciously a propagandist enterprise. Urban's name appears in the list of journalists, special correspondents and agency representatives who inhabited the press camp occupying the vast tented city in Delhi.[63] The Secretary of State for India, the Marquis of Crewe (who himself attended the durbar) and the Viceroy Hardinge were alert to the importance of press propaganda and gave every encouragement to the press corps.[64] No fewer than forty-six newspapers, countries and agencies were represented in this camp.[65] This included correspondents of all the leading London papers, as well as *The Scotsman* and *The Liverpool Courier* among regional ones. There were also British journalists from the principal Indian English-language journals, in addition to representatives of France, Italy, Holland, Hungary, Burma, Canada, South Africa and Australia. The Indian press camp (and later there was hostile comment on this racial distinction) contained forty-one Indians representing Indian vernacular papers and others.[66] These camps cannot have contained the entire press and photographic corps as there is no mention of the many cameramen, both still and movie, presumably accommodated elsewhere.

There can be little doubt that newspapers throughout Britain were more or less awash with reports of the durbar. Just as examples, this chapter will examine the coverage given to the durbar in some Scottish newspapers, notably *The Scotsman*, the Edinburgh paper which regarded itself as the Scottish equivalent of *The Times*, as well as the *Dundee Courier*, the *Dundee Advertiser* and the *Dundee Evening Telegraph*, together with the coverage in *The Times* itself.[67] In December of 1911 they were full of news of the preparations, of the arrival and progress of the King and Queen, of the grandeur of the events, and even of the shooting expedition and tours that followed. The *Dundee Courier* described Bombay, on the arrival of the King-Emperor, as offering 'one of the finest panoramas in the world', while in Delhi visitors witnessed 'scenes to which history has no parallel'.[68] Much was made of a 'tiny prince astride a huge camel' who got a 'great ovation' from the crowd when he saluted the King-Emperor with 'a sword larger then himself'.[69] It also described the unveiling of the All-India Memorial to Kind Edward by his son, who made an 'eloquent speech' matching the 'panegyric' on the inscription (in 1903, the Delhi statue of Queen Victoria had been unveiled).[70] Presumably other papers reported on these same events with equal breathlessness. These reports were frequently carried as the most prominent news items of the day, occupying three columns with larger headlines, unusually in bold print. The *Courier* carried sizeable photographs of Bombay, of Delhi and of hunting, on a daily basis. These were of course 'library photographs' rather than pictures of the actual events. *The Scotsman* was impressed that several members of European royal houses were to attend, providing regular details of the arrangements from February onwards.[71] The press corps and others were to be helped by the laying of the railway lines, as well as the thirty-one post and ten telegraph offices available for sending dispatches.[72] An exceptionally long report in December described the 'gorgeous spectacle', suggesting that here was a sovereign who arrived not as an old-style emperor 'of sword and burning' but as one 'clothed in the mantle of peace, and armed with the affection of his subjects'. 'The cold civilising power of the West met the abiding mystery and wonder of the East' while 'the East saw again a great legion thunder past, not in solemn, deep disdain, but in wonderment at its might and magnificence and in sure knowledge of its beneficence'.[73] Durbars always invoked purple prose – and there was a good deal more.

The *Dundee Advertiser*, which was the city's Liberal newspaper until it 'went Tory' in 1910 as a reaction to the Lloyd George budget, was equally lavish in its coverage. It carried virtually daily reports on its main international news page, covering two to four columns and it also printed large photographs of significant durbar visit locations.[74] Headlines included 'Gorgeous State Ceremonial', 'Unbounded Enthusiasm of Native Population', 'Scene of Oriental Splendour', 'Boundless Enthusiasm of India's People' and 'Royal Durbar Train: Last Word in Railway Luxuriance'. The Dundee *Evening Telegraph* also contained extensive reports with striking headlines such as 'Storm of Cheering. Gorgeous Scenes at Landing Stage' (on the arrival in Bombay).[75] Such headlines clearly carried powerful propagandistic messages, almost ensuring that there was little need to read the extensive report below. They also seemed to indicate that the indigenous population of India were not just overawed, but were willing and admiring participants in these events, something that may well have stretched journalistic licence too far. It may be suggested that the economy of Dundee was so closely linked to India (specifically Bengal) through jute that this city, of all in the United Kingdom, might be expected to give prominence to events in the subcontinent, but other newspapers indicate that this kind of coverage also existed elsewhere. Certainly no reader of newspapers in Dundee in these weeks could have been unaware of these events in faraway India, given the striking scale of coverage. And there were other media too.

Figure 8.2 'The Coronation Durbar, 1911: The King Emperor and Queen Empress attended by young Indian princes showing themselves to the multitude', postcard, 1911

While press reports could be telegraphed to Britain within hours and carried in the papers the following day, it took several weeks for the newsreels to be sent back, processed and edited. As well as Kinemacolor, Pathé and Gaumont were also there, together with other lesser known companies and some of their products survive – twenty-two minutes of the black-and-white Gaumont film can be viewed on the Web. It is important to establish just how popular these films were with the British public. The Kinemacolor film began to be shown in February of 1912 in spectacular circumstances. The Strand Theatre in London was decked out as the Taj Mahal and turned the newsreel into a two-and-a-half-hour show complete with a 48-piece band, a chorus and other musicians. It was described, admittedly in the Kinemacolor catalogue, as a sensational success and was then shown throughout Britain and the world. Reports were carried in all the London newspapers, the *Sunday Times* suggesting that all London would flock to see it. The Dundee *Evening Telegraph* reported that it was shown in that city and was attended by a crowded and enthusiastic house. The Belfast *Evening Telegraph* was equally enthusiastic and suggested that 'every child brought up under the serene protection and safety of the Union Jack' should see it.[76] Perhaps that was not a particularly surprising sentiment coming from a Unionist newspaper at an exceptionally fraught period in Irish politics. Indeed, in many papers the whole business of cinematography was a prominent and enduring one, the papers themselves offering showings, sometimes free. As in 1903, *The Scotsman* contained reports and advertisements for the black-and white-films of the Durbar, indicating that shows continued in a variety of theatres, as well as the new cinemas, from January until at least April.[77] These included the Picture House in Princes Street, the Empire Palace Theatre, the Royal Lyceum Theatre and others. Glasgow was similarly inundated with these performances, and the phenomenon must have been reproduced throughout the United Kingdom. The Dundee papers were proud of the fact that black-and-white film arrived in London on Sunday 1 January 1912 and was already on show in the Scottish city on the following day. The film was then shown in the New Electric, Palace and Cinema Theatres, sometimes continuously from 1.30 in the afternoon to 10.30 at night (with other things on the programme too). The *Advertiser* announced that

> the house was crowded all day and the audience showed special interest in the scenes at Delhi. There was a very fine picture shown of the actual ceremony of the Proclamation of King George as Emperor of India, and an idea of the pomp and brilliance of the scene was successfully conveyed.

The paper also carried a large photograph of the King-Emperor and Queen-Empress walking towards the durbar canopy. [78] On the 4th, the *Advertiser* carried details of the film, including the Proclamation, the Chiefs paying homage, the King and Queen reviewing troops, the Nizam of Hyderabad and the allegedly insulting mistake made by the Gaekwar of Baroda. There was also a large photograph of Indian Mutiny veterans attending the durbar. Advertisements indicated that ticket prices were 2*d*, 4*d* and 6*d*, providing evidence that almost any member of the population would have been able to attend. [79] In all these ways, films of the durbar perpetuated the long tradition of imperial theatre which begins in the eighteenth century and continues well into the twentieth. [80]

Yet we must remind ourselves that this was indeed a turbulent time in British political life. George Dangerfield's celebrated and seductive book *The Strange Death of Liberal England*, of 1936, suggested that Britain was almost on the verge of a revolution, when you put together the Irish nationalist movement and the threat of civil war proclaimed by Sir Edward Carson, the prominence of the trade unions influenced by syndicalism and the strikes encouraged by them, the suffragette agitation, not to mention the continuing disaffection of the right wing from the so-called people's budget of David Lloyd George and above all the Parliament Act of 1911 limiting the power of the House of Lords. [81]

Yet if we look at alternative contexts, we find that 1911 was a year of exhibitions. The largest was the Festival of Empire at the Crystal Palace Park at Sydenham. [82] This was an impressive display, both inside the Palace and out, including 300 buildings representing the British Empire with a railway line connecting them, offering the inevitable 'All Red Route'. There was also a grand pageant of Empire choreographed by the most celebrated pageant master of the day, Frank Lascelles. Fifteen thousand volunteers took part in this, recreating various events in imperial history and intriguingly it included a performance of the 1877 Delhi Imperial Assemblage. Perhaps the 1877 event was more prominent than we might think. It was said that the exhibition was extremely well attended, with no fewer than 144,000 people turning up on the first day, perhaps hoping to catch a glimpse of the new King and Queen. Nevertheless, figures for overall attendance are not available and the exhibition made a loss causing the bankruptcy of the Crystal Palace Company. This exhibition faced competition from another very impressive Coronation Exhibition at the White City in Shepherd's Bush, which also seems to have been well attended. We should not allow an all-too-common London focus to lead us to forget that there was also a major exhibition in Glasgow in 1911, held like its predecessors of 1888 and 1901 in Kelvingrove Park. Although this

Figure 8.3 'Coronation Durbar, Delhi: The King Emperor
and Queen Empress at the ceremony', postcard, 1911

exhibition has been seen as exhibiting aspects of the Scottish cultural
renaissance of the period, there were pavilions from many countries of
the Empire and it was alleged that attendances exceeded nine million
– clearly many of these were multiple visits. It made a reasonably
handsome profit.

How are we to reconcile the Dangerfield vision of crisis and supposedly near-national collapse with the celebrations of two coronations,
with three exhibitions and with a considerable public fascination
with the newsreels that followed? It is surely the case that two moods
can subsist at the same time. There are perhaps a number of parallels, but one obvious one is the situation at the end of the Second
World War. On the one hand there were the great celebrations in the
streets of London and elsewhere, complete with famous scenes on
the Buckingham Palace balcony and the Victory Parade in the Mall.
Churchill was at the centre of these, lauded as the great war hero and
yet he was about to lose, resoundingly, the general election that put
Labour into power with its policies of social reform, nationalisation
and decolonisation for India and other Asian territories. Two apparently conflicting tendencies can indeed coexist. The Dundee newspapers demonstrated this by carrying news of contemporary strikes in
the city, of dockers and of carters, serious enough to produce a clash
with the police and the deployment of 300 Black Watch troops, but,

[213]

even when coinciding on the same days, the strike news was no more prominent than that of the Delhi Durbar, even although the strikes clearly affected local people much more profoundly.[83]

It is perhaps interesting to conclude with one of the interpretations of Bernard Cohn. He suggests that the Indian National Congress took up some of the ceremonial forms of the Assemblage in its early meetings, but that this cultural inheritance from the British was overturned by the campaigns and style of Gandhi's movement.[84] He leaves it there, but just as Gandhi and Nehru represented very different visions for the future of India, so too can we find the durbar style re-emerging in post-Independence India. Anyone who has attended, as I have done, the Republic Day celebrations in New Delhi on 26 January will have seen durbar pageantry alive and well in modern Indian ceremonial, with its emphasis on troops, processions, splendid uniforms, bands, flags and banners, and also animals – the horses of the cavalry, the camels of the camel corps. We can find examples of durbar style elsewhere too. Sir John Lavery's painting of the visit of Queen Victoria to the Glasgow Exhibition of 1888 surely constitutes pure municipal durbar in its self-conscious magnificence.[85]

Of course it is true that a number of streams come together in this British-inspired ceremonial, including the state opening of Parliament and coronations themselves. These are reproduced in similar state openings in the former dominions to the present day – even the Afrikaner-dominated apartheid regime in South Africa maintained this tradition. To spread this suggestion out somewhat, we may also think of the inauguration of New Delhi as the Indian capital in 1931 once George V's 1911 announcement had worked its way through to the architecture of Edwin Lutyens and Herbert Baker; similar inaugurations of new planned capitals such as Canberra in Australia and Lusaka in Zambia; or for that matter the ceremonies associated with the royal tours of the interwar years (notably by the Prince of Wales, Edward VIII) and of George VI and Elizabeth II after the Second World War. We can add to that mix the decolonisation events throughout the British Empire, right down to the handover of Hong Kong to the Chinese in 1997, which also had the air of durbar about them, often including a British royal presence. It may be argued that the Assemblage and the two durbars had a considerable influence on all imperial ceremonials. Such ceremonies certainly had some popular resonance particularly through newsreels and later television. They all contributed to one of the myths of modern Britain, that the British can do grand pageantry and ceremonial, right down to the royal weddings of modern times. But what is striking about them is that the British got this imperial ceremonial act together so late in the history of empire, so close to its demise. Despite the protestations of Bernard Porter, it is surely hard to believe that the general public has been wholly indifferent to all of this.[86] Through this supposed British national obsession with pageantry and display, there can be little doubt that the fantasies of empire described at the opening of this chapter pass down to modern times. Surely the great popularity of television serials and films relating to the Raj, sometimes known as the 'heat and lust' school, of the last few decades helps to confirm this. The pageantry and fantasies of empire live on, not least because they exhibited empire in the most colourful and dramatic of ways. Through paintings, engravings, photography, newsreel cinematography and press reports they were deeply embedded in British popular consciousness.

Acknowledgements

An earlier version of this chapter was originally delivered as a keynote address at the conference 'Staging Empire, New Perspectives on the 1911 Coronation Durbar and Imperial Assemblage', held at Manchester Metropolitan University in September 1911. I am grateful to Dr Tilman Frasch for inviting me to this conference and to Professor Andreas Gestrich, Director of the German Historical Institute in London, co-organisers and funders. A number of significant papers were delivered at this conference on various aspects of the durbar.

Notes

1 Thomas Richards, *The Imperial Archive: Knowledge and the Fantasy of Empire* (London: Verso, 1993).

2 James R. Ryan, *Picturing Empire: Photography and the Visualisation of the British Empire* (London: Reaktion, 1997); Ann Maxwell, *Colonial Photography and Exhibitions: Representations of the 'Native' People and the Making of European Identities* (London: Leicester University Press, 1999).

3 For an elaboration of these ideas, see John M. MacKenzie, 'Empire Travel Guides and the Imperial Mind-Set from the Mid-Nineteenth to the Mid-Twentieth Centuries', in Martin Farr and Xavier Guégan (eds), *The British Abroad Since the Eighteenth Century, Volume 2: Experiencing Imperialism* (Basingstoke: Palgrave, 2013), pp. 116–33; see also John M. MacKenzie, 'Empires of Travel: British Guide Books and Cultural Imperialism in the 19th and 20th Centuries', in John K. Walton (ed.), *Histories of Tourism: Representation, Identity and Conflict* (Clevedon: Channel Publications, 2005), pp. 19–38.

4 Such pageants were a regular feature of the great exhibitions, reaching a great climax in the Wembley Exhibition of 1924–25 when a massive pageant of empire was staged in the newly completed stadium. Such pageants were also mounted throughout the Empire. Another example can be found below. See Deborah S. Ryan, 'The Man who Staged the Empire: Remembering Frank Lascelles in Sibford Gower, 1875–2000', in Marius Kwint, Christopher Breward and Jeremy Aynsley (eds), *Material Memories, Design and Evocation* (Oxford: Berg, 1999), pp. 159–79, and 'Staging the Imperial City: The Pageant of London, 1911', in Felix Driver and David Gilbert (eds), *Imperial Cities: Landscape, Performance and Identity* (Manchester: Manchester University Press, 2000), pp. 117–35.

5 Julie F. Codell, 'Introduction', in Codell (ed.), *Power and Resistance: The Delhi Coronation Durbars 1877, 1903, 1911* (Ahmedabad: Mapin Publishing, 2012), p.

17. This magnificently illustrated, beautifully produced book contains many photographs from the Alkazi and other collections. The essays in it (by a variety of authors) are of variable quality, with one or two containing some dubious judgements. However, it performs the useful function of highlighting both Indian photographers and indigenous reactions.

6   The 1911 durbar in particular was turned into a major postcard event with large numbers issued, although some were also published of the 1903 Curzonation. The author has a considerable collection of these.

7   For the photography of this durbar, see Codell (ed.), *Power and Resistance*, though, curiously, the 1903 durbar receives rather more attention that the 1911 one; for film, again concentrating more on 1903, but with some references to 1911, see Stephen Bottomore, '"An Amazing Quarter Mile of Moving Gold, Gems and Genealogy": Filming India's 1902/3 Durbar', *Historical Journal of Film, Radio and Television* 15 (1995), pp. 495–515.

8   Bernard S. Cohn, 'Representing Authority in Victorian India', in Eric Hobsbawm and Terence Ranger (eds), *The Invention of Tradition* (Cambridge: Cambridge University Press, 1983), pp. 165–210.

9   To a certain extent, Lytton's event emphasised medievalism, Curzon's modernity, while that of 1911 was more directly about displaying the monarchy to India and the world, utilising all modern technologies.

10 The durbars did a good deal more than 'serve to nationalize a local ceremonial idiom'. David Cannadine, *Ornamentalism: How the British Saw Their Empire* (London: Allen Lane, 2001), p. 109.

11 Cannadine, *Ornamentalism*, p. 122.

12 Cohn, 'Representing Authority', pp. 179–83.

13 Ibid., pp. 184–5.

14 Over three hundred ceremonies were held all over India on the day of the proclamation in 1877, ensuring the wider dissemination of the meaning of the Assemblage. Cohn, 'Representing Authority', p. 207.

15 David Cannadine, 'The Context, Performance and Meaning of Ritual: The British Monarchy and the "Invention of Tradition", c.1820–1977', in Eric J. Hobsbawm and Terence O. Ranger (eds), *The Invention of Tradition* (Cambridge: Cambridge University Press, 1983), pp. 101–64, particularly pp. 116–18.

16 John M. MacKenzie, *Propaganda and Empire: The Manipulation of British Public Opinion, 1880–1960* (Manchester: Manchester University Press, 1984), p. 4

17 *The Scotsman*, 19 December 1876, p. 2; 2 January 1877, p. 4; 2 January 1877, p. 6.

18 *The Scotsman*, 9 January 1877, p. 3.

19 *The Scotsman*, 2 January 1877, p. 4.

20 This description came from the *Saturday Review*, quoted in a round-up of the London weekly press in *The Scotsman*, 8 January 1877, p. 6.

21 *The Scotsman*, 11 January 1877, p. 5; 15 January 1877, p. 3; 15 January 1877, p. 3; 29 January 1877, p. 3; 31 January 1877, p. 4.

22 *The Scotsman*, 31 January 1877, p.4; 6 March 1877, p. 3; 3 December 1877, p. 3.

23 Cohn, 'Representing Authority', pp. 189 and 200.

24 Ibid., p. 205.

25 *The Scotsman*, 2 January 1877, p. 6; 14 May 1877, p. 3.

26 London: Longmans Green, 1877.

27 *The Scotsman*, 3 December 1877, p. 3.

28 My source for these census figures is Murray's *A Handbook for Travellers in India, Burma and Ceylon* (London: John Murray, 1919), pp. cxxxii–cxxxviii.

29 *The Times*, 18 December 1911, p. 8, column 1–2.

30 Press Association (PA) Report from Delhi 4 December 1902, quoted in *The Scotsman*, 29 December 1902, p. 8.

31 Chandrika Kaul, *Reporting the Raj: The British Press and India, c. 1880–1922* (Manchester: Manchester University Press, 2003), p. 105.

32 *The Scotsman*, 13 November 1902, p. 5. The report went on to suggest that, although the 1903 event might well cost double this, Eastern history was full of examples 'of

the inestimable value of prestige among tributary races'.

33 *The Scotsman*, 11 November 1902, p. 4, Editorial no. 2.

34 *The Scotsman*, 13 November 1902, p. 5; 30 December 1902, p. 4.

35 Kaul has indicated the extent to which Reuters and the other news agencies lavishly covered the durbars, as well as the extent to which major Fleet Street figures were sent out by the newspapers to report on them. Kaul, *Reporting the Raj*, pp. 43, 61, 63, 77, 109.

36 *The Scotsman*, 29 December 1902, p. 8.

37 *The Scotsman*, 30 December 1902, p. 4.

38 *The Scotsman*, 29 December 1902, p. 8.

39 Julie F. Codell, 'Gentlemen Connoisseurs and Capitalists: Modern British Imperial Identity in the 1903 Delhi Durbar's Exhibition of Indian Art', in Dana Arnold (ed.), *Cultural Identities and the Aesthetics of Britishness* (Manchester: Manchester University Press, 2004), pp. 134–63.

40 The first description of the arts exhibition was in *The Scotsman*, 26 December 1902, p. 4, with a further survey on 29 December 1902, p. 8; the opening of the exhibition and Curzon's speech were reported on 31 December 1902, pp. 6–7, together with the description of the building contained in a *Daily Telegraph* telegram quoted in *The Scotsman* that day, while Watt's knighthood appeared on 1 January 1903, p. 5.

41 Ram Singh's work was described in *The Scotsman*, 29 December 1902, p. 8.

42 London: John Murray, 1904.

43 Valentia Steer, *The Delhi Durbar 1902–3: A Concise Illustrated History* (Madras: Higginbotham; London: Marshall, 1903), pp. 3, 5, 10.

44 John Oliver Hobbes (Mrs Pearl Craigie), *Imperial India: Letters from the East* (London: Fisher Unwin, 1903), p. 20.

45 Lovat Fraser, *At Delhi* (Bombay: Times of India, 1903).

46 Sir George Watt, *Indian Art at Delhi, Being the Official Catalogue of the Delhi Exhibition 1902–3* (London: John Murray; Delhi: Government Printer, 1904; reprinted Delhi, 1987).

47 Mortimer Menpes, *The Durbar* (text by Dorothy Menpes) (London: Adam and Charles Black, 1903). Dorothy, it has been suggested, was Menpes's daughter.

48 Ibid., pp. 36–7, 42, 47, 55–7, 62, 65, 76, 126.

49 For a general account of audience reactions, see Jim Masselos, 'The Great Durbar Crowds: The Participant Audience', in Julie F. Codell (ed.), *Power and Resistance: The Delhi Coronation Durbars* (Ahmedabad: Mapin, 2012), pp. 176–203.

50 John Fortescue, *Narrative of the Visit to India of Their Majesties King George V and Queen Mary and of the Coronation Durbar held at Delhi on 12th December, 1911* (London: Macmillan, 1912), pp. 120–1, 151.

51 *The Times*, 14 December 1911, p. 10, column 5.

52 Fortescue, *Narrative*, pp. 2–3.

53 Information on Paul can be found in www.victorian-cinema.net/paul (accessed 14 June 2013). Other information on the film and extracts can be found on the Web.

54 *The Scotsman*, 22 January 1903, p. 1; 23 January 1903, p. 1; 24 January 1903, p. 2; 26 January 1903, p. 1; 27 January 1903, pp. 1, 5; 28 January 1903, p. 1. These advertisements and reports in 'amusements' round-ups appear almost daily. See also 3 February 1903, p. 1.They continue until 5 May 1903, p. 5.

55 South United Free Church, Forfar, *Delhi Durbar Bazaar Book*, printed by W. Shepherd, Forfar, 1903. The event was held between 29 and 31 October 1903.

56 The official programme of the durbar is available on the Web at www.archive.org/stream/coronationdurbar030742mbp#page/n5/mode/2up (accessed 14 June 2013). It has also been republished at least twice. See also Nayana Goradia, *The Delhi Durbar 1911: The Last Hurrah of the Raj* (New Delhi: Indian International Centre, 2011).

57 Official Programme, section XVI, pp. 79ff. The point about ownership of horses is on p. 84.

58 *The Times*, 19 April 1911, p. 7, column 3.

59 *The Times*, 8 December 1911, p. 11, column 1; 13 December 1911, p. 8, column 2.

60 This film can be found in various places on the Web.

61 Postcards were issued and widely sold of the *Medina* decked out as a royal yacht (its hull painted white, for example). One of these is in the author's collection.

62 *The Times*, 16 November 1911, p. 11.

63 Official Programme, list of all those allocated to the camps, p. 257.

64 Kaul, *Reporting the Raj*, pp. 109, 131, 142.

65 Official Programme, pp. 257ff., list of all those allocated to the camps.

66 Kaul, *Reporting the Raj*, p. 235.

67 *The Times* index for 1911 contains seven and a half columns of references to the durbar.

68 *Dundee Courier*, 5 December 1911, p. 6; 7 December 1911, p. 5. The *Dundee Courier* was a Tory paper, like *The Scotsman*. The Liberal paper in Dundee was the *Dundee Advertiser*. A.H. Miller, *The Dundee Advertiser, 1801–1901: A Centenary Memoir* (Dundee: J. Leng, 1901) claimed (p. 22) that in 1901 the *Advertiser* had a circulation of 250,000 per week.

69 *Dundee Courier*, 15 December 1911, p. 5.

70 *Dundee Courier*, 8 December 1911, p. 5.

71 *The Scotsman*, 1 January 1911, p. 1; 17 February 1911, p. 3; 3 March 1911, p. 9; 30 March 1911, p. 8, and many more during subsequent months.

72 *The Scotsman*, 15 December 1911, quoting a Reuters report.

73 *The Scotsman*, 8 December 1911, p. 7.

74 It carried major reports and/or photographs on 2, 4, 5, 8, 11, 12, 13, 14, 18 December 1911, all on either page 7 or 10. After that date, the news of the Dundee strike took over the prominent position in the paper. The *Advertiser* (18 December 1911, p. 7) carried a report of the alleged disrespect of the Gaekwar of Baroda complete with his letter of apology to the Viceroy – he had apparently been overcome by 'nervous confusion' and had missed seeing his only predecessor in giving homage, the Nizam of Hyderabad since he was second in precedence as a feudatory prince. He expressed 'sincere sorrow at the mishap'. Even the *Dundee Evening Telegraph* carried reports on similar dates, often running to more than a column.

75 *Dundee Evening Telegraph*, 4 December 1911, p. 2, cols 5–6. Or again 'King and Queen Make State Entry into Delhi amidst Scenes of Much Enthusiasm. Gorgeous Procession of Indian Chiefs', *Dundee Evening Telegraph*, 7 December 1911, p. 1, col. 4. There were also prominent reports on 2, 6, 9, 12, 13, 15 and 18 December 1911, among others.

76 Information on Charles Urban and the publicity material of the Kinema-color catalogue, with many quotations from newspapers, can be found in www. charlesurbn.com/documents-gallery.html and in www.charlesurban.com/sources. html.

77 *The Scotsman*, 28 December 1911, p. 1; 2 January 1912, p. 6; 3 January 1912, p. 1, and on many subsequent days right through until 23 April 1912, p. 4 and again succeeding days until 15 May 1912, p. 2. All of this was prefigured by pictures of Delhi at Poole's New Myriorama, *The Scotsman*, 27 December 1911, p. 6.

78 *Dundee Advertiser*, 2 January 1912, pp. 3 and 8. These showings continued in the Dundee theatres, always well attended, until the end of the month.

79 *Dundee Advertiser*, 4 January 1912, pp. 1, 8.

80 Marty Gould, *Nineteenth-Century Theatre and the Imperial Encounter* (New York: Routledge, 2011).

81 George Dangerfield, *The Strange Death of Liberal England* (London: Constable 1936; republished many times thereafter).

82 MacKenzie, *Propaganda and Empire*, ch. 4.

83 *Dundee Courier*, 19 December 1911, p. 5; 21 December 1911, p. 5; 25 December 1911, p. 5.

84 Cohn, 'Representing Authority', p. 209.

85 Sir John Lavery, *State Visit of Her Majesty Queen Victoria to the Glasgow International Exhibition, 1888–1890*, Culture and Sport Glasgow (Museums). This painting used to hang in the Royal Concert Hall in the city, providing a particularly celebratory ambience to that public building. It appears as the cover illustration of

John M. MacKenzie and T.M. Devine (eds), *Scotland and the British Empire* (Oxford, Oxford University Press, 2011).
86 Bernard Porter, *The Absent-Minded Imperialist: Empire, Society and Culture in Britain* (Oxford: Oxford University Press, 2006).

CHAPTER NINE

Elgar's *Pageant of Empire*, 1924:
An imperial leitmotif

Nalini Ghuman

The whole thing, besides being splendid to see, should have great Imperial value ... Never was there such a theme for a pageant in the world before.[1]

No soul & no romance & no imagination

One of the last great displays of the heyday of imperialism – the British Empire Exhibition – was held at Wembley in the summers of 1924 and 1925 and was visited by twenty-seven million people. It was, as the historian Jeffrey Richards has stated, 'in many ways, the culminating exhibition of Empire'.[2] *The Times* described its visual impact in vivid terms:

> What is Wembley but one great Pageant of Empire? – a pageant set among scenery as variegated as the Continents whence its inspiration comes. Here are the white minarets of India, and over there the Chinese signs of Hong-Kong. From the substantial Pavilions of Canada and Australia the eye strays to the carved ingenuities of Burma, rests for a moment on the colours of Malaya, and comes home by way of London Bridge to the massive Government Building ... Every day stages another scene in the eternal pageant of the Exhibition.[3]

The Exhibition opened on 23 April 1924, St George's Day, with a vast musical event directed by Sir Edward Elgar – rare home-movie film footage (and a striking photograph) shows the 67-year-old composer conducting the massed orchestral and choral forces in performances of *Land of Hope and Glory* and (unexpectedly) his old *Imperial March* of 1897. The assembled singers had memorably 'cheered the veteran conductor as he mounted the steps'. Privately, however, Elgar had deplored the vulgarity of the event in letters to Alice Stuart-Wortley, his 'Windflower', after rehearsals. The programme, he said, was 'short and lurid': there was 'no soul & no romance & no imagination'. 'Everything', he wrote, 'seems so hopelessly & irredeemably vulgar at

Court.'[4] The *Daily Mail* reported seeing Sir Edward as a 'lonely figure in black poised in his lofty pulpit', and his musical contribution has been described as 'a brave attempt to mend times that Elgar knew were thoroughly out of joint'.[5] For some, this became the enduring image of Elgar's participation not only in the Exhibition but also, by extension, in British imperialism more generally: a lonely figure with a tear rolling down his cheek at the sight of 'a group of real *daisies*' growing in the middle of the vast Empire Stadium.[6] Yet this romantic image of Elgar, as bravely carrying the musical burden of empire while holding its artificiality at arm's length from his artistic soul ('damn everything except the daisy'), tells only part of the story. Not least because he was, at the very same time, lobbying 'very strongly' for the position of Master of the King's Musick, beginning with a letter to Lord Stamfordham the day after Sir Walter Parratt's death on 27 March: 'I should feel it the greatest honour if I might be allowed to hold the position'.[7] Within the royal household it was known that 'Elgar is anxious for the appointment'.[8] When the post was finally offered to him, the composer gratefully accepted in a letter of 28 April, and pledged 'my loyalty and devotion at all times ... as a servant of His Majesty'.[9]

The question of whether Elgar threw body and soul into the Exhibition's opening ceremony while simultaneously urging the King to consider him for the royal post, though, has little historical significance. Of greater interest to historians today is, I believe, the central role his music played in one of the 'principal attractions' of the Wembley Exhibition – that is, in the elaborate Pageant of Empire, repeatedly staged in the specially constructed stadium over a six-week period in July and August 1924.[10] For it was Elgar's music which served to unify what was the most spectacular audiovisual display of empire that had ever been seen in Britain. The Pageant was conceived, according to the souvenir programme, as a 'Historical Epic', to tell 'The Empire's Story': 'to put forward in music, poetry, and movement a spectacle, as striking as we might conceive it, of our wonderful story; to show in pageant the whole moving tale of our achievement; to light the torches of the future at the glowing heart of the past'.[11] Each episode represented a direction of imperial expansion – first, *Westward Ho!* to Newfoundland and Canada; next *Eastward Ho!* to South Africa and India; and, finally, *Southward Ho!* to Australia and New Zealand – and the whole took three days to perform.[12] It was said that 'in three afternoons the spectator may learn more about the Empire, of which he is himself a unit, than he has been taught in his whole life before'.[13] 'Every school child in London', instructed *The Times*, 'ought to be sent to the Stadium for this three-day "course" in Imperial history'.[14]

The day after the pageant finally opened (it had been delayed because of poor weather), *The Times* published a celebratory account, shot through with imperial fervour, worth quoting at length:

> The Pageant of Empire is far more than a great spectacle. It is the gathering together of all the multitudinous lessons of the British Empire Exhibition into one whole, and the presenting of them afresh in a glittering argument of colour and movement. This is undoubtedly the way in which to teach British history – so much more amusing, so much more convincing and effective, so much more real than the way of ink and book and dates ... And the Pageant has recaptured atmosphere too. It reminds us that there was an England that was indeed merry. That then, as now, the orient was a mysterious and sun-soaked place. That the sea is the peculiar and special stage whereon the activities of our race should be rehearsed ... to [the name] of Mr Frank Lascelles, the pageant-master, may be added those of Mr Alfred Noyes, who has written special lyrics for the Pageant; of Sir Edward Elgar, who has composed music ... and of Sir Charles Oman, whose name is a guarantee of historical accuracy.[15]

The official programme further informed spectators that 'the various Dominions and Colonies will stage their own history, choosing the most spectacular scenes'.[16] This propagandistic framing – for it was an all-British committee, headed up by Oman, who took charge of 'staging their history' – has historically always been the way that European imperialism represented its enterprise for, as Edward Saïd has argued, nothing could be better for imperialism's self-image than 'native subjects who express assent to the outsider's knowledge and power, implicitly accepting European judgment on the undeveloped, backward, or degenerative nature of native society'.[17] In this context, the unintended irony of a remark in the glowing press reports of the first performance gains particular significance: 'Those who saw the counterfeit presentment last night at Wembley of some of our great national heroes and heroines must have believed in them as never before they did.'[18] Indeed, 'counterfeit presentment' was quite accurate: the spectacle was intended to deceive. By excluding the all-too-present challenges to British rule from India and other colonies, the Pageant, masquerading as a colourful depiction of the British Empire, was carefully inscribed with its creators' considered beliefs and suppressions.

A vivid picture emerges of the Pageant's scope and nature from press reports. 'The Pageant of Empire at Wembley', the *Illustrated London News* told readers, 'which is the greatest spectacle of its kind that has ever been organized, includes 12,000 performers ... Among the animals to be employed are 300 horses, 50 donkeys, 1,000 doves, 72 monkeys, seven elephants, eight camels and three bears.'[19] It was not only elaborate but also costly:

> The production of the Pageant has been very expensive. It will cost
> £100,000 of which the Government has contributed £65,000 ... It will
> not be possible to recover much of the expenditure from the public, as
> 10,000 seats in the Stadium are free, and none of the others costs more
> than four shillings.[20]

Of the Pageant's extraordinary venue, the Exhibition's *Official Guide*
boasted: 'The stadium covers a space over ten acres, accommodates
125,000 spectators; it is one and a-half times the size of the Coliseum
in Rome.'[21] Given these dimensions, *The Times* informed readers:

> There is a great deal of music in the Pageant, and as little speech as
> possible. The difficulty of introducing much dialogue or spoken verse
> will be obvious to all who know somewhat of the Pageant, if not to all
> who have yet to learn. Music pervades the various scenes.[22]

Indeed, music, which was performed by 'a choir of 400, and 110
instrumentalists', played a central role and accounted for £6,000 of
the overall expenses.[23] 'The *greatest* possible care', spectators learned
from the programme, 'had been taken ... in selecting the music.'[24]
And, although Elgar's emotive letters about (and the photograph of)
the Exhibition's opening ceremony in April have largely eclipsed
his participation in the Pageant, it was his music which appeared
most prominently (some twenty times) in this spectacular Pageant's
programme.[25] In addition to contributing existing works, Elgar wrote
a new *Empire March* and a series of songs setting poetry specially
written by Alfred Noyes (1880–1959) to introduce each of the pageant's
episodes and to 'link the scenes of the Empire Pageant together'.[26] Four
of these settings share the same music, thereby constituting a tangible
musical link – a leitmotif – which ran through the pageant.

A remarkable series of songs

Yet these important contributions to the British Empire Exhibition
by a composer of no small stature have largely been overlooked in
the literature on Elgar. One explanation for this neglect is that the
imperial fervour expressed in the music he wrote for the occasion was
becoming decidedly unfashionable among critics in the late 1920s and
early 1930s. They took their cue from the composer himself: 'I think
the pronounced praise of England is not quite so popular as it was',
he wrote in June 1928, 'the loyalty remains but the people seem to be
more shy as to singing about it.'[27] After the composer's death in 1934,
pastoral imagery began to dominate interpretations to such an extent
that associations of empire and war were dismissed from his music
in favour of the imagined virtues of a pre-industrial rural Britain that

many sought (and, indeed, still seek).[28] Sales of the *Pageant of Empire* songs, and of the *Empire March*, dwindled, and thus it was that, with the demise of their publisher, Enoch & Sons, and the subsequent loss of the source materials, manuscript scores and orchestrations, the songs were buried in the obscurity their imperial purpose seemed to deserve. However, Elgar's *Pageant of Empire* has sprung to life in the new millennium: 2010 saw the release of the first recording of seven of the songs in fine new orchestrations by Martin Tate, and the Elgar Society is planning to issue the complete music in a new edition. The reappearance of the music coincides with strenuous debate on how to interpret British imperial history – the very subject of the Pageant, and of Elgar's work.

This is not the only music by Elgar whose source materials or orchestral versions have not survived – *The Crown of India*, an Imperial Masque written to celebrate the durbar held in Delhi in December 1911 on the occasion of King George V's assumption of the title 'Emperor of India', of which I have written extensively elsewhere, and also published with Enoch, suffered the same fate.[29] There is, in fact, a particularly intense notion of ephemerality in relation to these *Pageant of Empire* songs. Not only has much of their source material disappeared, along with that of the *Empire March* too – which is surprising for the works of such a renowned composer – but there has been speculation, and even insistence, by some Elgarians that these songs written for Wembley were not actually performed at the Pageant at all, and that they never existed in anything more than an early 'draft' scoring. One commentator declared recently that 'all of the Elgar–Noyes songs were dropped from the Pageant', and concluded that the composer 'never g[o]t round to providing an orchestral accompaniment', thereby effectively writing them out of history.[30] Traces of such 'ephemeral' music as Elgar's *Pageant of Empire* music, as historians and ethnomusicologists have long understood, are found not among diaries, sketchbooks and letters in celebrated composers' archives but in more diffuse sources, such as the pages of newspapers which record vital social and cultural history. It is, I believe, this ephemeral music, and the issues raised by its reception, that offers the music historian a glimpse of popular beliefs concerning Englishness and empire.[31]

Elgar's settings of Noyes (contrary to the assertions of some Elgarians) were performed by the vast pageant choir and orchestra right through the six-week run, forming 'The Golden Chain' that united the whole spectacle, and which 'link[ed] the scenes of the Empire Pageant together'.[32] Moreover, the Elgar–Noyes contribution was noted in press reviews as being crucial to the pageant's beauty, coherence and intelligibility. 'The sound of these thousands of voices singing is wonderful', declared one writer in August, 'and it is fitting that the last impression should be of the voices and the music; for throughout the episodes the singing of Mr Noyes's ballads and the accompaniment of the music contribute in no small part to the beauty of the pageant.'[33] A critic for *The Times*, writing three days after the delayed opening, enjoyed the fact that a 'link in the scheme of pageantry is supplied by the choir, who sing the verses by Mr Alfred Noyes, set to music by Sir Edward Elgar'. He enthused about 'Over the Blue Mountains', 'the song [which] is a prelude to the Pageant of Australia', and 'The Islands', which introduces the Pageant of New Zealand:

> Verses by Mr Alfred Noyes set to music by Sir Edward Elgar give out the theme:–
>> 'Southward now, the radiant islands
>> O'er the golden ocean rise.'
> The change from the English Court to the Southern Seas has been swift.[34]

A review of the first performance on 25 July noted how apposite it was that the Pageant of South Africa began with 'the song' ('Cape of Good Hope') thus:

> Round the Cape our storm-beat galleons
> Strove to find the old sea-way.[35]

Speaking of how firmly rooted in history each episode was, one writer explained the function of the songs succinctly: 'Edward Elgar's music and Mr Alfred Noyes's verses contribute to [the Pageant's] solid [historical] foundation of material.'[36] The *Hull Daily Mail*'s particularly enthusiastic review is worth quoting at length:

> Messrs Enoch and Sons Ltd, the music publishers, have secured the rights of a series of songs and choruses each written for a special episode in the Empire's history, as included in the Empire Pageant at the Wembley Exhibition. I have received copies of these works which are most interesting, not only because of Mr Alfred Noyes' wonderful poems and Sir Edward Elgar's more wonderful music, but because of their educational value ... Here is the combination of literary and musical talent that goes to the making of successful numbers.[37]

After lively descriptions of each of the songs published as solos, the reviewer further notes that, in addition, 'the Enoch Choral Series (6d) has three choruses of the Empire Pageant, from the pens of the same author and composer, "Sailing Westward," "The Immortal Legions," and "A Song of Union" are their titles, and no mixed choral societies should be without them for the coming winter'. 'It is', he concluded, 'truly a remarkable series.'[38]

What shall be your profit?

By 1924, Elgar, who had a personal connection with the ventures of imperialism through his father-in-law, Major-General Sir Henry Gee Roberts KCB, had been making the spectacle of empire audible in music for nearly thirty years. He became known as an official imperial bard, a composer whose music glorified colonial policy, at Queen Victoria's Diamond Jubilee, thereby taking up 'The Composer's Burden' with all the gusto that Rudyard Kipling could have wished the White Man to show, subsequently composing music for many of the greatest imperial and national occasions for decades.[39] His contribution to the Jubilee celebrations included the *Imperial March* (attributed, as Robert Anderson notes, to *Richard* Elgar!) played by vast wind bands at the Crystal Palace early in 1897, and two cantatas – *The Banner of St George*, with its grand finale glorifying the Union Jack (not St George's banner) and *Caractacus*, its ancient context (about a Celtic hero) encompassing the fall of the Roman Empire and prophesying the rise of the British.[40] The Crystal Palace hosted yet another grand occasion that year when Elgar's *Characteristic Dances* were premiered and a horrific display of 'Ethnological Groups' including life-sized groups of 'Indians, Bushmen, Zulu Kaffirs, Mexican Indians, Hindoos, Tibetans' was placed in the south transept.[41]

Five years later, Henry Wood gave the London premieres of Elgar's *Pomp and Circumstance Marches* in D major and A minor. Of the former, he recalled: 'The people simply rose and yelled. I had to play it again – with the same result ... Merely to restore order, I played the march a third time.'[42] Charles Villiers Stanford remarked that 'they both came off like blazes and are uncommon fine stuff' that 'translated Master Kipling into Music'.[43] In October 1902, Elgar composed the *Coronation Ode* to commemorate the accession of Edward VII and his crowning as Emperor of India. At the King's suggestion, the *Ode* included the choral setting of the broad melody of *Pomp and Circumstance* March No. 1, a tune that would, in Elgar's words, 'knock 'em flat', and which became known across the world (with words by A.C. Benson) as *Land of Hope and Glory*, the anthem of British imperialism.[44]

At the second Festival of Empire at the Crystal Palace, which ran from May to July 1911, and which represented every corner of the Empire through exhibitions and displays, Elgar framed the musical programme with his arrangement of the National Anthem; the Epilogue and March, 'It comes from the misty ages' from *The Banner of St George*; and *Land of Hope and Glory*, performed by Clara Butt and the vast Empire choir.[45] It was at this time that Elgar was admitted to the Order of Merit (OM) – he had been knighted a few years earlier having been made Knight Bachelor in 1904.[46] (He waited thirty years for internal promotion to the highest level of Knight Grand Cross, when his title became 'Sir Edward Elgar Bt OM GCVO' – the very pinnacle indeed.) Undoubtedly, Elgar's most spectacular musical exhibition of empire was his Imperial Masque, *The Crown of India* of 1912, exemplified by 'the magnificent barbaric turmoil' of its *March of the Mogul Emperors*, which became a popular choice for patriotic and imperial occasions through the war years.[47]

It was unsurprising that Elgar was approached, in early January 1924, by Walter Creighton, Controller of the Wembley Exhibition, with a request for music ('we feel it unthinkable if we don't have your help').[48] His first thoughts about the vocal music he would contribute are found in letters to his 'Windflower' three days later:

> I have been trying to help this Wembley affair – an awful muddle – & I have had no moment. I have 'composed'! *five* things this week— one about 'Shakespeare' you will love it when I shew it to you: slight and silly.[49]

This notion of the songs as mere trifles dashed off for what he later termed the 'unfortunate Pageant' has proved durable – and no doubt accounts at least in part for their slight treatment in the literature on the composer.[50] The 'slight and silly' song he mentioned, entitled 'Shakespeare's Kingdom', has, in fact, as little to do with the overt representation of colonialism which characterised the Pageant as it has with the particular musical demands of the occasion. In the stadium, it introduced the allegorical Pageant of Learning, performed between the expansionist episodes on the first day, which commemorated the heroes 'who have made the Empire possible'.[51] Noyes's lyrics tell of Shakespeare coming to London unseen, and with 'no heraldic trumpet' to acclaim him. He passes unnoticed, carrying 'in his knapsack a scroll of quiet songs' which, although unknown, was 'wealth untold': 'the galleons of the Armada / Could not contain his gold'. Only in the last stanza is the imperial allegory unveiled:

> The kings rode on – to darkness,
> In England's triumphing hour,
> Unseen arrived her splendour,
> Unknown her conquering power.[52]

The *Sunday Times* reviewer, who had been attending the dress rehearsals, described how these lyrics were 'sung by a choir to a most captivating and whimsical melody by Sir Edward Elgar'.[53] Indeed, in its melodic subtlety and jaunty rhythms, and with voice and accompaniment

Example 9.1 'Shakespeare's Kingdom', from *Pageant of Empire*, music by Edward Elgar, words by Alfred Noyes. Voice and piano reduction published by Enoch, 1924: opening, bars 1–14

idiomatically trading phrases, it is more of an intimate art song – a skilful setting of poetry – than an imperial hymn for massed voices to sing to audiences of some fifty thousand (Example 9.1).[54] There was in it, the *Hull Daily Mail* noted, 'the mysterious sympathy that is such a feature of the composer's works'.[55]

All of its companion songs, however, are written in an entirely different musical style, in perfect tune with 'the stirring historical pageantry and Imperial symbolism' of the pageant itself. A review of the first concert performance of the orchestral songs 'composed by Sir Edward Elgar for the Empire pageant at Wembley' in October 1924 astutely points to the way their style was shaped by their purpose: 'This work was written for special conditions which necessitated, among other things, the greatest simplicity and lack of complication possible.'[56] Indeed, they resemble a string of *nobilmente* trio sections from marches – an Elgarian trick whose most famous example is *Land of Hope and Glory* from *Pomp and Circumstance* March No. 1. The first of the three days of the Pageant, *Westward Ho!*, was introduced by 'Merchant Adventurers', in which 'we are shown Raleigh, Gilbert, Drake, and their fellows, all "Merchant Adventurers chanting at the windlass ... All for adventure in the great new regions"'', memorably captured in the vivid images by Sir Frank Brangwyn, designer of the Pageant's scenery, and reprinted in the striking commemorative volume (Figures 9.1a and b).[57] Noyes's refrain sets the tone of imperial bravado:

Merchant Adventurers!
Merchant Adventurers,
what shall be your profit
in the mighty days to be?
England! England!
Glory, glory everlasting,
in the lordship of the sea.

'Merchant Adventurers', like its music-hall precursor, *The Fringes of the Fleet* – a song-cycle of Kipling settings which Elgar premiered at the Coliseum in June 1917 – is written in what the composer termed his 'broad saltwater style'.[58] For this seafaring swagger, he drew on several popular idioms of the late nineteenth and early twentieth centuries. The refrain's rousing melody and marching bass is akin to the 'crusader' hymn tradition as exemplified, for example, by Arthur Sullivan's 'Onward, Christian Soldiers', or Sidney Nicholson's 'Lift High the Cross' of 1916.[59] The militaristic idiom and lofty imperialism expressed in such hymns and patriotic songs had been caricatured in Gilbert and Sullivan's operettas to great acclaim since the 1870s. Elgar knew these productions well since he had either played in or conducted many of them in the 1880s and 1890s.[60] Ironically, or perhaps with original irony intact and intended, echoes of Sullivan's imperialist spoof 'He is an Englishman' (*HMS Pinafore*) can be heard in 'Merchant Adventurers' and the *grandioso* refrain appears to have strayed out of Lord Mountararat's song with chorus in *Iolanthe*, 'When Britain really ruled the waves ... in good King George's glorious days' – for this is music 'redolent of the sea' as one reviewer put it.[61]

Figure 9.1a/b Frank Brangwyn's 'Kings of the Sea' from *Westward Ho!*, the first day of the pageant, reprinted in the *Pageant of Empire Souvenir Programme* (London: Fleetway Press, 1924), pp. 6–7

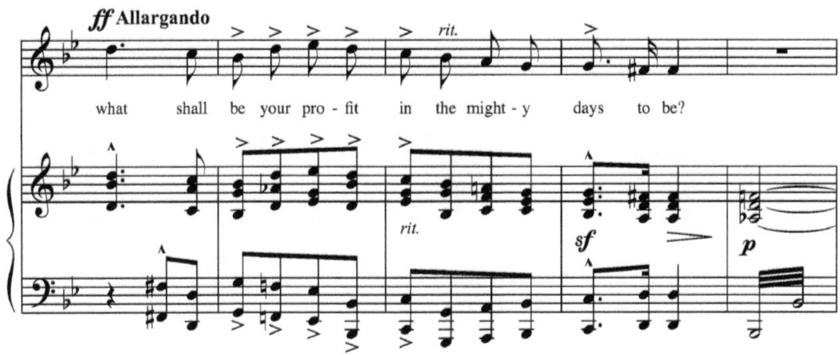

Example 9.2 Elgar–Noyes, 'Merchant Adventurers', from *Pageant of Empire*. Voice and piano reduction published by Enoch, 1924: Refrain, bars 37–67

Example 9.2 continued

Telling musical details reveal close attention to the verses, such as the plucky little grace note (an appoggiatura C sharp) which enlivens the dominant pedal (D) that grounds the repeated call to the plucky 'Merchant Adventurers' (Example 9.2, bars 37–41).[62] The question posed in Noyes's second line – 'what shall be your profit?' – might stand in for the whole imperial enterprise, whose principal driving force, in spite all of the propaganda about civilising and doing good, was ultimately profit. This is not lost on Elgar, who provides for it music of fitting import: fortissimo, heavily accented and broader (*allargando*) (bars 42–5). Next, he deftly delays the word 'England', preparing it with a sudden shift from the solid G minor to a trembling, hushed dominant seventh of a more heroic key, E flat major (bars 46–7) – while ensuring that the second, rhetorical, statement (bars 50–1), with its suspended dominant ninth harmony and characteristic descending seventh in the vocal line (C to D), would tug at the national heart-strings.[63] Finally, the answer – 'glory everlasting' – comes in a richly textured *grandioso* refrain in E flat, permeated with stately dotted rhythms in the march-like 2/4, and a hint of processional percussion – the tapping out of a side-drum.

Elgar made no secret either of his admiration for the words of 'Merchant Adventurers' and its companions in the 'Golden Chain' or of how amenable he had found Noyes as a collaborator. Four years later, he suggested that Noyes be approached about supplying another patriotic verse to fit the trio tune of *Pomp and Circumstance* March No. 4: 'He has a *feeling* for music & wrote some excellent "stuff", at a moment's notice' for the Wembley Pageant. Noyes was, he added, 'a very pleasant & understanding person to work with' and, in 1929, he again recommended the poet for a project involving an imperial 'March of Praise' for 'The King's Book'.[64]

The gorgeous East at Wembley

A particularly illuminating perspective on Elgar's contributions to the Pageant is gained from considering the musical context in which they were heard. While each colony was represented by its own elaborate pageant, it was reported that the Indian one, The Early Days of India – 'compiled from the historical notes of Sir Charles Oman, KBE, MP, *et al*, by the Pageant Master in Chief' – 'makes a spectacle that stands out in splendour even from its splendid surroundings'.[65] This episode depicting the conquest of India was also the one which featured Elgar's music most prominently and so a closer look will be particularly instructive. It seems, by all accounts, to have been the most spectac-ular and 'exotic' part of the whole Pageant. *The Times* reported:

Nothing that scholarship and knowledge of India can do to ensure accuracy of costume and atmosphere is being neglected, and the Indian Ruling Princes are giving all the help that they can, by the loan of splendid paraphernalia and otherwise, to make the scenes as brilliant as they deserve to be. Elephants in sumptuous trappings, camels, wild hillmen, … all [of] India's peoples and fighting races will be represented: all that is finest and most resplendent in India's chivalry and magnificence of colour.[66]

Indeed 'Elephants, llamas [*sic*] and bulls' were 'shipped from India' and the costumes and stage accessories used were the work of 'Mr Percy Anderson, the Oriental designer', who had designed the sets and costumes for *The Crown of India* at the Coliseum in 1912.[67] Figure 9.2 presents Frank Brangwyn's design for the scene which was described as follows:

India occupies the scene. At the west end of the Stadium is the throne of the Mogul Emperor Jehangir. While it is being erected an Indian market springs into being; buyers and sellers come to the bazaar, which swarms with musicians, snake-charmers, dancing girls, dervishes, and story-tellers. The Ambassador from King James I, Sir Thomas Roe, is at last ushered into the presence of the Emperor. Elephants and camels, soldiers and ox-drawn carts, with Indian bands, form an imposing procession.[68]

Figure 9.2 Frank Brangwyn's 'The Gorgeous East in Fee: The Court of Jehangir' from the Early Days of India episode of the pageant's second day, *Eastward Ho!* Reprinted in the *Pageant of Empire Souvenir Programme* (London: Fleetway Press, 1924), p. 17

[234]

Figure 9.3 'Indian' Dancers featured in the Early Days of India
on the second day of the pageant, *Eastward Ho!* 'The Empire in
Pageant', *The Times*, 29 July 1924, p. xi

Press photographs, such as the one shown in Figure 9.3, give us an
impression of the 'Indian' dancers.

This elaborate spectacle began with 'Indian Dawn', the link in the
'Golden Chain' written specially by Noyes and Elgar to introduce this
episode of expansion:

> Eastward now the sails of England
> Cleave their darkly shining way –
> Mighty sails that meet the sunrise
> Rolling westward from Cathay.[69]

These words, according to Enoch, were set to the same music as
another of the 'Golden Chain' songs, 'Sailing Westward!' – thereby
fitting neatly into typical Orientalist discourse in which any part of
'the Orient' can represent any other part or, indeed, the whole – with

Example 9.3 Elgar–Noyes, 'Indian Dawn', from *Pageant of Empire*: vocal line, author's reconstruction from companion piece, 'Sailing Westward' published by Enoch, 1924

the 'droning temples' and 'sacred river' of India here set to the same tune as 'Westward go the shining sailors!'[70] Yet as a piece of music, the song remains elusive. Since 'Indian Dawn' has, to my knowledge, scarcely been performed since the Pageant in 1924, and has received barely a mention in ninety years of Elgar scholarship, readers of this book will surely be interested in glancing at it. Example 9.3 presents the melody of 'Indian Dawn' in my reconstruction of the word-setting.[71]

To follow 'Indian Dawn', the selection committee chose scenes from Liza Lehmann's *In a Persian Garden*, the *Four Indian Love Lyrics* by Amy Woodforde-Finden, *Old Indian Dances* by 'Shankar' (undoubtedly Uday Shankar) and more music by Elgar, most spectacularly his *March of the Mogul Emperors* and other excerpts from *The Crown of India*. This unlikely combination of music suggests how crucial the Elgar–Noyes 'Golden Chain' was in maintaining coherence and intelligibility in the stadium. The odd one out is the Rajasthani dancer Uday Shankar, whose very name, misspelled in the press, has often been misidentified by subsequent writers as 'Shandar'.[72] Shankar had joined his barrister father in London in 1920 and took up studies at the Royal College of Art under Sir William Rothenstein.[73] His famous *Radha-Krishna Duet*, the second of two *Hindu Miniatures* forming Parts II and III of Anna Pavlova's ballet *Oriental Impressions*, was presented at the Royal Opera House, Covent Garden, in September 1923. Shankar's biographer, Mohan Khokar, states that it was through Lady Meherbai Dorabji Tata that Shankar got his big break to participate at the Wembley Exhibition. He danced Shiva, and composed the music for the orchestra.[74] How different from the rest of the music in the India Pageant Shankar's must have been!

But even the semblance of authenticity in either poetry or music was unnecessary, undesirable even, for these Indian musical depictions. After all, settings by both Liza Lehmann and Woodforde-Finden of *The Golden Threshold*, a collection of poetry published in Britain in 1905 by the celebrated Indian nationalist and feminist Sarojini Naidu, or Gustav Holst's choral *Hymns from the Rig Veda*, would have been ideal for inclusion in the Indian episode (not to mention more geographically appropriate than *In a Persian Garden*).[75] Moreover, the Indian music practitioner Maud MacCarthy was renowned in London not only for her fine renditions of music learned during travels in India in 1907–09 but also, with her second husband, John Foulds, for orchestral arrangements that suited staged dramas. In the summer of 1922, *The Musical Standard* lauded MacCarthy's 'intensely interesting' music for Niranjan Pal's play *The Goddess* at the Ambassadors Theatre produced by The Indian Players, and explained that: 'Miss MacCarthy and her husband had a very keen wish to arrange … music … which should prove as near the real thing as it is possible to have without the actual Indian instruments.'[76] Alongside Tyagaraja's *Karnatic kriti* entitled *Bhavanuta* which involved the collaboration of a *tabla* player, MacCarthy performed 'such gems' as an overture on an Agra *ghazal*, and 'Song of Ram Das', whose 'vital and telling' melody was in a style suggested by Tagore's singing when he had visited her some years earlier.

Yet despite London's rich seam of British-Indian music-making, the Pageant's musical choices reflected the reality that, for over two decades, India and its Orientalist projection, Indo-Persia, had been popularised to great appeal by Amy Woodforde-Finden (1860–1919), Liza Lehmann (1862–1918) and, of course, Sir Edward Elgar, whose *March of the Mogul Emperors* is a brilliant Russian-style polonaise representing perhaps the most magnificent scene of all British imperialism: the Great Elephant Procession of 1903, the State Entry into Delhi at the durbar.[77] With its trumpeting of elephants and second-beat accents (à la polonaise) suggestive of the measured tread of the two hundred elephants processing past the Jama Masjid, it was, perhaps, a fine choice for the state procession of Emperor Jahangir, the elephants and, of course, Sir Thomas Roe. The Mughal polonaise's companion pieces in the pageant were equally popular. Of Lehmann's *In a Persian Garden*, the critic Edwin Evans opined, seven years after the first performance in 1896, that its 'phenomenal success places it almost beyond the sphere of ordinary discussion'.[78] Lehmann's lively settings of FitzGerald's (mis) translation of the *Rubaiyat* of Omar Khayyam include such numbers for vocal quartet as 'They say the Lion and Lizard sleep' that no doubt fitted well with the India Pageant's sizeable menagerie.[79] Woodforde-Finden's *Indian Love Lyrics* had achieved even greater popularity. In an article whose appearance in the *Radio Times* coincided with the pageant's run at the Wembley Exhibition, A.B. Cooper declared:

> If sales are any criterion of popularity, the most popular songs ever published in the history of music are the 'Indian Love Lyrics' ... published over twenty years ago.[80]

Kashmiri Song in particular, had captured the English imagination, and had recently shaped a central episode of the 1921 Valentino film, *The Sheik*.[81] Although we do not know exactly where in the Pageant's action audiences heard the phrases, 'Pale hands I loved beside the Shalimar / Where are you now? / Who lies beneath your spell?', we might imagine that the song wove its own spell over the phantasmagorical proceedings. Even if 'romance' and 'imagination' were missing from the Exhibition's opening ceremony, they were, it seems, not in short supply in the Pageant's romantic (not to say romanticised) and imaginative depiction of British imperial expansion to India.

Sing we all as one!

The grand scale of the Wembley Pageant, portraying the expansion of the British Empire and showcasing thousands of actors and animals, was unprecedented. Kurt Koenigsberger argues that, with this vast spectacle at its core, the British Empire Exhibition 'marks the belated culmination of nineteenth-century exhibitionary practices'.[82] This is exemplified by the fact that it took three days to dramatise a unified narrative of the Empire, drawing the many disparate displays held at earlier exhibitions, such as the Indian one at the Great White City in 1908, into a single master-narrative. Deborah Hughes and other scholars have argued that the British Empire Exhibition 'deserves special attention … in the burgeoning study of imperial culture because it ushered in a new era of spectacle in which imperial unity … was the focus'.[83] It was an attempt to present the Empire as 'unitary and uniform'.[84] What is of particular interest for us here is Elgar's central role, in collaboration with Noyes, in generating that unity, in drawing the disparate narratives of imperial expansion together through the 'Golden Chain' which effectively gave musical life to the imagined episodes of the Empire's history. This unity was most spectacularly displayed through the final link in the chain, 'A Song of Union' – which was the ultimate musical unifier of the pageant and, by extension, of the entire exhibition – and by *The Empire March*.[85]

In his initial correspondence with Elgar, Walter Creighton had emphasised the role of the March:

> Might I come and see you? I would … explain the outline of the Pageant … What we want is a March of Empire from you which will be the Leit Motive going through the three days programme.[86]

Its importance was not lost on Elgar. A few days later, he wrote in a letter to his 'Windflower':

> I have to write *the* March for the Wembley affair, so have come here

> I begin thus – without any prelude &, with a great Military Band, should rouse people up – I *could* rouse Brazilians but not English.[87]

Example 9.4 Elgar, *The Empire March* (1924), from *Pageant of Empire*: Reprise of the 'frame', or opening theme. (Transposing instruments sound at pitch for ease of reading.)

On 7 February, he was still busy with the March: 'I have brought the "frame" of the March back & am working very hard at it'.[88]

Although the new March was replaced at the opening ceremony with his old *Imperial March* of 1897 because of rehearsal difficulties, the 1924 *Empire March* became, as the Controller of the Exhibition had originally envisioned, the Pageant's imperial leitmotif, regularly repeated during the three-day-long performances. The *Hull Daily Mail* certainly enjoyed the musical allegory of the colonial enterprise, declaring that '"The Empire March (1924)" ... is written in Elgar's grandest style, with broad, flowing melody, expressive of majesty, and sweeping rhythms indicating the wide expanse of our Empire'.[89] Thus, with this exuberant march Elgar did manage to rouse his stolid English audiences. At both the matinée and evening performances of *Southward Ho!* in July, *The Times* reported that the enthusiasm of the audience was unmistakable, and that a highlight was the orchestra of over one hundred playing the *Empire March* 'with rare precision'.[90] Despite the large scoring (in addition to full brass, woodwinds and strings, Elgar adds two harps and an organ for 'textural glue', as well as a large percussion battery), the 'frame' of the March demands precision and considerable skill from performers with its staccato articulation and cleanly notated dotted rhythms which characterise the main motif.[91] In the reprise, this 'frame' is even more *spiritoso* (Elgar's original marking), with the expanded percussion section, piccolo and organ now playing important roles in depicting 'the wide expanse of our Empire' (Example 9.4).[92]

What, though, of the 'broad, flowing melody, expressive of majesty' mentioned in the press? Elgar's marches, like most examples of the genre, and famously on account of *Pomp and Circumstance* No. 1, contain a central trio section of a less martial, more lyrical or *nobilmente* character. *The Empire March*, with a stately E flat major trio, is no exception. And it was this trio that Elgar drew on for the final link in the Pageant's 'Golden Chain': his setting of Noyes's 'A Song of Union' whose words evoke the myth of the destiny of the British Empire, that old fallacy of the *pax Britannica* – 'a vision of justice, peace, freedom' and, above all, of unity:[93]

> The stars that wheel around the Sun
> Proclaim the law that bound them.
> 'Twas love that linked our realms in one and Love in joy that crowned them!
> Then Freedom took her throne,
> And peace was breathed on ev'ry sea and music swelled around them;
> No more the dreams of war shall sound
> When hearts and realms in Love are bound:
> For Love binds all in one; Love binds all our hearts in one.

O Island heart of all the sea, though storm and cloud beset thee,
Thy children nations turn to thee, could e'en our dreams forget thee?
To thee O heav'nly sun.
Sing we all as one!
Earth, sky and ocean answer
Love shall bind all realms in one![94]

Each of the song's two stanzas comes directly out of the march and provides a fitting musical setting for this imperialist cant. Although the orchestration of the song has not survived, the relation of the two pieces enables us, from the scoring of the *Empire March*, to reimagine the crashing cymbals, descending cascades of tubular bells and swagger of trombones that brought the final unifying call of 'A Song of Union' to a close in the Pageant of Thanksgiving: 'Earth, sky and ocean answer – Love shall bind all realms in one!' (Example 9.5).[95]

But there is more to 'A Song of Union' (and thus to *The Empire March*) than overblown (musical) rhetoric. I referred earlier to the setting of words to an existing trio tune as an Elgarian 'trick', though it is not something he did unthinkingly. A few years later, in response to the publisher Leslie Boosey, who had sent words for the trio tune of *Pomp and Circumstance* March No. 4, the composer wrote: 'I have been having a long struggle with the enclosed words, I cannot by any help of Providence, or old Nick, make them fit.'[96] The setting of 'A Song of Union' reveals evidence of an inspired fit. A stately bass line (with only minor alterations of the march's more spirited accompanying figuration) underlines the crowning of 'Freedom' to a lyrical melody in the middle section (Example 9.6, bars 14–17). At the equivalent moment in the second stanza, 'sing we all as one!', the counterpoint created earlier by imitative entries calling for 'Freedom' is appropriately replaced by the homophonic union of all voices singing together, 'as one' (see Example 9.5, bars 42–5). The main melody which opens the piece aptly depicts the textual imagery of stars wheeling around the sun and the 'noble' destiny binding together the distant realms, with its *nobilmente*, distinctly angular contour permeated by falling sevenths (Example 9.6). It is these very sevenths that make up what the composer's biographer Michael Kennedy terms 'Elgar's signature' in the theme of that quintessentially Elgarian piece, the *Enigma Variations*, and which inspired a witty musician to comment 'Eh bien! Il est vraiment un "Angular Saxon", n'est ce pas?'[97]

Removed from their original context, the *Pageant of Empire* songs and the *Empire March* have been largely disregarded by commentators since the 1920s. Reviewing their release in print by Enoch, the *Musical Times* dismissed the songs thus: 'These show the popular side of the composer somewhat below its best.'[98] 'This is not a quality

mf
42
cresc.
To thee o heav'n-ly sun, Sing we all as
To thee heav'n-ly sun, Sing all as
To thee o haev'n-ly sun, Sing we all as
To thee O sun, Sing we as
mf
cresc.
cresc.
ff With much emphasis.
rit.
one! Earth, sky and o - - - cean an-swer
ff
one! Earth, sky and o - - - cean an-swer
ff
one! Earth, sky and o - - - cean an-swer
ff
one! Earth, sky and o - - - cean an-swer
winds (including flute 8va)
ff
rit.
horns, low brass, tubular bells
Timpani and snare drum roll,
cymbal crash on the third beat of these two bars.

[244]

Example 9.5 Elgar–Noyes, 'A Song of Union', from *Pageant of Empire*.
Choral version with piano reduction published by Enoch, 1924,
with scoring indications taken from the close of *The Empire March*:
bars 42–51

[of simplicity and lack of complexity] in which the composer shines most of all', opined a reviewer of the first concert performance two months after the Pageant's close, 'and no doubt the music lost a good deal of its broad effectiveness by being translated from large forces in the open air to a small orchestra and chorus in a concert-hall.'[99] In a similar vein, writers have generally passed over the *Empire March* as 'hardly a shadow of Elgar's earlier marches'.[100] 'It seems to lack the genuine inspiration of the *Pomp and Circumstance* marches', argues Richards, 'the confidence sounds forced, the tone bombastic.' 'It is', he concludes, 'Elgar imitating himself.'[101]

We might understand all this – as well as the strangely persistent notions that the *Pageant of Empire* songs were never performed or even orchestrated – as part of a more general, ambivalent approach to Elgar's music written for imperial occasions, which dates back some ninety years. In the same year as the Wembley Exhibition, the Scottish critic and composer Cecil Gray established, in his *Survey of Contemporary Music*, what was to become a trope in Elgar criticism:

A Song of Union

Edward Elgar

Example 9.6 Elgar–Noyes, 'A Song of Union', from *Pageant of Empire*: *nobilmente* melody, lyrical theme in imitation, and stately marching bass: bars 1–22

[247]

Example 9.6 continued

hearts and realms in Love are bound: For Love binds all in
hearts and realms in Love are bound: For Love binds all
hearts and realms in Love are bound: For Love binds al
hearts and realms in Love are bound: For Love binds all in
cresc.
sf
f
f
one; Love binds all our hearts in one.
Love Love binds all our hearts, our hearts in one.
Love Love binds all our hearts, our hearts in one.
one; Love binds all our hearts, our hearts in one.
rit.
Allargando
rit.
Allargando

the distinction between 'the composer of the symphonies' and 'the self-appointed Musician Laureate of the British Empire'.[102] Concluding that 'the one is a musician of merit; the other is only a barbarian', Gray denounced all of Elgar's marches, odes and other occasional pieces as 'perfect specimens' of jingoism.[103] By 1931, F.H. Shera, Professor of Music at the University of Sheffield, reported that some of the offending music written for such occasions had been 'allowed to fade into deserved oblivion'.[104] A.J. Sheldon declared that 'political ideas can never inspire the artist in the same way, or to a like extent, as poetical ideas can', and called for Elgar's entire output of imperialist works to 'be buried soon; at present it is a clog on the endearing place Elgar holds in our estimation'.[105] This construction of a 'two Elgars' theory (formulated by Frank Howes in 1935), aided by the oft-quoted letter the composer wrote to his 'Windflower' deploring the vulgarity of the Exhibition, has served to keep not only the composer's imperial works at arm's length from his 'abstract' compositions but also the realities of the Empire at a safe distance from us.[106] Yet while such dismissals reveal the contemporary attitudes of critics, they tell us little about the music's extraordinary role in the promotion of British imperialism, and of its popularity with the British public. Elgar's music for the Pageant was a particularly important element in 'the gathering together of all the multitudinous lessons of the British Empire Exhibition into one whole, and the presenting of them afresh in a glittering argument'.[107] By the time the Pageant closed at the end of August 1924, Sir William Furse, chief administrative officer, boasted that nearly one million people had seen the performances – an audience the size of which few of Elgar's 'poetic' instrumental pieces could aspire to.[108] Moreover, his imperial works – including *The Pageant of Empire* and *The Crown of India* – were among the most regularly broadcast pieces of his through the 1920s and early 1930s.[109]

But there is, I think, a broader conclusion to be drawn. To many people, the Wembley Exhibition, exemplified by the Empire Pageant, seemed outmoded in its revival of old imperial themes – a view expressed by Virginia Woolf, for whom the nineteenth century itself resembled the Exhibition's assemblages: 'a conglomeration ... of the most heterogeneous and ill-assorted objects ... globes, maps, elephants ... at once so indecent, so hideous, and so monumental'.[110] In his account of a visit to the Wembley Exhibition, E.M. Forster mocked the rhetoric of 'a high imperial vision', and the Won't Go To Wembley (WGTW) Society derided its aims.[111] These, and other representatives of 'intellectual culture', depicted the effort 'to reinvigorate popular imperialism' at Wembley, as John MacKenzie has stated, as 'a failure'.[112] If the maps, globes and elephants seemed to represent the Victorian era for Woolf and others (this was the era of the Rolls-Royce motor car in India; elephants had been eclipsed), then Elgar's music fitted the bill perfectly. Here was recycled 'imperial' music, for recycled imperial ideologies: his *Land of Hope and Glory* trio-like songs, and *The Crown of India*'s magnificent representation of the state procession of two hundred elephants from all over India in 1903 mapped somewhat anticlimactically with the Pageant's seven miserably cold elephants processing across the stadium in the pouring rain. Moreover, the musical context – 'a conglomeration ... of the most heterogeneous and ill-assorted objects' (dances by Shankar, *Love Lyrics* by Woodforde-Finden and *In a Persian Garden* by Lehmann) – certainly set the scene. And *The Empire March*, with its lavish scoring, including harps, organ and percussion battery, was quite at odds with the 'lean' back-to-Bach ideology of pared-down neoclassicism that had emerged from the war years across Europe – and in which Elgar himself had recently participated with his arrangement of Bach's Fantasia and Fugue in C minor (1921–22) – and, as such, it exemplifies the anachronism of empire itself.[113]

Thus, the sumptuous *Pageant of Empire* music, in its return to a *fin-de-siècle* musical language and performing forces, participates triumphantly in the attempt of the whole British Empire Exhibition to return to a prewar sense of the spectacle of empire – *The Empire March* could have been written in 1897; nothing in it suggests a musical vintage of 1924. Although the replacement of the 1924 *Empire* march with the 1897 *Imperial* one at the Exhibition's opening in April wounded the composer's pride, it was musically inconsequential.[114] Where the new march did matter, given the crucial relation between it and the final 'Song of Union' (that is, in the Pageant), it served its purpose magnificently. It was literally 'The March of Empire' as *The Times* put it, pressing Eastward, Southward, Westward – a musical manifestation of imperial expansion.[115] Finally, although Elgar's *Pageant of Empire* songs of praise to a 'heroic' and 'altruistic' imperialism are profoundly embarrassing today, there is no need to jettison them, to overlook their participation in the Exhibition, or to reinvent them as untainted pieces, mercifully uncheapened by the imperial occasion for which they were written. Elgar's pageant music is not only historically illuminating but also musically rich: even the most overtly imperialistic link in the 'Golden Chain', 'A Song of Union', shares with the composer's better-known works elements of his most celebrated style. It is, ultimately, the extraordinary *Pageant of Empire*, experienced by thousands of people from 25 July to 30 August 1924, which is surely the enduring sound and image of Sir Edward Elgar and the Wembley Exhibition.

Notes

1 *The Times*, 12 June 1924, p. 7.
2 Jeffrey Richards, *Imperialism and Music: Britain, 1876–1953* (Manchester: Manchester University Press, 2001), p. 194. The Exhibition ran from 23 April to 1 November 1924, and re-opened on 9 May 1925, running that year until 31 October.
3 *The Times*, 19 July 1924, p. xi.
4 Edward Elgar to Alice Stuart-Wortley, 9 March and 16 April 1924, in *Edward Elgar: The Windflower Letters. Correspondence with Alice Caroline Stuart-Wortley and Her Family*, ed. Jerrold Northrop Moore (Oxford: Clarendon Press, 1989), pp. 289–90.
5 The source of both quotations, the first from the *Daily Mail*, the second penned by Robert Anderson, in Anderson, *Elgar* (New York and Oxford: Maxwell Macmillan International, 1993), pp. 155 and 301.
6 Elgar to Stuart-Wortley, 16 April 1924, in *The Windflower Letters*, p. 290. For instance, John Norris writes: 'To most Elgarians, the musical festivities surrounding the Exhibition are now best remembered for Elgar's emotional outburst on the turf at Wembley as preparations for the opening ceremony continued around him.' See Norris, 'Tales from the Complete Edition – 5: A Pageant of Empire', *Elgar Society Journal* 17 (2011), p. 6. Jenny Doctor, writing about Elgar's role in the Exhibition's opening ceremony (which she erroneously calls the pageant), suggests that 'the pageant itself [*sic*] may have depressed Elgar's sensibilities' in her chapter, 'Broadcasting's Ally: Elgar and the BBC', in Daniel Grimley and Julian Rushton (eds), *The Cambridge Companion to Elgar* (Cambridge: Cambridge University Press, 2004), p. 201.
7 Edward Elgar to Lord Stamfordham, 28 March 1924, in *Edward Elgar: Letters of a Lifetime*, ed. Jerrold Northrop Moore (Oxford: Clarendon Press, 1990), p. 381.
8 The Lord Chamberlain, the Earl of Cromer (1877–1953) to the Treasurer to the King, 1 April 1924, in *Letters of a Lifetime*, p. 382.
9 Edward Elgar to Sir Frederick Ponsonby, 28 April 1924, in *Letters of a Lifetime*, p. 385. See also David Bury, 'Elgar and Queen Mary's Dolls' House', *Elgar Society Journal* 11 (1999), p. 93.
10 The quoted phrase comes from Richards, *Imperialism and Music*, p. 201.
11 *Sunday Times*, 27 July 1924, p. 7.
12 For a summary of the revival of the pageant as a genre (as a processional crossed with Elizabethan chronicle play), and its purpose as both entertainment and education in the context of the Festival of Empire of 1911 and the Wembley Exhibition, see Richards, *Imperialism and Music*, pp. 188–9.
13 *The Times*, 18 August 1924, p. 8.
14 Ibid.
15 *The Times*, 26 July 1924, p. 17.
16 *The British Empire Exhibition Official Guide* (London: Fleetway Press, 1924), p. 39.
17 Edward W. Said, *Culture and Imperialism* (London: Vintage, 1994), p. 180.
18 *The Times*, 26 July 1924, p. 17.
19 *Illustrated London News*, 2 August 1924, pp. 232–3.
20 Ibid.
21 'The Empire Stadium', in *The British Empire Exhibition Official Guide*, p. 38.
22 *The Times*, 29 July 1924, p. xi.
23 *The Times*, 18 July 1924, p. 12. The *Musical Times* was more optimistic about the acoustics in the stadium, suggesting that 'the musical results ought to be far better than those of the performances given by the Imperial Choir in Hyde Park in 1919. At Wembley the singers will be under cover, and the sound will be some extent confined to the Stadium, instead of being diffused.' See *The Musical Times*, 1 April 1924, p. 308.
24 Elgar Birthplace Museum, Worcester, Concert Programmes 1912, Ref. 1126: 5, 'Music for Pageant', *British Empire Exhibition Pamphlet, No. 7: Pageant of Empire Programme – Part II, July 21–Aug 30* (London: Fleetway Press, 1924). For listings of the music in each episode, see Richards, *Imperialism and Music*, pp. 202–4, and Norris, 'Tales from the Complete Edition', pp. 12–13.

25 *Pageant of Empire Programme* (London: Fleetway Press, 1924).
26 *Sunday Times*, 20 July 1924, p. 12. The songs are: 'Sailing Westward', 'Merchant Adventurers', 'The Cape of Good Hope', 'Shakespeare's Kingdom', 'The Islands', 'The Blue Mountains', 'The Heart of Canada' and 'The Immortal Legions'. 'Sailing Westward' also had 'four alternative poems': 'Indian Dawn', 'The Islands', 'The Cape of Good Hope' and 'Gloriana'. Enoch published the *Pageant of Empire* music in August 1924; the songs were published in various solo and choral arrangements, and the *Empire March* in a solo piano arrangement, in August 1924.
27 Edward Elgar to Leslie Boosey, 10 June 1928, in *Elgar and His Publishers: Letters of a Creative Life*, ed. Jerrold Northrop Moore, 2 vols (Oxford: Clarendon Press, 1987), vol. 2, p. 855.
28 For more on this reinterpretation of Elgar's music, see Jeremy Crump, 'The Identity of English Music: The Reception of Elgar', in Robert Colls and Philip Dodd (eds), *Englishness: Politics and Culture* (London: Croon Helm, 1986), esp. p. 184.
29 The Coliseum programme for the opening week (commencing 11 March 1912) of the masque is in the British Library: London Playbills (1908–13), ref. 74/436. Two copies are also held at the Elgar Birthplace Museum, Worcester: Concert Programmes (Jan.–Jul. 1912), ref. no. 1126.
30 The quotations are from John Norris: 'all of the Elgar–Noyes songs were dropped from the Pageant, for reasons which have now been lost to us'; and later: 'the orchestrations are not missing ... they have never existed'. See Norris, 'Tales from the Complete Edition', 10 and 14. This is the most recent of such erroneous claims. See also Moore: 'little of this music was ever to be heard at Wembley – owing (so it was said) to complications of rehearsal' in *Letters of a Lifetime*, p. 379; and Martin Bird: 'It is uncertain whether Elgar's orchestral versions were bulldozed along with the Enoch premises, or never existed in the first place'; CD Reviews, *Elgar Society Journal* 16.5 (July 2010), p. 56.
31 I purposely use the term *Englishness* here, for, although the term *English* to refer to the contemporary nation-state of the United Kingdom is problematic, I argue for its retention in relation to the historical period covered by this chapter. Robert J.C. Young, following Gargi Bhattacharyya, notes that the 'dutiful use' of *British* rather than *English* glosses over the fact that in terms of power relations there is no difference between them: British was imposed by the English on the non-English. Young, *Colonial Desire: Hybridity in Theory, Culture and Race* (London and New York: Routledge, 1995), pp. 1–29, esp. p. 4.
32 'The Golden Chain' is a phrase used several times in the press to refer to the Elgar–Noyes songs. See, for instance, the advertisement in *The Times*, 8 August 1924, p. 8; and *The Sunday Times*, 20 July 1924, p. 12.
33 *The Times*, 18 August 1924, p. 8.
34 *The Times*, 28 July 1924, p. 8.
35 *The Times*, 26 July 1924, p. 17.
36 *The Times*, 19 July 1924, p. xi.
37 *The Hull Daily Mail*, 22 August 1924, p. 6.
38 Ibid. On the final day of the pageant's run, *The Times* told readers that 'Enoch and Sons are issuing a special souvenir programme of the music of the British Empire Pageant' featuring 'the words of Mr. Alfred Noyes ... set to music specially composed by Sir Edward Elgar'. *The Times*, 30 August 1924, p. 8.
39 The reference is to Rudyard Kipling's poem, 'The White Man's Burden: The United States & Philippine Islands, 1899', which begins 'Take up the White man's burden / send forth the best ye reed ...'. *Rudyard Kipling's Verse: Definitive Edition* (Garden City, NY: Doubleday, 1929).
40 Anderson, *Elgar*, p. 39. Performances of the *Imperial March* during the Jubilee Year – at the Albert and Queen's Halls, at a royal garden party and a state concert, as well as at the Three Choirs Festival – placed Elgar in the position of laureate for imperial Britain.
41 Anderson, *Elgar*, p. 36.
42 Sir Henry Wood, *My Life of Music* (London: Gollancz, 1946), p. 154.

43 Quoted in Anderson, *Elgar*, pp. 49–50.

44 Anderson surmises that it was probably Clara Butt (rather than Edward VII) who suggested the use of the trio tune from *Pomp and Circumstance* March, No. 1; see Anderson, *Elgar*, p. 53.

45 Michael Musgrave, *The Musical Life of the Crystal Palace* (Cambridge: Cambridge University Press, 1995), pp. 211–12.

46 Elgar clipped and kept the following announcement in *The Bystander*: 'Sir Edward Elgar, strongest and most individual of all English composers, has, by assuming the Order [of Merit], redeemed knighthood from being the charter of mediocrity in music'. Elgar Birthplace Museum, Worcester, Cuttings Files, vol. 7 (Jun. 1911–Jun. 1914), Ref. 1332, 1 (15 November 1911).

47 The quotation comes from *The Musical Times*, 1 October 1912, pp. 665–6. For more on the masque, see Nalini Ghuman, *Resonances of the Raj: India in the English Musical Imagination, 1897–1947* (New York and Oxford: Oxford University Press, 2014), pp. 53–104.

48 Walter R. Creighton to Edward Elgar, 7 January 1924, in *Letters of a Lifetime*, pp. 378–9.

49 Elgar to Stuart-Wortley, 10 January 1924, in *The Windflower Letters*, p. 287.

50 The phrase 'unfortunate Pageant' is found in Elgar's letter to Boosey, 11 September 1928, in *Elgar and His Publishers*, pp. 855–6.

51 *The Times*, 14 January 1924, p. 7. Valuable reference to the learning pageant is made in *The Times*, 12 July 1924, p. 10.

52 'Shakespeare's Kingdom', words by Noyes, music by Elgar, from *A Pageant of Empire* (London: Enoch & Sons, 1924).

53 *Sunday Times*, 20 July 1924, p. 12. *The Times* specifically mentions that 'there have been dress rehearsals to which a certain number of the public have been admitted'. See *The Times*, 26 July 1924, p. 17.

54 Gerald Finzi's 'Who Is Silvia?', from his set of five Shakespeare songs written between 1929 and 1942, is in a similar vein.

55 *The Hull Daily Mail*, 22 August 1924, p. 6.

56 *The Times*, 13 October 1924, p. 12.

57 Quotation from *The Times*, 18 August 1924, p. 8. *Pageant of British Empire: Souvenir Volume* (London: Fleetway Press, 1924), pp. 6–7.

58 The composer's own description (of *Fringes of the Fleet*) is quoted in Charles Edward MacGuire, 'Functional Music: Imperialism, the Great War, and Elgar as Popular Composer', in Daniel M. Grimley and Julian Rushton (eds), *The Cambridge Companion to Elgar* (Cambridge: Cambridge University Press, 2004), pp. 214–24, p. 220.

59 'Stand Up, Stand Up for Jesus' is another such hymn popular at the time. See *Hymns Ancient and Modern Revised* (London: William Clowes and Sons, 1950), pp. 872–3.

60 Raymond Monk (ed.), *Elgar Studies* (Aldershot: Scolar Press, 1990), appendices 1 and 4, pp. 16–33.

61 The historian Jeffrey Richards brilliantly invokes J.B. Priestley's point that it is characteristic of the English to laugh at what they love most. Moreover, this may be an instance of a type of song which, as Richards puts it, 'starts out as satire, and ends up as celebration'. See Richards, *Imperialism and Music*, p. 34.

62 *The Hull Daily Mail*, 22 August 1924, p. 6.

63 E flat major was identified in this way as early as 1796 by Francesco Galeazzi, in *Elementi teorico-practici di musica*, and is well known as the key of Beethoven's *Eroica* Symphony, Richard Strauss's *Ein Heldenleben* and Mahler's vast 'Symphony of a Thousand' – the Eighth. For more on Elgar's 'signature' descending sevenths, see Ghuman, *Resonances of the Raj*, pp. 76–82.

64 Elgar to Boosey, 11 September 1928, and 26 August 1929, in *Elgar and His Publishers*, pp. 855–6, 864–5.

65 The two quotations are from, respectively, *British Empire Exhibition, Pamphlet No. 7*, p. 12, and 'The Pageant of Empire', *The Times*, 18 August 1924, p. 8. The subtitle for this section comes from *The Graphic*, 23 August 1924, p. 282.

66 *The Times*, 12 June 1924, p. 7.

67   *The Times*, 29 July 1924, p. 10.

68   *The Times*, 29 July 1924, p. xi.

69   This verse is quoted in *The Times* as the introduction to the scene change. *The Times*, 29 July 1924, p. xi.

70   The advertisement for Elgar's *Pageant of Empire* on the back of the published score of 'Merchant Adventurers' provides a note explaining that 'Sailing Westward' has 'four alternative poems', and the first listed is 'Indian Dawn' (London: Enoch & Sons, 1924).

71   Noyes's verse is taken from the *British Empire Exhibition Pamphlet No. 7: Pageant of Empire Programme – Part II Jul. 21–Aug. 30 1924*.

72   Both Richards (*Imperialism and Music*, p. 203) and Norris ('Tales from the Complete Edition', p. 13) repeat the mistake as it first appeared in *The Times*, 29 July 1924, p. xi. This is not a trivial matter as the meaning of Shankar is 'beneficent, the giver of bliss', while that of Shandar is 'pride'.

73   For critical studies of Shankar's work in London, see Joan L. Erdman, 'Performance as Translation: Uday Shankar in the West', *The Drama Review* 31 (1987), pp. 64–88; and Nilanjana Bhattacharjya, 'Aesthetic Fusions: British Asian Music and Diaspora Culture', unpublished PhD thesis, Cornell University, 2007.

74   Mohan Khokar, *His Dance, His Life: A Portrait of Uday Shankar* (New Delhi, Himalayan Books, 1983), p. 41.

75   Sarojini Naidu, *The Golden Threshold* (London: Heinemann, 1905). Both Lehmann and Woodforde-Finden set Naidu's 'Cradle Song', the latter's is entitled 'A Little Lovely Dream' (London, Boosey & Co. 1907 and 1917, respectively). Woodforde-Finden's 'In a Latticed Balcony' (1917) sets words from Naidu, and Lehmann's *The Golden Threshold. An Indian Song-Garland*, is scored for soloists, chorus and orchestra (London: Boosey & Co, 1906).

76   The quotation is from Julia Chatteron's review, 'Indian Music', *Musical Standard*, 29 July 1922, p. 43. For more on this subject, see Ghuman, *Resonances of the Raj*, pp. 11–52.

77   For a detailed discussion of this piece, see Ghuman, *Resonances of the Raj*, pp. 82–9.

78   'Modern British Composers: Liza Lehmann', *Musical Standard* 10 (17 October 1903), p. 243.

79   For more on the menagerie, see Donald R. Knight and Alan D. Sabey, *The Lion Roars at Wembley: British Empire Exhibition 60th Anniversary, 1924–1925* (London: Barnard & Westwood, 1984), and Kurt Koenigsberger, *The Novel and the Menagerie: Totality, Englishness, and Empire* (Columbus, OH: Ohio State University Press 2007).

80   A.B. Cooper, 'Songs that Moved the World: The Story of *The Indian Love Lyrics*', *Radio Times*, 15 August 1924, p. 310.

81   *The Sheik* (Famous Players-Lasky, Paramount, 1921).

82   Koenigsberger, *The Novel and the Menagerie*, p. 161, n. 61.

83   Deborah Hughes, 'Contesting Whiteness: Race, Nationalism and British Empire Exhibitions Between the Wars', unpublished PhD thesis, University of Illinois at Urbana-Champaign, 2008, pp. 24–5. See also Daniel Mark Stephen, '"The White Man's Grave": British West Africa and the Wembley Exhibition of 1924–1925', *Journal of British Studies* 48 (2009), pp. 102–28, esp. p. 127.

84   Koenigsberger, *The Novel and the Menagerie*, p. 166.

85   Ibid., pp. 57–8.

86   Creighton to Elgar, 7 January 1924, in *Letters of a Lifetime*, pp. 378–9.

87   Elgar to Stuart-Wortley, 21 January 1924, in *The Windflower Letters*, p. 287.

88   Ibid., 7 February 1924, p. 288.

89   *The Hull Daily Mail*, 22 August 1924, p. 6.

90   *The Times*, 28 July 1924, p. 8.

91   'Textural glue' comes from Julian Rushton, 'Review of the Acuta Edition of the *Empire March*', *Elgar Society Journal* 16 (2009), p. 48.

92   *Spiritoso* is the marking Elgar indicated in the opening bars of the march which he included in his letter to Stuart-Wortley, 7 February 1924, in *The Windflower Letters*, p. 287.

93 The quotations are all from Richards's reading of Elgar's vision of empire, which he describes as 'altruistic imperialism' and concludes that this was 'a far from ignoble dream'. Richards, *Imperialism and Music*, pp. 51, 53, 84.

94 'A Song of Union', words by Noyes, set to music by Elgar (London: Enoch & Sons, 1924).

95 *The Empire March* has been published in a limited edition full score by Acuta in 2008 from a set of printed draft orchestral parts which were discovered in the library of the Herefordshire Orchestral Society in the early 1990s. In the preface to the score, the editor surmises that, in the absence of Elgar's own manuscript, the set of parts could well constitute the prime surviving source material for the *Empire March* orchestral score.

96 Elgar to Boosey, 10 June 1928, in *Elgar and His Publishers*, p. 855.

97 John Foulds relates the French remark, made by a distinguished musician after playing through some of Elgar's melodies on the piano, in his book *Music To-Day* (London: Ivor Nicholson and Watson, 1934), p. 233, n. 2. Michael Kennedy writes: 'the falling thirds and sevenths of the G minor section of the original theme ... pervade the whole work as clearly as if they were Elgar's signature', Kennedy, CD notes Deutsche Grammophon CD 413, 490-2 (1982).

98 *The Musical Times*, 1 October 1924, p. 917.

99 *The Times*, 13 October 1924, p. 12.

100 Moore, *Elgar and His Publishers*, p. 838. See also Anderson, *Elgar*, p. 301.

101 Richards, *Imperialism and Music*, p. 205. Yet Rushton rightly states that, 'as an example of Elgar's instrumental thinking, this piece remains as exuberant as ever'. See Rushton, 'Review of the Acuta Edition of the *Empire March*', p. 48.

102 Cecil Gray, *A Survey of Contemporary Music* (London: Oxford University Press, 1924), pp. 78–9.

103 Ibid.

104 F.H. Shera, *Elgar: Instrumental Works* (London: Oxford University Press, 1931), p. 6.

105 A.J. Sheldon, *Edward Elgar*, with an introduction by Havergal Brian (London: Office of 'Musical Opinion', 1932), p. 16.

106 Frank Howes claimed that 'the two Elgars may be roughly described as the Elgar who writes for strings and the Elgar who writes for brass'. See Frank Howes, 'The Two Elgars', *Music and Letters* 15 (1935), pp. 26–9.

107 *The Times*, 26 July 1924, p. 17.

108 *Sunday Times*, 24 August, 1924, p. 11.

109 See, for instance, *The Times*, 7 November 1924, p. 21. Ronald Taylor, 'Music in the Air: Elgar and the BBC', in Raymond Monk (ed.), *Edward Elgar: Music and Literature* (Aldershot: Scolar Press, 1993), pp. 336–7, 351–5. See also *The Times*, 13 October 1924, p. 12.

110 Virginia Woolf, *Orlando: A Biography* (1928) (Orlando, FL: Harcourt Books, 2006), p. 170.

111 Benita Parry quotes from Forster's mocking account of 1924 (entitled 'The Birth of an Empire') in her book *Postcolonial Studies: A Materialist Critique* (London and New York, Routledge, 2004), p. 228, n. 41. For the WGTW Society, see John M. MacKenzie, 'Introduction', in MacKenzie (ed.), *Imperialism and Popular Culture* (Manchester: Manchester University Press, 1986), p. 7.

112 MacKenzie, 'Introduction', p. 7.

113 Notwithstanding Rushton's astute point that some of the *Empire March* scoring was 'essentially for show'. See Rushton, 'Review', p. 48. In fact, it made sense that the scoring was large, and that it included an organ part to 'glue it all together', given the ten-acre stadium.

114 This comes through most obviously in the letter to his Windflower of 16 April 1924: 'I have been at Wembley & am overwhelmed with etiquette & red tape. My March will not be done as there are difficulties in the way of the Brigade Bands co-operating etc etc – so the Military Bands will play the old Imperial March.' *The Windflower Letters*, pp. 289–90.

115 *The Times*, 12 July 1924, p. 7.

CHAPTER TEN

Representing 'Our Island Sultanate' in London and Zanzibar: Cross-currents in educating imperial publics

Sarah Longair

Visitors exploring the East African pavilion at the British Empire Exhibition in 1924–25 entered the imposing whitewashed Arab-style palace through an ornately carved 'Zanzibar' door (Figure 10.1). This replica was modelled on the door to the old Italian Consulate in Zanzibar, admired as one of the most impressive examples of this art form. Inside, the Zanzibar Court celebrated the Busaidi dynasty's harmonious rule with the British Protectorate Government and proudly exhibited the island's key exports – cloves and coconut products. The full-length oil-painted portraits of the current Sultan, Khalifa bin Harub, and his formidable pro-British ancestor, Sultan Barghash bin Said, presented an image of opulent regal rule and a stable and productive local economy.

This confident image of Zanzibar was in large part illusory. Since the late nineteenth century, Zanzibar's pre-eminence in the region had waned. The Sultan's government no longer dominated mainland territories and, in the wake of the abolition of the slave trade and slavery, Zanzibar ceased to be the hub of economic activity in the region. Since becoming a British Protectorate in 1890, the island maintained the key clove trade at a steady level. However, unlike the vast new imperial mainland territories of Uganda, Kenya and, after the Great War, Tanganyika which seemed rich in potential, Zanzibar's 'Golden Age' lay in the past. As if to underline this, in the central court of the pavilion, where each territory exhibited a small stall of key produce, Tanganyika Territory displayed a new 'Zanzibar' door carved by the students of the Tanga Government School.[1] The prominent placement of this second door made clear that the skill of its manufacture and consequently potential for the future lay with the youth of Tanganyika. During the 1920s, the Zanzibar government asserted its significance in contemporary affairs by configuring the island as the 'mother' to its East African 'daughters'.[2] From this vantage point, Zanzibar could claim responsibility for the success of the region through its

Figure 10.1 East Africa pavilion at the British Empire Exhibition, Wembley, postcard, 1924–25

long history of trade. While the economic and political reality was somewhat different, then, the representation of Zanzibar in Wembley sought to advertise and emphasise the island's continued centrality and historical importance in the region.

In common with exhibition practice at the time, a handbook was produced by the Zanzibar Organising Committee to contextualise the Court. This publication was intended to be more than just 'a pleasing Souvenir'.[3] In Britain, according to the booklet, Zanzibar was little known 'to the man in the street who remembers it chiefly as a musical-comedy name and secondly as vaguely connected with Heligoland'.[4] During the nineteenth century, the island was better known for associations with the slave trade and as the starting point for many of the major expeditions into the African interior. The organisers were eager to dispel such impressions – either that of an exotic name exploited for comedic purposes on the stage or an association with some ill-remembered episode during 'the Scramble for Africa'. Through this text, the educational mission of the Organising Committee was clear: readers should 'gain a correct impression of our Island Sultanate'.[5] The Empire Exhibition at Wembley, and its interpretation of Zanzibar's past and present, was envisaged as a crucial tool for achieving this.

The historical narrative presented at the Wembley exhibition was also a key component of the new educational movement in Zanzibar. It formed the basis of the displays in Zanzibar's new Peace Memorial

Museum, opened in 1925, and was repeated in the first *School History of Zanzibar*, also published in 1925, and the *School History of East Africa* in 1930.[6] This moment, therefore, when territories across the British Empire were invited to represent themselves to the British public, also coincided with various projects of representation in Zanzibar which had local, regional and global dimensions.

The 'correct impression' of Zanzibar – in particular the historical narrative and its dissemination both in Britain and Zanzibar through exhibitions and printed texts – is the subject of this chapter. It reveals how these displays of material culture and the interpretative narratives associated with them offer new insights into the construction of Zanzibar's imperial identity at home and abroad in the first half of the twentieth century. The chapter will examine the nature of this representation and how it can be seen as a response to the regional anxieties prevalent in 1920s Zanzibar. In the context of the island's diminishing role, this history was a method of claiming individuality among the British Empire's African territories.

As will be demonstrated, the British interpretation of the island's history was critically informed by local oral histories in Zanzibar, by intellectual movements and by the personal interests of its administrator-authors, W.H. Ingrams and L.W. Hollingsworth. Such men acted as cultural mediators between the territory and the wider empire, carefully constructing the island's complex society and history through objects and text. Its diverse communities defied simple categorisation and included the indigenous Swahili islanders, former slaves, recent migrants from the African mainland, Arab and Indian elite communities and a small but influential European contingent. The history related by Ingrams and Hollingsworth through the exhibitions and in print traced the island's history back to the era of the Ancient Sumerians and Assyrians and progressively described the development of Zanzibar's culture, culminating in the benevolent rule of the Omanis and the British.

The term 'our Island Sultanate' echoed Marshall's *Our Island Story* and invited comparison between Great Britain and Zanzibar, islands which through maritime and commercial aptitude were able to command influence far beyond their shores.[7] While Zanzibar's heyday lay in its past, British rule was presented as the latest in a long history of overseas interventions which forged its vibrant cosmopolitan society. The *School History* also reused the 'our island story' phrase, 'our' here suggesting a shared history between the British colonialists and the various peoples of Zanzibar. In the context of the Wembley Exhibition, however, the term can be interpreted as a claim of ownership by the imperial centre. This chapter explores the significance of these shifting contexts first by examining the Zanzibar Court at Wembley and its handbook, then by investigating their manifestations in Zanzibar itself, through the *School History of Zanzibar* and the island's new Peace Memorial Museum.

Exhibiting Zanzibar at Wembley

The British Empire Exhibition staged at Wembley in 1924 and 1925 was a spectacle on a scale unprecedented in Britain.[8] Fifty-six of the fifty-eight territories in the Empire exhibited in pavilions and courts alongside a fairground with thrilling rides and refreshment kiosks. The Exhibition's organising committee had a clear agenda, with aspirations to reinvigorate the spirit of empire in the minds of the British public in the decade after the Great War and to encourage new commercial networks between imperial territories. Wembley represented an apogee of the exhibition model, where the spectacle simultaneously entertained and instructed. It rendered in physical form the interlocking commercial body of the British Empire. While the Exhibition was notoriously unprofitable and the funfair might have been the key attraction, twenty-seven million visitors explored the Empire through carefully managed pavilions designed to project individual territories' culture, arts, crafts and potential for productivity, trade and future investment. This awe-inspiring expression of imperial dominance lingered in memory, buildings and a vast array of exhibition ephemera.[9]

The African section of the Wembley exhibition, with three large pavilions devoted to 'the Three Africas' (West Africa, East Africa and South Africa), reflected the renewed interest in the continent in the interwar period.[10] The capabilities and proficiencies of African populations were demonstrated through exhibits of raw materials, manufactured objects and, in certain cases, African artists and craftsmen undertaking practical work.[11] Images of Africa and the presence of Africans at exhibitions in metropolitan centres have been the subject of works by several scholars, including Annie Coombes, Sadiah Qureshi and Jonathan Woodham.[12] Deborah Hughes and Jinny Prais have demonstrated how exhibitions were the focus of boycott and resistance by Indians and West Africans respectively.[13] Within the wide-ranging literature on imperial exhibitions, the representation and participation of Zanzibar has rarely been addressed. This absence is itself instructive – existing work has tended to focus on mainland sub-Saharan Africa and depictions and denigrations of peoples from territories which corresponded to the stereotypical trope of 'the Dark Continent' and 'black Africa'. Zanzibar, while subject to its own set of characterisations, did not fit into this discourse at the time and it has since been overlooked within the scholarship on exhibiting Africa. In fact, as this chapter will suggest, such distinctions were reinforced by the Wembley exhibit and its handbook. The island's reputation as 'the Pearl of the Indian Ocean', redolent with the atmosphere of the *Arabian Nights*, aligned it in the European imagination with 'the Orient' – an image which cultural projects such as exhibitions and education textbooks served to perpetuate.[14]

The Zanzibar government's attempt at self-representation through Wembley must be considered within the context of economic anxiety. The prosperity which built Zanzibar town's magnificent palaces and narrow atmospheric streets had passed. The city from which the first Omani Sultan, Seyyid Said, maintained control of mainland territories from Lamu to northern Mozambique and into the interior, was no longer the economic centre of the coast. The incorporation of Tanganyika into the British Empire as part of the peace settlement after the Great War united British control of the coastline, and Zanzibar's strategic role in the Empire diminished still further. Its economy was a source of concern in the Colonial Office.[15] The vulnerable clove industry remained the principal source of finance for the government. From 1913 to 1927, the British Resident in Zanzibar was answerable to the High Commissioner in Nairobi. The Exhibition as a whole represented many views of British Africa, and the design of the Zanzibar room demonstrates how the Organising Committee sought to differentiate it from its East African neighbours in the adjacent halls between Kenya and Uganda.[16] To promote the island effectively, the Protectorate Government chose to highlight the attractive qualities of Zanzibar's history and reputation alongside its key produce while presenting it as the most sophisticated culture of the East African region.

The organisation of the Zanzibar section was led by Dr Francis Charlesworth, the representative in London, nominated in 1922. A committee in Zanzibar, convened in 1923 to collect exhibits, was headed by William Hendry, Director of Education with William Harold Ingrams among its members.[17] It was allocated by the Zanzibar government £3,000 with which to organise the exhibits.[18] It was an entirely British committee, unlike the London Advisory Committee for the India pavilion, which included several leading London-based Indians.[19] Charlesworth had been a surgeon in Zanzibar from 1887 to 1921, arriving in the last year of the reign of the charismatic Sultan Barghash. With memories of Zanzibar's precolonial years and the splendour of Barghash's court, Charlesworth brought his own experience to bear on the display while being conveniently located to oversee activities in London.

In contrast, William Hendry, local chair of the Organising Committee, had been in Zanzibar only since 1921. He was appointed as Director of Education, having previously served in Egypt.[20] In this post he led a much more active education policy after many years of inactivity by the government in this area.[21] An important legacy of his work, as well as the creation of many more town and district schools, was the establishment of the Teacher Training School, opened in 1923 under the direction of Lawrence W. Hollingsworth. One aim of this institution was to train promising young Arabs to become teachers and divert them from the temptations of the town.[22] As Jonathon Glassman has shown, this institution became an important meeting point for young Arab intellectuals who were themselves influential upon Hollingsworth.[23] He directed the centre until 1935 when its functions were transferred to the first Government Secondary School, of which Hollingsworth was appointed headmaster. He was a remarkable and inspiring teacher in his years on island from 1922 to 1944, and taught many students who came to prominence in public life in the 1950s and early 1960s.[24]

William Harold Ingrams was a critical figure in the research into and representation of Zanzibar's history and culture. Posted initially to Pemba as Assistant District Commissioner, he relocated in 1924 to Zanzibar town to act as Clerk of the Protectorate Council and then Private Secretary to the British Resident. His time in Zanzibar, from 1919 to 1927, was characterised by his 'vigorous investigation into the history and ethnology of these islands'.[25] As well as working on the Wembley display and contributing key chapters to the handbook, he participated in the planning of the Peace Memorial Museum and subsequently worked in the museum in his spare time enthusiastically from 1925 to 1927. Ingrams analysed Zanzibar's culture as an enthusiastic amateur anthropologist, collecting information, artefacts and oral histories in his various postings. His publication on *Zanzibar: Its Native Industries and People* was one of the first ethnographic surveys of the island and he, with Hollingsworth, authored the *School History* based on the Wembley handbook. It is significant that these were two of the more liberal-minded officers in Zanzibar, noted for their good relations with the local community.

The Zanzibar Court

We are fortunate that four photographs of the Zanzibar Court survive in the Zanzibar National Archives. These can be analysed alongside reports in the newspapers in Zanzibar and the UK and the few remaining records relating to the Court in the official records. The key themes in the display were the twin cultural and commercial strengths of Zanzibar: the Busaidi dynasty and clove production. These were echoed across the material culture created by the British in Zanzibar. The Sultan's signature and the clove tree and flower created a recognisable 'brand' for the island, distilled to these two elements of the clove, as seen on the new banknote of 1907 and the medal for the Zanzibar Exhibition of 1905.[26]

The Zanzibar Court retained the regal essence of the joint government of the Sultanate, with the Union Jack and the Sultan's flag crossed over the entrances and the Sultan's coats of arms displayed between portraits of Sultan Barghash and the current Sultan, Sir Khalifa bin Harub (Figure 10.2). The portrait of Barghash is likely to be that which was housed in the British Residency since the early 1900s and is currently on display in the Zanzibar Museum. These formal portraits were atypical of displays in the East and West African pavilions, and served to present the unique identity of Zanzibar: a sophisticated Arab state as well as a productive island with trading possibilities within the Empire. Clothing of two Arab dignitaries and an Arab woman provided material examples of the typical clothing of Zanzibar's elite, together with their daggers, swords and jewellery which gave material examples of the formal clothing worn in the Sultans' portraits. The woman's outfit included the eye-mask worn by elite Arab women in Zanzibar, an item often remarked upon by European visitors in describing the exotic otherness of the island. Alongside the portraits of the Sultan were Swahili drums, stools and a so-called Zanzibar chest – brass-embossed dark wood chests popular since the Omani period although often made in the Persian Gulf rather than in Zanzibar itself.

On the wall facing the formal display of the Sultanate was a diorama depicting clove production (Figure 10.3). A panoramic watercolour of an avenue of clove trees provided the backdrop in a composition similar to that on the Zanzibar Exhibition medal from 1905. In front, batches of cloves were laid out, as if drying, under a *makuti* (palm-leaf) roof. The panorama included pieces of stone wall and larger painted figures on freestanding flats to create a sense of depth. Unlike the 'African village' where some territories arranged for local craftsmen to undertake their work for the British public to observe, no Zanzibar locals formed part of the exhibit. They were instead represented by these painted depictions. Their clothing formed a marked contrast with those of the Arab costumes in the cases opposite. The aroma from the cloves was strong – as a *Times* correspondent wrote in 1924: 'The odour of cloves hangs around the Zanzibar court', which would have evoked the ambience of the spice island.[27]

The display in the centre of the room exhibited products made from

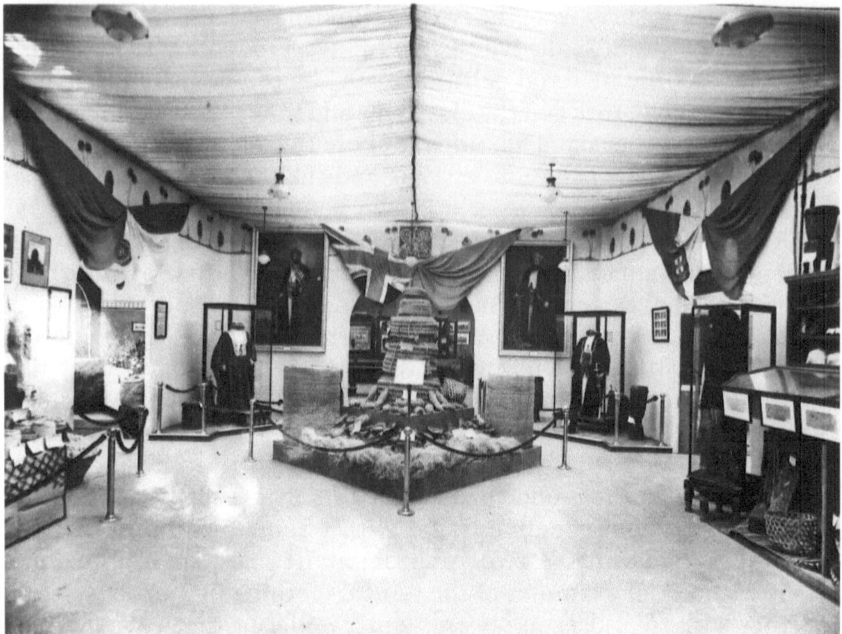

Figure 10.2 Zanzibar Court at Empire Exhibition in Wembley, 1924–25

coconuts, including coir – fibre from the husk of the coconut which was a growing industry in Zanzibar. Rope was the principal commodity produced in Zanzibar from this source. Large coils of rope were piled into a central tower with baskets and examples of thinner twine at its base. Large rolls of matting were positioned on the corners, along with rustically arranged baskets of halved coconuts and the husks fringing the section. Coconuts also provided the basis for soap production and copra – the dried kernel of the coconut – was exported from Zanzibar, for example for the production of oil.[28] In this case, the organisers may have realised that the size of the coir rope made it a useful focus for the room and employed an alternative mode of display to the clove exhibit.

On one of the two remaining walls, a large wooden cabinet provided a means to display a range of other goods of local origin, including mats, musical instruments, fishing baskets, domestic utensils, such as brass coffee pots, and a model of a dhow. Also on display were four *kofia* caps, the traditional Swahili form of headgear, worn along the East African coast. While the Arab outfits were displayed in their entirety, these much more commonly and widely used items were included

Figure 10.3 Clove diorama in the Zanzibar Court at the Empire
Exhibition in Wembley, 1924–25

in a display of 'crafts' and divorced from their use.[29] On the opposite
wall was a selection of different goods, such as spices and foodstuffs,
arranged in open sacks and baskets as if at a bazaar. These included
'rice, ground-nuts, castor seeds, mangrove-bark, kola, palm kernels,
beeswax, nutmegs etc.'[30] On the walls throughout were photographs,
watercolours and prints, while a frieze painted around the top of the
walls used an alternating pattern of a coconut and clove tree.

In 1925, 'dainty bags' of cloves sold in the Zanzibar section of the
exhibition for 6*d*, along with mats and baskets.[31] Pemba stools were
also on sale – it was noted in the *Zanzibar Gazette* that, in 1925,
'the range of comfortable Pemba stools' for sale caused 'quite a sensation'.[32] Such sales were important as evidence of public popularity and
to spread awareness of the territory as well as bringing in some small
sums of money. Each territory's government hoped to attract public
and commercial interest and their exhibits competed for the attention
of the visitors.

A number of the exhibits were transported back to Zanzibar,
including the portraits and some of the smaller items. Others were
dispersed 'to lands and places which before knew nothing of them'.[33]

The clove panorama was moved to the office of the Trade Commissioner for East Africa in London, the photographs to the Imperial Institute for their museum and the dhow model to the Science Museum in South Kensington. The carved Zanzibar door was installed in a public building in Hull: the city had supported the Zanzibar section financially as it held 'from a commercial aspect, the interest of East Africa'.[34] In this instance, the artefact provided material evidence of commercial relationships, whether or not these connections had any great economic significance.

In the British press reports, the Court was acknowledged but rarely attracted more than passing interest. Among the vast number of displays and exhibits to review at Wembley, the Zanzibar Court was regularly listed in the array of courts to see, its name doubtless adding to the allure as attested in a report of the opening ceremony: 'East Africa (which includes the Sudan, Kenya, Tanganyika, Nyasaland, Zanzibar, Mauritius, and the Seychelles – which a dictionary of romance the very names are!) …'.[35] In general, Zanzibar and sometimes the production of cloves were mentioned briefly during descriptions of exploring the exhibition. One of the more expansive references to the Zanzibar Court was given in a report for housewives on the origins of household and culinary products:

> The tale of what the larder and the many needs of the home owes to the Empire is found in every pavilion, and the roaming housekeeper learns in Zanzibar that from here her grocer, by many intermediary channels, secures her pepper, rice, nutmegs, beeswax, cloves and other spicy things.[36]

Such a description captures an essence of the connectivity of empire, from the distant tropical island to the domestic sphere, that a visitor might have experienced in Wembley. One reporter offered an insight into perhaps a more realistic response to the display of commercial products:

> The casual visitor, however, may be pardoned for turning from these reminders of East African industry and wealth – impressive as they may be – to the fascinating collection of big game trophies in the Central Court. They will surely make every sportsman sigh that the 'Never-stop' railway does not run from Wembley to Mombasa.[37]

Zanzibar's display could not compete with the spirit of adventure evoked by the attractions of big game hunting and the thrill of the fairground ride, which were, disappointingly for some, not yet connected. The commendation of the Court by a writer from the *African Industries* journal was received warmly in Zanzibar and quoted proudly in the local *Gazette*:

> The general arrangement of the Zanzibar Court merits high praise. The grouping of the practical with the artistic; the mingling of the commercial aspect with the needs of the sightseer, and the definite illustration of the many industries, all combine to impress the public.[38]

The image of the island presented in the Court, with the magnificent oil paintings, the opulent traditional Arab costumes and the bazaar of exotic goods, reinforced the generalised cultural tropes associated with Zanzibar – those of the exoticism of the spice island and colourful Arab rulers. The coir exhibit was clearly an 'industrial' rather than artistic presentation, while elements of Swahili culture – musical instruments, baskets and caps – were positioned as 'native craft' to add an authentic 'African' aspect of the display. The painted panorama of the clove plantation and strong aroma emanating from it conjured a powerful multi-sensory experience of the tropical landscape. This served as a contrast to the images of contemporary East Africa exhibited by the mainland African territories. Kenya in particular hoped to attract settlement from Europe, and thus emphasised the prospects of ranch-life and hunting wild game through exhibits of animal trophy heads and images of idyllic Rift Valley rolling hillsides. Both constructions were fantasies, but represent the diverse needs of the East African territories in the interwar period.

The exhibition handbook

As we have seen, the Organising Committee was anxious to educate the British audience about the intricacies of Zanzibar's history and culture. This was manifest not just in the display of material culture but also in the accompanying interpretative handbook. In his Preface, Hendry evoked the island's *Arabian Nights* charm: 'there is an Eastern atmosphere and glamour not possessed by any other settlement on the coast' with its bazaar 'reminiscent of the Mouski of Cairo'.[39] It was at this point that Hendry explained the text's purpose: to contextualise the image created within the Court, and to reclaim the island's reputation back from the music-hall and assert its rightful place as the historical trading emporium of the Indian Ocean.

Of the six chapters in the eighty-page book, three were written by Ingrams: 'Ethnology', 'History' and 'Native Industries and Occupations'. Together they formed more than three-quarters of the text. The remaining chapters were 'Trade' (three pages), 'Agriculture' (seven pages) and 'Economic Minerals' (two pages). These latter three were broadly factual and designed to encourage commercial interest by highlighting, for example, the greater capacity for export in the coming years thanks to the harbour improvements. Handbooks for other African pavilions devoted the majority of their texts to the economic potential of the territories with short summaries of history, often dismissive of the precolonial period. In the case of Zanzibar, however, presenting the lengthy history of the island was one ambition the organisers had for the Court itself. As the officer with the most enthusiastic and extensive interest in the island's people and history, Ingrams's personal research and interpretation therefore dominated the text. His sources included Arab manuscripts, so-called 'Native Histories of Zanzibar and Pemba' (manuscripts of transcriptions of indigenous histories), local informants and interviewees, and the writings of his British predecessors.[40] This part of the discussion will consider the 'History' chapter of the exhibition handbook as it subsequently provided the basis for the teaching of Zanzibar's history in schools and the arrangement of the museum in Zanzibar.

Ingrams's account of the history of Zanzibar was informed by the Arab intelligentsia in Zanzibar and by the narrative model typical of British writers about the island, as well as indigenous histories. At this time, the Arab interpretation of history was developing in the new Teacher Training School, led by Hollingsworth, Ingrams's co-author on the *School History of Zanzibar*. A variety of sources influenced these young men, including the Arab Association founded in 1911 which itself was inspired by pan-Arab movements, the *ulamaa* scholars who had been debating Islamic modernism in Zanzibar since the nineteenth century, and Hollingsworth and other British administrators.[41] Their universal interpretation of Zanzibar's history, in which 'the attributes of civilization had been introduced to East Africa by outsiders' was influenced by pan-Arabist ideas as well as long-held indigenous beliefs.[42] In his examination of racial thought in Zanzibar, Glassman traces the long history on the coast of these customs which located claims to authority in exotic origins. The spread of Islam reinforced this sense of coastal exceptionalism and difference from the peoples of the hinterland. While this did not imply a unifying Swahili identity, a notion existed throughout the region that 'assigned prestige to all things connected to the distant Islamic heartland'.[43] When analysing the British interpretation of these histories, it is vital to recognise their complex origins.

It is possible that Ingrams encountered these ideas via Hollingsworth. Ingrams supported this educated Arab elite in their claim for their future role in guiding the development of Zanzibar.[44] His research into Zanzibar's history led him to look positively upon the Arab rule prior to the British Protectorate. In an article published towards the end of his career, he stated that Zanzibar should not be described as 'misruled, backward and all the other derogatory things one can say of places which have not "enjoyed the benefits of enlightened western rule"'.[45] His conclusions settled on the benefits of Arab rule rather than calling for a drive for greater empowerment or enfranchisement of the population at large.

Ingrams opened the 'History' chapter by explicitly highlighting the island's external connections: 'Zanzibar owes its history mainly to its insularity, to its convenience as a jumping-off place for the East Coast of Africa, to its proximity to Asia and to the trade winds or Monsoons which account to a large extent for its close political and commercial connections from the earliest times, with India, the countries bordering on the Persian Gulf and the Red Sea.'[46] He began by introducing the ancient trading origins of the island, thereby associating it with the Sumerians, the Assyrians and the ancient cultures of the Near East. Ingrams noted links with the ancient Egyptians and to ancient Arabian trade. He included lengthy descriptions from the Greek guide to Indian Ocean trade, known as the *Periplus of the Erythraean Sea*. He subsequently explained the 'invasions' of the Bantu peoples before the arrival of Arabian peoples from the Persian Gulf and the advent of Islam.

The next phase was that of the 'Zenj Empire' where Ingrams recounted prevailing traditions about the Swahili city-states originating with the arrival of Persian merchants from Shiraz, from whom centuries later Zanzibaris claimed descent and took the name 'Shirazi'.[47] The visitations of other peoples from the Far East, for example the Chinese and Malayans, were also highlighted. He briefly described the characteristics and temperaments of the 'native tribes' and the differences between them, before commencing a detailed narrative from the arrival of the Portuguese in the sixteenth century onwards and their struggles on the coast with the Omani Arabs. These sections featured figures such as Seyyid Said, the Omani Sultan who moved his capital to Zanzibar in the 1830s, and Sultan Barghash and their dealings with the British, as well as the nineteenth-century European explorers, Sir John Kirk and General Sir Lloyd Mathews. Tippu Tib, 'the great traveller, trader and ruler', was also considered.[48] Several pages were devoted to this latter figure, who, by the time of his death in 1905, was a popular member of Zanzibar's elite societies, respected by Arabs and the British alike.[49] Significantly, Ingrams does not once in this account mention Tippu Tib's involvement in slavery, merely his supreme influence over caravans trading in the interior. He did not draw attention to the history of slavery in Zanzibar – merely factually noting the treaties in the nineteenth century – which may have been a tactful omission to satisfy Zanzibar's ruling Arab elite.

A passage which played explicitly to the British audience was his reference to Zanzibar's contributions to the Great War effort, which were 'for her size, by no means negligible'. Ingrams highlighted Sultan Khalifa's 'steadying influence' over the Muslim populations of East and Central Africa, which 'largely contributed to the maintenance of peace among the Mahommedans of mid-Africa during the critical periods of war in these regions'.[50] Ingrams made clear to the British public that the war effort had been global throughout the imperial community. He concluded the historical section with positive news of future works to bring further development in education and commerce to Zanzibar.[51]

This handbook, then, situated the British Protectorate government as the latest in the line of ruling elites whose origins lay overseas. It was this responsiveness to outside influence, so the argument went, which distinguished Zanzibar from other African societies. Such a concept suggests a simultaneous understanding of the Zanzibar population, determined both by race and by class, complicating the concept set out in David Cannadine's *Ornamentalism*.[52] The relationships between Zanzibar's political and financial elites – the British, Arabs and Indians – were close and were reinforced by elaborate rituals, ceremonies and bestowal of honours, supporting Cannadine's thesis. Their economic and honorific status differentiated them from the majority of local peoples. However, as the written history of Zanzibar demonstrates, these ideas of commonalities between the elite communities, whose origins lay overseas, coexisted with the longstanding indigenous perception, accepted and promoted by the British and Arab population, of racial difference between the people of Zanzibar and the Swahili coast and those of the African interior.

History and education in Zanzibar: textbook and the museum

While the Wembley handbook was prepared for publication in 1924, just one year later Ingrams co-authored the *School History of Zanzibar* with Hollingsworth. With a new history syllabus appearing in schools, Hollingsworth noted that a local textbook was essential for teaching the subject: 'In the past there have been no facilities for the study of local history. According to modern educational practice the study of both history and geography should be based on a foundation of local knowledge.'[53] Since the appointment of Hendry in 1921 and the opening of the Teacher Training School, the Protectorate Government was hoping to improve the standard and scale of education in Zanzibar. Producing suitable textbooks of local relevance was one aspect of this project.

Ingrams explained his contribution in his section of the preface and the book's relationship to the earlier publication:

> For the bulk of the subject-matter of this book I must be held entirely responsible, and should there be any mistakes of fact or conjecture they are mine. The book has been derived chiefly from the Historical Section in *Zanzibar: An Account of its People, Industries, and History*, supplemented from the longer and fuller chapters on Zanzibar history of which the book referred to is an abbreviation. But apart from this and revision of the written chapters, the book and the labour of it has been Mr. Hollingsworth's. He has written it in a form adapted to the needs of pupils of the Govt Schools.[54]

The two texts correspond closely – the overall organisation is the same, with only a few sections reordered to improve the chronological flow. Throughout, the same historical events are reported in both texts and the emphasis upon external influences upon Zanzibar remains. The key difference is the tone in which the *School History* is written. While Ingrams's prose in the Wembley handbook was direct and factual, the language of the *School History* is more varied, evocative and readable – with regular use of 'we' to explain the direction of the narrative: 'we must now look at ...', 'we know this because ...' These following sentences from the 'Native tribes of Zanzibar' section provide useful comparative examples. They are remarkably similar, but the text for schools phrased more expansively and elegantly:

> *Wembley handbook:* 'From traditions and investigations into the native Customs and written histories of these peoples it is apparent that they have both an Asiatic and an African origin.'[55]
> *School history:* 'From traditions and investigations into their customs and written histories, it is apparent that these three tribes are not entirely of Bantu origin, but are also partly of Persian descent.'[56]

Such changes are typical – the content often does not vary, but the narrative voice is more engaging and descriptive. The final paragraph of the book is worth quoting in full as it makes clear its intent as a celebration of the transformation of Zanzibar by external rulers and as a centre of key historical events:

> We thus come to the end of our island story, the romantic tale of a tiny unimportant coral island which for centuries was visited by all kinds of merchants, traders and conquerors from distant lands; which in the nineteenth century, through the genius of a remarkable prince, Seyyid Said, was transformed into one of the richest spice islands in the world, and became the capital of a great East-African Empire and the trade market of the East Coast; which was the very centre of the stirring drama of the final suppression of the slave trade; which later was the centre of

the great European race for the acquisition of land in Africa; and which, finally, though retaining its own Sultan, came under the protection of Great Britain, and became part of the great British Empire.[57]

The 'we' is partly that of the storyteller – the teacher talking to the class – but as mentioned earlier it also suggests a collective island identity which included the colonisers and colonised, which in many cases was the teacher (whether British or Arab) and the pupil.

The *School History* was used by higher classes in schools and in the Teacher Training School.[58] Hollingsworth updated the text in 1929 with expanded sections on the mainland and republished it as the *Short History of East Africa*.[59] These texts became the standard historical textbooks for schools across the East African region. The historical narrative was also included in Ingrams's most widely known work, *Zanzibar: Its History and Its People*, published in 1931.

Assessing the impact of such a textbook is a much wider project than can be explored here but it is clear that the text was used extensively in the region from its publication until the end of the colonial period. A revealing reminiscence by a former student in Zanzibar offers a glimpse into how this narrative was absorbed. This woman vividly recalled learning from Hollingsworth's school history textbook. She remembered feeling disappointed when she attended Makerere College in Uganda in the 1970s and was taught history from an Africanist perspective. The 'heroes' from her school days, such as Vasco da Gama, were turned into villains.[60] Only two chapters in the *School History of Zanzibar* were devoted to 'The Origins of Local Tribes' and 'The Local Dynasties'. The clear message from the textbooks was that Zanzibar's history was the story of civilised foreign figures and explorers from overseas, a story which was rightly challenged in the postcolonial period.

The historical display in Zanzibar's museum

The publication of the *School History* in 1925 coincided with the opening of the Peace Memorial Museum, which provided the opportunity to represent this historical narrative in material form. As it was designed specifically to be an educational institution for the local population, the historical exhibits in the museum replicated precisely the chronology from the *School History* to ensure consistency with classroom work.[61] The main source for reconstructing this original display in the museum are a series of photographs and another of Ingrams's publications, the pamphlet produced for visitors as a 'Guide to the Historical and Ethnological sections', which also reproduced text from the Wembley handbook and the *School History*. Fitting with

Ingrams's overall historical perspective on Zanzibar, these sections were structured around the interventions, incursions and influences from peoples beyond Africa.

The museum's interpretation of pre-Omani history, in particular Shirazi immigration from the Persian Gulf, perpetuated the accepted paradigm of history for this period. The section was dominated by photographs, maps, drawings and text – as few objects remained – where Ingrams sought to stress the influences from the great civilisations of antiquity, including the Phoenicians, the Sumerians, the Greeks and the Assyrians. A small section was included on 'the Origins of the Native Tribes', in which he described the 'natives' as being 'of mixed African and Asiatic origin'.[62] Ingrams's particular focus in this section was the development of the 'Zenj Empire' of the East African coast following the arrival of Persian or 'Shirazi' immigrants which he dated to AD 965. This corresponded with the popular belief that the Swahili city-states were created by an alien people from Shiraz in Persia. He also discussed the Indian Ocean trade and visitors from the Far East although only a few coins and pottery fragments remained to represent this story.[63]

In spite of Ingrams's meticulous discussion of the early period, for the majority of European and Omani visitors this was 'prehistory'. For them, the arrival of Omani rule marked the beginning of Zanzibar's era of significance. The subsequent British involvement was presented as a seamless transition of rule which drew on the best of both cultures.[64] The nineteenth-century objects were therefore placed in the central hall, giving physical and material prominence to this period. There was also more material available from this period and much of it visually enticing and in good condition. Such a display reaffirmed and rendered permanent the widely held opinion that the nineteenth century represented the zenith of Zanzibar's history.

A significant subsection was the 'Explorers' exhibit which was expanded in the late 1920s. In this narrative, Zanzibar could be depicted as integral to the imperial mission rather than simply an exotic island. The famed heroes of the mid-nineteenth century proceeded from Zanzibar 'to the hinterland, which, largely owing to their pioneer efforts, has been opened up to civilisation and made a prosperous part of the British Empire'.[65] These explorers were mythologised in Britain and in East Africa.[66] Connections with them, through buildings, objects and letters, were eagerly sought by Zanzibar's European residents. The most prized exhibits were the original autographs of Speke, Livingstone and Stanley, and Livingstone's medicine chest, which he and Kirk used on the 1858 Zambesi Expedition.[67] Evelyn Waugh, visiting in 1929, noted with scepticism that this contained 'practically no quinine, but an enormous variety of pharmaceutically valueless poisons'.[68]

The focus on the explorers, the work of 'enlightened' sultans who signed the important abolition treaties and the role of Sir John Kirk, the British Consul who negotiated the 1873 treaty with Sultan Barghash, bypassed any controversies about slavery. Notably the only object relating to slavery was a set of stocks – not mentioned in the guides and placed at ground level, easily ignored. The museum did not engage in a more rigorous examination of the tense machinations between the British and the Arab rulers in the nineteenth century and the delay over abolition.[69] Nor did they dwell upon slavery as a source of Zanzibar's nineteenth-century prosperity.[70]

Other key 'protagonists in Zanzibar's history', including Sultan Barghash, the Mwinyi Mkuu (a notable precolonial local leader), Tippu Tib, Sir John Kirk and Sir Lloyd Mathews, were depicted in detail.[71] The historical section included many accoutrements, including Omani jewellery, ornaments and costume. Such objects perpetuated the pomp and splendour of the Sultanate. The 'Arab dress' referred to in the guidebook, displayed on dummies made by the museum carpenter, consisted of the three costumes displayed in the British Empire Exhibition at Wembley. Through their reinstallation, these objects would have been read in different ways by the two audiences. In London, as the only costumes on display, they were exotic curiosities and aligned Zanzibar with 'the East' rather than its East African neighbours. The museum in Zanzibar gave them a different meaning. These elaborate costumes projected Arab superiority by the inclusion of their clothing in the Historical section while clothing worn by the Swahili population, such as the *kofia* caps, was located in the 'Native Industries' section. In only a few sections did the Swahili population feature in the 'Historical Section' – the regalia of the Mwinyi Mkuu being a notable exception. In the main, 'history' as written for the British public and displayed and taught in Zanzibar was dominated by waves of arrivals in Zanzibar.

Conclusion

Reflecting on the Zanzibar Court at the Wembley Empire Exhibition and the accompanying handbook, Charlesworth believed the people of Zanzibar should be gratified in taking 'an adequate share in the carrying out of a great Imperial idea'.[72] Furthermore, 'the widespread interest taken in the Court and its exhibits has had a considerable educational value, which will react beneficially to the Sultanate in its status in the public estimate, and in the knowledge gained of its products, its activities and its individuality'. Such impact is impossible to measure precisely but this passage is most telling for its perceptions of success. Transmitting the impression of the uniqueness of Zanzibar to the British audience was a central priority for the Protectorate Government. Although limited by the exhibition space in describing Zanzibar's cultural individuality, the handbook provided the opportunity for detailed description to ensure that 'the correct impression' of the island was given. Attention was drawn to Zanzibar's cultural and historical significance to prevent it being overshadowed and subsumed by its powerful neighbouring territories. As Ingrams wrote in his report of the East African Governor's conference in 1926: 'Zanzibar stands aloof in the sense of her age-long civilization and history'.[73]

Ingrams and Hollingsworth played vital roles in projecting this image of Zanzibar to the Wembley audience and subsequently to the island's inhabitants. As this chapter has shown, a single room at the Wembley exhibition was just one aspect of educational projects which spanned imperial territories. This chapter represents a new perspective on the legacy of Wembley by considering the cultural and educational impact within the Empire itself. At the same time as the Wembley Exhibition was under construction in London, back in Zanzibar in 1923–24 visual material was being collected and prepared to illustrate this same story for the people of Zanzibar as part of the education programme of the 1920s. The resulting narrative laid down the official history of the island for the next forty years in the island's museum and in schools. The history of Zanzibar was prepared initially by the island's administrators for the metropolitan audience, then returned and repackaged for local use. The perspective of the narrative, one which incorporated precolonial and local intellectual concepts, explicitly demonstrated the benefits of synthesising ideas and influences from beyond Africa, a perspective which well-suited the then rulers of 'our island Sultanate'.

Notes

1 'Tanganika at Wembley', *East Africa (Souvenir Number)* 1 (1925), pp. 23–28 (pp. 18, 27).
2 For example, 'Report from the 1926 East African Governors' Conference', *Zanzibar Gazette*, 20 February 1926, pp. 37–8. The Zanzibar Protectorate included both the larger island of Unguja – often called Zanzibar Island – and the neighbouring island of Pemba. This chapter mainly refers to Zanzibar Island.
3 William Hendry, 'Preface', in Local Committee of the British Empire Exhibition (ed.), *Zanzibar: An Account of Its People, Industries and History* (Zanzibar: Zanzibar Government Press, 1924), p. i.
4 Ibid.
5 Ibid.

6   The museum was also known as the Beit el Amani and later simply as the Zanzibar Museum. For a full account of this museum's history, see Sarah Longair, '"A Gracious Temple of Learning": The Museum and Colonial Culture in Zanzibar, 1900–1945', unpublished PhD thesis, University of London, 2012.

7   See Peter Yeandle, *Citizenship, Nation, Empire: The Politics of History Teaching in England, 1870–1930* (Manchester: Manchester University Press, 2015), in particular Chapter Four on imperial values and seafaring.

8   Texts on Wembley and imperial exhibitions which have informed this study include Donald R. Knight and Alan D. Sabey, *The Lion Roars at Wembley: British Empire Exhibition 60th Anniversary 1924–1925* (London: Barnard and Westwood, 1984); John M. MacKenzie, *Propaganda and Empire: The Manipulation of British Public Opinion, 1880–1960* (Manchester: Manchester University Press, 1985); John M. MacKenzie (ed.), *Imperialism and Popular Culture* (Manchester: Manchester University Press, 1986); Christine Boyanoski, 'Selective Memory: The British Empire Exhibition and National Histories of Art', in Annie E. Coombes (ed.), *Rethinking Settler Colonialism: History and Memory in Australia, Canada, Aotearoa New Zealand and South Africa* (Manchester: Manchester University Press, 2006), pp. 156–71; Peter H. Hoffenberg, *An Empire on Display: English, Indian, and Australian Exhibitions from the Crystal Palace to the Great War* (Berkeley, CA: University of California Press, 2001); Jeffrey A. Auerbach, *The Great Exhibition of 1851: A Nation on Display*, (New Haven, CT: Yale University Press, 1999); Patricia A. Morton, *Hybrid Modernities: Architecture and Representation at the 1931 Colonial Exposition, Paris* (Cambridge, MA: MIT Press, 2000).

9   Knight and Sabey, *The Lion Roars at Wembley*, p. 18.

10 Donald Maxwell, *Wembley in Colour* (London: Longmans, Green, 1924), p. 23; Andrew D. Roberts, *The Colonial Moment in Africa: Essays on the Movement of Minds and Materials, 1900–1940* (Cambridge: Cambridge University Press, 1990), p. 41.

11 Jonathan Woodham, 'Images of Africa and Design at the British Empire Exhibitions between the Wars', *Journal of Design History* 2 (1989), pp. 15–34 (p. 19). Woodham also discusses the impact the objects from Africa had on contemporary designers seeking inspiration.

12 Annie E. Coombes, *Reinventing Africa: Museums, Material Culture and Popular Imagination in Late Victorian and Edwardian England* (New Haven, CT: Yale University Press, 1994); Sadiah Qureshi, *Peoples on Parade: Exhibitions, Empire, and Anthropology in Nineteenth-Century Britain* (Chicago: University of Chicago Press, 2011); Woodham, 'Images of Africa and Design'.

13 Jinny K. Prais, 'Imperial Travelers: The Formation of West African Urban Culture, Identity, and Citizenship in London and Accra, 1925–1935', unpublished PhD thesis, University of Michigan, 2008, pp. 52–64. Deborah Hughes discusses how this episode undermined the image of racial unity. See Deborah L. Hughes, 'Kenya, India and the British Empire Exhibition of 1924', *Race and Class* 47 (2006), pp. 66–85.

14 Sharae Deckard, *Paradise Discourse, Imperialism, and Globalization: Exploiting Eden* (London: Routledge, 2010); Longair, '"A Gracious Temple of Learning"', pp. 65–74.

15 Garth A. Myers, 'From "Stinkibar" to "The Island Metropolis": The Geography of British Hegemony in Zanzibar', in Anne Godlewska and Neil Smith (eds), *Geography and Empire* (Oxford: Blackwell, 1994), pp. 212–27 (p. 219).

16 The Official Guide does not give a map of the country displays so the internal layout is not clear, but the other countries in the East African section were 'the Sudan, Zanzibar, Nyasaland, the Seychelles, Tanganyika, Kenya, Uganda and Mauritius'. See *The British Empire Exhibition, 1924: Official Guide* (London: Fleetway Press, 1924), p. 58.

17 *Zanzibar Gazette*, 7 August 1922, p. 452.

18 Zanzibar National Archives (hereafter ZNA), BA 83/5, Report by John Sinclair, 'Report on the Zanzibar Protectorate from 1911–1923', 31 August 1923, p. 28.

19 Daniel M. Stephen, '"Brothers of the Empire?": India and the British Empire Exhibition of 1924–25', *Twentieth Century British History* 22 (2011), pp. 164–88 (p. 172).

20 Roman Loimeier, *Between Social Skills and Marketable Skills: The Politics of Islamic Education in 20th Century Zanzibar* (Leiden: Brill, 2009), p. 595.
21 William Hendry, 'Some Aspects of Education in Zanzibar', *Journal of the Royal African Society* 27 (1928), pp. 342–52.
22 Ibid., p. 346.
23 Jonathon Glassman, *War of Words, War of Stones: Racial Thought and Violence in Colonial Zanzibar* (Bloomington, IN: Indiana University Press, 2011), p. 78.
24 Loimeier, *Between Social Skills and Marketable Skills*, p. 354.
25 *Zanzibar Gazette*, 9 July 1927, p. 160.
26 For further discussion of this first major exhibition during the period of the British Protectorate in Zanzibar, see Sarah Longair, '"A Grand Show⊠ for East Africa: The Zanzibar Exhibition of 1905', *Ex Plus Ultra* 2 (2012), online journal: http://explusultra.wun.ac.uk/images/issue3/2012Longair.pdf (accessed 30 August 2013).
27 'Our Crown Colonies: A Tour of the Globe, Riches from the Tropics', *The Times*, 24 May 1924, p. xii.
28 *Zanzibar Gazette*, 3 August 1925, p. 288.
29 By the early twentieth century, many such handcrafted objects were being manufactured on the coast and several administrators in the 1920s warned against the loss of local handicraft skills.
30 *Zanzibar Gazette*, 3 August 1925, p. 288.
31 Ibid.
32 Ibid.
33 *Zanzibar Gazette*, 3 April 1926, p. 71.
34 Ibid.
35 'To-day's Opening Ceremony, The King's Visit, An Imperial Enterprise', *The Times*, 23 April 1924, p. 15.
36 'Women at Wembley. Inventions for the Home. Drapery and Food', *The Times*, 24 May 1924, p. xxii.
37 'Our Crown Colonies: A Tour of the Globe, Riches from the Tropics', *The Times*, 24 May 1924, p. xii.
38 *Zanzibar Gazette*, 3 August 1925, p. 288.
39 Hendry, 'Preface', p. i.
40 Glassman, *War of Words, War of Stones*, p. 78.
41 Ibid.
42 Ibid., p. 84. Glassman notes that this should not be equated to a shared sense of a Swahili identity – individuals identified with clans, villages and city-states. 'Still, the townspeople's devotion to Islam helped cement a notion among them that they lived a world apart, connected more with their trade partners and coreligionists overseas than with their cultural cousins of the near interior.' Glassman, *War of Words, War of Stones*, p. 25.
43 Ibid., p. 25.
44 Ibid., p. 43.
45 Rhodes House Library, MSS.Brit.Emp.s.428 (5), Extract from article by W.H. Ingrams, 'Zanzibar in Retrospect' (n.d.).
46 W.H. Ingrams, 'History', in Local Committee of the British Empire Exhibition (ed.), *Zanzibar*, p. 35.
47 'Shirazi' ancestry was claimed by many indigenous people in the nineteenth and twentieth centuries as a means to combat Arab domination. 'Shirazi' became a complicated identity marker in nascent nationalist discourse. See Glassman, *War of Words, War of Stones*, pp. 26, 52–3.
48 Ingrams, 'History', p. 69.
49 *Zanzibar Gazette*, 14 June 1905, p. 3.
50 Ingrams, 'History', p. 76.
51 Films to accompany the exhibition were made with particular countries featured: www.colonialfilm.org.uk/node/1050 (accessed 15 October 2011). The silent black-and-white Zanzibar film opens with images evoking the old town and the Sultan and focuses on the clove production process, another example of the 'brand' of Zanzibar.

52 David Cannadine, *Ornamentalisn: How the British Saw Their Empire* (London: Allen Lane, 2001).

53 W.H. Ingrams and L.W. Hollingsworth, *School History of Zanzibar* (London: Macmillan, 1925), p. vii.

54 Ingrams and Hollingsworth, *School History of Zanzibar*, p. viii.

55 Ingrams, 'History', p. 46.

56 Ingrams and Hollingsworth, *School History of Zanzibar*, p. 23.

57 Ibid., p. 130.

58 ZNA, BA 18/15, 'Zanzibar Government Administrative Reports for 1925', p. 70.

59 L.W. Hollingsworth, *A Short History of the East Coast of Africa* (London: Macmillan, 1929), p. v.

60 Corrie Decker, 'Reading, Writing, and Respectability: How Schoolgirls Developed Modern Literacies in Colonial Zanzibar', *International Journal of African Historical Studies* 43 (2010), pp. 89–114 (p. 97).

61 *Annual Report of the Zanzibar Museum, (Beit-el-Amani) 1939* (Zanzibar: Government Printer, 1940), p. 3.

62 ZNA, BA 106/8, W. H. Ingrams, 'Guide to the Historical and Ethnological Section', 1927, pp. 11–12.

63 Like others at the time, Ingrams attributed the construction of Great Zimbabwe to the South Arabian peoples. See ZNA, BA 106/8, Ingrams, 'Guide to the Historical and Ethnological Section', p. 9. David Randall-MacIver was the first to state in 1906 that the site was unquestionably of African origin, but it was not until Gertrude Caton-Thompson's groundbreaking archaeological research in 1928–29 confirmed this that the idea was more widely accepted. See David Randall-MacIver, *Medieval Rhodesia* (London: Macmillan, 1906); Gertrude Caton-Thompson, *The Zimbabwe Culture: Ruins and Reactions* (Oxford: Clarendon Press, 1931). My thanks to John MacKenzie for bringing Randall-MacIver's work to my attention.

64 This has comparisons with British cultural representation in India. Thomas Metcalf describes how the British used architecture to articulate their image as heirs to the wise and tolerant Emperor Akbar. See Thomas R. Metcalf, *An Imperial Vision: Indian Architecture and Britain's Raj* (London: Faber, 1989), p. 47.

65 *Zanzibar Gazette*, 2 October 1926, p. 215.

66 Clare Pettitt, *Dr Livingstone, I Presume?: Missionaries, Journalists, Explorers and Empire* (London: Profile, 2007); Sarah Worden (ed.), *David Livingstone: Man, Myth and Legacy* (Edinburgh: National Museums of Scotland, 2012).

67 R.H. Crofton, *Zanzibar Affairs, 1914–1933* (London: Francis Edwards, 1953), p. 63.

68 Evelyn Waugh, *Remote People* (London: Duckworth, 1931), p. 169.

69 For a fuller discussion of the significance of this politically charged object, see Sarah Longair, *Cracks in the Dome: Fractured Histories of Empire in the Zanzibar Museum, 1900–1964* (Farnham: Ashgate, 2015).

70 See Lindsay Doulton, 'Anti-slavery and the Royal Navy in the Indian Ocean, 1860–90', unpublished PhD thesis, University of Hull, 2010.

71 ZNA, BA 106/10, 'A Short Guide to the Zanzibar Museum', 1933, p. 6.

72 *Zanzibar Gazette*, 3 April 1926, p. 71.

73 *Zanzibar Gazette*, 20 February 1926, p. 38.

INDEX

EU authorised representative for GPSR:
Easy Access System Europe, Mustamäe tee 50,
10621 Tallinn, Estonia
gpsr.requests@easproject.com

www.ingramcontent.com/pod-product-compliance
Ingram Content Group UK Ltd.
Pitfield, Milton Keynes, MK11 3LW, UK
UKHW041843150726
7214IPUK00015B/134